INDONESIA
BEYOND
SUHARTO

Society

www.asiasociety.org

INDONESIA BEYOND SUHARTO

Polity
Economy
Society
Transition

Donald K. Emmerson , Editor

Published in Cooperation with the Asia Society

An East Gate Book

M.E. Sharpe
Armonk, New York
London, England

An East Gate Book

Copyright © 1999 by the Asia Society

All rights reserved. No part of this book may be reproduced in any form
without written permission from the publisher, M. E. Sharpe, Inc.,
80 Business Park Drive, Armonk, New York 10504.

Library of Congress Cataloging-in-Publication Data

Indonesia beyond Suharto : polity, economy, society, transition / edited by Donald K. Emmerson.
  p. cm.
Includes bibliographical references and index.
ISBN 1-56324-889-1 (hardcover : alk. paper) —ISBN 1-56324-890-5 (paperback : alk. paper)
  1. Indonesia—Politics and government—1966–1998. 2. Indonesia—Politics and
government—1998– 3. Indonesia—Economic conditions—1945– 4. Indonesia—Social
conditions. I. Emmerson, Donald K.

JQ770.I57   1999
320.9598′09′045—dc21   99-023949
                                     CIP

Printed in the United States of America

The paper used in this publication meets the minimum requirements of
American National Standard for Information Sciences
Permanence of Paper for Printed Library Materials,
ANSI Z 39.48-1984.

BM (c) 10   9   8   7   6   5   4   3   2   1
BM (p) 10   9   8   7   6   5   4   3   2

Contents

INDONESIA UNDER SUHARTO

Part One: Polity

Part Two: Economy

THE FALL OF SUHARTO AND AFTER

Foreword

On May 21, 1998, Indonesia's President Suharto resigned, forced from office by sustained and overwhelming popular protest in the face of deteriorating social and economic conditions. In so doing, the man who assumed the mantle of power from Indonesia's founding president Sukarno and ruled Indonesia for over 30 years became perhaps the most spectacular casualty of the economic crisis that has swept across Asia and beyond.

Suharto's resignation came at a time of wrenching social, political, and economic upheaval in Indonesia, the world's fourth-largest country and home to the largest Muslim population of any country. Suharto's successor, B.J. Habibie, endorsed greater political participation, but the country remained mired in rising poverty, and ethnic, regional and religious tensions.

Indonesia Beyond Suharto provides both a survey of Indonesia's post-independence development and a multidisciplinary assessment of the pressing issues now confronting the country. This volume is not an attempt to predict Indonesia's future; rather, it provides a wide-ranging examination of the key social, political, and economic factors that have shaped Indonesia's developmental successes and its latest crisis.

Many people have contributed in bringing this volume to publication. The Asia Society thanks Don Emmerson and his outstanding team of authors whose dedication to their study is reflected in these chapters. Thanks are due to Deborah Washburn, who conceived the idea and paved the way for the volume; Karen Fein, who skillfully edited and shaped the manuscript in its initial stages; and Mai Shaikhanuar-Cota, who managed the production. Andrew Thornley submitted valuable comments on the volume. Angela Che provided indefatigable administrative support. Robert Radtke and Kevin Quigley provided constructive recommendations. Finally, we wish to acknowledge our colleagues at M.E. Sharpe, especially Douglas Merwin, Patricia Loo, and Angela Piliouras for their patience, encouragement, and generosity in making this volume a success.

Marshall M. Bouton
Executive Vice President
Asia Society

Preface

During the preparation of this book, its title came true. On 21 May 1998, after more than thirty years in power, President Suharto resigned. His vice president, B.J. Habibie, took over. At last Indonesians could move "beyond Suharto."

Or could they? As the first anniversary of his resignation neared, Suharto was alive, reasonably well, and still living in Jakarta. On the streets near his home, students shouted his name, demanding that he be tried for corruption and repression during his rule. In coffee shops, talk shows, newspaper columns, and over the Internet, rumors circulated that he was manipulating politics from behind the scenes. The new president, after all, owed his entire political career to Suharto. The more he insisted that he was not a puppet of his former patron, the more Habibie implied the strength of suspicions to the contrary.

That such suspicions should endure was not surprising. In 1998, eight years after Augusto Pinochet Ugarte had ceased being their president, Chileans were noisily divided over whether he should be tried for crimes committed during his rule. A dozen years after Ferdinand and Imelda Marcos had fled Manila, the extent let alone the disposition of the wealth they had acquired during his presidency still had not been settled. Pinochet had ruled for seventeen years, Marcos for twenty. But Suharto had held full title to the presidency of Indonesia for thirty years—three decades in which to put his stamp on the country. Suharto's legacy was virtually certain to be felt, in one way or another, well into the twenty-first century.

And yet, if it would take years for Indonesians to move fully beyond Suharto, there was an obvious sense in which even during his rule they had lived their lives beyond him. His regime had achieved unprecedented ubiquity and authority over its subjects. But the fourth most populous country in the world could never be shrunk to fit the shadow of its leader, no matter how authoritarian he might be. "Suharto's Indonesia" had never been more than a metaphor. The country was far too vast and diverse to belong to any one man.

The coverage and composition of this book reflect these contrasting ideas: not only the post facto political importance of Suharto and his decades of autocratic rule; but also, during those decades, the autonomy and vitality of Indonesia's economy and society, including its cultures, which were never merely clay for shaping by the regime.

Because it will not soon escape his legacy, Indonesia after Suharto cannot be understood without knowing what the country was like during his rule. Indonesia under Suharto is therefore the main subject of this book. And understanding the "New Order," as his regime from 1966 to 1998 was known, requires knowledge of the archipelago before—long before—Suharto. Robert Cribb in Chapter 1 ("Nation") opens his historical interpretation of the making of Indonesia with the peopling of its islands by Austronesians some 5,500 years ago. In Chapters 2 ("Regime") and 3 ("Regions"), respectively, R. William Liddle and Michael Malley focus on the politics of the New Order nationally and subnationally. But they also spotlight Indonesia's first and failed experiment with democracy in the 1950s, including the importance of perceptions of that failure to the chance for success the second time around, at century's end, with Suharto no longer blocking the way.

Because even under Suharto, Indonesia was always more than his political domain, understanding the country during the New Order requires extrapolitical knowledge. That is the purpose of the book's second and third parts, concerned as they respectively are with Indonesian economy and society from the 1960s through the mid-1990s, and they also provide historical context as needed. In Chapter 4 ("Development") Anne Booth charts and evaluates the economic transformation of the archipelago, while Richard Borsuk does the same for deregulation and privatization in Chapter 5 ("Markets"), and Ahmad D. Habir in Chapter 6 ("Conglomerates") describes and questions the role and reputation of large business groups.

The authors of Part Three also go "beyond Suharto." Robert Hefner in Chapter 7 ("Religion") traces the evolution of religious pluralism from the initial diffusion of Hinduism and Buddhism into the archipelago some two millennia ago. In Chapter 8 ("Women"), Kathryn Robinson contrasts the actual diversity of gender relations with official images of women as mothers and wives, while Virginia Hooker uses Chapter 9 ("Expression") to chart the variety and creativity of Indonesian writers, artists, and performers in the face of Suharto's censors.

In the fourth and last part of the book I focus on events from 1997 through mid-September 1999. Chapter 10 ("Exit and Aftermath") is an effort to fathom the multifaceted crisis that ushered Suharto out of power, brought in Habibie, and opened the way to national legislative elections in June 1999. Chapter 11 ("Voting and Violence") tentatively scans the balloting and its results for signs of continuity and change. "Voting and Violence" also shares my provisional understanding of the August 1999 plebiscite in East Timor and its catastrophic aftermath. (Users of the index and list of additional reading under "Sources" should note that, for lack of time before publication, the contents of this final chapter are not covered in these parts of the book.) These final chapters also revisit earlier themes in assessing the process and prospect of reform.

Authors were selected for their expertise, and to ensure a range of backgrounds and perspectives. It was important that the essays be analytic; drafts were solicited and edited with this criterion in mind. Authors were also encouraged to refer to each other's chapters. The aim was to minimize uneven quality and unrelated content—the banes of multiply authored works—in a volume palatable to diverse readers, from students and travelers with little or no prior exposure to Indonesia, to scholars and other professionals wanting to augment what they already know. For readers interested in learning still more, additional sources are listed at the back of the book.

Many people and organizations deserve gratitude: especially my coauthors, for their acuity, insights, cooperation, and patience; Leonardus Eko Sudibyo, for invaluable research and computer assistance; and the Asia Society, which proposed the book, furnished honoraria for its contributors, and did not give up on the project when it took much longer to complete than expected. Especially helpful at the Society were Karen Fein, Mai Shaikhanuar-Cota, and Deborah Washburn. Robert Cribb graciously and skillfully prepared maps to fit the book's contents. For administrative assistance, thanks are due to Diane Morauske, Laura Weeks, and Pat Whipple in the University of Wisconsin-Madison Department of Political Science; and Anne Marie Kodama, Zera Murphy, and James Raphael at Stanford University's Asia/Pacific Research Center.

I am also grateful to the Carter Center and the National Democratic Institute. Without their cooperation and support, I could not have monitored the events in 1999 on which Chapter 11 is focused: Indonesia's national elections in June, and East Timor's fateful plebiscite in August.

In addition to my coauthors, many other colleagues shared knowledge and advice. At the risk of inadvertent omissions, for which I apologize in advance, I must acknowledge my debts to Dewi Fortuna Anwar, Syafi'i Anwar, Medea Benjamin, Judith Bird, Arief Budiman, James Castle, Marzuki Darusman, Wayne Forrest, Vedi Hadiz, Bambang Harymurti, Sidney Jones, Suzaina Kadir, Aristides Katoppo, Dwight King, Andrew MacIntyre, Nurcholish Madjid, Andi and Rizal Mallarangeng, Ed and Alleen Masters, Goenawan Muhammad, Buyung Nasution, Mari Pangestu, Steve Radelet, Mohammad Sadli, Adam Schwarz, Laurie Sears, Hadi Soesastro, Frank Supit, Jean Taylor, and Mary Zurbuchen. Since only two of the eleven chapters herein are mine, readers may imagine how much longer this list would be if it included the names of those who in one way or another helped my coauthors. However numerous our creditors, of course, they are not responsible for whatever shortcomings may survive.

Last, and first, there is my wife. Thanking her in this context is like appreciating oxygen. Without her loving grace and good humor in the face of extreme preoccupation, you would not be reading this.

Donald K. Emmerson
Madison, Wisconsin
September 1999

Contributors

Anne Booth is a professor of economics in the University of London School of Oriental and African Studies. She has been a senior research fellow at the Australian National University, and has taught in the University of Singapore Department of Economics and Statistics. She is the author of *The Indonesian Economy in the Nineteenth and Twentieth Centuries: A History of Missed Opportunities* (1998) and *Agricultural Development in Indonesia* (1988). Among her other publications are several edited books on the Indonesian economy. Her research interests include the impact of economic growth on living standards in Southeast Asia since 1960.

Richard Borsuk is Singapore bureau chief of *The Asian Wall Street Journal*. He was the newspaper's correspondent in Indonesia from October 1987 through July 1998, and its Thailand correspondent for six years prior to that. Earlier assignments included Malaysia, for *Asiaweek* magazine, and Hong Kong, for Agence France-Presse and the Press Foundation of Asia. He received his bachelor's degree in Asian Studies from the University of Wisconsin-Madison. A conference paper based on his reporting during the last years of Suharto's presidency is being published by the Australian National University Research School of Pacific and Asian Studies in *Post-Suharto Indonesia: Renewal or Chaos?* (1999).

Robert Cribb is a reader in Indonesian history at the University of Queensland in Brisbane, Australia. He has held research positions at the Australian National University, the Netherlands Institute of Advanced Study, and the Nordic Institute of Asian Studies in Denmark, and has taught at Griffith University in Australia, and at Leiden University in the Netherlands. His publications include a *Historical Atlas of Indonesia* (1999), *Gangsters and Revolutionaries* (1992), a *Historical Dictionary of Indonesia* (1992), and an edited volume, *The Indonesian Killings of 1965–1966* (1990). Indonesian topics covered by him in other published work include the colonial era, environmental issues, and contemporary politics.

Donald K. Emmerson is a senior fellow at Stanford University's Asia/Pacific Research Center and a professor of political science at the University of Wisconsin-Madison. He holds advisory positions with the National Bureau of Asian Research and the Social Science Research Council. In 1998 articles by him on Indonesia and the East Asian crisis appeared in the *Cambridge Review of International Affairs, Foreign Affairs,* and *NBR Analysis.* He has chapters in *Asia's New World Order* (1997), *Southeast Asian Security in the New Millennium* (1996), and *Southeast Asia in the New World Order* (1996). Earlier writings include *Indonesia's Elite: Political Culture and Cultural Politics* (1976).

Ahmad D. Habir is a founding faculty member of the Indonesian Institute for Management Development in Jakarta, where he also directs the Ecolink Center for Business and the Environment. He is affiliated with the University of Auckland's New Zealand Asia Institute and several management consulting firms, and has held visiting positions at the University of Sydney and the Institute of Southeast Asian Studies in Singapore. His publications include *Managing Indonesia* (AustAsian Paper No. 2, RIAP, University of Sydney, 1995) and chapters on business education and state enterprise reform, respectively, in *Indonesia Assessment 1991* (1991) and *Indonesia Assessment 1992* (1992).

Robert W. Hefner is a professor of anthropology at Boston University and associate director of the Institute for the Study of Economic Culture. His publications include: as author, *The Political Economy of Mountain Java* (1990) and *Hindu Javanese: Tengger Tradition and Islam* (1985); as editor, *Democratic Civility: The History and Cross-cultural Possibility of a Modern Political Ideal* (1998), *Market Cultures: Society and Morality in the New Asian Capitalism* (1998), and *Conversion to Christianity: Historical and Anthropological Perspectives on a Great Transformation* (1993); and as coeditor, *Islam in an Era of Nation-States: Politics and Religious Renewal in Muslim Southeast Asia* (1997).

Virginia Hooker is a professor and head of the Southeast Asia Centre in the Australian National University Faculty of Asian Studies, where she teaches courses on contemporary Indonesia and traditional Malay culture and society. Her research interests include representations of women and the family in Indonesia and Malaysia in the context of Islam-state relations. Among her recent publications are *Writing a New Society: Social Change through the Novel in Malay* (1999) and a chapter on public discourse in *Indonesia: Dealing with a Neighbour* (1996). Earlier work includes an edited volume, *Culture and Society in New Order Indonesia* (Kuala Lumpur: Oxford University Press, 1993).

R. William Liddle is a professor of political science at Ohio State University and a visiting lecturer at the Foreign Service Institute in Washington, DC. He has taught, done research, and been a consultant in Indonesia on many occasions since 1962. Among his recent publications on Indonesia are *Islam, Politik, dan Modernisasi* [*Islam, Politics, and Modernization*] (1997) and *Leadership and Culture in Indonesian Politics* (1996); chapters in *Government Policies and Ethnic Relations in Asia and the Pacific* (1997) and *The Politics of Elections in Southeast Asia* (1996); and an article on Islam and politics in the *Journal of Asian Studies* (1996). Earlier work includes *Ethnicity, Party, and National Integration: An Indonesian Case Study* (1970).

Michael Malley is a visiting assistant professor in political science at Ohio University. He wrote his University of Madison-Wisconsin dissertation on the centralization of political power in Indonesia since the 1950s. His publications include a survey of President Suharto's final cabinet (*Indonesia*, 1998) and a biography of one of Suharto's advisers, Soedjono Hoemardani (*Indonesia*, 1989). Hoemardani was the subject of Malley's MA thesis at Cornell University (1990). Malley's writings have also appeared in *Editor, Forum Keadilan*, and *Prisma*, among other Indonesian-language journals. He received his BA degree cum laude in foreign service and Asian studes from Georgetown University (1987).

Kathryn Robinson is a senior fellow in anthropology at the Australian National University Research School of Pacific and Asian Studies. Her research on Soroako, a mining town in South Sulawesi, has yielded chapters in *Gender and Power in Affluent Asia* (1998), *Resources, Nations and Indigenous Peoples* (1996), among other recent publications. She has also published on traditional architecture in South Sulawesi (*Australian Journal of Anthropology*, 1997) and Australian-Asian gender relations (*Feminist Review*, 1996). Earlier work includes *Stepchildren of Progress: the Political Economy of Development in Indonesia* (1986).

Tables

Names

In this book all Indonesian words, including names of places and organizations, are spelled according to the orthography that has been in effect since 1972. Among other changes, the letter "u" replaced "oe" under the 1972 reform. Names of people, however, are spelled herein the way their owners sign or signed them or as printed in historical accounts or contemporary local media. There is an exception, however. The man who held the title of president of Indonesia from 1968 to 1998 still signs his name "Soeharto." Nevertheless, bibliographic references aside, the "oe" in his name is rendered "u" in this book, in keeping with Western journalistic practice. The spelling of names in bibliographic references and quotations, of course, has not been altered.

Readers unfamiliar with Indonesian may wish to note these pronunciations: The vowel sounds "oe" and "u" are like "oo" in the English word "too"; "sy" (e.g., in the organization called Masyumi) resembles the "sh" in "she"; "i" (as in the island of Timor) sounds like the "ee" in "tree"; and "c" (for instance, in the province named Aceh) is pronounced "ch" as in "check." To avoid mixing languages, in this book Indonesian nouns are not pluralized by adding "s"; instead, following Indonesian practice, the context implies whether a singular or plural form is intended.

Finally, the selection of a single name to refer to a person without repeating his or her full name conforms to no rule other than common Indonesian usage. Among the ministers in Suharto's cabinet in 1997, for example, Bacharuddin Jusuf Habibie is given as Habibie, but Ginandjar Kartasasmita is rendered Ginandjar. The anticolonial activist Tan Malaka, on the other hand, is neither Tan nor Malaka but always Tan Malaka. The choice does not arise, of course, in the case of Indonesians who have but one personal name. An example is Indonesia's first president, Sukarno. Suharto, late in his life, added the name Muhammad, but because he rarely uses it, it is omitted here.

Abbreviations

ABRI	Angkatan Bersenjata Republik Indonesia (Armed Forces of the Republic of Indonesia)
Apodeti	Timorese Popular Democratic Association (Associaçao Popular Democrática Timorense)
ASEAN	Association of Southeast Asian Nations
Bapepam	Capital Markets Supervisory Agency (Badan Pengawas Pasar Modal)
Bapindo	Indonesian Development Bank (Bank Pembangunan Indonesia)
Bappenas	National Development Planning Agency (Badan Perencanaan Pembangunan Nasional)
BPIS	Strategic Industries Management Agency (Badan Pengelola Industri Strategis)
BPPC	Clove Support and Marketing Agency (Badan Penyangga dan Pemasaran Cengkeh)
Bulog	Food Supply Agency (Badan Urusan Logistik)
CBS	Central Bureau of Statistics (Biro Pusat Statistik)
CE	common era
CGI	Consultative Group on Indonesia
CIDES	Center for Information and Development Studies
CNRM	National Council of Maubere Resistance (Conselho Nacional da Resistência Maubere)
CPI	consumer price index
CPR	crude [school] participation rate
CSIS	Centre for Strategic and International Studies
DDII	Council for Indonesian Muslim Proselytization (Dewan Dakwah Islamiyah Indonesia)
DI	House of Islam (Darul Islam)

DPR	People's Representative Council (Dewan Perwakilan Rakyat)
DPRD I	Level I Regional People's Representative Council (Dewan Perwakilan Rakyat Daerah Tingkat I)
DPRD II	Level II Regional People's Representative Council (Dewan Perwakilan Rakyat Daerah Tingkat II)
DW	Ladies' Duty (Dharma Wanita)
Falintil	Armed Forces for the National Liberation of Timor (Forças Armadas de Libertação Nacional de Timor)
FDI	foreign direct investment
Fretilin	Revolutionary Front for an Independent East Timor (Frente Revolucionária do Timor Leste Independente)
FY	fiscal year, set by the Indonesian government to run from 1 April through 31 March
GAM	Free Aceh Movement (Gerakan Aceh Merdeka)
GDP	gross domestic product
GNP	gross national product
Golkar	Functional Groups (Golongan Karya)
HKBP	Batak Christian Protestant Church (Huria Kristen Batak Protestan)
HMI	Islamic Students' Association (Himpunan Mahasiswa Islam)
IAIN	State Institute [for Higher Education] in Islamic Religion (Institut Agama Islam Negeri)
IBM	International Business Machines
ICMI	Indonesian Muslim Intellectuals' Association (Ikatan Cendekiawan Muslim Indonesia)
IDT	Presidential Directives [to Develop] Left-behind Villages (Inpres Desa Tertinggal)
IGGI	Inter-Governmental Group on Indonesia
IMF	International Monetary Fund
IMPM	"Noble Vow" Management Institute (Institut Manajemen Prasetya Mulya)
Inco	International Nickel Company
Inpres	Presidential Directives (Instruksi Presiden)
IPMI	Indonesian Institute for Management Development (Institut Pengembangan Manajemen Indonesia)
IPPM	Institute for Management Education and Development (Institut Pendidikan dan Pembinaan Manajemen)
IUD	intrauterine device
JSX	Jakarta Stock Exchange
Kadin	Chamber of Commerce and Industry (Kamar Dagang dan Industri)
KKN	collusion, corruption, nepotism (*kolusi, korupsi, nepotisme*)
Koanda	Interregional Command (Komando Antar Daerah)
Kodam	Regional Military Commands (Komando Daerah Militer)

Kopassus	Special Forces Command (Komando Pasukan Khusus)
Kostrad	Army Strategic Reserve Command (Komando Strategis Angkatan Darat)
Kowilhan	Regional Defense Command (Komando Wilayah Pertahanan)
LEKRA	Institute of People's Culture (Lembaga Kebudayaan Rakyat)
LKAAM	Consultative Body for Minangkabau Customary Law (Lembaga Kerapatan Adat Alam Minangkabau)
Masyumi	Consultative Assembly of Indonesian Muslims (Majelis Syuro Muslimin Indonesia)
MBA	Master's in Business Administration
MI	Indonesian Muslims (Muslimin Indonesia)
MPR	People's Consultative Assembly (Majelis Permusyawaratan Rakyat)
MPRS	Provisional People's Consultative Assembly (Majelis Permusyawaratan Rakyat Sementara)
MPR-SI	Special Session of the People's Consultative Assembly (Sidang Istimewa Majelis Permusyawaratan Rakyat)
Muspida	Regional Leadership Consultative Council (Musyawarah Pimpinan Daerah, or Muspida)
Nasakom	Nationalism, religion, and communism
NU	Revival of Islamic Scholars (Nahdlatul Ulama)
NYSE	New York Stock Exchange
OPM	Free Papua Organization (Organisasi Papua Merdeka)
PAN	National Mandate Party (Partai Amanat Nasional)
Parmusi	Indonesian Muslims' Party (Partai Muslimin Indonesia)
PDI	Indonesian Democracy Party (Partai Demokrasi Indonesia)
PDI-P	Struggle PDI (Partai Demokrasi Indonesia Perjuangan)
Pefindo	Indonesian Finance Rating Agency (PT Pemeringkat Efek Indonesia, or Pefindo)
Permesta	Universal Struggle Charter (Piagam Perjuangan Semesta Alam)
Pertamina	Perusahaan Tambang Minyak dan Gas Bumi Nasional
Perum	wholly government-owned corporation (Perusahaan Umum)
PKB	Nation's Revival Party (Partai Kebangkitan Bangsa)
PKI	Indonesian Communist Party (Partai Komunis Indonesia)
PKK	Family Welfare Movement (Pembinaan Kesejahteraan Keluarga)
PNI	Indonesian National Party (Partai Nasional Indonesia)
PP	Government Regulation (Peraturan Pemerintah)
PPP	Development Unity Party (Partai Persatuan Pembangunan)
PRRI	Revolutionary Government of the Republic of Indonesia (Pemerintah Revolusioner Republik Indonesia)
PSI	Indonesian Socialist Party (Partai Sosialis Indonesia, or PSI)
PT	limited liability company (Perséroan Terbatas)
PT	Pindad PT Army Industries (PT Perindustrian Angkatan Darat)
PT INKA	PT Railroad Industry (PT Industri Kereta Api)

PT Inti	PT Indonesian Telecommunications Industry (PT Industri Telekomunikasi Indonesia)
PT IPTN	PT Indonesian-Archipelagic Aircraft Industry (PT Industri Pesawat Terbang Nusantara)
r.	reigned
RIS	Republic of the United States of Indonesia (Republik Indonesia Serikat)
Rp	rupiah, the currency of Indonesia
RPR	refined [school] participation rate
SME	small or medium-sized enterprise
SPSI	Pan-Indonesian Workers' Union (Serikat Pekerja Seluruh Indonesia)
Supersemar	Letter of Instruction of 11 March (Surat Perintah Sebelas Maret)
TMII	Beautiful Indonesia in Miniature (Taman Mini Indonesia Indah), also sometimes shortened to Taman Mini
TVRI	Republic of Indonesia Television (Televisi Republik Indonesia)
UDT	Timorese Democratic Union (Uniao Democrática Timorense)
UN	United Nations
VOC	United East Indies Company (Vereenigde Oost-Indische Compagnie)
YPM	"Noble Vow" Foundation (Yayasan Prasetya Mulya)

The symbol $ refers to United States dollars unless specified otherwise.

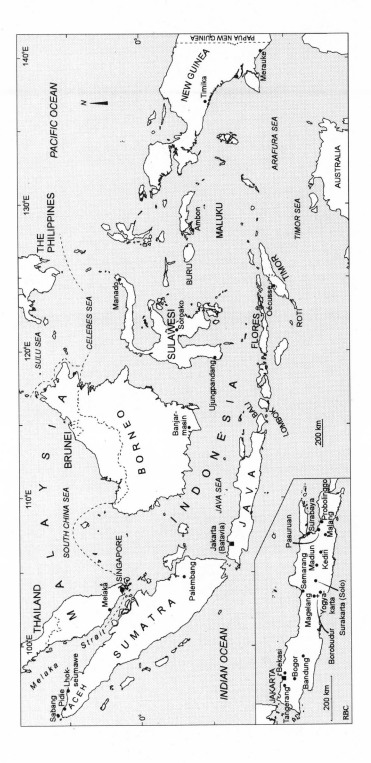

Map 1. Indonesian Seas, Islands, and Sites

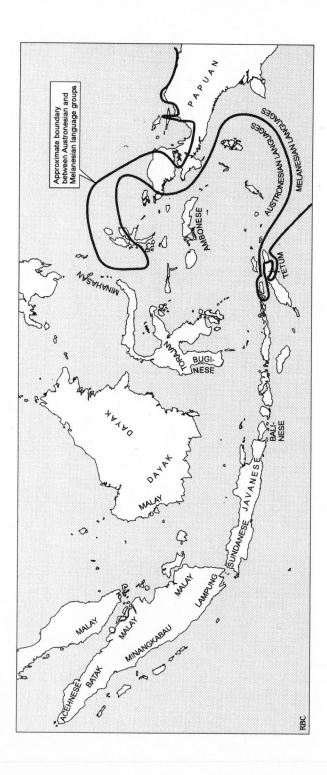

Map 2. Indonesian Peoples and Languages

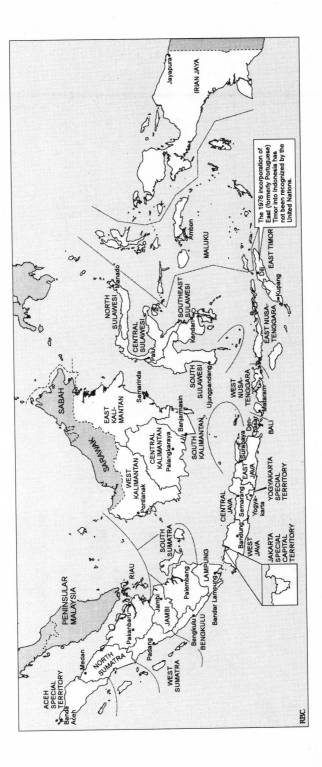

Map 3. Indonesian Provinces and Capitals

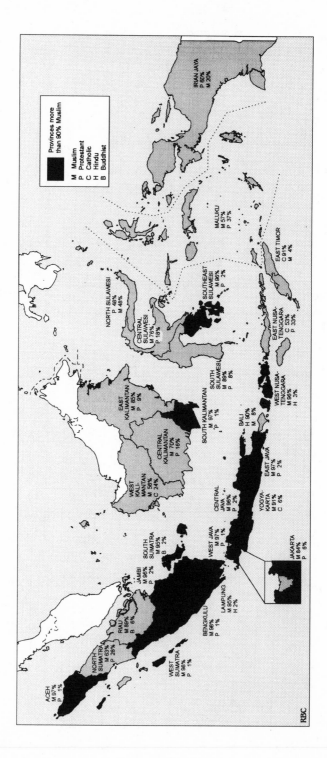

Map 4. Indonesian Religious Affiliations

PART ONE: POLITY

Chapter 1

Nation: Making Indonesia

Robert Cribb

A glance at a map might seem to be enough to suggest the improbability of Indonesia. With more than 13,000 islands, stretching west-to-east for more than 5,000 kilometers across three time zones, Indonesia is the world's largest archipelagic state. One might expect to find in such a vast assemblage at least several countries. Instead there is but one, the Republic of Indonesia. This chapter tries to explain why.

Surprise at the survival of one Indonesia, on the other hand, lies in the eye of the map's beholder. For the country's first president, Sukarno, the unity of Indonesia was not anomalous; it was foreordained. He liked to say that by looking at a map even a child could see how natural the physical integrity of the Republic was. In accounting for the making of Indonesia, this chapter will emphasize the strength of this claim—the power of national unity as an idea.

In Indonesia, citizenship and ethnicity coexist. Most of the more than 200 million people who call themselves Indonesians also identify with one of their country's more than 200 ethnic groups. These groups range in size from the Javanese, roughly 100 million strong, who live on the politically focal island of Java, to tiny, disappearing language communities on the islands of eastern Indonesia beyond Sulawesi (or Celebes). The intertwining with and separation of these local identities from the idea of a united Indonesia is a major part of the story of how the nation-state was made. It is appropriate, therefore, to begin with the ancient peopling of the archipelago.

The vast majority of today's Indonesians are the descendants of Austronesian migrants to the islands, who began moving southward from what is now Taiwan about 5,500 years ago. They traveled in sturdy outrigger canoes, and their migration took them not only to the Philippines and the Indonesian archipelago, but also out into the Pacific, where they became the ancestors of the modern Polynesians, and across the Indian Ocean to Madagascar, whose people are still predominantly Austronesian in ancestry.

The Austronesians were not conquerors. For the most part, they settled on empty islands and uninhabited coasts. Their impact was weakest, therefore, in those parts of the Indonesian archipelago where human settlement was already established. On the island of New Guinea and on neighboring islands to the west, such as Timor, Melanesian peoples had been living for millennia. Their ancestors probably had arrived in the region 50,000–60,000 years earlier and their ways of life had changed with the changing climate (see Maps 1 and 2).

Seventeen thousand years ago, during the last ice age, when sea levels were as much as 200 meters lower than they are today, what is now western Indonesia was a subcontinental plain probably covered with dry forest well suited to hunting societies. At that time the Melanesians probably were evenly spread over much of what would eventually become Indonesia. By the time the Austronesians arrived, however, sea levels had risen, creating an archipelago, and a wetter climate had allowed tropical rain forest to displace the existing dry forest, especially on the large western islands of Java, Sumatra, and Borneo. Rain forest was a less tractable environment for hunters, so the centers of Melanesian population shifted to the east. By about 7000 B.C.,[1] a millennium or so prior to the Austronesians' arrival, Melanesians in the highlands of New Guinea had begun to cultivate taro and other root crops, which allowed much greater population density than before. In terms of their ancestry, therefore, the peoples of the Indonesian archipelago form an uneven continuum from Austronesian predominance in the west to Melanesian preponderance in the east, with zones of transition between.

Today in Indonesia, people of predominantly Austronesian origin still can be distinguished from their Melanesian co-citizens. Concentrated on the easternmost islands, the Melanesians have dark skin and curly hair, and their languages differ from those of the vastly more numerous, lighter-skinned, and straighthaired Indonesians of Austronesian descent. These differences, between Java and the western islands on the one hand and the islands of Timor and New Guinea on the other, have persisted as an element in the political conflicts that marked the recent histories of the provinces of Irian Jaya and East Timor (see Map 3).

Trade and Politics

The Austronesian communities appear to have been generally small, with chiefs or *datu* who drew their authority from the direct consent of the community as a whole, both men and women. There seems to have been no aristocracy; indi-

---

1. "B.C.," "A.D.," and "the Christian era" are used in this chapter for convenience alone, without reference to the actual historical importance of Christianity.

vidual leaders apparently rose and fell on the strength of their own skills and prestige. Technological and cultural innovations such as metalworking spread rapidly once they reached the Austronesian world, suggesting that these communities were in regular contact with each other, but there was no overarching Austronesian polity.

Around A.D. 100 an extensive trade in spices and tropical forest products began to develop. Austronesian traders in large outrigger vessels carried tree products such as camphor, benzoin, pine resins (used in medicines, incense, and perfumery), and gold to the ports of India and southern China to be exchanged for cloth, porcelain, and metalwork. Cinnamon and other spices were taken directly across the Indian Ocean to the eastern coast of Africa and passed on through Egypt to the markets of the Roman Empire.

In the wake of long-distance trade, larger political units arose. Trading wealth overthrew the balance of power within the small Austronesian settlements. *Datu* who could bring the new commerce under their authority soon became far more wealthy and powerful than the other members of their communities. Trade created a compelling incentive to form larger political units that could more closely control the selling of products from a single region.

The Austronesian communities of the archipelago were in trading contact with both India and China, but without exception they turned to India for political models to deal with the new situation. Whereas Chinese political ideology offered allegiance to a single emperor and a powerful administrative bureaucracy, Hindu-Buddhist cosmology afforded each ruler the status of a reincarnated god and a strong but flexible hierarchy that fitted much more easily the dispersed and fluid politics of the Austronesian world. Thus *datu* invited brahmans and other Indian religious experts to help them establish courts and acquire the trappings and rituals of Indian kingship.

Archaeological remains suggest the sudden appearance of a multitude of such political units in western Indonesia during the first centuries of the Christian era. Most of these polities counted for little, but two regions developed into significant centers of power. First was the Melaka (also Malacca) Strait between Sumatra and the Malay Peninsula (see Map 1). By the seventh century, the kingdom of Srivijaya had become a trading outlet for the rich hinterland of southern Sumatra and a major naval power controlling the strait and the surrounding waters. Trading vessels seeking a port of call came, willingly or not, to the main port of Srivijaya, close to the site of the modern city of Palembang (shown on Map 1). Although Sanskrit was used in the Srivijaya court, the language of the kingdom was Malay. One of Srivijaya's most important legacies was the consolidation of a broad Malay-speaking zone on both sides of the Melaka Strait.

The other power center to emerge at about this time was central Java, where a series of kingdoms developed on the fertile rice-growing plain of Kedu. From Sumatra to Maluku (the Moluccas), rice from Java fed port cities that had grown beyond the agricultural resources of their hinterlands. The cultivation of rice in wet paddy-fields (*sawah*) sustained the greatest concentration of population in the archipelago and allowed Javanese rulers to build Indonesia's most spectacular ancient monuments. The Buddhist temple of Borobudur, erected and intricately carved over sixty years during the seventh and eighth centuries using more than a million blocks of volcanic rock, is both a masterpiece of Javanese art and a measure of the power of Javanese rulers to mobilize their subjects. In the tenth century the center of Javanese civilization moved to eastern Java, perhaps as a result of disease or volcanic catastrophe. But the island retained its preeminence in population and civilization, and Javanese became the most spoken language of maritime Southeast Asia.

Srivijaya on Sumatra and its rivals on Java were warlike states. They raided each other and attempted to establish spheres of influence beyond their Malay and Javanese heartlands. Javanese forces were even engaged briefly in Cambodia. None of these polities was able to conquer the rest; their political control outside the heartlands was always tenuous. Even within these kingdoms the authority of rulers was far from evenly felt. Hindu-Buddhist cosmology gave the monarch unassailable authority as the divine incarnation and representative of divinity, but political realities in the Indonesian world made his position much less eminent or secure. The authority of a ruler was, in practice, negotiated and renegotiated with powerful regional leaders. The position of rulers in Srivijaya rested on a carefully constructed balance between chieftains in the interior, merchants and officials in the capital, and the leaders of semi-piratical "people of the sea" (*orang laut*) who formed the core of the Srivijayan navy. A king on Java had to keep looking over his shoulder at regional warlords (*bupati*) who formed a potential nucleus for revolt.

The cultural authority of Srivijaya and the Javanese states, on the other hand, stretched well beyond their spheres of political influence. Sumatra and Java were twin pinnacles of political power and cultural achievement in an archipelago where power and refinement were highly valued. Many of the peoples of Southeast Asia became accustomed to looking beyond their immediate political horizons to such "exemplary centers," as they have been called: glittering and attractive foci of power, wealth, and civilization.[2] This respect for the cultural power of greater states transcended without canceling the individual claims of local rulers to divine status. In the archipelago, for example, god-kings could offer tribute from time to time to Chinese emperors without conceding the political subordi-

---

2. On the idea of an "exemplary center," see Barbara Watson Andaya, "Political Development between the Sixteenth and Eighteenth Centuries," in Nicholas Tarling, ed., *The Cambridge History of Southeast Asia* (Cambridge, UK: Cambridge University Press, 1992), vol. 1, pp. 442–445; Clifford Geertz, *Negara: The Theatre State in Nineteenth-century Bali* (Princeton, NJ: Princeton University Press, 1980), pp. 11–19; and Robert Heine-Geldern, "Conceptions of State and Kingship in Southeast Asia," *Far Eastern Quarterly,* 2 (1942), pp. 15–30.

nation that Chinese authorities tried to read into such actions. Centuries later, in parallel fashion, Indonesian nationalists could admire the modernity of Japan or the West without being any less committed to their own country's identity and independence.

The archipelago's politics in premodern times were thus diverse but patterned. The islands sustained a multitude of local polities of widely varying size and character—some of them clearly states, some of them semi-autonomous tributaries, some of them no more than statelets, and some of them stateless societies such as the Batak of northern Sumatra. But there was at the same time a strong sense of a larger world, involving centers inside and outside the archipelago, centers whose key feature was not their military strength but their civilization— their power to represent and deliver higher and more attractive levels of meaning and livelihood to the islands' peoples.

Competing Exemplary Centers

Between the fifteenth and the seventeenth centuries this political order came under new strains. The volume and value of trade expanded, as clove, nutmeg, pepper, fragrant aloeswood and sandalwood, bezoar stones, and trepang joined the older staples of camphor and benzoin in the marketplace.[3] More and more of the archipelago was drawn in one way or another into the global economy, including the previously isolated east that now gained fame as the Spice Islands. New cities arose, especially in northern Sumatra and along the north coast of Java, and increasing numbers of foreign traders came to visit them. It was a time of economic and cultural quickening when merchant aristocracies, often known simply as *orang kaya,* or "rich people," became increasingly influential in urban politics.

By the thirteenth century a new religion, Islam, had taken firm root in the archipelago, having come in over the trade routes. Merchants were particularly receptive to Islam, with its straightforward message of human equality before God and its usefully explicit rules regarding commerce. One can imagine such itinerant converts feeling uncomfortable with the conventions of Hindu-Buddhist royal absolutism and attracted by a faith whose Allah stayed with them wherever they went, unlike the local gods and spirits of older beliefs.

Traders of Indonesian origin had once dominated commerce in the archipelago. Now, however, Chinese, Japanese, Arabs, and Indians, among other nationalities, became more prominent. For the first time, too, powers outside Southeast Asia began to take a sustained political interest in the region. Before 1400 the archipelago

---

3. Highly valued at the time as an antidote to poison, bezoar stones are formed by the accretion of a kind of tannin around a nucleus of wood or bark in the stomach of an animal such as monkey. Trepang are worm-like sea creatures related to starfish; boiled, dried, and smoked, they were prized, especially by the Chinese, as an ingredient in soup.

had been attacked by such forces only twice: In the eleventh century men from the Chola Kingdom in southern India ventured across the Bay of Bengal to raid Srivijaya. Late in the thirteenth century the Mongols dispatched an army to Java to assert their right to exact tribute from the eastern Javanese kingdom of Singosari—a right the Mongols believed they had acquired from the Chinese.

The Chola attack sent Srivijaya into an abrupt decline. Srivijaya's economic role and cultural standing were taken up first by neighboring Jambi and, in the fifteenth century, by Melaka (or Malacca), on the peninsular coast of the strait of the same name. Melaka's authority as an exemplary center survived its ruler's conversion to Islam and the Melaka sultanate came to define much of the high culture of Indonesian Islam. The Mongol raid achieved little more than a dynastic succession from Singosari to the kingdom of Majapahit. But Majapahit would come to be regarded as the greatest of the early Javanese states.

Beginning early in the fifteenth century the archipelago's polities were more subject to intrusion from the outside world. In 1405 the Chinese emperor sent the first of seven naval expeditions into maritime Southeast Asia and beyond in an effort to affirm Chinese hegemony over this increasingly wealthy region. The Chinese expeditions ceased after 1433, but Chinese traders remained.

In 1511 the Portuguese captured Melaka, Srivijaya's successor, adding to the Southeast Asian political mix a new European element that would in time become decisive for Indonesia. An intermittent and protracted European conquest of the archipelago ensued. The process would be completed only in the early twentieth century, but its most consequential events took place early on. The fall of Melaka in particular dealt a crucial blow to the Melaka Strait as an exemplary center of political-cum-cultural authority. Melaka declined rapidly under Portuguese rule, but the Portuguese were strong enough to prevent any indigenous rival from donning the mantle of Srivijaya. The northern Sumatran state of Aceh (pronounced "Acheh") and the remnants of the Melaka royal court in Johor (in present-day Malaysia) became significant local powers, but neither ever approached the standing of Melaka in its pre-Portuguese heyday.

In 1610, a century following the Portuguese seizure of Melaka, the Dutch established a permanent presence in the archipelago by opening a trading post on the northwestern coast of Java. That outpost, Batavia, would eventually become the capital of the Netherlands Indies. Still later the city would be renamed Jakarta and declared the capital of the Republic of Indonesia (see Map 1).

In the course of the seventeenth century the political authority of Java as an exemplary center was destroyed. The dominant power on Java when the Dutch arrived was the recently emerged Muslim kingdom of Mataram, based in the center of the island. Mataram, however, quickly came into conflict with the Dutch traders' agency, the United East Indies Company (Vereenigde Oost-Indische Compagnie, or VOC). Deftly using military force and diplomatic maneuver, the Dutch were able by mid-century to reduce Mataram to client status. Mataram survived for another century until it was partitioned at Dutch hands in 1755, but its ability to provide a model for the rest of the archipelago was gone. Nor did the Dutch allow a new indigenous polity to emerge. Their control of the sea gave them sway over trade and the main sources of revenue for state-building.

Batavia became a major metropolis, a center of trade and administration, and the Dutch were able to establish enough hegemony over the archipelago to keep their European rivals out. (The Portuguese colony on the eastern half of the small island of Timor was an exception.) But the dour, practical merchants of the VOC had no interest in turning Batavia into an exemplary center of cultural display or in using their own business to spread European learning and civilization. For the most part, in fact, the VOC was indifferent if not hostile to proposals to spread Western learning, language, and religion among its subjects.

Initially, therefore, the West as a new exemplary center held relatively little appeal for the peoples of the archipelago. One of the few indigenous leaders to see Western civilization in a clearly positive light was Karaeng Pattingalloang, chief minister of the southern Sulawesi state of Gowa from 1639 to 1654. He learned five European languages, collected European books, maps, and globes, and had European works on gunnery translated into the local language to improve his army's skills.

Pattingalloang's interest in the West was doubly unusual as he was a Muslim. For most leaders in the islands at the time, Islam offered a more attractive exemplary center than did the West. The Ottoman Empire was at the height of its powers, and direct trading communication between the archipelago and the Arabian peninsula had become an important conduit for Muslim traders and missionaries who actively proselytized on behalf of their religion. The late sixteenth century had been a golden age of Islamic learning in Southeast Asia, with Mecca, Cairo, and Istanbul the most important external points of reference. Neither the Portuguese nor the Dutch could compete with Islam for broad cultural appeal.

Growing Dutch Dominance

Colonial historians writing in the nineteenth and early twentieth centuries tended to treat the arrival of Europeans as the start of a new era in Southeast Asian history. Mid-to-late twentieth-century scholars have reacted against such "Eurocentrism" by pointing out the relative insignificance of the European presence before the nineteenth century and the concomitant "autonomy" of indigenous societies.[4] As noted above, the conquest of the archipelago was gradual.

---

4. An influential example of "Eurocentrism" was Bernard H.M. Vlekke, *Nusantara: A History of the East Indian Archipelago* (London: Benn, 1977). Arguments for "Indonesia-centric" approaches were made, for example, by John R.W. Smail, "On the Possibility of an Autonomous History of Modern Southeast Asia," *Journal of Southeast Asian History,* 2:2 (1961), pp. 72–102; and J.C. van Leur, "A History of the Netherlands East Indies: Three Reviews," in *Indonesian Trade and Society: Essays in Asian Social and Economic History* (The Hague: Van Hoeve, 1955 [orig. in Dutch, 1939–1940]), pp. 249–289.

Many regions experienced colonial rule for no more than a few decades. The early loss of Melaka and Java did, however, remove from maritime Southeast Asia not just its most powerful states but its foci of political and cultural authority. No such magnetic centers would be restored within the archipelago until the rise of the idea of Indonesia in the early twentieth century.

The slow expansion of Dutch colonial rule over the Indonesian archipelago was driven by a changing tangle of motives and imperatives. At the beginning of the seventeenth century the Dutch were mainly interested in the spice trade to Europe. Their territorial conquests accordingly were confined to the areas of spice production and a few strategically located fortresses. As the century progressed, however, trade between Asian ports grew into an increasingly important source of Dutch income, and the VOC's ability to enforce a monopoly over commerce between specific ports, and in particular commodities, became the basis of its profits. Later still, the Dutch gradually shifted their economic presence inland as they involved themselves in growing high-volume plantation crops such as sugar and coffee, and much later tobacco, tea, rubber and palm oil, for processing, sale, and resale in markets around the world. In the twentieth century, petroleum, too, became an important export.

Pieced together over three centuries, the administrative structure of the Netherlands Indies was a baroque monument to complexity in which successive attempts at reform never entirely succeeded in removing the vestiges of earlier structures. At the core of the Indies administration stood a relatively straightforward administrative hierarchy headed by a governor general and a Council of the Indies and staffed by a few hundred European men appointed for their general administrative skills. In each region of the colony this European hierarchy interacted variously with one or more indigenous political institutions. In many places, especially outside Java, the local polities thus enmeshed were so-called native states—once independent entities that, by treaty or conquest, had fallen under Dutch control.

In managing the affairs of their own subjects, the rulers of most of these states enjoyed a fairly high degree of autonomy, so long as they did not attract the attention of the colonial authorities by hindering European economic interests, dallying with foreign powers, or unduly afflicting their own people. Elsewhere, in what were called regions of "direct" rule, the Dutch used local hierarchies of officials drawn whenever possible from indigenous aristocracies. On Java these officials were the *bupati,* the former regional lords of Mataram; their counterparts on other islands were known by a variety of titles. These officials were somewhat more closely supervised than their counterparts in the native states, but they were allowed and even encouraged to use the rituals and regalia of traditional royalty to secure the loyalty and obedience of their subjects.

The authority of these quasi-traditional rulers extended only over indigenous peoples. Europeans, wherever they traveled in the archipelago, came under the direct authority of the central administration. Other Asians, mainly Chinese, were administered separately again: The colonial government appointed locally promi-nent Chinese as civilian officials with military titles such as *majoor, kapitan,* and *luitenant* and gave them responsibility for administering the affairs of their own communities. Still different regulations governed the position of Christian Indo-nesians.

The VOC formula for profit was simple: Buy cheap and sell dear. In applying this strategy to Maluku the Company tightly monopolized the production of spices, to the extent of launching raids to destroy spice trees not under VOC control. On Java, where most of the coffee and sugar plantations came to be established, the strategy involved forcing peasants to tend and harvest crops on behalf of the Company for little or no remuneration. Although slaves provided an important part of the labor force in the seventeenth century, especially in the vicinity of Batavia, the VOC for the most part preferred to place legal obligations on nomi-nally free peasants. During the first half of the nineteenth century, under the so-called Cultivation System, communal tax obligations tied Javanese peasants to their villages and set them to work for the colonial government. In the late nine-teenth century in Sumatra, a system of "penal sanctions" enabled private planta-tion owners to use criminal law to enforce employment contracts with plantation workers.

On the other hand, from about the middle of the eighteenth century, liberal ideas of labor management began to exercise some influence in colonial policy. Especially after the VOC collapsed into bankruptcy at the end of the century and the colony was taken over by the Dutch government, the colonial administration tried to build an element of incentive into its production strategies by allowing peasants and laborers to profit from working on colonial projects. Whether these measures were of any real consequence to either peasants or wage laborers has been a matter of scholarly debate.[5] Controversial, too, is the thesis of "agricul-tural involution" advanced by Clifford Geertz: that the Cultivation System led to the lasting impoverishment of the Javanese peasantry by locking its members into increasingly elaborate value-sharing structures that made economic devel-opment based on value-accumulation virtually impossible.[6]

What is not controversial is that in the nineteenth century the living standards

5. Compare, for example, V.J.H. Houben, "History and Morality: East Sumatran Inci-dents as Described by Jan Breman," *Itinerario* [Leiden, Netherlands], 12:2 (1988), pp. 97–100; Jan Breman, "Controversial Views on Writing Colonial History," *Itinerario,* 16:2 (1992), pp. 39–58; and Houben's "Colonial History Revisited: A Response to Breman," *Itinerario,* 17:1 (1993), pp. 93–97.

6. Geertz, *Agricultural Involution: The Process of Ecological Change in Indonesia* (Berkeley: University of California Press, 1963). Benjamin White reviewed the debate in his "'Agricultural Involution' and Its Critics: Twenty Years After," *Bulletin of Concerned Asian Scholars,* 15:2 (1983), pp. 18–31. For recent archival research that puts to rest many of the speculative lines of argument for and against Geertz's thesis, see R.E. Elson, *Village Java under the Cultivation System* (Sydney: Allen and Unwin, 1994).

of a great many indigenous people in the Indies declined. As population density grew and employment opportunities failed to keep pace, famine became more and more common, especially on Java. By the beginning of the twentieth century, the evidence of declining welfare was compelling enough to prompt the Dutch to announce a new "ethical" approach to colonial policy. Palliative measures such as improved health care at the village level were introduced, alongside longer-term programs to raise agricultural production and even to encourage industrial development.

These programs had only a limited material impact. They took time to plan and they cost money. They were largely abandoned at the start of the Great Depression of the 1930s, which badly damaged the Dutch economy. But the "Ethical Policy," as it was called, was significant as the first concerted effort by a European government to address what would later be described as the underdevelopment of the Third World. The policy also illustrated a developmentalist or welfare-promoting conception of modernity for Indonesia that would later attract some nationalist leaders.

The Dutch faced resistance to their rule from time to time in virtually every part of their colonial empire. Sometimes this resistance was aimed at remedying specific grievances or reversing unwanted colonial actions: Local elites fought to recover power lost to the Dutch; peasants fought to be relieved of harsh overseers or unreasonable regulations. Much of such opposition, however, took place within the broad and related ideological frameworks of Islam and messianism. The most tenacious rejections of Dutch rule, in areas such as Banjarmasin in southern Borneo and in Aceh, were led by Muslims unwilling to submit to an infidel state. The most destructive uprising occurred in the Java War of 1825–30 in which at least 200,000 people died. The Javanese insurgents were led by a charismatic Muslim prince, Diponegoro. His followers believed he had been commanded by Allah to conquer the island and create a new Javanese empire.

The effectiveness of Islamic and messianic movements was limited by the difficulties they faced in projecting themselves and their beliefs as plausible alternatives to Western power and culture. In the nineteenth century Islam was at a low ebb in world affairs. The Ottoman Empire was in terminal decline. Muslim societies throughout the world faced defeat and domination at the hands of the Christian West. Muslims might well decide that life under Christian rule was intolerable, but nowhere could an Islamic society point to itself as a shining example of civilized achievement.

Galvanized by precisely this issue, Islamic reformers tried to purify their religion: to rid Islam of what they saw as medieval accretions in order to make it again a basis for greatness. Reformism became a major intellectual and political force in the Muslim world in the nineteenth century. But the reformers' agenda was by no means dominant; other Muslims contested their diagnosis and their proposed treatment. As for messianism, Diponegoro's project and the many much smaller-scale instances of millenarian resistance that peppered the nineteenth and early twentieth centuries on Java simply did not acknowledge, and thus could not learn from, the technological advantages of the West or the social changes that colonialism had already wrought in the archipelago.

Modernity and the Idea of Indonesia

The technological prowess and cultural and intellectual virtuosity of the West attracted admirers and imitators in nineteenth-century Asia. In the still independent states of the mainland, a string of capable reformers arose with plans to transform their societies according to a Western model. In Southeast Asia, the reformism of the Siamese kings Mongkut (r. 1851–68) and Chulalongkorn (r. 1868–1910) most strikingly illustrated this vision of modernity.

In the Indonesian archipelago the impulse to copy if not catch up with the exemplary West was felt weakly and late, for two main reasons. First, accelerated modernization relied on a strong, autonomous, and well-funded state. Many of the modernizing movements on the mainland foundered because they could summon neither the political authority nor the finances to implement their visions. In the archipelago there were no independent states with the wherewithal for serious reform.

Second, in the nineteenth century the Netherlands Indies was something of an international backwater. The hub of the trade in goods moving through Southeast Asia was not Batavia but British-held Singapore. Holland was no longer a great power, militarily, economically, or culturally. Language barriers and the reluctance of the Dutch to spread Western education severely limited their subjects' access to the world of European ideas.

Only in the late nineteenth century did this situation begin to undergo significant change. The growing complexity of administration required the Dutch authorities to recruit increasing numbers of indigenous people into the middle levels of the colonial civil service, and that meant educating a small pool of young Indonesians from whom such officials could be recruited. At the same time the colonial administration began to hear the siren call of a *mission civilisatrice*. An important part of the ideology of late European imperialism, this was the idea that Europeans had a duty to impart to those whom they ruled the supposed blessings of Western civilization. The resulting expansion of European-language education opened a hole in the colonial edifice through which Western ideas could be transmitted to and diffused among large numbers of people in the archipelago. These changes made the first two decades of the twentieth century an intellectually lively time of learning and questioning in the archipelago.

Central to this ferment was the question: How could the Indies become modern? Those who answered were distributed across a wide spectrum of opinion. Some accepted the notion of a Dutch civilizing mission and envisaged a kind of apprenticeship in which the people of the Indies would gradually become more responsible for their own affairs as they mastered Western civilization one step at a time. Others took inspiration from Marxism with its promise of liberation for oppressed peoples in the name of an eventual socialist order that would be even more modern and progressive than the existing capitalist one. In the eyes of still others the best chance for modernity lay in Islamic reform: reanchoring the great Muslim majority in the basic, eternal, and thus necessarily ever-up-to-date values of the Qur'an (or Koran).

Increasingly among the indigenous population, this diversity of views and projects was tempered by agreement, first, that ending colonial rule was the most important step the Indies could take to become more modern. Second, that the transition to modernity should nevertheless occur inside, and thus acknowledge, the territorial frame that colonialism itself had created.

The first two decades of the twentieth century saw the breakup, temporarily or permanently, of the Austrian, Ottoman, Russian, and Chinese empires. Against this Eurasian backdrop of nationalism and revolution, the national movement in the Indies became committed to the idea of independence for an Indonesian nation-state encompassing the entire territory of the Netherlands Indies and all of its indigenous ethnic groups. This outcome was not foreordained. It was one thing to break the Netherlands Indies into its unequal components—the small Netherlands and the huge Indies. But why stop there? Why not finish the anticolonial project by dismantling the Indies itself in the name of smaller, regional nationalisms?

But if the pan-archipelagic colonial state was a problem for Indonesian nationalists, it presented a far greater opportunity as well. In the Indies the early twentieth century was a time of socioeconomic management. Colonial authorities made unprecedented intrusions into the daily lives of ordinary people. In the space of a few decades the rather backward colonial state of the nineteenth century was transformed into a touted model of supposedly scientific colonialism, exemplified most notably by the development programs of the Ethical Policy. As already explained, the Great Depression undercut the policy's ambition, but not before it had become clear that the twentieth-century Indies state could deliver modernity to its subjects—in principle, to all of them—if only it had the will and wherewithal to do so.

The increasing numbers of Indonesians who worked within that state grew confident not only that they could manage it as well as the Dutch had in a technical sense, but that they could supply the missing political will. As for wherewithal, the Indonesians grew convinced as well of their ability to exploit the islands' abundant natural resources for the good of the entire indigenous population of the Indies—a frame therefore worth retaining. Thus was the Dutch-made, archipelago-wide apparatus of government reconceived as a means of lifting all Indonesians toward better and more meaningful lives. And thus did the idea of Indonesia begin to acquire the connotations of an exemplary center in the legacy if not the image of Melaka and Majapahit.

The framework of the Indies was also attractive because the Dutch had deliberately sought to exclude Indonesians from it. During the decades when Western education was at last opening up the modern world to Indonesians, the colonial authorities were refining a system of racial-legal classification in the colony intended to limit indigenous participation in the facilities of modernity. The earlier distinctions between Europeans, non-indigenous Asians (mainly Chinese), and the indigenous subjects of local rulers were eventually systematized into a classification of all residents of the Indies as Europeans, "foreign orientals" (mainly Chinese), or "natives." To each of these groups the authorities assigned distinctive legal rights and responsibilities.

There were anomalies and loopholes: For example, the growing power of Meiji Japan persuaded the Dutch to grant to Japanese residents of the Indies a status equivalent to that of the Europeans. A Chinese or even a "native" who met certain criteria for being European—Western language and dress, monogamous marriage, and the like—could acquire equivalent-to-European status for a small fee. The laws also gave some protection to the indigenous population, notably by banning the purchase of land by non-indigenes.

But the system implemented discrimination: "Natives" received lower salaries within the colonial administration, could expect unequal treatment by the police, and faced restricted access to public facilities ranging from schools to swimming pools. The system's codifications were a standing affront to modern Indonesians who correctly saw that racial discrimination could not be ended unless colonialism itself were done away with.

Another reason why the archipelago-wide idea of Indonesia could stand for the promise of modernity was that Dutch colonial policies had largely disabled less inclusive alternatives based on regional ethnic identities. The Dutch had preserved the rulers of native states and employed the *bupati* in part because they believed that the traditional authority of these elites would make colonial domination less obtrusive and more palatable. In this context the main indigenous ruling elites in the archipelago did best by not being modern. In Java especially, the coopted aristocracy sponsored an elaboration of traditional culture and philosophy that emphasized the refinement of esoteric, sometimes mystical, skills rather than mastery of the material world through science, technology, and modern administration.

Its close association with modernity gave the idea of Indonesia a special relationship with the many ethnic identities across the archipelago. The national idea was not a composite projection of advanced versions of each regional culture; the name "Indonesia" labeled the potential that all Indonesians had to become modern. At the same time, being Indonesian did not mean ceasing to be Javanese or Acehnese or Manadonese; it meant augmenting one's ethnic self with participation in the modern world. The nearest analogy is perhaps the self-confidence with which the United States took on for itself an identity as exemplar of modernity, admitting people from many ethnicities and allowing them to acculturate at their own pace, confident in the eventual solvent power of the American nation running "from sea to shining sea"—or, in the Indonesian phrase, "from Sabang to Merauke."[7]

The national movement in Indonesia, therefore, was two things at once: a movement of individuals who saw themselves and their future as trans-ethnically Indonesian, and a coalition of ethnic or regional groups prepared to fit into the national frame. Some of the largest mass organizations of the first half of the twentieth century were explicitly ethnoregional, but did not advocate secession. In West Java, for example, the Sundanese Association (Paguyuban Pasundan) aimed to revitalize Sundanese culture and restore prosperity to the Sundanese people. Yet it never confronted the national movement with demands for a political future separate from the rest of Indonesia.

Unity as Necessity

For the national movement, the idea of unity quickly acquired crucial symbolic value. It meant, first of all, that none of the indigenous ethnic groups of the archipelago was to be excluded from the idea of Indonesia in the way that the Dutch had kept "natives" from participating fully in the Netherlands Indies. Unity was also appealing because the national movement saw that its main strength lay in numbers. Having come to realize that Holland was a relatively minor power in world affairs, Indonesians had to explain a conundrum: How could such a small country have come to dominate so vast an archipelago? Part of the solution was to attribute to the Dutch a strategy of "divide and rule," and from this it followed that unity must be a top priority of the national movement to end colonialism.

The emphasis on unity had major consequences for the ideology of the national movement. The need to rally disparate identities made it difficult for nationalist leaders to make any pronouncement on specifics—just what sort of modernity an independent Indonesia ought to have. The constituents of the Indonesian state-to-be were diverse not only ethnically but also religiously. Some 90 percent of Indonesians were Muslim, but there were strong Christian communities among, for example, the Bataks of northern Sumatra in the archipelago's far west. Just east of Java, the Balinese were almost all Hindu. Farther east, Christians in substantial number could be found among the Ambonese, Minahasans, Timorese, and Florese (see Maps 2 and 4).

Even Indonesians who considered themselves Muslim displayed enormous variation in religious practice. Many Javanese, for instance, followed an Islam that had incorporated Hindu-Buddhist and other pre-Islamic beliefs, while Muslims in some other regions prided themselves on following an orthodoxy associ-

---

7. As shown in Map 1, Sabang in northwestern Aceh and Merauke in southeastern Irian Jaya symbolize the territorial breadth and integrity of Indonesia. After World War II the phrase was used to assert national unity against the Netherlands, first during the revolution and later in the campaign to recover Dutch New Guinea (now Irian Jaya).

ated with the Middle East. A national movement aiming to include all of these communities, therefore, could not take Islam as its substantive guiding principle.

Just as important, class issues in different regions varied greatly. The polar-ized plantation society of northern Sumatra had little in common with the communities of independent smallholders in southern Sumatra. The accomplished Minangkabau traders of western Sumatra shared little of the worldview of Javanese peasants. With their high levels of out-migration, economic backwaters such as Ambon and Timor were unlike the social environment in East Kalimantan, where a developing oil industry attracted growing numbers of immigrants. A broadly Marxist analysis of class contradictions could make powerful sense in parts of Java yet hold little appeal for Indonesians in more entrepreneurial regions.

Any section of the national movement that pressed a too-specific understanding of Indonesia's national identity and modern future faced the risk of splitting the anticolonial coalition and endangering its numerical advantage over the Dutch. In 1920–21 the hazards of division were brought home to many of the movement's leaders by a bitter falling out between Marxists and Muslims inside one of the leading national organizations, the Islamic Association (Sarekat Islam). There was also a danger that excluding any portion of the archipelago from the national movement might drive that part to declare its own independence or negotiate a separate autonomy based on cooperation with the Dutch.

The seriousness of this risk should not be underestimated. Neither the relative ethnic homogeneity of their populations nor their traditions of political unity could save China and Vietnam from being partitioned in the mid-twentieth century. Great-power rivalry abetted these civil wars, to be sure, internal differences played major contributing roles: In both cases national unity fell victim to the alienation of certain social elements by the radicalism of a key section of the national movement. In retrospect, in the Indies, appealing to unity as an anticolonial goal without specifying the kind of postcolonial society that would be used to achieve it was a way of trying to avoid such an outcome.

Accordingly, the central principles of the Indonesian national movement, when they were finally defined at a national youth congress in 1928, were simple: one country, one people, one language. Ideological or cultural conformity to a particular vision of Indonesia was not required. Nor, in 1928, was the "one language" chosen, Indonesian, associated with the ambitions of any particular ethnic group. *Bahasa Indonesia,* the Indonesian language, had evolved from the Malay language of the Melaka Strait region. But the latter medium had been expanded into a lingua franca for trade across the archipelago and then used and popularized by the Dutch as the Indies' main indigenous language. No longer the property of a single ethnicity or region, *bahasa Indonesia* became a widespread, practical, neutral, and therefore unifying medium.

Because of the need for unity, preeminence in the national movement went to those personalities who could articulate a message that included all and antagonized none. The most important of these figures was Sukarno. Trained as an engineer in the city of Bandung south of Batavia, captivated by the wealth of ideas that Western learning opened to him, Sukarno distinguished himself from his peers in the national movement by excelling as an orator and an ideologist. Characteristically, in his most important early essay, *Nationalisme, Islamisme dan Marxisme*, first published in 1926,[8] he emphasized not how these three philosophical systems differed but what they had in common. His purpose was to blend nationalism, Islam, and Marxism into a single though multi-stranded national ideology for modern Indonesia. The eclectic modernity thus envisaged by Sukarno would subsume ideological, cultural, and religious divisions under a sole rubric: Indonesia, united and free.

But it was easier to imagine Indonesian freedom than achieve it. In the 1920s and 1930s the nationalists tried in various ways to unseat the Dutch. Nothing worked. Sarekat Islam tried popular confrontation, even sharpening it with some small-scale terrorism, but was easily checked by the authorities. The Indonesian Communist Party (Partai Komunis Indonesia, or PKI) tried armed revolution in 1926–27, but was quickly suppressed. Sukarno advocated mass mobilization and withholding cooperation from the Dutch, but he was soon arrested and condemned to internal exile. So were two of his nationalist colleagues, Mohammad Hatta and Sutan Sjahrir, who had sought to begin the long-term task of constructing a revolutionary cadre party. More moderate nationalists could become members of the People's Council, or Volksraad, a semirepresentative parliament with limited powers that the Dutch had established in 1916. But this was a more or less coopted venue. In the 1920s, and through most of the 1930s, Indonesian nationalists had few good options.

Global conditions, however, had begun to favor the nationalist project. By the 1930s the tide of world affairs had begun to turn against colonialism. The Americans had promised independence to the Philippines, while the British policy of devolving power to elected Indian representatives in their Indian colony pointed clearly toward future self-rule.

Indonesia's passage to independence was more turbulent. By 1941 there were at last signs that the Dutch were beginning to take seriously the Indonesian thirst for freedom. But by then the Netherlands had fallen under German occupation. The Dutch had no political will to do more than promise a serious look at reform some time in the future. Early in 1942, anxious to secure oil supplies from Sumatra and Borneo for their war effort elsewhere in Asia, Japanese forces seized the Indies.

The occupation shattered the power and authority of the Dutch in the archipelago. Once Japanese military preeminence was clear, the colonial administra-

---

8. Translated by Karel H. Warouw and Peter D. Weldon as *Nationalism, Islam, and Marxism* (Ithaca, NY: Cornell University Modern Indonesia Project, 1970), with an introduction by Ruth T. McVey.

tion decided not to take a stand. Merely ten days elapsed between the landing of Japanese forces on Java and the surrender of the Dutch. The decision may have been wise from a humanitarian point of view, but it made the Dutch appear to have abandoned their colony to Asian invaders with virtually no resistance. During the occupation, moreover, the Japanese treated the Europeans with contempt. Herded into detention camps, the Dutch suffered arduous and demeaning conditions. The comfortable assumptions of European superiority and dominance that had prevailed before the war could never be restored.

The ruining of their myth of prowess did not stop the Dutch from attempting to reestablish authority over the islands in the wake of Japan's defeat in 1945. But the manner and timing of that defeat opened a unique chance for Indonesia's nationalists to thwart recolonization. The dropping of atomic bombs on Hiroshima and Nagasaki led the Japanese to surrender on 15 August 1945 while their forces were still in control of much of the archipelago. Some weeks elapsed before the Dutch and the other Allies against Japan were in a position to bring more than token military forces to reoccupy the islands. The Indonesian nationalist leaders Sukarno and Hatta used this window of opportunity to proclaim their country's independence in Jakarta (formerly Batavia) on 17 August. A day later the two men were named president and vice president, respectively, of the newly formed government of the Republic of Indonesia.

In a remarkable display of political agility, Sukarno would manage to keep his presidency intact through the turbulent early decades of independence. For twenty-three years, until General Suharto fully replaced him in 1968, Sukarno remained, at least in name, president of: (a) the original, unitary Republic (1945–49); (b) its ill-fated federal successor state (1949–50); (c) the original state revived, but with a different constitution (1950–59); and (d) the fully restored original Republic (1959–68) that Indonesia still is today.

This future could hardly be foreseen by Indonesian nationalists in late August 1945. But they knew they were living in a time of change and opportunity. Sukarno's first government faced a political climate that had been transformed by three and a half years of Japanese occupation. The Dutch authorities had prized peace and order in the colony. But the Japanese had taken a more dynamic view, seeking to engage their new subjects in the war effort by involving them in a series of mass organizations. Indonesians had been encouraged to believe that they were an integral part of a movement of Asian peoples fighting for liberation from Western imperialism. For the first time since the imposition of colonial rule in the Indies, a government had publicly courted its subjects, showered them with slogans, and galvanized them to political ends. Those ends were driven by Japan's wartime needs, not by an Indonesian desire for freedom. Nevertheless, especially among younger Indonesian nationalists, heady political mobilization fired by accumulated grievances against colonialism created a mighty conviction that Indonesians had not only the right but also the power to make their own future.

Meanwhile the potential for disunity and conflict within nationalist ranks had risen precipitously. The movement before 1945 had been a coalition of ethnic and ideological groups whose leaders had read into the idea of Indonesia differing conceptions of modernity. As argued above, to preserve unity during the struggle for freedom, the hard task of reconciling these diverse views had been kept in the background as much as possible. But now that independence had been declared, decisions on basic political structures and basic government policy had to be taken—at a time when the number of voices demanding a say in such decisions had never been greater.

Three Meanings of Modernity

Inside the anticolonial movement, nationalists of diverse ethnoregional and ideological stripes had coalesced around two convictions: that an Indonesian nation-state could deliver modernity, and that Dutch rule blocked this aspiration. The resulting coalition spanned over a dozen major ethnic identities and, broadly speaking, three main outlooks: Marxist, Muslim, and developmentalist.

Marxist nationalists argued that modernity and prosperity would come to Indonesians only if the economic system were radically overhauled. In particular, Indonesia's subordination to the global economy had to be overthrown. Foreign-owned enterprises, which had been the source of such wealth to the West, had to be seized by and for the Indonesian people.

What mattered for Muslim nationalists was that fundamental aspects of the relationships of individuals with Allah, and with each other under Allah, be correctly understood and carried out. Only by deepening its Islamic character could Indonesian society bolster political with moral independence from the West. Because an Islamic modernity presupposed the operation of Islamic laws, the launching of an independent state created an opportunity for Muslim leaders to demand the official enforcement of religious duties for the vast majority of Indonesians who were already Muslim in name—and could now become fully Muslim in practice as well.

Adherents of the third ideology in the nationalist coalition may be described as developmentalists. They largely accepted the conception of modernity embodied in the Ethical Policy that the Dutch had pursued. From this standpoint the priority lay in expanding and improving education, infrastructure, and investment so that Indonesians could reduce, as quickly and as far as possible, the gap between their living standards and those of the West. The colonial state would be renamed Indonesia, staffed by Indonesians, and redeployed on behalf of Indonesian betterment, but the developmentalists saw no need substantially to change its basic structures.

After independence had been proclaimed in 1945, two factors worked to preserve the modi vivendi among these three constructions of modernity. First, Sukarno continued his efforts to compress and bind Marxism, Islam, and developmentalism into an intellectual whole. In a speech delivered shortly before he declared Indonesia's independence, Sukarno outlined what he called the Pancasila, or Five Principles. These generally are summarized as: Belief in God; Nationalism; Humanitarianism; Democracy; and Social Justice. Because all Indonesians subscribed to its elements, asserted Sukarno, Pancasila could and should become a common doctrine underlying and unifying the new nation-state.

A second and more important factor working to dampen or postpone ideological conflict was the rapid realization that declaring independence on paper was one thing, winning it quite another. The Dutch immediately made clear their intention to reestablish their presence on the islands. When Allied troops landed in the eastern Javanese port city of Surabaya in November 1945, they created a potential foothold for the Dutch return. Heavy fighting broke out between British-Indian and Indonesian nationalist forces. Obliged to retreat into the countryside, the Indonesians began a guerrilla war. (The Battle of Surabaya is still celebrated in Indonesia as Heroes' Day.) By early 1946 Allied troops were firmly established in the seven main cities of Java and Sumatra, while most of Kalimantan (on Borneo), Sulawesi, and the islands of eastern Indonesia were fully restored to Dutch rule.

These events temporarily sustained the need to downplay ideological differences for the sake of the common struggle for national freedom. Nevertheless, pronouncing Indonesia independent had abruptly highlighted the uncomfortable fact that the new country could not be simultaneously Marxist, Islamic, and developmentalist—except perhaps in the mind of Sukarno. Marxism and Islam gave contradictory answers to the basic question of God's existence. If the developmentalists hoped Western capitalists would invest in Indonesia to help make it modern, Marxists opposed capitalism and championed socialism. Compared with the developmentalists, Muslim nationalists were less complacent about giving infidel foreigners a stake in the economy. Unlike the secular Marxists, Muslims resented partly on ethnoreligious grounds the economic stature of the archipelago's racially Chinese minority, almost none of whose members had embraced the majority faith of their adopted country. Divergent understandings of class and the need for class struggle further divided the three groups.

The ideological crisis was immediate. It emerged in 1945 during the drafting of Indonesia's new constitution, even before independence was announced, when strongly Muslim leaders sought to create a special place for Islam in the new document. An outright proclamation of Indonesia as an Islamic state was too controversial to be realistic: The Christian minorities would have objected and those in eastern Indonesia might have been tempted to secede. Muslim leaders therefore fell back on what they considered a more feasible request. Let the constitution merely affirm, they argued, that Indonesia's Muslims were obliged to comply with Islamic law.

After an emotional debate in the committee charged with drafting the new charter, this seemingly reasonable request was rejected. For even the reduced language—a mere seven words—implied that the full power of the state could be used to enforce orthodoxy for all Muslims, including those, especially numerous on Java, whose beliefs and practices could be said to ignore, if not violate, Qur'anic law.

Demographically, Muslims were a huge majority in the new country. But politically, Islamists were a minority both within that majority and among the new state's founders. Nor did the idea of officially implementing Islam reassure non-Muslims, who saw it as an invitation to use the state to transform the archipelago's statistically Muslim majority into a formidable and, from their standpoint, dangerous political force. The defeat of the Islamists' project and the consequently non-Islamic character of the new state, in turn, profoundly disappointed the more self-consciously Muslim segment of Indonesian society.

Also soon thwarted were the plans of radical and mainly secular Indonesians to make social transformation a priority of Indonesia's national revolution against the Dutch. The Marxist Tan Malaka argued that thoroughgoing social changes were needed if the mass of Indonesians was to be given a stake in the fight for freedom from the Dutch. By instigating a social revolution inside the national one would, he believed, win such fervent support from formerly exploited Indonesians as to doom the designs of the returning Dutch.

But Indonesia's first prime minister, Sjahrir, disagreed. In his opinion, pursuing such radical goals would undercut a republic already too weak to confront the Allies who had so recently won a global war. At least for the time being, Indonesia would have to set aside the hope of social transformation and defend its very survival by constructively engaging the West. Indonesians needed the West; they could not go it alone; they could not reject Western investment and still hope to become modern. For Sjahrir, pragmatic cooperation within a Western-dominated economic order would benefit Indonesians more than radical idealism or revolutionary confrontation.

Whatever the merits of transformation versus adaptation as alternative paths to modernity, Tan Malaka the Marxist activist soon found himself outmaneuvered by Sjahrir the prime minister. Early in 1946 Sjahrir had him jailed. Under Sukarno, Sjahrir's developmentalist ideology would first be tried, then discredited and rejected. But elements of it would return to inspire the economic policies of the "New Order" under Indonesia's second president, Suharto, as recounted by Anne Booth in her chapter in this book.

Identity and Revolution

These setbacks for the Islamist and Marxist projects within Indonesian nationalism were at least partly a result of the determination of the just-declared republic's leaders not to endanger the ethnoregional coalition. Indonesia's Christian and Hindu communities were concentrated in certain ethnic communities, typically on islands outside Java. In 1945 most of the drafters of the new constitution feared that any kind of special recognition for Islam would leave these communities in a second-class status that might encourage them to think of becoming independent states in their own right.

Ethnoregional arguments against Tan Malaka's program were even stronger. His radical proposals might have consolidated Republican authority on Java and Sumatra, where colonial exploitation had gone the farthest toward creating class inequalities and grievances. But by this same token his ideas offered little prospect of recovering the other islands, where traditional elites and Dutch influence were still relatively strong.

These arguments made sense, and the fears of disintegration they relied on were real. In retrospect, however, it seems clear that even those regions least mobilized by the Indonesian revolution could not offer more than parochial alternatives to the archipelago-wide state that the Republic was, from the beginning, intended to be. The fact that the government in Jakarta had very little effective authority in the early months of the revolution actually may have facilitated the expression of regional loyalty to the Republic. Within each region, local leaders were free to shape the revolution as they chose, settling local scores and changing the local political landscape, while all the time professing utmost loyalty to the center.

Strikingly, there was no pressure at all in 1945 to acknowledge Indonesia's ethnic diversity by creating a federal system. Ethnicity had been compartmentalized as "tradition"—a valued part of every Indonesian's identity but not something that required protected status in the unitary modern polity of Indonesia. Ethnoregional identities were strong enough to warrant sensitivity; their importance had helped to undercut the viability of Marxist and Muslim visions of modernity. But regional cultures remained points of local and not national reference.

The imposing size of the one ethnic group large enough to have aspired to hegemony, the Javanese, may in fact have helped to restrain its nationalist leaders from doing so. The Javanese leaders of the Republic were committed to archipelago-wide unity as a matter of nationalist principle. But they also understood that no other regional culture had a better chance to shape the character of a unified Indonesian state. In this sense, it was the Javanese and not the "outer islanders" who had the most to lose from secession.

The priority on preserving unity within Republican ranks could not prevent efforts to try out Tan Malaka's more radical vision of modernity. A wave of social revolution swept virtually the whole length of Sumatra and Java in late 1945 and early 1946. But Republican leaders such as Sukarno were not radicalized by these events. Class consciousness did not oust national unity as the basis for the Republic. The social forces involved in the uprisings in 1945–46 in Indonesia were too diverse—not only communists, but also Muslim groups, labor unions, bandits, militias, young intellectuals, progressive aristocrats—and the mix varied from region to region. They thought of themselves, in any case, not as opposing the Republic but implementing it.

The ethnoregional coalition sustaining the Republic was first put at risk only later in the revolution. By early 1946, the Dutch authorities had given up as unrealistic the idea of resurrecting the Netherlands Indies and begun to accept, however reluctantly, the probability of some kind of Indonesian autonomy. Their main concern was to ensure that their eventual Indonesian successors would not be unduly hostile to Dutch interests. But to ensure this they insisted on exercising more authority during and over the process of succession than most Indonesians were willing to accept.

Negotiations between the two sides began early in 1946. Two agreements were achieved—one in 1947 in a resort town in western Java, the other a year later aboard the USS *Renville,* which the United States had provided as a neutral venue. But the terms of these documents were quickly violated.

Mistrust abounded on both sides. The Dutch feared that the Republicans would sign any agreement merely to win a recognition of sovereignty, and then use that asset to radical ends contrary to the agreement's provisions. The Republicans too feared perfidy: that the Dutch would use any transitional period to purge the national movement and set up a puppet state. The negotiations were constantly blighted on both sides by suspicion, bad faith, and military action.

Between Federalism and Radicalism

By 1948 the Dutch had gained control of extensive territory on Java and Sumatra, in addition to what they held elsewhere in the archipelago. Unwilling to transfer authority to an independent, archipelago-wide Republic, the Dutch began to develop an alternative successor to the Indies by erecting a framework of federated states on its outer islands.

At first the Dutch had seen these federal states as a politically conservative counterweight to Republican radicals on Java—and also as a way of easing the reunification of the archipelago following its administrative division under Japan's occupation. During the course of the revolution, however, Dutch opinion shifted toward the idea of actually fragmenting the Indies. During 1948 the Dutch seriously considered granting independence to a federal state that would exclude a nationalist Republic and would be reduced to parts of Java and Sumatra, and toyed with encouraging separatist movements in West Java, Ambon, and the Minahasa area of northern Sulawesi. Not coincidentally, the Ambonese and Minahasans were (and remain) largely Protestant populations.

The Dutch experiment with promoting ethnic separatism was remarkably unsuccessful. The idea of Indonesia continued to hold the same promise of modernity in 1948 that it had two decades earlier. Most Indonesians were not attracted by the prospect of living in a small but ethnically homogeneous state with neither the cultural appeal of a new exemplary center nor the material resources to deliver modernity. By the end of 1948, moreover, fears that the Republic would fall into the hands of radicals on Java had abated.

This is not to underestimate the turbulence of Republican politics. Sjahrir's policies of accommodation with the Dutch had proven deeply unpopular. In 1946–47 governments led by him fell three times over concessions that he wanted to make to secure Dutch recognition. In July 1947 a Dutch "police action" against the Republic dealt a further blow to the case for accommodation. On Java the Dutch attack shrank Republican territory down to a few narrow and crowded zones.

Tensions rose further, not only between Dutch and Indonesians, but even among the latter. With the Republic in increasingly dire economic straits, its prime minister at the time—Mohammad Hatta, who had declared Indonesian independence with Sukarno in 1945—took austerity measures, dismissing many government employees and demobilizing segments of the Republican armed forces. More radical elements were prime targets of these measures. Clashes broke out between centrists and leftists within the Republic.

In this worsening atmosphere in September 1948 in the city of Madiun in eastern Java, leaders of the Indonesian Communist Party unilaterally declared their own government. Amid brutalities on both sides, progovernment army units suppressed the coup, and for the time being the PKI ceased to be a significant force in Indonesian politics.

In the 1950s the Party would make a stunning comeback. Later still, apologists of Suharto's regime would cite the "treachery" of the PKI in Madiun as an omen of a supposedly communist plot to murder army leaders in Jakarta in 1965—killings that Suharto would use to justify destroying the party. But seen from Madiun at the end of 1948, the defeat of the PKI, far from presaging a reinvigoration of communism, not to mention its later destruction, gave the lie to Dutch accusations that Sukarno was leading the Republic radically leftward.

When the Dutch attempted to eliminate the Republic once and for all by launching another "police action" against it at the close of 1948, they were surprised by the nearly universal condemnation that their action received from the ostensibly conservative leaders they had tried to coopt into a federal framework. Nor were the Dutch prepared for the effectiveness of Republican guerrilla resistance to their assault. Politically and militarily at a loss, and under pressure from the United States to forestall a communist recovery by reaching a quick settlement with more moderate Indonesian nationalists, the Dutch agreed to forego the period of transition to independence that they had previously demanded. In December 1949 they transferred their sovereignty to an Indonesian state: a Republic of the United States of Indonesia (Republik Indonesia Serikat, or RIS).

Republik Indonesia Serikat was a federal state, in keeping with Dutch desires. But by far its most popular and hence potentially most powerful constituent unit was the unitary Republic of Indonesia. The territory of that Republic had been truncated and its sovereignty caged within a federal frame. But it was still powerfully legitimated by its origin in the pan-Indonesian nation-state that Sukarno and Hatta had declared in 1945.

In 1950 the Dutch flirtation with ethnic politics did stimulate a short-lived but serious secessionist movement among Christian Ambonese, a group traditionally favorable to Holland. Indonesian authorities were able to suppress the resulting Republic of the South Moluccas, but the attempted breakaway showed how far the centrifugal force of ethnicity mixed with region and religion could go. By far the more enduring consequence of the Dutch experiment with federalism, however, was the stigmatizing of that concept by association with foreign intrigue to divide the country the better to rule it.

The federal RIS lasted less than a year. Under nationalist pressure, all but one of its constituents dissolved themselves, finally leaving the original unitary Republic as the only member of the federation. This anomalous situation ended on 17 August 1950, when Sukarno, who was president of both the Republic and the RIS, formally abolished the latter. Similar to the original 1945 constitution, the charter of the now reenlarged Republic called for a unitary state. But whereas the earlier document had allowed for power to be concentrated in the hands of the executive, the later one provided for parliamentary democracy.

To people in the regions of Indonesia, the failure and tarnishing of federalism and secession in 1948–50 made these options even less attractive than they had been at the start of the revolution. Meanwhile, a Dutch effort to prevent the western half of New Guinea from becoming part of the Republic triggered a nationalist reaction that expressed and reinforced the popularity of the vision of a single, exemplary Indonesia stretching "from Sabang to Merauke."

Western New Guinea had been part of the Netherlands Indies. But the Dutch had refused to permit the territory's incorporation into the federal RIS, so when the Republic replaced the RIS and took over its borders, western New Guinea remained beyond Indonesian reach. Nor would the Dutch then relinquish their New Guinean colony to independent Indonesia.

The position of Netherlands New Guinea was slightly different in international law because it had never been fully occupied by the Japanese; Merauke had remained under Dutch rule throughout World War II. Reserves of gold, copper, and oil made the territory economically attractive, but its remote location and lack of infrastructure made it costly to administer. In retaining western New Guinea the Dutch government was driven, in any case, far less by the legal niceties or the material prospects than by a desire to salvage its national pride by not appearing to have surrendered all of the Indies to Indonesian nationalists.

Important, too, was the Dutch conviction that among all of the archipelago's peoples, the Melanesians of western New Guinea were the most distinctive, the least advanced, and thus the most vulnerable to "Javanese imperialism" in the guise of Indonesian nationalism. The Melanesian peoples of western New Guinea, many of them Christian and most of the rest animist, were ethnically and religiously distinct from the Muslim Austronesian majority of Indonesians to the west. The solution in Dutch eyes was to prevent their Melanesian charges from falling prey to Jakarta while preparing them for an eventual separate independence.

Indonesians excoriated this Dutch policy. Many of them read it as evidence that Holland had not given up its "divide and rule" designs on Indonesia. Would the Dutch use their fallback position in western New Guinea as a base from which to try to reconquer the archipelago? Dutch insistence that Melanesians could not be Indonesians contradicted a basic understanding of the national movement: That "Indonesia" was not an ethnic category at all but an exemplary project to achieve modernity through unity. To exclude Melanesians from Indonesia was as racist, in this Indonesian view, as the then-current "White Australia" policy against Asian immigration.

Dutch sympathy for preserving indigenous Melanesian culture in western New Guinea—relabeled West Irian by Sukarno—disturbed Indonesians all the more. Seen from Jakarta, this sympathy appeared to signal not sensitivity toward these New Guineans—in Indonesian parlance, Irianese—but an insidiously neocolonial desire to immobilize them in a kind of massive open-air museum and thus deprive them of the chance for modernity they would have had inside Indonesia. The Dutch could not compete with the promise of modernity-within-Indonesia; they had no workable alternative model to offer. Even regional leaders who might have turned their backs on Java and, in effect, faced West concluded that secession would not deliver the modernity they desired.

Nothing demonstrates the strength of this conclusion more than the fact that Indonesian unity survived the enormous disappointments of independence. Regional rebellions would occur, as this chapter will show. But their aim was not to shatter the national idea. Rather their leaders wished to rescue the implementation of that idea from centralizing forces on Java that appeared to be exploiting the regions materially while moving the country dangerously to the left.

Disappointment and Mistrust

Indonesia's promise of material modernity—welfare—for its people was not fulfilled in the decades following independence. There were many reasons why. Roads, buildings, and ports available to the new Republic, for example, had suffered a decade of damage and neglect under wartime occupation and ensuing revolution—infrastructure already worn down by the depression of the 1930s. Yet popular expectations were high. So much hope had been pinned on the removal of the Dutch, as if freedom were a panacea, that it was hard to avoid disappointment when it became clear just how much had to be done and how difficult the task would be.

The heritage of a colonial economy, moreover, severely constrained the Republic's leaders. Indonesia still depended, as the Indies had, on the export of primary produce from plantations. How could an equitable kind of modernity be delivered to plantation laborers, smallholders, and peasants while keeping them at work in enclaves outside the urban areas, in forms of agriculture rather than industry, given the association of modernity with cities and manufactures? With local capital still scarce, how could the country free itself of the priorities of foreign traders and investors?

Indonesia's polycentric politics under a democratic constitution also made economic planning difficult. Of the seventeen parties and groups represented in the parliament of the Republic in 1951, for example, the largest held only one-fifth of the seats. In the 1950s all governments had to be coalitions pieced together in laborious negotiations between factional leaders—and vulnerable to collapse over contentious issues. The political authority of such governments was also diminished by the fact that none of the members of these parliaments had undergone popular election: The legislative branch was a motley hybrid, its members drawn from the generally unelected assemblies of the original Republic and the various Dutch-sponsored federal states. This was not a political environment in which hard decisions could readily be made.

Economic management was also hampered by uncertainty over how to treat Indonesia's ethnic-Chinese minority. They had been settled for centuries in certain parts of Indonesia. Many of them had married locally and their descendants had merged without trace into indigenous society. However, where Chinese settlers were most numerous—especially in places to which they had migrated in large numbers as laborers—they had formed their own lasting communities.

Many of these communities had adopted major elements of local culture such as language, cuisine, or dress. By the twentieth century many such descendants were identifiable as Chinese only by their names and their Confucian, Buddhist, or Christian—that is, non-Muslim—culture. In contrast, more recent arrivals tended to be more "Chinese" in their lifeways and to maintain stronger connections with China. This link to what they tended to see as a superior culture, together with the Dutch practice of separating them from the "natives" for purposes of law and administration, helped to preserve the distinctiveness of the Chinese minority. Economic inequality reinforced these differences as ethnic Chinese came to dominate middle-level retail trade and money lending in many parts of the archipelago, especially on Java. In this process the Chinese minority became the focus of great resentment among less affluent Indonesians, especially Muslims. And that resentment, in turn, made many Indonesians of more or less "Chinese" descent more inclined to consider themselves a community apart, thus augmenting the exclusiveness for which self-described "indigenous" Indonesians had blamed them in the first place.[9]

Most important from a nationalist standpoint, the idea of Indonesia never held the promise of modernity among ethnic Chinese that it did for non-Chinese Indonesians. The government of China had unilaterally granted Chinese citizenship to all Indonesian Chinese, whether they wanted it or not. Their notions of moder-

---

9. In this context, the term "indigenous" refers not to place of birth but to an ethnic background perceived by most Indonesians as distinct from "Chinese." Used here sparingly and for convenience alone, these categories are not fully exclusive. Many people of "Chinese" descent consider themselves to be, and therefore subjectively are, every bit as "indigenous" as their "non-Chinese" compatriots.

nity had reached them through the ideas of Sun Yat-sen, the promise of the Chinese revolution of 1911, and the nationalism of the Kuomintang formed the following year—all before the idea of Indonesia had begun to take political shape. The first explicitly Indonesian students' association, for example, was not formed until 1917.

In one way or another, many Chinese took part in the nationalist movement. But the Chinese community as a whole never matched the unstinting commitment to the national idea shown by non-Chinese Indonesians. After independence this difference in support cast some doubt on the loyalty of the ethnic Chinese to the new Indonesia. Secession had been forced off the political agenda. But nothing so categorical had occurred to rule out "repatriation" as an option for Chinese Indonesians—the chance that they might want to "return" to their ancestral homeland. With the economy in difficulty, and with national pride affronted over the New Guinea issue, indigenous politicians were constantly tempted to restrict the economic power of the Chinese in the name of national integrity. Such steps, in turn, weakened the allegiance and the capacity of the group best positioned to get the Indonesian economy moving.

Rebellion without Secession

The political stalemate, while it made economic management difficult, had initially positive consequences for national unity. In the divided parliaments of the early 1950s no one among the contending ideologies within Indonesian nationalism could hope to dominate, and thus alienate, the others. The largest party was the Consultative Assembly of Indonesian Muslims (Majelis Syuro Muslimin Indonesia, or Masyumi). Masyumi's modernists wanted economic development and a greater role for Islam in public life. In the cabinets of the period, however, their ministers had to work alongside ministers from other parties and backgrounds, including representatives from Christian and secular nationalist parties and traditionalist Muslims suspicious of Masyumi's modernist interpretation of Islamic principles. Similarly, the Indonesian Communist Party (PKI), rehabilitated under the leadership of D.N. Aidit after the Madiun debacle, had a significant political presence but no hope at all of forming a coalition through which to implement its ideas. The colonial-era truce between ideologies, partially disrupted during the revolution, was now largely restored, not by the discipline of a common struggle toward shared goals but by the polycentrism of the political system.

The only major movement to stay outside these parliamentary arrangements was the House of Islam (Darul Islam, or DI). Its strength in the regions made it appear secessionist, but its aspirations at any rate were pan-Indonesian. The movement had emerged in West Java in 1948 out of Islamic dissatisfaction with the Republic's concessions to the Dutch. Darul Islam's leader, S.M. Kartosuwirjo, argued that Islamic principles could never be achieved within the compromised independence for Indonesia that Sukarno and Hatta were trying to negotiate.

In 1949 DI declared an Islamic State of Indonesia. During the early 1950s the movement spread from West Java to South Kalimantan, South Sulawesi, and Aceh, with smaller manifestations in other regions. These rebellions were eventually defeated by military action. Yet DI did not seek modernity through secession as such. While advocating an uncompromisingly Islamic future and criticizing what they saw as the unprincipled eclecticism of Sukarno and the craven diplomacy of Hatta, DI's leaders nevertheless projected their ambitions onto a national Indonesian canvas. In contesting its too-secular content, they reaffirmed the Republic's value as a frame.

The greatest strain on Indonesian unity came not in the early 1950s but later, in reaction to political changes at the center that began in 1955. In September of that year, for the first time since independence had been declared a decade before, Indonesians went to the polls to choose a national parliament. The result shifted the balances of regional and ideological power somewhat toward Java and the left, respectively—a prospective realignment unwelcome to anticommunists on the outer islands.

Four parties dominated the newly elected parliament: the reformist-Muslim Masyumi; the secular-nationalist Indonesian National Party (Partai Nasional Indonesia, or PNI); the rural-conservative Revival of Islamic Scholars (Nahdlatul Ulama, or NU); and the communist PKI. Of these four, only the anticommunist Masyumi drew a large part of its vote from the islands outside Java. Compared with Masyumi, the others relied proportionally much more for their support on Javanese.

The coalition government that resulted from the 1955 election was led by a Javanese, Ali Sastroamidjojo of the PNI. The nature of his support base in parliament enabled him to favor the interests of Java, notably by overvaluing Indonesia's currency, the rupiah. With perhaps three-fifths of Indonesians living on Java and most of the country's exportable resources located on the outer islands, overvaluing the rupiah appeared discriminatory: Imported goods became cheaper for consumers, who were disproportionally on Java, while the country's main exports, disproportionally located off Java, became costlier and therefore less competitive on world markets.

The 1955 election also shifted politics to the left. The communist party won 16.4 percent or one-sixth of the vote. The new premier, Ali Sastroamidjojo, came from the influential left wing of the PNI. The Catholic and Protestant parties were anti-Marxist. But their combined vote did not even reach five percent, and the small size of the Christian minority limited their potential to expand.

The PKI meanwhile made clear its desire to grow. Foreshadowing later trends in Western European communism, PKI leaders argued that they could come to power in Indonesia using democratic means. By appealing to Javanese peasants in particular, the party earned over 27 percent of the vote in the regional elections held on Java in mid-1957. Had that result been repeated or bettered in the next national election, due in 1959, no ruling coalition could have been formed without the participation, or at any rate the consent, of the PKI. The 1955 contest—independent Indonesia's first national experience of electoral democracy—had broken the ideological stalemate of the colonial era and the early 1950s along a fault line that coincided, dangerously, with the division between Java and the other islands.

Making matters more critical was the accessibility of weapons to regional leaders. The Indonesian army had emerged from its armed struggle against the Dutch with a command structure that was, in practice, highly decentralized. Out in the provinces, troops were often personally loyal to local commanders. A lack of funds from the central treasury in Jakarta led these officers to help finance their units by engaging in business deals. These operations further increased the practical autonomy such men already enjoyed. Smuggling with military connivance in and out of Sumatra and Sulawesi grew in scale to the point where it began seriously to diminish government revenues. In 1956 the Ali government therefore supported the head of the army, General A.H. Nasution, in an ambitious program of transfers designed to break up the fiefdoms of the regional commanders.

In reply, officers mutinied, first in Sumatra and later in Sulawesi. They declared martial law and repudiated the authority of the central government. A wave of political arrests in Jakarta led a number of civilian politicians to flee to Sumatra where they joined the mutineers in demanding that President Sukarno's powers be reduced; that former Vice President Hatta form a new cabinet; and that General Nasution be dismissed. In February 1958 the rebels in Sumatra declared themselves the Revolutionary Government of the Republic of Indonesia (Pemerintah Revolusioner Republik Indonesia, or PRRI).

The mutinies in Sumatra and Sulawesi reflected the grievances of the regions: The rebels wanted a better economic deal for the islands outside Java. They advocated creating a senate in Jakarta to safeguard regional rights. But, as the "RI" in PRRI implied, they remained committed to the national idea of Indonesia. The main demand of the rebels was not to detach the regions from Indonesia but to change the government in Jakarta.

The central government replied with force. Like the Darul Islam, these rebellions were suppressed militarily. But President Sukarno also defeated them politically, and he did so not by defending Indonesia's experiment with electoral democracy but by attacking it. Knowing that the rebellions had been prompted by resentments and suspicions accompanying the breakdown of the former ideological balance, President Sukarno intervened in the name of harmony and against divisive proceduralism. He denounced the party system for encouraging strife and "fifty percent plus one" elections for allowing a bare majority to dictate to a large minority.

Gradually Sukarno unveiled an alternative model that he came to call "Guided Democracy." He tried to legitimate the new format as a reincarnation of supposedly ancient Indonesian ways of making decisions. These ways, he contended, gave a say to all in the community and did not permit the views of any minority to be overridden. But Sukarno did not rely on the weight of tradition to animate his new system. He placed himself squarely at the heart of "Guided Democracy" as the conciliator of competing views—the indispensable guide who would make it work.

In effect, Sukarno offered a return to an equilibrium that would, this time, be stable—a guarantee that no ideology would prevail in Indonesia as long as he was there to balance it against other ideologies. In 1957 Sukarno prepared for this concentration of power by declaring martial law throughout the country. He appointed as prime minister a capable nonparty politician, Djuanda Kartawidjaya, and freed him from responsibility to the fractious and Java-dominated parliament.

Finally, on 5 July 1959—Sukarno cut the Gordian knot of ideological confrontation. Preempting the constituent assembly that had been elected in 1955 to draft a fresh constitution for the country, he unilaterally replaced the parliamentary-democratic constitution of 1950 with the strong-executive document of 1945 as the blueprint of the Republic. The assembly had become deadlocked over a variation of the same question that had sown such controversy among the new state's founders in 1945: Should the sovereign state of Indonesia be based upon Islam or Pancasila? Sukarno dissolved the assembly and answered the question himself: The Republic would rest on Pancasila, including respect for Islam. But it would not be an Islamic state.

From Guided to Pancasila Democracy

Sukarno's measures resolved the regional crisis of 1957–59, but they set Indonesia on the path to political disaster. The fundamental contradiction between Marxism, Islam, and developmentalism was not resolved. The truce between them now depended not on a common national project, overthrowing Dutch rule, but on the balancing act of a single man. No sooner was Sukarno's Guided Democracy in place than a new question loomed: What would happen when, sooner or later, Sukarno departed the scene?

Sukarno tried to submerge ideological differences in a single national belief. He called it Nasakom—from *nasionalisme, agama* (religion), and *komunisme*. If Sukarno could persuade Indonesians that Nasakom entailed more than a truce among ongoing enemies, then it would survive even his own mortality. As Guided Democracy evolved, therefore, Indonesians who engaged in public discourse found themselves increasingly obliged to use the vocabulary of Nasakom and related acronyms evoking unity and struggle.

But such controls on expression, instead of convincing people, raised the level of political uncertainty and anxiety. Muslims and Christians, officers and civilians, communists and anticommunists all used Sukarno's vocabulary, as required, but to say different things. The more opaque political language became, the less sure one could be that an ideological equilibrium in fact existed and was being maintained—in short, that Guided Democracy was working as Sukarno had promised it would. To many observers, inside and outside Indonesia, the PKI appeared to be poised on the threshhold of power. But to others, the communists appeared to be deluding themselves with rhetorical incantations and ignoring the real threat posed by the anticommunist leadership of the army. Meanwhile, the economy began to give way under the combined weight of official neglect, statism, and ineffectiveness, and that too heightened the atmosphere of crisis.

In late 1965 the teetering structure of Guided Democracy finally collapsed. In the predawn hours of 1 October, units from Sukarno's presidential guard kidnapped and killed six senior anticommunist generals, seized state radio and telecommunications facilities, and announced the formation of a Revolutionary Council with full power to safeguard Sukarno and maintain the integrity of Guided Democracy. A smaller takeover occurred in Central Java involving units of the Diponegoro Division. Ostensibly led by the palace guard's commander, one Lieutenant Colonel Untung, the conspirators said they had acted to destroy a plot that army commanders were planning against Sukarno. Circumstantial evidence linked the conspiracy to the PKI.

Many questions still surround what happened that night and, still more elusively, why. Few observers believe that Untung and his soldiers acted entirely on their own initiative. The plotters may, according to various versions, have been prompted or directed by the PKI, by Sukarno, or even by the general who took charge of the army and suppressed the ostensible coup—Suharto himself. Suharto's own judgment was unambivalent. For him and the other surviving generals, the PKI had masterminded the conspiracy and murdered their colleagues. That charge served powerfully to justify the anticommunist New Order that Suharto and his supporters would proceed to put in place.[10]

Whoever was or was not responsible for it, the conspiracy abruptly ended the play acting of Guided Democracy and precipitated a sweeping crackdown on the left. With army encouragement, Muslim and other vigilantes took to the villages and massacred perhaps half a million real or accused communists; another million and a half were arrested and kept in military prison camps for periods ranging from weeks to years. The PKI was banned and Marxism was expunged from the state ideology.

Without communism to balance against Islam and developmentalism, Sukarno's position, too, was fatally weakened. General Suharto slowly but methodically edged him from power. In March 1966, under duress, Sukarno gave emergency authority to Suharto to restore order. A year later a Provisional People's

---

10. In the eyes of Benedict R. O'G. Anderson and Ruth T. McVey, writing with Frederick P. Bunnell shortly after the event, the PKI was an unwitting victim of guilt by association with an intramilitary conspiracy. Articulating the New Order's version of events, Nugroho Notosusanto and Ismail Saleh blamed the PKI. W.F. Wertheim tried to implicate Suharto. See, respectively, *A Preliminary Analysis of the October 1, 1965, Coup in Indonesia* (Ithaca, NY: Cornell University Modern Indonesia Project, 1971 [written 1965–66]); *The*

Consultative Assembly (Majelis Permusyawaratan Rakyat Sementara, or MPRS), its members not elected but its role provided for in the 1945 constitution, stripped Sukarno of his powers, leaving him president in title alone and making Suharto acting president in his stead. In March 1968 when his New Order was already fully under way, the anticommunist general finally was named president of Indonesia. Politically outmaneuvered and marginalized, his movements severely restricted by the new authorities, Sukarno died in 1970.

What path to modernity was left for Indonesia to follow? Having destroyed the PKI and banned Marxism, Suharto and his fellow generals had precluded a Marxist future for the archipelago. And although they welcomed the anticommunist piety of Islam under the first principle of Pancasila—Belief in God—they also ruled out an Islamic state. Instead they drove Indonesians down the third road to modernity: developmentalism.

The new president, his army colleagues, and the civilian technocrats who advised them did not consider their commitment to economic growth a matter of ideology. They thought of themselves as rational pragmatists trying to end once and for all the country's irrational fascination with ideology. Reviewing the history of strife between communists on the left and Islamists on the right of the political spectrum, they came to the view that ideologies tapped into primitive, dangerous impulses that led inevitably to social conflict and should not be allowed to distract the Indonesian people from the unity that was necessary if they were ever to acquire modernity. They defined modernity not as a utopian outcome but incrementally in a practical sense: stabilizing prices, repairing physical infrastructure, making agriculture more productive, encouraging industry, expanding employment, improving education, and raising per capita income.

To ensure that ideological conflicts would not again betray the developmental promise of modernity, Suharto built on the ruins of Guided Democracy an authoritarian "Pancasila Democracy" with the armed forces at its core. He equipped the new system with the forms of political competition and participation, so that people would feel a sense of engagement with the developmental mission of the state. National legislative elections would be held in 1971, 1977, and every five years thereafter. But these and other channels—parties, courts, media—would be constrained and, if necessary, repressed to prevent the system from being led by anyone except Suharto, or in any direction other than the developmentalist one that he wanted Indonesia to follow.

A repertoire of such methods kept the New Order anticommunist, anti-Islamist, and committed to development, or *pembangunan*—the leitmotif of the re-

---

Coup Attempt of the "30 September Movement" in Indonesia (Jakarta: Pembimbing Masa, 1968); and "Suharto and the Untung Coup: The Missing Link," *Journal of Contemporary Asia,* 1: 2 (1970), pp. 50–57. A more dispassionate review of the conspiracy and its causes may be found in Harold Crouch, *The Army and Politics in Indonesia* (Ithaca, NY: Cornell University Press, 1978).

gime. From about 1974, these techniques were augmented with the full-scale promotion of allegiance to Pancasila as the sole basis of the Indonesian state. In 1985 all private nonbusiness associations were obliged by law to adopt Pancasila as their own chief guiding principle.

Development and Discontent

The developmentalist New Order paid spectacular material dividends. The modernization of Indonesia's economy was rapid and dramatic. But there were costs. Less authoritarian, less elitist, and less materialistic visions of modernity were repressed or set aside. Political repression and socioeconomic inequalities led more than a few Indonesians to argue that true modernization required their government to become democratic in practice, not just in name, and to curb corruption and narrow the gap between rich and poor.

What is more, for all its impact in filling the national frame with modern content, developmentalism did not render Indonesia immune to possible future fragmentation. Unlike their predecessors, the most important centrifugal movements faced by the central government in the mid-1990s were explicitly secessionist: one in Irian Jaya (formerly West Irian), the other in East Timor. As noted above, the Dutch had retained control of western New Guinea after 1949 with the intention of developing it toward a separate independence. But American diplomatic pressure and Indonesian military action finally forced the Dutch out; Indonesian administration began in 1963. An independence movement was formed in 1965 and has been skirmishing intermittently with Indonesian forces ever since.

The eastern half of the island of Timor remained a Portuguese colony until 1974, when a newly democratic regime in Lisbon offered independence to Portugal's overseas empire. Seizing the occasion, a popular left-wing movement took power in the colony in 1975. Indonesia promptly invaded and annexed the territory. The ensuing violence and disruption exceeded in scale and intensity the unrest in Irian Jaya.

The Indonesians who took them over expected that the solvent power of the Indonesian national idea would work as effectively in these new regions as it had elsewhere in the archipelago. This was not the case. Irianese mainly, and East Timorese wholly, were bystanders during the crucial years of common struggle against the Dutch. They found it difficult to identify with an Indonesian state born from an experience that did not significantly involve them. Especially for the East Timorese, who never were part of the Netherlands Indies, Indonesia was and remains an alien, imposed idea.

Indonesian policy in these regions was also part of the problem: Substantial regional development budgets could not compensate for brutality, cultural insensitivity, and the expropriation of natural resources by Indonesians, especially those who differed doubly from the local population in being Javanese and Muslim.

Finally, the international environment changed in ways that did not make incorporation easier. Indonesia had become independent at a time when it was widely believed that only large states could deliver prosperity to their people. Small independent countries created by breaking up one larger colony would suffer diseconomies of scale, including a scarcity of trained local experts. The point of the anticolonial struggles of the post–World War II period typically was to end Western rule while retaining intact the boundaries Westerners had drawn. It was a time when the rights of ethnic groups to self-determination within such postcolonial states were not given a high priority.

In subsequent decades, however, a number of small states proved their viability, including Brunei and Singapore in Southeast Asia. In 1991 the Soviet Union broke up into its constituent republics, many of them defined along ethnic or religious lines. No longer constrained by the strategic imperatives of the Cold War, the governments of the United States and other democratic countries felt freer to advance a global agenda for human rights, including the right to self-determination for culturally distinct regions oppressed or mistreated by central authorities inside sovereign states.

For people seeking their own road to modernity in small places such as East Timor, or ones as sparsely peopled as Irian Jaya, a vast and unitary state such as Indonesia became an increasingly less attractive vehicle to ride. Meanwhile, the rise of Islamic consciousness in many countries, including Indonesia, strained relations with adherents of other faiths, including the Christians who form majorities within East Timor and Irian Jaya but are vastly outnumbered by Indonesia's Muslims. Generally rising incomes gave Indonesians a stake in the country. But as the New Order aged, juxtapositions of rich and poor created new economic grievances with a potential to exacerbate ethnoregional ones.

This context suggests that Indonesia may have caught the boat of multiethnic and trans-religious nationalism none too soon. Another few decades and the archipelagic polity that was the Indies might have fractured along its ethnolocal and religious fault lines into several or more independent countries.

The Unmaking of Indonesia?

The tumultuous events of 1996–98 that badly damaged the Indonesian economy and obliged Suharto to resign his presidency are described elsewhere in this book. Suffice it here to note the hope of many Indonesians, that this transition will yield a successfully democratic "Indonesia beyond Suharto." Such an outcome, were it to occur, could also imply decentralization, conceivably to the point of allowing peoples on the periphery of the archipelago to choose their own futures: full independence, continued incorporation, or something in between.

Does this mean that Indonesia, having been made, will now be unmade? If the people of East Timor are allowed to exercise their right to self-determination, and if they choose to secede, will their decision provoke a general rush to the exits?

The Indonesian revolution began in 1945, more than half a century ago. Yet one ought not underestimate the power of the national idea that motivated it. That idea, whose fortunes this chapter has recounted, was to build an integral state within ex-Dutch boundaries—boundaries that never encompassed East Timor. For Sukarno and his fellow nationalists, the modernity of the Indonesian state necessitated unity: one people in one country speaking one language, to paraphrase the youth oath of 1928 and the song written for it, "Great Indonesia," which became and remains the national anthem. For Suharto and his fellow generals and technocrats, the modernity of an already unified Indonesia required development, or *pembangunan*: the New Order's promise of a better life to Indonesians. The successes of these struggles—first the making, then the betterment of Indonesia—made the country's dismemberment hard to imagine.

Nor has the sudden reversal of material progress in 1998 assured the disintegration of Indonesia. Democracy held pride of place in neither Sukarno's nor Suharto's conception of the modern. But on the threshhold of the twenty-first century, more and more Indonesians have begun to wonder whether the time has come to redefine the modern yet again: to make their country, already unified and (until 1998) developing, truly democratic. Far from dismantling Indonesia, such a process, if it takes place, could satisfy the growing desire of Indonesians for a greater say in public life. And that could cement the unity of the republic and facilitate its further development—once the economy begins to recover, as eventually it must.

Nevertheless, it may be fitting to end this chapter on a historically derived note of skepticism that the mere removal of Suharto will assure political liberalization. The failure of electoral democracy in the 1950s and its association with civil strife will continue to be read by antidemocrats, especially within the armed forces, as reasons not to experiment with it again. If violence and disorder spread over the course of a prolonged recession, the economically vital ethnic-Chinese component of what—in historical perspective—is still a rather small middle class could be frightened into withholding needed capital and skills. The partly anti-Chinese riots that took more than 1,000 lives in Jakarta in May 1998 are a case in point.

And even if the movement for reform does manage to introduce democratic procedures, they could worsen the prospect for national unity, if they are again seen as facilitating a polarization of political life between the center and the regions, or between Islamist and competing visions of Indonesia's future. As argued above, the historical experiences of the weakest links in the national chain, Irian Jaya and East Timor, were either peripheral or external to the evolution and the revolution of Dutch-demarcated Indonesia, making these places relatively indifferent to the national idea. And compared with "the generation of 1945" for whom the revolution was a defining experience, future generations will be able to live the lesson of unity as a founding imperative only vicariously from books.

Ultimately, however, not one of these intimations of autocracy or disunity will be realized without the force of political events behind it. The future of Indonesia cannot be known. If the disintegrations of Pakistan in 1971 and the

Soviet Union in 1991 are any guide, it would seem that a large, multicultural country is especially likely to come apart under the stress of rapid and basic political change. To be sure, compared with these examples, the idea of Indonesia has broader and deeper historical roots. But history can carry the observer only so far toward a sense of how likely—or unlikely—future changes may be. Accordingly, the next few chapters will seek the shape of "Indonesia beyond Suharto" not in the farther past, but in the New Order and how it worked.

Chapter 2

Regime: The New Order

R. William Liddle

By 1997 the authoritarian political system built and run by Indonesia's second president, Suharto, had lasted more than thirty years. Yet it was still called the "New Order"—a name originally meant to distinguish it from its immediate predecessor, the "Old Order" of President Sukarno. The economic and political crisis of 1997–98 finally brought Suharto down. On 21 May 1998 he resigned and was replaced by his vice president and protégé, Bacharuddin Jusuf Habibie.

In mid-1998 it was still not clear to what extent this change of leaders might have set in motion a chain of events that would successfully transform Indonesia's polity from an autocracy into a democracy. But whatever system does ultimately emerge, its character will have been affected in no small measure by the nature of the New Order. For Suharto's regime must be the point of departure for Indonesians, whether in the end they replace it, revamp it, or merely renew it behind a facade of reform.

The main aims of this chapter are, therefore, to describe how the New Order worked and explain how it came about. Particular attention will be paid to the second, historical topic, because it conditions the first. One cannot adequately understand the workings of the New Order, or consider alternative futures beyond it, without knowing its past. The mainly national frame of this essay will also serve as a bridge to the subnational focus of the next chapter—Michael Malley's review of how the New Order allocated power between central and provincial authorities.

Controlled Participation

If by 1997 the "New" Order had grown old, another name for it also was misleading: "Pancasila Democracy." This is what its rulers and propagandists called the regime. But their use of "democracy" amounted to an Orwellian deception. In fact the regime was a complex hierarchy of authoritarian institutions designed to curtail political participation and enable Suharto and the military to control society. One of the five principles of Pancasila is democracy, but only of a constrained kind, "guided" by the "wisdom" of "unanimity" arising from "deliberation among representatives."

A brief explanation of Pancasila will be helpful at this point. As officially translated, the five principles are, in official order: "Belief in the One and Only God," "Just and Civilized Humanity," "the Unity of Indonesia," "Democracy Guided by the Inner Wisdom in the Unanimity Arising out of Deliberation amongst Representatives," and "Social Justice for the Whole of the People of Indonesia."[1] Sukarno launched the principles in a famous speech on 1 June 1945 during a debate between those Indonesians who wanted their new state to be Islamic and those who wanted it to be secular, or at any rate trans-religious.

Sukarno offered Pancasila as a compromise: Its first principle would commit the new country to faith in God, which Muslim spokesmen wanted. But it did not mention Islam, and that implied toleration of Christian and other non-Muslim beliefs. The first principle could also be interpreted to include syncretic understandings of what God might be. In the 1950s and 1960s Pancasila became an ideological weapon, wielded against militant Muslims for their religious intolerance and against communists for refusing to believe in God at all. President Suharto made Pancasila the basic credo to which all Indonesians had to adhere. In the 1990s, at least until his resignation in 1998, virtually all politically active Indonesians supported the credo, although proponents and opponents of his regime often read its vaguely worded principles differently.

On 18 August 1945, some two and a half months after the birth of Pancasila, the Republic of Indonesia promulgated its first constitution. According to this charter, in effect from 1945 through 1949 and reinstated in 1959, the People's Consultative Assembly (Majelis Permusyawaratan Rakyat or MPR) is the country's highest governing body. It meets every five years to elect the president and vice president and to adopt a general program of state policy. The president holds a mandate from the assembly to carry out this program.

Below the assembly, according to the constitution, is a parliament, the People's Representative Council (Dewan Perwakilan Rakyat or DPR), which meets at least annually. Parliament is responsible for legislation and must approve the budget submitted to it each year by the government. All members of parliament are automatically members of the assembly, which is also to contain "additional delegates from the regions and groups, according to

---

1. *The Process and Progress of Pancasila Democracy* ([Jakarta]: Department of Information, [1991]), p. 14.

rules to be determined by law" (Chapter II, Article 1).[2] The New Order determined these rules in statutes and regulations covering not only the assembly and parliament but elections, parties, the media, interest groups, and other organizations as well. The net result was to create the appearance but not the reality of popular control.

The number of seats in the assembly was set at twice that of parliament. In 1997 these figures were 1,000 and 500, respectively. In a process of appointment ultimately controlled by President Suharto, the government filled the assembly seats not already occupied by members of parliament. Under the New Order, Indonesians went to the polls in 1971, 1977, and every five years thereafter. Yet parliament was never a wholly elected body. In 1987 and 1992, for example, only 400, or 80 percent, of its seats were filled in this way; the remaining 100 were reserved for appointed military officers. (For the 1997 balloting, the number of elective seats in parliament was increased slightly to 425, or 85 percent.) Technically speaking, polling procedures such as the counting of votes were for the most part implemented honestly. But substantively, the government was favored: Less than a month was allowed for campaigning, for example, and regulations restricting campaign activities were used to harass nongovernment parties.

Official control over the party system was especially pervasive and intrusive. Only three entities were permitted to contest the elections: the state party, called Functional Groups (Golongan Karya, or Golkar); the Development Unity Party (Partai Persatuan Pembangunan, or PPP); and the Indonesian Democracy Party (Partai Demokrasi Indonesia, or PDI). Golkar was the partisan political face of the state bureaucracy. Once every five years, all public employees, including elected village leaders, were mobilized to get out the vote for Golkar. These officials were effectively prohibited from joining either of the other two parties. Civil servants and retired military officers were recruited to lead Golkar nationally and at provincial and local levels.

In 1971, following its first campaign, Golkar won 62 percent of the vote. Its best performance in the next four elections came in 1987, at 73 percent. In 1992 its share fell back to 68 percent. Government spokespersons denied that Golkar was a political party at all, calling it instead an "election-participating organization." They claimed that Golkar represented the interest of the whole nation, and was therefore unifying, while the parties represented only a part of that interest, and were therefore divisive.

The nongovernmental PPP and PDI felt the impact of this hostile portrayal, beginning with the way they were created. Each was the product of a 1973 fusion forced upon several preexisting organizations in order to simplify the party system and make it more manageable from the government's point of view. PPP was

---

2. This and all following citations from the 1945 constitution are from its translation in *Indonesia 1990: An Official Handbook* (Jakarta: Department of Information, 1990).

formed by merging four Islamic parties, of which the Revival of Islamic Scholars (Nahdlatul Ulama, or NU) and the Indonesian Muslims' Party (Partai Muslimin Indonesia, or Parmusi) were the most important. Upon entering PPP, Parmusi dropped the word "party" from its name and became simply Indonesian Muslims (Muslimin Indonesia, or MI).

Nahdlatul Ulama had demonstrated its ability to win nearly one-fifth of the vote both in 1955, in the one genuinely free parliamentary election that has been held in Indonesia, and in 1971. In 1984, feeling outmaneuvered within PPP by MI, NU reclaimed its autonomy from the larger body. In the 1990s NU claimed thirty million members. That would make it the largest Islamic organization in the country.

Muslimin Indonesia was an indirect descendant of the Consultative Assembly of Indonesian Muslims (Masyumi), whose 21 percent of the vote in 1955 had made it at that time the largest Muslim party by a small margin over NU. President Sukarno had disbanded Masyumi in 1960 for participating in regional rebellions against the central government. In the early years of the New Order an effort to re-create the original Masyumi had foundered when President Suharto refused to lift the ban. Instead, in 1968, a successor to Masyumi was approved under a new name, Parmusi, without the participation of former Masyumi leaders whom the regime considered too likely to prove uncooperative.

Compared with its famed ancestor, Parmusi fared badly in the 1971 election. But following the amalgamation of Parmusi into PPP, Parmusi's successor MI managed to hold most of the key positions within the composite party. As noted, that helps to explain why NU eventually left PPP and declared itself a nonpartisan social and educational organization. The break did not prevent politicians with backgrounds in NU from continuing to compete for influence within PPP.

The second "party of parties," PDI, merged three nationalist and two Christian organizations. Of these the most important was the Indonesian National Party (PNI)—at 22 percent the most successful vote-getter in the 1955 elections. Sukarno had once been a PNI leader, and the party's popularity depended in part on its identification with him and his record as a nationalist. The party adopted Sukarno's vaguely populist ideology, which he called Marhaenism in honor of a kind of Indonesian everyman. Marxist but not communist, pan-religious rather than Muslim, Marhaenism illustrated Sukarno's desire to position himself on the middle ground between the Indonesian Communist Party (PKI) and its Islamic rivals.

Most PNI leaders were state or village officials, and their easy access to patronage funds was a major reason for its success in 1955. But they deserted the party en masse in the New Order's first election, in 1971, to comply with the government's requirement that all officials join Golkar. The PNI won merely 7 percent of the vote that year, and its successor, the PDI, did little better until 1987 and 1992, when it received 11 percent and 13 percent, respectively. The party's fortunes appeared to brighten under the leadership of Sukarno's daughter

Megawati Sukarnoputri, elected party chair in 1993. But, apparently fearing her popularity, the authorities engineered her ouster at a state-approved party congress in June 1996. On 27 July a successful effort to expel her supporters from PDI headquarters by force, an eviction instigated by the regime, triggered the worst rioting Jakarta had seen in more than twenty years.

As Megawati's fate illustrates, time and again PPP and PDI suffered government manipulation and intervention to curb their ability to mobilize people and criticize government policies. In the 1970s and 1980s, PDI was generally pacified by these interventions, although PPP was still able on occasion to voice the grievances of parts of the Islamic community. Both parties were also used as pawns by major players in intra-elite political conflicts, which sometimes created the impression that the parties were more important than they really were.

Neither PDI nor PPP was allowed to have branches below the district level, while Golkar existed wherever there was a government office, which included every village in the country. (The district is the administrative tier below the province.) Party nominees for legislative office in the five-year election cycle were screened for possible "extreme left" (communist) or "extreme right" (militant Muslim) connections or tendencies, and at least several candidates were always rejected.

The state was further insulated from society by statutes and decrees that permitted the regime to restrict the activities of any organization. There was no press censorship in Indonesia, according to law, but the government could issue, or retract, a publishing license. In 1994, to cite a notorious example, the government withdrew at a single stroke the licenses of three major newsweeklies. One of these was *Tempo,* the prestigious 23-year-old local equivalent of *Time* or *Newsweek* in the United States. The crackdown followed a pattern, repeated on several occasions since the early 1970s, in which relatively independent and adversarial newspapers and magazines emerged, acquired readers, developed a reputation for independent coverage, and were cut down when they appeared to threaten powerful elite interests.

Many social groupings whose members might be mobilized against the government were controlled through communist- or fascist-style corporatist organizations. Nationwide there was only one legal labor union, the government-sanctioned Pan-Indonesian Workers' Union (Serikat Pekerja Seluruh Indonesia, or SPSI), and only one Chamber of Commerce and Industry (Kamar Dagang dan Industri, or Kadin). Women, youth, the professions, and other social categories were organized in the same way. Churches and religious organizations were able to maintain some autonomy, but only at the cost of staying out of politics. In the 1990s the leaders of both the Batak Christian Protestant Church (Huria Kristen Batak Protestan, or HKBP), Indonesia's largest Protestant church, and Nahdlatul Ulama, the largest association of "traditionalist" Muslims, were targets of government subversion. On the other hand, Muhammadiyah was left alone. The largest association of "modernist" Muslims, with a claimed membership of over twenty million "followers of Muhammad," Muhammadiyah concentrated on building and running schools and hospitals.

These labels should not be misunderstood. Nahdlatul Ulama has been "traditionalist" in the narrow sense of adherence to a school or tradition of legal interpretation—in Indonesia, the Syafi'i tradition. Members of NU and other traditionalists call themselves *ahlus sunnah wal jama'ah,* observers of the customs of the Prophet and the community. Like the traditionalists, modernist Muslims are also Sunni—the term is derived from *sunnah* for customs—as are most Muslims worldwide. (Unlike Shi'i Muslims, Sunnis accept the legitimacy of the first four caliphs.) But modernists downplay traditional legal interpretation in favor of *ijtihad,* direct individual judgment of the meaning of the Qur'an. Compared with traditionalists, who tend to rely on the advice of respected religious teachers, called *kiai,* modernists defer less to religious authority.

Modernists tend to be urban, middle-class, and educated mainly in secular subjects in Western-style settings very different from the rural, *kiai*-centered religious schools that underpin NU and other traditionalist organizations. But the spread of Western-style education to the remotest parts of the archipelago during the New Order has narrowed this gap in backgrounds. A new generation of urban, middle-class, Western-trained traditionalists has emerged to challenge the intellectual dominance of the modernists. Some traditionalist and modernist leaders have even called for a new blend of the best in both camps. (For more on this subject, see the chapter by Robert Hefner on religious pluralism and revival.)

Military Intervention

Vital to the New Order and how it worked were Indonesia's armed forces. They maintained the domination of the state over society. They justified their intervention in civilian politics under a doctrine known as *dwifungsi,* the dual function. According to this idea, the armed forces has two closely related roles: to defend the country not only from conventional military threats originating abroad, but also from domestic dangers of any kind, military, political, socioeconomic, cultural, or ideological. Underscoring the importance of this sweeping second aspect of *dwifungsi* in Suharto's Indonesia is the fact, admitted publicly by General Leonardus B. ("Benny") Murdani when he commanded the armed forces, that Indonesia had no significant external enemies and was unlikely to have any soon.

In armed forces propaganda, whether written for officers or for the general public, the nation's main foes were communists and militant Muslims, liberals (sometimes derogated as excessively Westernized intellectuals), and separatists. The last category included the Free Aceh Movement (Gerakan Aceh Merdeka) in northern Sumatra, the Free Papua Organization (Organisasi Papua Merdeka) in Irian Jaya, and those fighting for the independence of East Timor, the former Portuguese colony forcibly annexed by Indonesia in 1976.

The armed forces implemented the interventionist dual-function doctrine by placing active and retired military personnel in the assembly, parliament, and provincial and district legislatures; in executive and staff positions in central, provincial, and district administration; in positions of formal and informal authority over Golkar; and by keeping the population under surveillance through territorial commands that covered the country from Jakarta to the outermost islands and down to every village. Serving officers occupied roughly one-fifth of the seats in every regional legislature, where they reported to their local commander, and in the national parliament and assembly, where they were responsible to the armed forces commander. Being thus formally represented in the political process by appointment, active-duty military personnel—some 300,000 in 1996—were not allowed to vote or be elected to public office.

Serving and retired officers were appointed to posts in civilian government for reasons of patronage and control. In the 1980s and 1990s, as the number of educated and experienced civilians rose, the proportion of military appointees tended to decline. However, certain key ministries, such as the Department of Home Affairs, which administered regional government and had a directorate-general for keeping tabs on political and social organizations in the provinces and districts, were never led by civilians. In 1996 a quarter of cabinet-level posts and a somewhat larger number of second-echelon ministerial positions were held by retired or serving officers. Nearly half of the provincial governorships and district headships, by far the most important civilian government positions in the regions, were also in military hands.

When the armed forces founded Golkar in 1964, before the New Order began, they hoped it would limit the growing influence of the Indonesian Communist Party (PKI) and its affiliated organizations. The new Joint Secretariat of Functional Groups (Sekretariat Bersama Golongan Karya), as Golkar was first called, mobilized under military auspices all of the noncommunist organizations that had been given representation by President Sukarno in the national and regional legislatures of the time. In the late 1960s, President Suharto, on the advice of his chief political aide, Brigadier General Ali Murtopo, decided to hold parliamentary elections and to convert Golkar into a government-sponsored political party.

For the 1971 election, Murtopo recruited an able cadre of civilian political operatives, including a number of ethnic-Chinese Catholics, to organize and coordinate Golkar's campaign. At the president's direction, most government ministries required their subordinates to join and support Golkar. (The major exception was the Department of Religion, then controlled by Nahdlatul Ulama.) A key role was played by the Department of Home Affairs, which could apply pressure to elected but dependent village officials who were in daily contact with most of the voters. The armed forces' territorial commands, described below, were also pressed into service. Territorial chiefs-of-staff working directly under each regional commander became Golkar chairs in their respective areas.

The government prepared for the 1971 poll with impressive organizational skill. Every province, district, subdistrict, village, and hamlet in the country was assigned a Golkar quota, based on the estimated local strengths of the other parties. Quotas tended to be lower in strongly Muslim areas, where Islamic parties were thought to be entrenched, and higher in former nationalist or communist strongholds. Nationalist leaders, mainly government officials, were coopted, while ex-communists and fellow travellers were too frightened to oppose the Golkar juggernaut. The strategy worked. In a field of ten contending organizations, Golkar won a stunning 62 percent of the national vote, triple the showing of the most successful party in the 1955 elections.

This process was repeated with minor variations in five parliamentary elections after 1971, including the last one held, in 1997, under Suharto's presidency. After the 1977 contest, active-duty military personnel moved into the background. But often they were replaced not by civilians but by retired officers who continued to implement *dwifungsi*'s second, catch-all function. And the serving commander of the armed forces remained a major player, nominating and vetoing candidates for party and legislative office at all levels.

The military's relationship to Golkar was controversial, even inside the regime. In the 1980s Suharto moved one of his long-time assistants, retired Lieutenant General Sudharmono, into the leading political role previously played by Ali Murtopo. Sudharmono, most of whose career had been spent in the office of the president, was unpopular among line (troop-commanding) army officers. Nevertheless, over these objections, Suharto chose—and the assembly ratified—Sudharmono to be vice president of Indonesia from 1988–93. In 1993, over vigorous but again unavailing armed forces' dissent, Suharto chose another long-loyal associate, Minister of Information Harmoko, to lead Golkar nationally from 1993 to 1998. Harmoko being a civilian, his appointment broke with precedent. But in the provinces and districts, retired officers still headed the great majority of Golkar branches.

A system of ten territorial commands, unchanged as of mid-1998, backstopped the power of the armed forces. Of these military zones, the four on Java correspond to the provinces of West Java, Central Java (including the province-level Special Territory of Yogyakarta), East Java, and the province-level Special Capital Territory of Jakarta (see Map 3). The remaining six commands subsume the twenty-two less populous provinces of the outer islands. Each command is divided into several levels of subcommand. The lowest of these matches the government's subdistrict, a unit comparable to a township or suburb in the United States. The subdistrict commander is responsible for recruiting village-level "guidance officers," typically retired noncommissioned officers.

The armed forces' initial justification for this system was the doctrine of territorial warfare, formulated in the late 1940s during the revolution for independence, whereby the Indonesian army would rely for logistical support primarily on villagers who shared its commitment to the Indonesian nation-state. First erected in the 1950s ostensibly to maintain this revolutionary link between the armed forces and the people, the territorial command structure had from the start political surveillance and police functions as well.

These functions grew in importance during the 1960s, and were paramount throughout the New Order. In the run-ups to elections the commands made sure that civilian officials carried out their Golkar assignments, provided security for Golkar campaign events, and obstructed PPP and PDI meetings and rallies. In matters of "state security," the territorial commanders—not the governors—were the real regional heads, and they interpreted the phrase broadly. In 1992–93, for example, the commander of Sumatra intervened in the election of the head of HKBP, the Protestant church, to the point of having several of the church's ministers arrested and tortured in a district command headquarters. District commanders routinely terrorized independent labor organizers, especially in the more industrial provinces such as West and East Java. A notorious instance of the latter practice came to light in East Java in 1993 when a female labor organizer in East Java named Marsinah was tortured and murdered. At first, her employers were arrested for the crime, but they were released when evidence collected by the Legal Aid Institute (Lembaga Bantuan Hukum) pointed to officers in the local military command. The case became a cause célèbre in the press.[3]

Suharto's Political Impact

The mind behind this elaborate political structure, the single intelligence that built it, maintained it, and kept it stable and in overall control of Indonesian society for more than thirty years, was President Suharto's. Opinions vary on the extent to which he was a strategist, a long-range builder and planner, or merely a tactician responding incrementally to challenges and opportunities as they arose, and on the extent to which he accepted or rejected advice. But there is no doubt that every critical decision in the history of the regime was made by Suharto himself.

A man with firsthand knowledge of the president's role is retired General Murdani. When I interviewed him in Jakarta on 1 March 1995, he argued that Suharto had been much more of a tactician than a strategist, reacting to events as they occurred with little thought of the larger consequences. Murdani's opinion must be taken seriously. He led the armed forces in 1983–88 and served as minister of defense and security in 1988–93. Long before he played these and other formal roles, including a stint as the president's chief intelligence officer, Murdani had gained notoriety as the New Order's éminence grise, a Machiavellian plotter against Suharto's enemies, especially those on the Islamic "right."

Certainly Murdani knew Suharto well. But Murdani's deprecation of the president's role in conversation with me in 1995 could also reflect pique at having lost favor with Suharto. Murdani had been ostracized for having raised with Suharto two sensitive issues: the presidential succession and the security problems caused by the greed of the first children. Several of Suharto's three sons and

---

3. For more on the Marsinah case, see Human Rights Watch/Asia, *The Limits of Openness* (New York: Human Rights Watch, 1994), ch. 4.

three daughters had entered into business ventures that had profited handsomely from association with the presidential name.

My own view, which may benefit too much from hindsight, is that the president deserved more credit for long-range political thinking than Murdani gave him. As I observed him over more than thirty years, and ignoring his actions in the crisis of 1997–98 that finally bought him down, Suharto behaved strategically in four basic ways: First, he coerced his opponents by using the armed forces as his main base of support. Second, he fostered regime-legitimating economic growth and used its material benefits to win friends and coopt potential enemies within the state and, more broadly, in society. Third, he promoted a set of legitimating symbols for consumption inside and outside Indonesia. Fourth and finally, he built the state into an effective apparatus for implementing his policies and transmitting his message of authoritarian development and national unity to the Indonesian people. Each of these strategies bears elaboration.

In the mid-to-late 1960s the main target of New Order coercion was communism. As noted by Robert Cribb in the preceding chapter, perhaps half a million members of the PKI or its affiliated labor, farmer, youth, student, women's, and other organizations were killed in the aftermath of the assassination of six senior army generals on 1 October 1965. Many of these killings were carried out spontaneously by civilians, particularly the religiously devout who feared atheistic communism and local economic elites who feared expropriation of their land. But the armed forces, effectively headed after 1 October by Major General Suharto, played a key role in stimulating and organizing the massacre. Hundreds of thousands of other communists and fellow travelers were arrested. The great majority of these were released by the late 1970s. But even toward the end of Suharto's rule—prior to the crisis of 1997–98—a few of these detainees remained in prison, the ban against the PKI remained in effect, former political prisoners were closely watched, and officially stoked "red scares" still broke out from time to time, driven more by intra-elite conflict than by realistic fear of a communist revival.

No one was repressed more harshly than the communists. But from the late 1960s until the mid-1980s militant Islamists were the second most important target of coercion by Suharto through the armed forces. Former leaders of Masyumi were not allowed to return to politics. Other Muslim leaders deemed too independent were purged. Muslim daily newspapers were closed down or taken over. Preachers in mosques were closely watched and subjected to interrogation. Even so, "green scares" were common, as the regime exaggerated the threat posed by small-scale, highly localized Islamic cults in order to justify repressing them.

The atmosphere changed in the mid-1980s. President Suharto relaxed his and his regime's suspicion of Muslims as a social force. In the 1990s the fruits of the new toleration were widely felt: Female students in state schools were allowed to wear Muslim head scarves along with their school uniforms. Muslims could observe the Qur'anic injunction against usury by placing their savings in interest-free banks that paid depositors a return on investment. When most Muslim organizations opposed a state lottery, it was dropped. A Catholic newspaper editor was jailed for insulting the Prophet Muhammad. Suharto, himself a Muslim, further boosted his popularity among cobelievers by making the pilgrimage to Mecca. To mark the occasion he took the name of the prophet, Muhammad, as his own first name. In 1997, hard liquor sales were restricted in deference to the Qur'anic injunction against alcohol.

Perhaps most significantly, in 1990 the president allowed his favorite cabinet official, State Minister for Research and Technology B.J. Habibie, to head up a new Indonesian Muslim Intellectuals' Association (Ikatan Cendekiawan Muslim Indonesia, or ICMI). The Association soon became the most important elite-bureaucratic faction inside the regime. Friends and enemies alike of ICMI saw it as the opening wedge of a new Islamic political movement—a movement that could empower the intellectual descendants of the long-ostracized modernist Muslims who had given Masyumi its mass base back in the 1950s.

Suharto's opening to Islam did not, however, augur relaxation across the board. The president still was willing to use coercion against perceived challengers, individual dissidents, and critics who stepped over the line—and it was he who drew the line. As already noted, when *Tempo*'s accurate coverage of a policy conflict between Minister Habibie and Minister of Finance Mar'ie Muhammad proved unflattering to Habibie, the president shut down the magazine. Underground newspapers had their offices searched and their assets seized. Two members of parliament, a Golkar and a PPP representative, were removed from office for "vocalism," to cite the media's euphemism.[4] One dissident intellectual, George Adicondro, fled the country to escape punishment for speaking out against Suharto and the repression of East Timor. A small-time Javanese mystic with PDI connections was put on trial for calling the Prophet Muhammad a dictator. Meanwhile, on a far deadlier scale, Suharto continued to rely on armed force to subdue the East Timorese people.

Suharto's Economic Impact

It was not just coercion that made the New Order work. Prior to the crisis of 1997–98, development was a second and no less effective instrument of the president's power and, therefore, his regime's staying power. As detailed by Anne Booth in her chapter, for some three decades the New Order under Suharto's leadership kept the Indonesian economy growing. In this respect, Indonesia's experience differed markedly from that of nearby Burma, ruled by despotic generals since the early 1960s but remained one of the poorest countries in Southeast Asia in the 1990s.

---

4. "Vokalis Yang Turun Panggung" ["Vocalists Who Leave the Stage"], *Tempo,* 14 September 1991, pp. 31–33.

The New Order's material success is attributable to a decision made by Suharto at the outset of his regime to follow the advice of a group of University of Indonesia–based economists led by Professor Widjojo Nitisastro. Several members of this group had been trained at the University of California-Berkeley and other Western universities. They believed in the developmental power of market-based economics and enjoyed good international connections.

In the mid-1960s the Indonesian economy was in steep decline. Productivity was falling. Inflation raged. Indonesia could no longer pay interest on the debt owed to foreign governments and banks. Suharto's economists, dubbed the "Berkeley Mafia," worked with teams of foreign advisers from the United States and international lending agencies to fashion a massive structural adjustment program. The program relied on a bargain: The debt was rescheduled and new loans were offered in return for austere monetary and fiscal policies including moves toward market-conforming rates of foreign exchange to stabilize the rupiah and attract foreign capital. Within a few years inflation had been curbed and new domestic and foreign investment had begun to flow. Without these initial steps, the New Order might not have survived.

In 1974 and again in 1979, as a major exporter of petroleum, Indonesia benefited from sharp increases in the world price of oil. Government revenues surged, as did the supply of concessional foreign loans that could be used for domestic development projects. Notwithstanding a near-collapse of the state oil company, Pertamina, the New Order in the 1970s enjoyed an unprecedented windfall of resources with which it could, and did, strengthen the state while coopting discontented elites and impressing the larger population with more and better schools, roads, and jobs.

The boom did not last. In the early-to-mid 1980s, the world price for Indonesian oil plunged, from $32 per barrel at its peak in 1982 to a low of $9 per barrel in 1986. Suharto and his economists responded with a series of deregulation measures designed to encourage private-sector exporters of nonpetroleum products. Exports surged and the economy continued to grow. The share of government revenues earned from oil dropped from a high of over 70 percent in the early 1980s to a low of under 25 percent in the 1990s, despite the rise of the oil price in the latter decade to highs above $20 per barrel. Meanwhile, over the life of the regime, the absolute size of the state budget expanded dramatically, from perhaps $500 million in the late 1960s to an officially projected $44 billion in 1997, while the incidence of poverty declined, according to the World Bank, from 60 percent to less than 15 percent.

Before the collapse of 1997–98 dragged many Indonesians back down below the poverty line, the New Order's long if not unbroken record of economic success enabled millions upon millions of Indonesians to participate as producers, consumers, and investors in predictable and reliable markets. Most Americans take a smoothly running market economy for granted, but no such thing existed in Indonesia in the mid-1960s. Assuring a functioning economy and spreading economic opportunities were crucial to the political stability of the New Order, just as the loss of these achievements in 1997–98 was instrumental in ending Suharto's reign.

Suharto's policy on rice, for example, brought stable incomes and prices to millions of farmers and consumers of that politically sensitive foodstuff. Along with the activities of millions of entrepreneurs, regional and village development projects initially funded by the oil boom transformed the countryside. By the mid-1990s virtually every Indonesian child lived within walking distance of an elementary school and a professionally staffed health center. New roads, bridges, and grids of electrification and telecommunication had vastly improved the accessibility of a modern life.

I witnessed this transformation. In 1971, while doing fieldwork on that year's election, I lived for several months in a village on the south coast of Java, twenty miles from Yogyakarta. There were in the village no automobiles, not even motorcycles. The villagers had no electricity, no health center, one state elementary school, no middle school, and only a few small shops on the one main street. When I revisited the village in 1991 I counted several state and private elementary and middle schools, a government health center, a bustling commercial area, homes and businesses equipped with electricity, asphalt roads, and many locally owned cars and other motorized vehicles. Furthermore, and crucial to the political value of Suharto's economic strategy, the villagers were fully aware that they owed these improvements in large measure to the New Order and its policies.

The president also channeled economic benefits more narrowly to key elites and potential counterelites. High-ranking military officers, top civilian officials, and members of parliament and the assembly all received attractive salaries and allowances through the state budget. Informal, extrabudgetary payments and opportunities were even more important.

These favors did not necessarily involve the president directly. Some of them illustrated a long-standing pattern of ethno-economic bargaining. It had long been common practice for military officers and civilian officials to offer private entrepreneurs, typically Indonesians of Chinese descent, political protection and facilities such as cheap state credit, import monopolies, and other privileges in exchange for payments of various sorts, in cash or in kind. Ethnic-Chinese Indonesians are, as a group, proportionally more successful in business than other Indonesians, but also more vulnerable politically. The nationalist credentials of the ethnically Chinese minority have never been fully accepted by other Indonesians. As recounted by Robert Cribb in the previous chapter, the roots of this mix of suspicion and resentment can be traced back to colonial times.

But while this pattern long predated the New Order, Suharto adapted it to his own political purposes and made it a key element in the working of his regime. The president collected large sums of money from his personal friends and business associates in the ethnic-Chinese community, ostensibly for charitable giving through the several foundations that he controlled. These funds were then dispensed to selected organizations and individuals in return for political support. Recipients included not only Golkar but the two "opposition" parties as well.

The president also saw to it that lucrative business opportunities were channeled to his political friends and away from potential adversaries. An Indonesian official, newly appointed to a high post, confessed to me (in an interview on 15 May 1994) that after many years of service to the state he had really wanted to become a private businessman. But when his minister told the man that Suharto himself had chosen him for his new assignment, he knew that he had no choice: "Had I refused," he said, "the president would have made it impossible for me to succeed in the private sector."

Finally, Suharto used economic favors such as preferential credit and monopoly licenses to encourage the growth of an ethnically non-Chinese or "indigenous" Indonesian business community.[5] Such "affirmative action" was most common in the oil-soaked 1970s, but it continued in more modest form in the 1990s, despite the new climate of deregulation for global competition. While questionable from the standpoint of market-oriented Indonesian economists, heirs to the liberalizing tradition of the original Berkeley Mafia, the result made political sense: the creation of a prosperous but beholden group of indigenous businessmen. For to the extent that these entrepreneurs depended on state contracts and other official privileges, they had good reasons to want to maintain the regime. (For evidence that in the New Order's last years this pattern may have begun to change toward somewhat greater professionalism, see the chapter by Ahmad Habir.)

Suharto's Ideological Impact and Institutional Legacy

After coercion and development, legitimating symbols formed a third instrument of Suharto's power. These were used to identify the New Order with national unity, progress, and consensus. These symbols included the two chief doctrinal achievements of Indonesian nationalism, Pancasila and the constitution of 1945, and the regime's own "trilogy of development": growth, stability, and equalization. All public officials were obliged to take repeated courses in these subjects, which were also a staple of state and private school curricula from elementary through tertiary levels. Instructors in the armed forces academy taught the finer points of the seven pledges (*sapta marga*), the dual function, and the soldier's oath. Graduating officers were subject to refresher courses at key points in their careers, and required to listen to frequent speeches from their superiors, including Suharto himself, at regular commanders' calls, conferences, and seminars. The general public got a steady dose of government propaganda on television, in state-owned print media, and on holidays celebrating milestones in Indonesian history.

---

5. On the use of "indigenous," see Robert Cribb's chapter, n. 9.

The essence of these messages was that the political institutions of the New Order—a strong and autonomous presidency; a managed assembly, parliament, and three-party system; a politically involved military; controlled media and social organizations—reflected and fulfilled the true intentions of the framers of the 1945 constitution and the original meaning of Pancasila. Pancasila was lauded as a concept with deep roots in Indonesian history and culture. The New Order was described as an "integralist" state whose interdependent parts were coordinated by a powerful center to achieve consensus. This happy outcome was contrasted with the chaos of the "Old Order" in the period from 1950 to 1965 when opponents of Pancasila—communists, liberal democrats, militant Muslims, and regional separatists—had jeopardized the very existence of the nation.

To what extent did Indonesians, at the time, accept this wielding of symbols and history to justify Suharto's regime? Before Suharto's fall, this question could not be posed and debated in public or asked in opinion surveys. Clearly, however, not everyone bought the official line. Throughout the New Order a small number of intellectuals and activists, mostly outside the state, nurtured a liberal vision of politics. Prominent members of this group included the legal rights activist Buyung Nasution, *Tempo* editor and poet Goenawan Mohamad, and the head of Nahdlatul Ulama, Abdurrahman Wahid.

Alongside these liberal thinkers, a much smaller democratic left maintained a precarious existence, notably in the writings of a Harvard-trained sociologist, Arief Budiman. Still fewer and more harrassed by the state were the handful of young people brave or foolish enough to express their disgust for the New Order in radical Marxist terms. In the mid-to-late 1990s the best known of these was Budiman Sudjatmiko, a drop-out from Gadjah Mada University who had illegally launched a tiny People's Democratic Party (Partai Rakyat Demokratis). In 1996 he was arrested and blamed, implausibly, for masterminding the antigovernment riots in July of that year in Jakarta against regime connivance in the ouster of Megawati from PDI.

Most significant among these secular critics were the liberals. They kept alive the possibility of an alternative national ideology centered not on the state but on the individual. In his long leadership of the Legal Aid Institute, Nasution tirelessly defended the rights of defenseless persons to due process under the law. At its peak, *Tempo* enjoyed a circulation of some quarter of a million readers. As editor, Goenawan kept high standards of journalistic integrity and independence while arguing for a national identity based on the appreciation of Indonesians as individuals not members of particular groups.

It would be wrong to portray these critics as modern or Western to the point of being un-Indonesian. On the surface, Abdurrahman Wahid, the grandson of NU's founder, appeared anomalous: a thoroughly modern man at the head of an organization of traditional, rural-based Muslim teachers and scholars. But in a deeper sense he was a natural outgrowth of the accommodative values of Javanese village Islam, including respect for forebears, deference to religious experts, and tolerance of differing paths to religious truth. Arief Budiman articulated a social-ist vision of an egalitarian Indonesia much closer to that of the country's found-ing fathers than was Suharto's East Asian–style capitalism. Its resonance with nationalist values helped to explain the appeal of Arief's vision to successive generations of university students inspired by their own readings of Pancasila and Indonesian history.

Yet the influence of these democratic intellectuals should not be exaggerated. Suharto seems to have been fairly successful at convincing most Indonesians of the relative merits of his system. Admittedly, just as his regime failed to survive the economic shocks of 1997–98, it had previously relied on legitimacy by asso-ciation with prolonged economic growth and rising living standards for the great majority of the population. During those years, many sophisticated Indonesians privately admitted that Pancasila democracy was not democratic. But many of these same people also sincerely believed that some degree of authoritarianism in politics was a necessary condition for economic development. As for the less sophisticated, they tended to care more about their personal economic circum-stances than about politics. They passively accepted, more for convenience than from conviction, the regime's self-description as democratic.

By the time he resigned in May 1998, economic breakdown had delegitimated Suharto's regime. Yet, even after the end of his presidency, the ideological ratio-nale for his long tenure retained some appeal. Suharto's antiliberal integralism—his symbolic fusion of state and society in a single organism—continued to resonate deeply with armed forces officers, civilian bureaucrats, and a number of others outside the state. The latter included those Javanese who took pride in relating such rhetoric to what they imagined to have been the organic unity of their own royal traditions dating back to precolonial times. The historical source of the New Order's integralism is more plausibly traced to German and Japanese fascism, a powerful intellectual force when Suharto and his cohort were young.[6] But the important point for behavior in the immediate aftermath of Suharto's resignation is how many Indonesians, even among those who decried the influ-ence of the New Order's political culture, were inclined to attribute it at least in part to deeply rooted Javanese and other indigenous traditions.

The fourth and final instrument of Suharto's power was his ability to build and use institutions to carry out his will. Chief among these institutions were the armed forces and the government agencies responsible for economic develop-ment. One of Suharto's major goals upon taking power was to reorganize and unify a military establishment that had suffered a decade and a half of debilitat-ing intramilitary conflict. In the late 1960s he moved to consolidate his personal control by promoting allies and removing officers still loyal to former president

---

6. Marsillam Simandjuntak makes this argument in his *Pandangan Negara Integralistik* [The Integralist View of the State] (Jakarta: Grafiti, 1994).

Sukarno. Suharto also introduced or strengthened regular procedures for recruitment into the armed forces academy, officer promotion and assignment, advanced training, appointment to civilian posts, and mandatory retirement at age fifty-five.

Throughout the New Order the president was personally and closely involved in internal armed forces affairs. He chose his adjutants carefully and saw to their further progress through the ranks and into key commands. Retired General Try Sutrisno, for example, selected to become vice president in 1993, had been an adjutant to Suharto in the early 1970s. Promotions were not free of the appearance of nepotism. In 1992 a brother-in-law of the president, Major General Wismoyo Arismunandar, was promoted to chief of staff, the second highest position in the army. In 1997 it appeared as though one of Suharto's sons-in-law, Major General Prabowo Subianto, having risen on a fast track into the higher ranks of the army, was being groomed to command the armed forces. But these signs of political control through personal favoritism were visible within a well-established framework of military professionalism that the president had taken care to foster.

Suharto's commitment to economic development required him to strengthen much of the civilian bureaucracy as well. Substantial investments in upgrading the agencies for national planning, food distribution, and family planning, and the ministries of agriculture, education, finance, health, home affairs, industry, public works, and research and technology made these arms of government much more effective implementers of development policy than they had been thirty years earlier. Similar to the more professional military, and notwithstanding persistent inefficiency and corruption, these agencies formed an important institutional legacy that President Habibie would inherit from his predecessor in 1998.

The political institutions described earlier in this chapter were a different matter. Suharto invested heavily in shaping the People's Consultative Assembly, parliament, and Golkar, and the regular national elections on which these bodies ostensibly depended. But he denied them autonomy in order to keep them under control. The assembly and parliament survived him; they are central institutions in a constitution that is still widely accepted. But without successfully undergoing major reforms—discussed by Donald Emmerson later in this volume—these bodies will remain tools of the wielders and brokers of power, including behind-the-scene actors in the armed forces. Golkar could prove especially vulnerable to such maneuvering, given that prior to the fall of Suharto almost none of its cadres were independent of its military and civilian-bureaucratic factions.

In describing how the New Order worked I have stressed the role of Suharto and the instruments of power that he crafted and used to underpin and maintain his regime. I have done this because, to a large extent, the system was his personal achievement. But the New Order was not so beholden to its authoritarian founder as to imply that his removal would necessarily clear the path to a democratic future for Indonesia. In the second half of this chapter I want to explore the balance between continuity and change in the post-Suharto era as it appeared on the eve of the crisis of 1997–98.

In this context, I will consider three prospects for Indonesia beyond Suharto: A return to the relatively liberal democracy that the country enjoyed in the 1950s; a shift in the center of political gravity toward Islam; and a contrary movement away from Islamism toward a more pluralist, secular, and inclusively nationalist Indonesia. In doing this I will refer to history and to the views and choices of key actors on the political scene as of mid-1997.

Back to the Future?

The fact that a constitutional democracy existed in Indonesia from 1950 to 1959 can be used to support opposing conclusions about the chance that Indonesia beyond Suharto will move in a democratic direction: What has happened before could happen again. But what has already failed may not seem worth reattempting, especially if the conditions that caused the failure still exist and remain influential.

As Robert Cribb writes in this book, "the failure of electoral democracy in the 1950s and its association with civil strife will continue to be read by antidemocrats, especially within the armed forces, as reasons not to experiment with it again." Of course, not all Indonesians are antidemocrats. And, as Cribb implies, prodemocrats need not blame political pluralism for previous civil strife nor believe that democracy will prove destabilizing in the future. In 1997 democratists typically placed the onus for the earlier failure on President Sukarno and the armed forces, and this judgment led them to be optimistic that Indonesia beyond Suharto could become and remain democratic after all. The subsequent resignation of Suharto in 1998 did remove a key barrier to democratization. But his departure left intact a second potential obstacle, the military. The difficult though not impossible trick for the future will be to ensure that the armed forces do not inhibit in post-Suharto Indonesia what they helped to undermine in the earlier period.

Whatever the future may hold, four contextual factors crucially shaped the behavior of the major players involved in the failure of democracy in the 1950s. First and most generally, there was at that time a vast gap between popular expectations and the administrative capability of government. Indonesians in 1950 had lived through three years of Japanese occupation followed by five years of national revolution—a near-decade of terrible hardship mixed with great hopes for the future. During the 1920s and 1930s, nationalist leaders had assured their followers that Dutch (and Chinese) affluence and Indonesian poverty were a direct result of colonial exploitation. Independence, in Sukarno's words, would be a "golden bridge" to justice and prosperity. Expectations were high.

Perhaps no government—certainly none in the developing world in 1950—could have met such lofty aspirations, and the new Indonesian government was weaker than most. Its Dutch predecessor, though known for efficient administration, had barely laid the foundation of a modern state. Only a handful of Indonesians had been trained above the secondary level, and even fewer had been entrusted with high-level administrative responsibilities. Moreover, government agencies had been created by colonial officials for their own purposes, not the purposes of Indonesians. Occupation and revolution had severely weakened this already poor foundation. Democratic or not, the Indonesian state was not yet capable of governing effectively.

Second, commitment to a democratic form of government was neither broad nor deep. A few national-level politicians, journalists, intellectuals, and officials did appear to be convinced democrats. But many more were either skeptical from the start or adopted a wait-and-see attitude. What mattered to many in this larger category was not democracy in principle but whether the government was acting in the way they claimed it should. And while these claims typically were justified as national needs, they tended to reflect the narrower preferences of the claimants' own ethnoregional, religious, economic, or ideological group.

A third major culprit in the demise of parliamentary democracy was its lack of structural focus. The trouble lay not so much in the extent to which the multiple-party system reflected major cultural, regional, and class cleavages in Indonesian society. As Cribb emphasizes, national and even local politicians shared a deep loyalty to the idea of the Indonesian nation-state. The depth of that consensus could not prevent disagreements over the country's problems and how to address them, but it did contain them. It was not a fragmented political culture that doomed democracy. Rather it was the absence of any widely accepted, central decision-making or problem-solving agency or procedure that could have resolved these differences on behalf of the national idea—or, in Cribb's terms, on behalf of a compelling but workable conception of modernity.

The 1955 elections might have played that role. But neither of the deliberative bodies they produced—neither the parliament nor the constituent assembly—enjoyed the working majority, whether made up of one party or a stable coalition of parties, that could have made it effective. In Indonesian democracy 1950s-style, there was no one place of which it could be said, as U.S. President Harry Truman could say of his oval office, "The buck stops here."

Finally, the parliamentary system and the 1950 constitution underlying it were unsuited to Indonesian conditions in the sense that they provided no place for two of the most powerful actors of the time, President Sukarno and the armed forces. What if Indonesia in the 1950s had been a democracy with an elected president but no prime minister, akin to the system the nearby Philippines had inherited from American rule? Or a democracy without a president, but with an elected prime minister who ruled by virtue of heading the one party with a clear-cut legislative majority, along the lines laid down by the British in India? Had Indonesia in the 1950s been a presidential or a parliamentary democracy, the experiment might not have failed and the New Order might never have been born. Under such conditions, Sukarno might have provided the vital center the system did not have. Instead, he held the presidency through most of the 1950s in a constitutional arrangement that gave his office no authority. In such a system, his ambition to lead the country necessarily put Sukarno at cross purposes with the parties, parliament, the constitution, indeed with representative democracy itself.

The armed forces were another part of the problem. Their leaders felt constrained by the 1950 constitution and the power it gave to civilians in general and party politicians in particular. From the first months following the declaration of independence in 1945, these officers had clashed with civilian politicians, including President Sukarno, over many issues, including the right to choose their own commanders and whether to advance the revolution through military force or international diplomacy. The armed forces were themselves divided along various lines. Among these differences were prior training by the Dutch versus the Japanese, experience in conventional versus guerrilla units, rivalries between regionally defined military formations, and contrasting religious and social-class origins.

These splits bedeviled the military's political behavior in the 1950s. A few middle-ranking officers mutinied, took their troops with them, and declared war on the central government including their own former commanders. More typically, officers used political connections within the political elite to promote their own careers and views. At the same time armed forces leaders as a group were inclined to decry civilian involvement in internal military affairs as partisan intervention and to press for a greater collective say in decisions with military implications. In 1952, when the political system was barely two years old, armed forces leaders went so far as to point their cannons at the presidential palace and demand that Sukarno dismiss parliament.

Sukarno recovered from this experience to make himself increasingly indispensible to the system in which he had so little formal authority. Through a combination of skill and luck he managed to restore central control over the armed forces, blunt the ambitions of some Muslims for an Islamic state, and both stimulate and ride a tide of nationalism against the Dutch specifically and Western imperialism generally. By 1959 Sukarno had become the centripetal pivot missing from the parliamentary system. That July, with the support of the armed forces, he terminated parliamentary democracy by returning Indonesia to the strong-executive constitution of 1945. In 1997, having served Sukarno's authoritarian plans for Guided Democracy and Suharto's for the New Order, the charter remained in force.

Do the four conditions that helped to doom the parliamentary experiment still exist, and could they again imply change, this time not away from democracy but toward it? My answers are mixed, but not encouraging. Prior to the calamitous events of 1997–98, the gap between popular expectations and the system's ability to meet them was probably narrower than it had been in the 1950s. Certainly the developmental capacity of the New Order greatly exceeded that of the earlier regime, while socioeconomic development presumably had satisfied to some extent the hopes of the millions of Indonesians whose life chances had improved. But the severe shocks to the economy in 1997–98, coming as they did on the heels of prolonged material betterment, surely reinflated the gap, and with it the expectations that a future democratic regime would need to meet if it were to succeed.

But there was also a positive case to be made. By 1997 the idealism of the national revolution had receded too far back in time to heighten disappointments the way it had in the 1950s. By 1997 a whole new generation with no memory of Indonesia before the New Order had been exposed to Western ideas and grown critical of, or simply bored with, prolonged authoritarian rule. Inequality and corruption further tarnished Suharto's regime in the eyes of many in this genera-tion. Arguably, its members, unrestrained by personal experience of the imperfections and fate of their country's first experiment with democracy, were better able to support, even to lead, a second attempt. In the 1990s compared with the 1950s, decades of involvement with the outside world appeared to have broadened support for democracy among older Indonesians too.

Nor did the rise of Islamic consciousness and politics, which will be discussed next, swing the citizenry against democracy. In 1997 there was in Indonesia no necessary contradiction between Muslim and democratic politics—although a more Islamic climate had begun to put somewhat on the defensive those Indonesians for whom political pluralism was preferable not only to the New Order but also to a more Qur'anic society and state.

At the same time, however, the commitment to democracy among the middle and working classes should not be overestimated. During the New Order, their burgeoning size made these strata prospectively influential. Yet their incomes and jobs depended on economic growth, which in turn depended in significant measure on the policies and the stability of the regime. By endangering growth and stability alike, the crisis of 1997–98 appeared to jeopardize this incremental path toward democracy. Even before the crisis, strikes had become more common, raising the hope that workers might spearhead reforms. But the surplus of labor over employment weakened the capacity of labor activists to improve wages and working conditions, let alone achieve broader political goals. While the political climate following Suharto's fall made it easier to organize independent labor organizations, steeply mounting unemployment undercut their economic clout.

Events could outdate these remarks. Democratization could well occur. As detailed elsewhere in this book, socioeconomically and culturally Indonesia is a vastly different place in the late 1990s compared to what it had been four decades before, when Sukarno and the armed forces had terminated the country's first experiment with democracy. This transformation may have rendered moot any comparisons with earlier conditions. Nor does the question "democratic or not?" adequately portray the range of possible futures facing Indonesia. In the rest of this essay I want to deal with conditions on the eve of the crisis of 1997–98 as they may shed light on some of these other prospects for Indonesia beyond Suharto.

An Islamist Future?

In mid-1997 President Suharto appeared reasonably healthy for a man of his 76 years. He was leading an active life and keeping a full schedule. In reality his long tenure in office was almost over. But in Jakarta the crisis that would so soon and so quickly bring him down was not foreseen. Instead, less dramatic expectations were widely held. In mid-1997 it seemed plausible that, at its scheduled meeting in March 1998, the People's Consultative Assembly would renew Suharto's presidency, his health permitting, for a seventh term. Many observers also doubted, however, that his presidency would be renewed for an eighth term in March 2003, when (if still alive) he would be almost 82 years old.

From this scenario, it followed that whoever occupied the vice-presidency between 1998 and 2003 would be in the best position to succeed Suharto should the president die or be incapacitated before 2003, or should he decide not to run again in that year. Under the 1945 constitution, a president who dies, resigns, or cannot fulfill the obligations of office "is replaced by the vice president until the end of the term" (Chapter III, Article 8). Prior to the crisis of 1997–98, observers of Indonesian politics overestimated Suharto's longevity in office. But they correctly focused on his impending selection of a vice president. What they could not know was that this choice—B.J. Habibie, as it turned out—would ascend to the presidency not years later, but in May 1998, barely more than two months after his inauguration as vice president in March.

In 1997, broadly speaking, two large but only very loosely cohering groupings were competing to influence Suharto's choice of a vice president in 1998—and thus, more broadly, Indonesia's post-Suharto future. I will label these political constellations, following the practice of Indonesian commentators but with major reservations of my own, the "Islamic group" and the "nationalist group." The "nationalist group" may also be seen as part of a wider "rainbow coalition" hostile to the Islamization of political life.

In the historical portion of this chapter I distinguished "modernist" from "traditionalist" Muslims. The "Islamic group" in Suharto's Indonesia consisted mainly of modernists who resented what they took to be official discrimination against their views and affiliations. In their opinion, the New Order, and especially the leadership of the army, had been too willing to brand them as "extreme rightists" disloyal to the nation. These were not recent vexations. The Islamic group had inherited the mantle of Masyumi and the successive resentments of its leaders, first against President Sukarno for outlawing the party, then against President Suharto for reaffirming the ban. In applying the conventional local label, "Islamic group," to these neo-Masyumi activists I mean neither to homogenize them—they disagreed on many issues—nor to exaggerate their numbers or importance within Indonesia's vast and diverse Muslim majority.

The rise of the Islamic group had begun in the mid-1980s, when Suharto began taking the steps noted above to accommodate the desires and sensitivities of Indonesian Muslims while deepening his own identification with Islam. The group's chief political vehicle was ICMI, the organization of Islamic intellectu- als led by Habibie, then Suharto's minister for research and technology. The founders of ICMI were ex- and neo-Masyumi activists outside the state, many of them long-standing critics of the New Order's policies toward Islam and even of the regime itself. Before agreeing to lead ICMI, Minister Habibie had been care- ful to obtain Suharto's approval. Once ensconced, the minister recruited allies and aides from the state bureaucracy into key ICMI posts, largely displacing the social activists who had created the association. Nevertheless, most of these ac- tivists continued to support ICMI under its new management.

Habibie did not have a history of Islamic activism. He came from South Sulawesi, a strongly Muslim region. But his core identity was that of a West German-trained aeronautical engineer who wanted Indonesia to become a player in high-value-added manufacturing. He believed that Indonesia must build its own sophisticated industries such as aircraft and shipbuilding. Indonesia in his view could and should break free of dependence on imported planes, ships, weap- ons, and other high-technology items while gearing up to challenge foreign com- panies in the world markets for these products. His speeches contained few references to Islam. He stressed instead the need to train the scientists and engi- neers who could create the cutting-edge industries that Indonesia would need to survive and compete in the future world economy. Habibie presided over Indonesia's military-industrial complex, and in the 1990s Suharto appointed sev- eral of Habibie's associates to cabinet and other positions.

In the 1950s Masyumi leaders had often found themselves debating ideol- ogy: Should the state be explicitly Islamic in character? Many of them thought it should. Or should it cleave to the trans-religious principles of Pancasila, as Sukarno and his secular-nationalist and Christian supporters wished? In the 1990s the Islamic group centered in ICMI was willing to set aside talk of an Islamic state and work instead for an Islamic society within the framework of Pancasila. The group was also less focused on debating and implementing Islamic law than Masyumi had been. Muslims in and around ICMI saw themselves as striving to realize an ethical society characterized by prosperity, equality, and democracy— conditions that embodied, in their view, the authentic core values of Islam.

In the terms favored by Robert Cribb in this book, the Islamic group had a particular vision of modernity for Indonesia. Underlying that vision was Islam. But religion was more to these Muslims than a juridical list of prohibitions and requirements; it was a way of life that was moral in principle and beneficial in practice. The group was also pragmatic. The high value placed by Habibie on advanced education and technology appealed to them partly because of their own higher degrees and skills and exposure to the wider world. In Habibie's kind of Indonesia, they could expect to do well. To the extent that their association with Islam had kept them from enjoying the economic opportunities that the New Order had provided to so many other Indonesians, Islamic group members resented their outsider status. They saw in Habibie's ICMI their chief hope to become insiders and make up for time lost and influence foregone.

The Islamic group was internally diverse. Some of its members were genuine democrats. They hoped to use ICMI and Muslim politics to move Indonesia toward representative democracy. But many others, perhaps most, appeared to object more to their exclusion as individuals from the state and its opportunities, than to its authoritarian character and putative bias against Muslims in general. A few diehards, retaining the legalistic commitment of Islamist hard-liners in the 1950s, sought a fully Islamic state. The rhetoric of democratization for them had only tactical value. Still others had no political goals at all, but were content to exploit ICMI and its patron, Habibie, as vehicles to personal wealth, status, and power. Some true believers in high-tech "Habibie-nomics" were elitist. Others held egalitarian views inspired by various mixtures of leftist-Muslim thought from abroad with Indonesia's own traditions of radical populism and nationalism. In 1997 all of these people were still within the ICMI fold. But it was not hard to imagine them, under changed political conditions, breaking up and striking out on different paths.

As I have emphasized, the "Islamic group" by no means grouped all Muslims, nor was it monolithic. Tens of millions of traditionalist Indonesian Muslims, for example, lived well outside ICMI's variously modernist orbit. And they too were diverse, as illustrated by the composition of NU: Its dominant wing, led by NU head Abdurrahman Wahid, opposed ICMI. Wahid and his followers were also active in the "nationalist group" (described below), notwithstanding its non-Muslim label. In the meantime another wing of NU, critical of Wahid and less worried than he was about being coopted by the regime, continued to struggle for position and influence within PPP. Followers of this older tendency within NU tended to focus instrumentally on access to patronage: getting the state to provide jobs for NU members, fund NU projects, and protect NU as an established social and educational organization operating within the existing political system.

An estimated 87 percent of Indonesians are Muslims. Yet Masyumi and NU each won only about one-fifth of the votes cast in the elections of 1955. Even if the shares received by the smaller Muslim parties in 1955 are added to these two-fifths, roughly half of all Indonesian Muslim voters chose parties without Islamic labels, including the PNI and the PKI. Apparently, many if not most Indonesian Muslims at the time did not identify politically with Islam. This is thought to have been especially true of Javanese Muslims. Compared with their co-religionists in other ethnic groups, Javanese Muslims are said to have taken their religious obligations more lightly, and to have deemphasized Qur'anic legalism in favor of more relaxed attitudes, including tolerance for the juxtaposition and even the mixing of Islam with other traditions in a basically Javanese matrix of identity.

In the 1990s, it was thought, this situation was undergoing a reversal, with Islamic pietism increasing while Javanese syncretism declined. This perception led many ICMI activists to argue that in a truly democratic election a neo-Masyumi party could well win an absolute majority. Nevertheless, to the limited extent that the New Order's heavily managed elections can be used to speculate about the distribution of public opinion in Indonesia at the time, the optimism of these neo-Masyumi activists may not be warranted. Golkar, controlled until 1993 by officials hostile to political Islam, did consistently well at these polls. One may attribute this success to intimidation and manipulation. But it is harder to explain why the pseudo-opposition PDI, which shared with Golkar the non-Muslim or lightly Muslim if not syncretically Javanist heritage and appeal of the old nationalist and Christian parties, should have steadily improved its showing at these polls. Meanwhile, the noticeably Muslim PPP's vote share shrank by 11 percent from 1982 to 1987, as a result of the formal departure of NU from PPP in 1984, and failed to regain lost ground in 1992.

Nevertheless, on the eve of the 1997 election, the PDI's prospects for power were not bright. The weakening of the party by state interference against Megawati in 1996, along with Suharto's and Golkar's prior efforts to coopt self-consciously Muslim Indonesians, recommended caution against betting that the heirs to either tradition, Masyumi's or PNI's, would be able to control the transition to a post-Suharto regime.

The role of the armed forces especially must be taken into account when estimating the prospects of any group in post-Suharto politics. If in 1997 the Islamic group around Minister Habibie claimed to enjoy the support of top military leaders, those leaders had increasingly been recruited from among officers with Islamic backgrounds. In 1993 President Suharto had appointed General Feisal Tanjung to head the armed forces. An ethnic Batak from North Sumatra, the new commander's clan name suggested an Islamic upbringing. Two years later the president named General Raden Hartono army chief of staff. Hartono is an ethnic Madurese with a devoutly Muslim if aristocratic family background. In the mid-1990s Tanjung was widely rumored to have known Habibie when they both lived in Germany, while Hartono himself acknowledged being personally close to, and long acquainted with, Habibie.[7] (The cabinet announced by Habibie in May 1998 after his inauguration as president included Tanjung as coordinating minister for defense and security.)

In 1997 Generals Tanjung and Hartono were thought to be sympathetic to the views of other officers with similarly "green," that is, Islamic backgrounds, officers who believed that their careers had been slowed during the "Murdani era" of the 1970s and 1980s. Himself a Catholic, Murdani had both illustrated and implemented Suharto's desire to exclude Masyumi-stream Muslims from national political life, including the upper echelons of government. The other architect of

---

7. See the interview with Hartono subtitled "Saya Menaruh Harapan Pada ICMI" ["I Place My Hope in ICMI"], *Media Indonesia Minggu* [Jakarta], 19 February 1995, p. 8.

this exclusion had been Murdani's army patron, the late Lieutenant General Ali Murtopo, who had masterminded the development of Golkar in the late 1960s and 1970s with the help of ethnically Chinese-Indonesian Catholic intellectuals in the Centre for Strategic and International Studies (CSIS), a Jakarta think tank formed with Murtopo's help.

Notwithstanding their religious hue, "green" officers did not adhere to an Islamic political ideology. They did not advocate replacing Pancasila with an Islamic state. Unlike many civilian ICMI activists, they did not even discuss filling Pancasila with Islamic ethical content. Their commitment to military values, including the dual-function doctrine, appeared to be no weaker than that of their non- or nominally Muslim peers. What distinguished them was their sense of having been discriminated against because of their Islamic background—a feeling that made these green officers more sympathetic to the similar complaints of the civilian Muslim activists in and around ICMI than Murtopo, Murdani, and their associates in CSIS would have been.

In 1993 the Islamic group campaigned hard for Habibie to be named vice president. The minister was rumored to be high on Suharto's own list, perhaps even his personal first choice. And if that were so, given the president's power, one might have thought that the minister's promotion to vice president was a sure thing. Instead, the armed forces' delegates to the 1993 assembly stole a march on the president by declaring early their united support for their commander, Try Sutrisno, who ultimately received the job. Yet since the president's preference prior to Try's success had not been clear, it was not possible to conclude that Suharto's choice and power had been overridden. Try had, after all, once been Suharto's personal aide.

By 1997 Habibie's name had again surfaced as a possible candidate for vice president in 1998. Other names included Siti Hardiyanti Rukmana ("Tutut"), the president's oldest daughter and a prominent Golkar campaigner in the run-up to the 1997 parliamentary election. But a growing number of Muslims in the Islamic group appeared to believe that their future would be more secure if a sympathetic military officer could be placed in line to succeed Suharto. A green general such as Hartono appealed to them more than did Habibie or Tutut.

In 1997 an Islamist future for Indonesia seemed unlikely. The Muslims around ICMI were too diverse and possibly too opportunistic to move the country any significant distance down the road toward becoming an Islamic state. The green generals might have been raised in pious Muslim families but that background had not compromised the sincerity of their commitment to a diverse and tolerant Indonesia, or to the trans-religious, Pancasila-based role and ideology of the armed forces in guarding that ideal. Finally, as the next section will show, alongside the greens there were "red and white" officers and civilians—the so-called nationalists—who appeared to be more concerned about Muslims discriminating against non- and nominal Muslims than vice versa.

A Nationalist Future?

Although green is the color of Islam, and the national flag is red and white, the contrast between "Islamic" and "nationalist" thinkers and actors in Indonesian political life is far less stark. These are broad, loose groupings whose boundaries in principle overlap—good Muslims can be good nationalists, and vice versa—and they are both diverse. Like the Islamic group, for example, the nationalists include officers and civilians alike. However, nationalist officers do tend to worry that the growing influence of the Islamic group could endanger national unity, and warn against replaying the divisively Islamist politics of the 1950s. To be a nationalist in this sense is to have a religiously inclusivist vision of the character of the Indonesian nation.

In the New Order's last decade, the most vocal public spokesmen of the nationalist officers' views were two retired generals: Vice President Try Sutrisno, the ethnic Javanese from East Java with a devoutly Islamic background who rose from adjutant to President Suharto to become armed forces commander (1988–93); and Minister of Defense Edi Sudrajat, an ethnic Sundanese from West Java who served as army chief of staff (1988–93) before briefly replacing Sutrisno as head of the armed forces (1993). Arguably, the intellectual leader of this red-and-white wing of the military was still General Murdani, although he stayed in the background after Sudrajat succeeded him as minister of defense in 1993.

Active-duty officers may not, and do not, challenge their superiors in public. They do not like to be interviewed, least of all on sensitive topics, and even when an unguarded conversation does occur, the serving officer is extremely unlikely to risk his career for the sake of candor. Nor can an officer's opinions be inferred from his background, as Sutrisno's Islamic origin and nationalist outlook illustrate. Certainly no outsider knows just how much influence red-and-white officers exert within the military, or the extent of antagonism between them and their green colleagues.

Nevertheless, in the late New Order period, a shift did occur: The nationalists became somewhat less influential, the Islamic group more so. Before Suharto first reduced Murdani's influence in 1987 by removing him from command of the armed forces, their top levels had been staffed mainly by nominally or syncretically Muslim Javanese and non-Muslim non-Javanese. In the years following Murdani's removal, Suharto systematically weeded the former commander's closest allies out of the senior ranks and promoted as rapidly as possible junior officers who were too young to have been directly influenced by Murdani. Moreover, retired officers appeared to have relatively little influence and virtually no leverage over their still active colleagues. The public statements of Edi Sudrajat, Try Sutrisno, and other prestigious retired generals in the red-and-white camp thus may not have reflected a substantial body of opinion within the armed forces. But military discipline and secrecy made it virtually impossible to know for sure.

Prominent among the civilians in the nationalist group was NU's Abdurrahman Wahid. The traditionalist NU had long been hostile toward modernist-dominated Islamic political organizations, partly because of the tendency of urban modernist intellectuals to look down on rural Islamic teachers as old-fashioned country folk uninterested in religious reform. Partly for such reasons, NU had quit the modernist-controlled Masyumi in 1953 and resented modernist domination of PPP from 1974 until 1984. In 1984, as already noted, NU left PPP as well. Nor did ICMI, clearly led by modernists, attract many traditionalist members.

Meanwhile, since the late 1970s, apart from the traditionalist-modernist split within Islam, Abdurrahman Wahid had been pursuing a political vision of his own. Wahid condemned religion-based political parties. They were, to him, disturbingly primordial and sectarian. He believed in a tolerant, pluralist Indonesia where religion was a source of ethical inspiration and cooperation not only within but also across differing faiths. His first reply to ICMI was to challenge it by announcing the formation of a Democracy Forum (Forum Demokrasi), a proto-party to which he recruited traditionalist Muslims, Christians, secular nationalists, and others. Strategy aside, Wahid was a skilled tactician and infighter who loved the political game. A Murdani ally in many elite political conflicts in the 1980s, Wahid in the 1990s remained close to the red-and-white officers who shared his concern over the rise of the Islamic group.

After separating Nahdlatul Ulama from PPP in 1984, Wahid had tried to expand NU's influence in all three parties. Golkar was a primary focus in the late 1980s, but it was captured by the Habibie group. In 1996–97 Wahid worked hard to organize support for PDI's 1997 campaign among local-level NU leaders and the growing cadre of university-educated NU youth, who were among his most enthusiastic followers. It was not easy to build alliances across the cultural gap separating the secular-nationalist, Christian, and syncretist PDI from the traditionalist-Muslim NU. But in east and central Java, where NU and PDI were particularly strong, their respective constituences were at least not estranged from each other, in contrast to the intra-Muslim division between modernists, who claimed to reject all local accretions to religious belief and practice, and syncretist traditionalists, who tended to share a Javanist understanding of the world.

PDI was also a target of political opportunity for red-and-white officers who feared the rise of political Islam and resented Suharto's refusal to let them retain control over Golkar. Murtopo and Murdani were reported to have channeled funds to PDI and cultivated its leaders in the 1970s and 1980s. Megawati's selection to head the PDI in 1993, apparently over the objections of Suharto and Armed Forces Commander Tanjung, may also have reflected behind-the-scenes maneuvering on her behalf by red-and-white officers, just as Suharto's and Tanjung's hands may be seen in her subsequent ouster from that role.

The removal of Megawati in 1996 lowered the expectations of the nationalist group, or at any rate those of the PDI-NU coalition. The coalition had hoped to boost the PDI's vote share in the 1997 parliamentary election at Golkar's expense while building a base for Megawati as a contender for higher national office; weaken the Islamic group around Habibie and ICMI; and thus pressure Suharto into naming a vice president acceptable to the nationalists in 1998. In 1997, with Megawati out of contention, Vice President Sutrisno or another more or less red-and-white general seemed a more realistic choice for the nationalist group.

The red-and-white officers, Wahid's NU, and Megawati's PDI were all linked to a number of other political actors loosely referred to as the "rainbow coalition." These actors included human rights lawyers, democratic activists, disaffected journalists, grass-roots development organizers, socialists and other leftists, activists at non-Islamic universities, dissident artists, Christian groups, environmentalists, a tiny feminist movement, and individuals with personal and political grievances, some of long standing, against the government. What the nationalists appeared to share with these disparate groups was a common fear of rising political Islam combined with an "anyone but Suharto" attitude and a probably naive willingness to think that red-and-white officers, were they to take power, would rule more democratically than he had. Many in the rainbow coalition believed that as president, Try Sutrisno or someone like him would be less authoritarian, more consensual, and more attentive to the needs of ordinary Indonesians than Suharto had been.

Claims and counterclaims were advanced by all sides of this competition among the Islamic group, the nationalist group, and the members of the rainbow coalition. Led by the civilian engineer Habibie, most Islamic group members were unafraid of Muslim majority rule; they desired it as a democratic alternative to military control. Green officers might not agree that the armed forces were politically dispensable, but they appeared to support Suharto's decision to cultivate the Muslim community. Habibie and his entourage also believed that state-led intervention would create a modern economy more surely and quickly than the market-based policies of the professional economists.

The nationalists generally opposed Islamization and Habibie-nomics, but had no clearly articulated or widely accepted blueprint of their own for Indonesia's future. They claimed a higher regard for national unity and Pancasila-based tolerance than they imputed to the Islamic group. But their attitudes toward democracy ranged from Murtopo's and Murdani's elite-level manipulations to Wahid's and Megawati's hopes for political liberalization. As for economic policy, red-and-white generals resented Habibie's growing military-industrial empire and its encroachment on their power over military planning and procurement. Within the broad rainbow coalition, however, many shared Habibie's antipathy toward the economists' policies for having exacerbated the gap between rich Chinese and poor indigenous Indonesians. Such critics favored redistributive policies that would slow down or even reverse the trend toward deregulation. (For more on the opponents of deregulation, see Richard Borsuk's chapter in this book.)

In 1997 the wide range of interests and policy positions among these groups suggested that Indonesian politics before and after the New Order could look very different. Despite more than thirty years in power, Suharto still had not institutionalized his regime. Its performance had earned it some legitimacy, but its procedures lacked support. Arguably, it had no life of its own apart from the political forces competing to control it. Unlike, say, American constitutional bodies, laws, and alternating parties, the New Order's entities, rules, and means of allocating power did not substantially constrain aspiring presidents and president-makers. This indeterminacy made substantial political change a real possibility for Indonesia beyond Suharto.

The extent of such change will depend on the outcomes of choices by political actors seeking to form a coalition that will enable them to secure and hold power. Sukarno and Suharto were such actors, and the coalitions they mobilized, respectively, against representative democracy and Guided Democracy brought about great change. In mid-1998 it remained to be seen whether President Habibie, or whoever might in time succeed him, could once again reorient the country. But with the crisis of 1997–98 still not over, one could at least plausibly speculate that Indonesia without Suharto might eventually differ significantly from what the country had been like with him in charge.

Classes and Leaders

It is not my purpose here to discuss the economic recession and political decompression of 1998, subjects taken up at the end of this book. But it is appropriate here to note that the crisis of 1997–98 had by no means made democratization inevitable. A shrinking economy is obviously not conducive to democracy. The armed forces remained a crucial institution whose leaders continued to claim a political role. They had accepted a civilian president, Habibie. But they had not given up the dual function, including the right to reestablish order should reform, in their estimation, degenerate into revolution.

Nor could the economic blows that Indonesian society absorbed in 1997–98, for all their severity, drive the country back through time to what it had been like in the 1960s. The archipelago's transformation under Suharto had diversified the pool of resources available to contenders for national power. Among these new resources, perhaps the most important, and least well understood, was class. Economic growth under the New Order had yielded a new and highly complex class structure with multiple differentiated components.

Within the category "business," for example, one could distinguish enterprises according to whether they were located on the more developed western islands or on the eastern frontier; on or off Java; urban or rural; indigenous or Chinese-Indonesian; large, medium, or small; exporters, importers, or import-substituters; and so on. "Farming" could be upland or lowland, smallholder or plantation, subsistence or commercial, and traditional or industrial, among other kinds of agriculture. The "labor" force included urban professionals and landless villagers, office staffs and factory workers, schoolteachers and slum scavengers, rock stars and prostitutes.

By the end of the New Order, the fissures and overlaps within and across these categories had created potentials for conflict and alliance that simply did not exist in the 1950s or 1960s. In this chapter I have tried to draw lessons from Indonesia's democratic past for the country's possibly democratic future. But the novel complexity of the society's changing class structure and related changes in patterns of opposing and converging interest amount to a reason to question whether the past will be repeatable. If parliamentary democracy is revived, it will not happen merely because it existed before. Nor will democracy be retried merely because the first trial failed. Rather, the effort will be made because it serves in some sense the interests of rising and emboldened groups. And the country's sudden impoverishment in 1997–98, other things being equal, is unlikely to persuade these groups to be quiet.

Notwithstanding this picture of increasingly complex diversity and polycentrism, however, many Indonesian intellectuals and activists cleave to the hope that one class, the middle class, will be of one mind in wanting democracy, and will spearhead a transition to democracy, as the middle classes of South Korea, Taiwan, Thailand, and the Philippines are said to have done. Less optimistic observers question whether the indigenous members of this new middle class are up to such a risky role: whether they are numerous and wealthy enough relative to the Chinese-Indonesian segment of the business community; or autonomous enough from the state and its preferential credit, licenses, and contracts, which Suharto was able to use, despite deregulation, to coopt those who might have changed the political status quo earlier on.

Politically more visible in the 1990s, because it was more militant, was a new industrial working class concentrated in the export manufacturing zones in and around Jakarta, Surabaya, and Medan. Toward the end of the New Order, an explosion of wildcat strikes and illegal organizing to improve wages and conditions and to protest layoffs was labeled communist and met with repression. The downturn of 1997–98 has further hurt workers. But as long as its leaders continue to promote industrialization, the working class is likely to expand and become harder to contain through coercion alone. If its leadership is not coopted, urban industrial labor could become fertile ground for mobilization by future aspirants to national power. If movements based in working rather than middle classes played the key role in Latin America's democratization, as analysts of that region's politics have argued,[8] this too could occur in Indonesia.

I will end this chapter on a personal note. I first lived in Indonesia from 1962 to 1964. I studied ethnic and class politics in a small north Sumatran town. From

---

8. For example, Paul Drake, *Labor Movements and Dictatorships: The Southern Cone in Comparative Perspective* (Baltimore, MD: Johns Hopkins University Press, 1996); and Ruth Berins Collier and David Collier, *Shaping the Political Arena* (Princeton, NJ: Princeton University Press, 1991).

that vantage point, I could not imagine the immediate future: a more-than-thirty-year-long unified military regime, under a single leader, steadfastly pursuing market-oriented economic growth. In 1964 it was much easier to predict the waging of a real-life Bharata Yudha—the final bloody war in the Javanese version of the Indian epic *Mahabharata*—from which only soldiers or communists would emerge victorious. But I thought that if the military won, Indonesia was likely to remain a weak state: that the armed forces would stay divided; that the inconsistent, even incoherent economic policies of the 1950s would continue to thwart development; and that noncommunist civilian politicians would retain some capacity to inhibit the exercise of military power.

More than any other factor, it was the leadership of Suharto that made the difference between my expectations and what actually happened. Whatever happens in Indonesia beyond Suharto, structural explanations and predictions have their limits. Neither the strength of the status quo nor the potential for changing it need determine the future. Much will still depend, as it did in the mid-1960s, on the fateful choices of political actors responding to contingent—that is, unpredictable—events.

Chapter 3

Regions: Centralization and Resistance

Michael Malley

In Pekanbaru, the capital city of Riau province in central Sumatra, a large statue depicts the "revolutionary heroes" of Riau—the native sons who joined their counterparts from around the Indonesian archipelago in the struggle for freedom from Dutch rule. The sculpture is meant to be an imposing symbol of local pride. Yet it stands at an intersection of streets named after two Javanese heroes: Gadjah Mada and Diponegoro.

Gadjah Mada was the chief minister of the fourteenth-century Javanese kingdom of Majapahit. So expansionist was he, it is said, that he swore to abstain from *palapa*—possibly a fruit or spice, perhaps a metaphor for sex—until Sumatra and the other regions off Java had been brought, by force if necessary, under his empire's dominion. The idea of austerity as a path to power was embedded in Java's Hindu-Buddhist past. The popularity of Diponegoro, a nineteenth-century Javanese prince, was bound up with another Javanese idea: the messianic promise of a "just king" who would arise to make the world right. Diponegoro arose to lead, and lose, the anticolonial Java War (1825–30). The Dutch exiled him to another outer island, Celebes (now Sulawesi), where he died.

Those who see the statue are meant to recall Riau's contribution to the struggle for a single Indonesian nation. The names of the surrounding streets are meant to commemorate forerunners of Indonesian nationalism and statehood. Schoolchildren are taught that Gadjah Mada's Majapahit was a glorious precursor to a unified Indonesia, and that Diponegoro's anti-Dutch struggle prefigured the Indonesian revolution.

Statues and street names are symbols, but in Riau little stands between them and political realities. Located directly behind the monument to Riau's heroes is the official residence of the province's governor. From 1978 to the end of 1998, all of its occupants hailed from Java. Like nearly every other region, Riau was peripheral and subordinate to the country's Javanese center. To understand how Indonesia's regions were ruled in Suharto's Indonesia, one must first understand that the center ruled the regions.

The New Order regime embodied centripetal power. It justified itself as guardian of the integrity of the nation-state. This justification was rooted in the official memory of the 1950s as a strife-ridden time that pitted the upholders of national unity against fomenters of disunity who were emboldened by the supposedly too liberal democratic system then in effect. As the preceding chapters in this volume have noted, New Order leaders used this diagnosis to justify strict limits on personal and political freedom—saying, in effect, "Never again."

The challenges to national unity in the 1950s were real enough. The ideological and economic conflicts of that era had clear regional dimensions. Those who supported the creation of an Islamic state were concentrated outside Java, while supporters of secular nationalism and communism were more numerous on Java. In addition, in regions outside Java that were relatively rich in natural resources, many people resented the imposition of economic policies that funneled those resources toward poorer Java.

Although it allowed Indonesians to challenge the national government on these issues, constitutional democracy was not the cause of such grievances. Nor was democracy responsible for the disorganization and indiscipline in the armed forces, which enabled regional challengers to ally with discontented local military officers and units against Jakarta, resulting in the series of regional rebellions that marked the 1950s.

To prevent a repetition of this centrifugal history, the founders of the New Order designed a center-out, top-down regime. They concentrated power in Jakarta as opposed to the regions, and in the state rather than society. Crucial to this imbalance was the ability of the central government to centralize control over financial and military resources. Such centralization enforced the dependence of regional leaders on Jakarta, orienting them away from their local constituencies and toward the national capital. In this way, the New Order succeeded in reducing the opportunity for regional groups to express their views within the formal political arena. Nearly eliminated was the chance that regionally mobilized political interests could gain control, and exploit the power, of the regional state apparatus.

Politically, administratively, and financially, regional governments in the 1990s enjoyed less autonomy than at any time since independence. In 1997, on the eve of the end of his long rule, the chief question for Indonesia beyond Suharto was whether the institutions of central dominance constructed by the New Order were strong enough to withstand significant changes in central government leadership. After examining the evolution of these institutions and assessing the pressures for continuity and change, I will argue in this chapter that they were. Already by mid-1998, in the wake of Suharto's resignation in May, moves to revise these institutions were underway. It appeared likely, nevertheless, that the institutional legacy of the New Order would powerfully influence regional politics for at least several years into the post-Suharto era.

On the eve of the crisis of 1997–98, the New Order's top-down, center-out framework was under growing strain. The nature of the structure had become the cause of frequent tensions between Jakarta and the regions. Regional leaders' resignation to the sharp limits on their authority was increasingly mixed with resentment toward the long arm of Jakarta. These strains, and the potentials they represent for future change, underscore the importance of understanding how center-regional relations were managed in Suharto's Indonesia.

In explaining how Indonesia's regions were ruled during the New Order, I will not delve into details of administration. Rather, I will take up in succession three broad themes: the institutionalization of central dominance; regional political and military reactions to it; and emerging pressures for change.

Indonesia beyond Suharto will not crumble. But just as the concentration of political power under Suharto spawned demands that it be democratically dispersed, the centralization of power produced a range of dissatisfactions and demands that it be decentralized. In Aceh, Irian Jaya, and East Timor, movements fought for the ultimate decentralization—independence. Elsewhere, apparently more mundane pressures were building that had the potential not just to split one part of the country from the rest, but to restructure the relationship between the center and all of the regions.

Central Dominance

The centralization of the New Order was a product of long historical development. As noted by Robert Cribb in his chapter, it took more than three centuries for the Dutch to expand their control over the scattered and disparate insular societies that would eventually be renamed Indonesia. Some of these territories were brought under Dutch control only a few decades before Japan seized, held, and lost the Indies in World War II. During the revolution against Dutch recolonization, regional power groups under different leaders with varying agendas proliferated across the archipelago. Despite the unitary form of the insurgent nationalist republic, in the negotiations to end the revolution the departing Dutch were able to exploit the weakness of central authority to compel the new national government to accept a federal structure. This experience emphasized to Indonesian leaders the difficulty of acquiring and maintaining centralized authority, and the costs of not being able to do so.

In 1950, less than a year after the Dutch had departed, Republican leaders adopted a new, provisional constitution that jettisoned federalism in favor of the unitary structure first adopted during the revolution. This time, however, the unitary state structure was paired with a parliamentary system of government rather than the strong-presidential form for which the 1945 constitution had called. But because the new central government lacked the administrative, financial, and military resources to make its constitutional authority effective nationwide, for most of the 1950s the country was unitary only in law. In practice, regional governments and military formations enjoyed high degrees of autonomy.

Most accounts of the 1950s focus on the parliamentary conflicts that bedeviled the republic during that time. Yet before falling prey to these rifts and Sukarno's authoritarian response to them, Indonesia's constitutional democracy had resolved, at least in law and partly in practice, the tension between the unitary pretensions of the center and the actual autonomy of the regions. And the resolution distinctly favored the latter. In fact, just prior to the outbreak of the rebellions in Sumatra and the eastern islands (PRRI/Permesta),[1] Indonesia's freely elected parliament had adopted two decentralizing laws—one on regional government, the other on regional finance.

One of these measures (Law No. 1 of 1957) permitted provincial and district assemblies to elect their own leaders. That would have ended the practice, dating to colonial times, of allowing the central government to appoint regional executives. As a result, it would also have put an end to the practice of treating regional government as an administrative arm of national government. For the first time, provincial and district government, though not local government, would be placed in the hands of elected politicians rather than career bureaucrats.

The law on financing (Law No. 32 of 1956) provided a formula for allocating fiscal resources from the central government to regional governments. The formula was unworkably complex. It required data that did not exist and which the government was not readily able to compile. The law's passage reflected the political parties' view that dependable sources of financing were a prerequisite for the exercise of true autonomy. But the measure's impracticability testified to the enormity of the task of redirecting official revenues from the center to the regions and from administrative to political goals.

Despite the ideological discord that afflicted the constituent assembly then meeting to write a replacement for the provisional 1950 constitution, its members were in agreement that a new constitution should accord significant autonomy to the regions within the framework of a unitary state. Nevertheless, the reforms in the 1956–57 laws on elections and finance were never fully implemented.

In 1959, Sukarno declared martial law and returned the country to the 1945 constitution and its strong-presidential system of government. After dissolving

---

1. In March 1957 in a Universal Struggle Charter (Piagam Perjuangan Semesta Alam, or Permesta), army mutineers unilaterally declared martial law in eastern Indonesia. They later joined their counterparts in the PRRI rebellion on Sumatra described by Robert Cribb.

parliament and the constituent assembly, he overturned the provisions of the law that allowed regional legislatures to elect regional executives. Once again, regional executives would be appointed by and accountable to the central government, and the primary role of regional governments would again be to administer central government policies.

Sukarno's declaration of martial law ended Indonesia's experiment with parliamentary democracy and marked a turn toward authoritarian, army-dominated politics that would last into the 1990s. The declaration also marked the end of all efforts to grant substantive political autonomy to subnational units of government. The major long-term effect of the legal changes made in the late 1950s was the creation of new provinces and districts in response to demands from various groups for local administrative jurisdictions to match their own, mainly ethnic identities.

During the country's fleeting moment of rule by a freely elected parliament, that body approved laws to grant significant political and fiscal authority to regional government. At all other times, national governments dominated by military and bureaucratic interests consistently centralized power. The difference in approach stems from the contradictory interests of political party leaders and heads of state institutions. Governments headed by political parties viewed the regions as sources of power, while those dominated by the military and the bureaucracy saw them as arenas for the exercise of power.

Relaxation of central control was not on Suharto's agenda when he took over from Sukarno in the aftermath of the abortive conspiracy by left-wing officers in 1965. The incoming government's priorities ran in the opposite direction: toward establishing central control over a divided and politicized military and bureaucracy, including steps further to centralize relations between Jakarta and the regions. Parallel policies to depoliticize society and limit political competition further reduced the ability of regional actors to mobilize support for local interests. This centralizing strategy included three crucial moves to be discussed below: a major reform of the armed forces to bring regional commanders firmly under control of the central army command while eliminating interservice rivalries; the appointment of military officers as governors, mayors, and rural district heads (*bupati*); and, in 1974, the adoption of a new law on regional government that formalized central dominance.

Reorganizing the military to reduce its autonomy was the most important early step Suharto took to consolidate his regime and ensure that regional rebellions would not reoccur. Under martial law the regions had been subject to the authority of leadership councils that generally placed the regional military commander above the governor. In 1967, as acting president of Indonesia, Suharto abolished these bodies and replaced them with Regional Leadership Consultative Councils (Musyawarah Pimpinan Daerah, or Muspida) that included the military commander but were headed by the governor (himself often an even higher-ranking officer). Two years later, as full president, Suharto took operational control of the armed services away from their respective commanders and assigned it to the Department of Defense and Security. And since the president himself was Indonesia's minister of defense and security (until 1973), this reform located power over the military in his own hands, leaving the headquarters of the army and the other armed services with merely administrative responsibilities.

Similarly centralizing reforms changed the spatial balance of power within the military. Previously, the largest and highest-level military zones, known as Interregional Commands (Komando Antar Daerah, or Koanda) had been limited to coordinating the activities of their constituent Regional Military Commands (Komando Daerah Militer, or Kodam). The Kodam had always been the most important elements in the army's territorial structure, which roughly paralleled the structure of regional government. And during the 1950s and much of the 1960s, they enjoyed substantial amounts of autonomy. Suharto sought to reduce this autonomy by replacing the old Koanda with new Regional Defense Commands (Komando Wilayah Pertahanan, or Kowilhan), to which he assigned operational control over the Kodam. By rotating and replacing the Kodam commanders every few years, he prevented them from developing bases of power independent of the center. He was also careful not to appoint as commander of a military region outside Java anyone who was a native of that same region.

Civilian administration was also tightened. An overstaffed and politicized bureaucracy spread out across the archipelago could not be adequately controlled so the New Order purged the rolls of public employees, singling out those who might have had leftist affiliations. Those who remained were forced to join a civil servants' organization that professed "monoloyalty" to the government's political party, Golkar.

Meanwhile, military officers, serving and retired, were placed in key governmental positions. Scholars have long recognized the impact of such appointments to higher central administrative and cabinet posts. But the extent of militarization, and thus its consequences, may have been greatest in the regions. In 1970, twenty of the country's twenty-six governors were from the military, and a survey of six provinces suggests that about 60 percent of all district heads (*bupati*) including mayors (*walikota*) also hailed from the armed forces.[2] Moreover, thirteen of the twenty military governors in 1970 were later appointed to second five-year terms, further entrenching military influence.

As a proportion of all governors, military appointees remained stable at around four-fifths until 1977. The fraction then gradually declined to around half in 1992, remaining at roughly that level over the next five years. In mid-1997, for

---

2. The six provinces are East Java, North Sulawesi, and Riau, as well as Central Java, South Sulawesi, and West Sumatra. I compiled data on the first three and took data on the second three from Theodore McRoberts Smith, "The Indonesian Bureaucracy: Stability, Change, and Productivity," Ph.D. dissertation, University of California, Berkeley, 1971, pp. 126–127.

example, the armed forces supplied fourteen of the country's twenty-seven governors. Yet eleven of these fourteen regions had had only military governors during Suharto's era, while in the key province of East Java an unbroken series of officers had succeeded the civilian who had held that governorship for the New Order's first decade.

Institutionalizing Control

In 1974 the New Order established the legal foundation for this pattern of central dominance. Law No. 5 of that year set forth the relationship between central and regional governments, the procedure for selecting regional executives, and the nature of regional autonomy. The new measure reinforced the strong centralizing trend on which Sukarno, with military backing, had embarked in 1959. Technically, the 1974 measure replaced a law on regional governance that had been adopted just weeks before the outbreak of events in 1965 that had led to Sukarno's downfall. Substantively, however, Law No. 5 of 1974 was a direct rejection of the decentralizing and democratizing thrust of Law No. 1 of 1957.

In 1966, a special session of the Provisional People's Consultative Assembly (MPRS), convened under Suharto's influence, issued a series of decisions that overturned major policies of the previous regime. Decision No. XXI called for a review of the 1965 law on regional governments and asked the central government to grant them autonomy that was "as broad as possible."[3] The decision recalled the language of the 1957 law, which had promised regional autonomy that was "real and as broad as possible." Between 1968 and 1970, when Sukarno was under house arrest and Suharto had succeeded him as president, central authorities submitted three bills to the MPRS to fulfill the terms of its 1966 decision.

By 1973 Suharto felt more firmly in control. That year the newly installed regular assembly (People's Consultative Assembly or MPR) annulled the 1966 decision of its provisional predecessor (MPRS) and replaced the latter's call for "broadest possible" autonomy with an offer of "clear and responsible" autonomy. According to the new criteria, which a colonial regime would have understood well, regional governments were meant to be "responsible" not to their own constituents but to the center in Jakarta. In 1974 central authorities submitted to the national legislature (People's Representative Council or DPR) a comprehensive bill on "government in the regions." After only forty-four days of debate, the bill became a law—No. 5 of 1974—that would remain in force for the duration of the New Order.

The phrase "government in the regions" captured the tone of the New Order's

---

3. "Ketetapan MPRS tentang Pemberian Otonomi Seluas-luasnja kepada Daerah" [MPRS Decision Regarding the Granting of Broadest Possible Autonomy to the Regions], No. XXI/MPRS/1966, 5 July 1966.

plan for revamping regional governance. If previous laws had at least pretended to create meaningful "regional governments," that was not Suharto's aim. Instead, regional governments would be treated as administrative extensions of the central government in the regions.

The president and his lieutenants accomplished this goal in ways that were even more complex than they were clever. As a result, some apparently arcane distinctions came to lie at the root of important structural tensions in relations between central and regional governments under the New Order. Two parallel structures of regional governance were created. One structure, called "regional administration," was intended to undertake the top-down implementation of central government policies in the regions and would answer directly to Jakarta. Supposedly, the second structure, termed "autonomous regional government," would engage in the bottom-up political representation of regional interests and be accountable to itself.

Administrative and autonomous regions had existed prior to the New Order, as allowed by the constitution. But these had been mutually exclusive territorial jurisdictions. In practice, of course, the central government had insisted on appointing regional government leaders, such that regional governance had retained its colonial—administrative—character. Under the New Order, however, the two types of regions were made to coexist inside the same territorial unit.

Between Jakarta and the villages lay three tiers of regional governance. Existing territorial jurisdictions at these three levels—provinces, districts (*kabupaten* including municipalities [*kotamadya*]), and subdistricts (*kecamatan*)—were declared to be purely administrative regions. But the central government established supposedly "autonomous" regions, known as "Level I Regions" and "Level II Regions," which, respectively, corresponded to these provincial and district jurisdictions. The two structures, in effect, occupied the same spaces. The province of East Java and, within it, the district of Banyuwangi, for example, were declared administrative regions but also given labels denoting "autonomy": the Level I Region of East Java and the Level II Region of Banyuwangi.

The New Order did not grant even ostensible autonomy to subdistricts. Sukarno had tried to extend governmental autonomy down to that level. But the new regime's anticommunist army leaders reversed his effort, believing it to have been designed to benefit the communist party (PKI) and its superior grass-roots organizational strength.

Although the two structures coincided, they differed fundamentally. Regional administration consisted of branch offices (*kantor wilayah*) of central government departments and a governor (*gubernur*) or district executive (*bupati* or mayor). Regional government, on the other hand, had its own bureaucratic departments (*dinas*), a legislature—a Level I or II Regional People's Representative Council (Dewan Perwakilan Rakyat Daerah Tingkat I or Tingkat II, abbreviated DPRD I or II), and a regional executive called a level I or II regional head (*kepala daerah tingkat I or tingkat II*).

The critical political difference between regional administration and regional government was the concentration of fiscal resources and executive authority on the administrative side and the confinement of legislative authority to the "autonomous" governmental side. Historically, Indonesia's central government held a near-monopoly on official revenues, such that regional governments depended almost entirely on central government grants to fund their own operations. The New Order exploited this advantage by creating an entire structure of regional administration insulated from regional government—and therefore from politics. Regional governments oversaw their own bureaucracies, largely mirror images of the national bureaucracy, but could do little on their own because they depended so heavily on the central government for funding. Meanwhile, the central government was free to funnel resources in large amounts to the regions, as it wished, via the separate administrative apparatus.

This neat separation of administration from politics was breached in only one key—but all-important—respect: the position of regional executive. Law No. 5 of 1974 required that the same person serve simultaneously as head of regional administration and regional government. In a phrase repeated endlessly by government officials, that person was "the representative of the center in the region, and of the region to the center." Regional executives would be appointed by and accountable to the national government, as they had been under the Dutch, in the early years following independence, and for the life of Sukarno's Guided Democracy. The brief moment between the passage of Law No. 1 of 1957 and the declaration of martial law in 1959, during which some regional legislatures had been allowed to elect their own regional executives, was not to recur.

In contrast to the dual position of regional executives under the New Order, regional legislatures—the Level I and II DPRDs—belonged only to the "autonomous" structure of regional government. Technically, there were no "provincial legislatures" or "district councils," since a province or a district, as a purely administrative unit, had no legislative component. In consequence, regional legislatures held very weak positions.

Legally, regional governments had both an executive head and a legislative body, and legislative consent was required for the creation of regional laws. But a DPRD's ability to make laws was severely limited. It could not legislate on a matter of concern to its constituents if that matter fell under the jurisdiction of regional administration. And even on matters on which it could pass laws, its rights to enact legislation were tightly controlled. It had many rights, including the right to propose legislation. But how a DPRD carried out those rights—its rules of order, what form its bills took, who would head its secretariat—were either decided by the minister of home affairs or could only be decided by the DPRD with the minister's consent.

The 1974 law on regional government did not change the nature of financial relations between the center and the regions. Instead, central authorities allowed a 1956 law on this subject to remain on the books for decades before it was superseded by Law No. 18 of 1997 on Regional Taxes and User Fees—the product of legislation submitted to the national-level DPR by the Department of Finance as part of a package of fiscal reforms.

Based on the provisional constitution of 1950 in effect at the time, the 1956 law reflected the priorities of the parliamentary-democratic experiment then underway. The parliament of the time had passed the 1956 law mainly to tie the hands of the national executive in hopes of assuring a firm fiscal basis for meaningful regional self-government. Precisely because he wanted to limit regional autonomy as much as possible, and could do so by funding the regions administratively rather than politically, Suharto refused to replace the seemingly generous 1956 law until fiscal conditions made it necessary to do so.

Materially, Jakarta could afford to be generous toward the provinces. The oil booms of the 1970s and the upswing in non-oil and non-gas receipts beginning in the late 1980s enabled the central government to meet the fiscal needs of the regions to a far greater extent than ever before. A variety of developmental activities were put in motion, based on Presidential Directives (Instruksi Presiden, or Inpres) and called Inpres programs, to supply the regions with predictable flows of funds for various specific purposes such as building roads and primary schools, and in the form of general grants to provinces, districts, and still lower levels of administration. Such an ad hoc approach to financing regional governance gave central authorities greater flexibility than they would have enjoyed had specific legal guidelines on the distribution of revenues between central and regional government been laid down. Unrestrained by such guidelines, the central government could more easily keep regional governments beholden to it.

In redistributing the returns from national economic growth, especially windfall profits from oil exports, the Inpres programs benefited the poorer provinces, and that enhanced the legitimacy of Suharto's regime. But the unprecedented abundance of funds available to the central government also allowed it to continue to sidestep the issue of the regional governments' inability to raise enough resources on their own to cover more than a small fraction of their expenditures. All major revenue-producing instruments, including income and value-added taxes as well as levies on oil and gas, were assigned to the central government. Inferior sources of revenue were left to the provinces and districts: motor vehicle registration and title-transfer charges for the former; and for the latter, dozens of minor duties and taxes, most dating to colonial times and some not even economic to collect.

Even after the central government began to reform the financing of regional government in the early 1990s, enormous disparities between the center and the regions remained. The central government's domestic revenues (excluding foreign assistance) were nearly twenty times the total amount of revenues raised by all district governments, and almost fifteen times the amount raised by the provinces.[4] Not surprisingly, regional governments could meet only a small share of their expenses out of such limited resources. Through the early 1990s, provincial governments managed to raise only about one-quarter and districts about one-fifth of their total budgetary requirements. The rest of their revenue came from the national government in the form of various transfers. Some regional governments borrowed from multilateral lending institutions, but in order to incur any debt, regional governments had to secure the approval of the Department of Home Affairs.

To summarize, then, militarily, administratively, legally, and financially, the New Order enforced the dependence of regional government on the center. Unlike the 1950s, economic and military resources were no longer directly susceptible to regional control. The New Order organized Indonesia into regions that were legally "administrative" and "autonomous" at the same time, and used the ambiguity to treat them in practice as administrative extensions of central power, as they were under the Dutch. The irony is clear. Historically warranted as a nationalist reaction against Dutch efforts to impose divide-and-rule federalism on the archipelago following World War II, Indonesia's strongly unitary New Order came to resemble in this respect the earlier colonial example.

The continuity was significant, but it should not be exaggerated. During the New Order, Indonesia was a rather more democratic place than it had been under colonial rule, although less so than in the early years following independence. The New Order also accumulated a far larger material and coercive capacity than either Dutch or post-independence Republican rulers ever dreamed possible. And it was this capacity that enabled Suharto's regime to achieve a historic level of centralized control over the regions.

Compliance and Ambition

From the onset of the New Order, coercion underpinned its centralizing moves. The lack of outright resistance in the regions to the new regime's initial efforts to impose central control reflected Jakarta's willingness to compel compliance with its policies. This was especially true for those regions where the PKI had been strongest and the country's new rulers were therefore least tolerant of dissent. Almost all of these provinces were on Java and Bali. On the other islands, the process of consolidating central

---

4. Calculated from Central Statistical Bureau documents, these figures compare the central government's total domestic receipts with the combined (own source and shared) revenues of each level of regional government for fiscal years 1992–93 and 1993–94, the latest for which data were available at the time of writing.

power involved more negotiation and compromise over a longer time.[5]

The New Order's first task was to choose regional elites on whom it could rely. In the late 1960s local Muslim leaders, for example, were well disposed to cooperate with the new regime because it shared their opposition to communism. In parts of the country where Islam was relatively strong, such figures and their supporters quickly found positions in regional government. In political terms, however, this welcome was only superficially warm. Its historic association with regional strife and the struggle for an Islamic state made political Islam suspect in the eyes of the new authorities in Jakarta. Many of the Muslim leaders whom the New Order first favored were soon shunted aside in favor of emerging technocratic elites who, from Jakarta's viewpoint, seemed more reliably to endorse, and appeared more willing to implement, political stability and economic development—the New Order's core priorities.

Some of these new elites were well regarded in their communities. This seems to have been the case, for example, in West Sumatra, which had been in the 1950s a stronghold of the Islamic Masyumi party and a site of the PRRI rebellion. Early in the New Order period in that province—almost wholly Minangkabau by ethnicity and Muslim by religion—the new leaders emphasized their ethnic rather than their Islamic identity, partly to avoid being stigmatized by Jakarta as heirs to a tradition of Islamist opposition to the center. At the same time, however, these new local leaders were careful not to appear out of step with the moderately Muslim mainstream of provincial society. Such an approach enabled Harun Zain, the first governor of West Sumatra to serve under the New Order, to attract large amounts of aid from Jakarta for the development of his province while maintaining close ties with important Muslim organizations such as Muhammadiyah.

A main theme in Minangkabau social history had been the interaction between Islamic law (*syariah*) and customary law (*adat*). This difference had come to symbolize the respectively religious and ethnic aspects of West Sumatran identity. Under the New Order, the province's main organization for *adat,* the Consultative Body for Minangkabau Customary Law (Lembaga Kerapatan Adat Alam Minangkabau, or LKAAM), was used to reorient local identity away from political Islam and the notion that the state should enforce *syariah.* Partly in consequence, LKAAM's influence over regional politics grew. The success of Minangkabau leaders in adapting to the New Order, and thereby appearing to deserve the center's resources, along with the relative social tranquillity that West Sumatra enjoyed, made the province a strong base of support for the national government. In the 1992 election, West Sumatrans marked 81 percent of their ballots for Golkar, compared with Golkar's 68 percent share of the vote

---

5. At least while the New Order was still in progress, scholars showed only limited interest in its regional politics. See, however, the chapters by I. Amal and B. Magenda in D. Bourchier and J.C. Legge, eds., *Democracy in Indonesia: 1950s and 1990s* (1994); and T. Kell, *The Roots of Acehnese Rebellion, 1989–1992* (1995).

nationwide, and in 1997 they gave 91 percent of their votes to Golkar in contrast to the much lower national average of 74 percent.

East Kalimantan, on the large island of Borneo, affords an instructive contrast to West Sumatra. Ethnic, political, and economic conditions in the two provinces differed greatly, and East Kalimantan had not rebelled against Jakarta in the 1950s. But in late Sukarno times the province had experienced intensifying political conflicts. In large part these resulted from the practice of appointing military commanders from Java and from an influx of Javanese laborers into the province's oil fields. As the workers were organized by a communist labor union, tensions similar to those between the army and communists on Java developed in East Kalimantan as well.

The governor of East Kalimantan in the mid-1960s was a civilian from the Banjarese ethnic group. Native to southern and eastern Borneo, the Banjarese constituted about a third of East Kalimantan's population (see Map 2). In 1967, considering him too close to Sukarno and the Indonesian National Party (PNI), the new regime in Jakarta replaced him. The new governor, Wahab Sjahranie, was also Banjarese, but not a civilian. An army colonel still on active duty, he had been a young civil servant under the Dutch.

Sjahranie established his control over the apparatus of provincial government by building bridges among many of the competing political groups in East Kalimantan while shunting aside those too closely associated with Sukarno. He replaced his fellow Banjarese from the PNI with others from the Indonesian Socialist Party (Partai Sosialis Indonesia, or PSI), a more reliably anti-leftist party than the PNI despite its name. He also rehabilitated part of the local Kutai aristocracy by recruiting some of its members as well into his administration. (The Kutai sultanate had been located on the lower Mahakam river in and around the site of East Kalimantan's capital city, Samarinda. In 1960 Sukarno had abolished the sultanate and purged many of its descendants from positions of local authority.) The sultanate had been so weakened during the early 1960s that its minor revival did not threaten the interests of its Banjarese rivals. For his closest advisers, Sjahranie drew on Banjarese associates from his native South Kalimantan.

Out of such constituencies, Sjahranie began to build a base of power that was potentially independent of Jakarta. He exploited the weakened position of the regional military command in Samarinda that resulted from Suharto's policy of rotating Kodam commanders frequently to prevent the recurrence of 1950s-style warlordism. During Sjahranie's tenure as governor from 1967 to 1978, East Kalimantan had five different Kodam commanders. The weakening of the Kodam created opportunities for regional political entrepreneurship that the new governor capitalized on by coopting key groups to gain control of the regional bureaucracy. The local police were one such constituency. In return for cooperating with him, they were able to establish their own political foothold at the district (kabupaten) level, where several police officers became bupati.

Centralizing economic policies and rising military influence eventually undermined Sjahranie's position. Along with oil and gas, forests had been a major provincial resource, and licensing the forests' exploitation had given its beneficiaries access to great wealth. In the 1960s regional elites had controlled the licensing process. But in the 1970s the authorities in Jakarta implemented their centralizing bent by taking control over timber licensing away from Samarinda. Governor Sjahranie lost a key source of patronage that he had used to reward local Banjarese officials and entrepreneurs.

Meanwhile the Kodam commanders in Samarinda, who were not Banjarese and looked more to Java, or at any rate Jakarta, began to lobby to redirect the allocation of licenses away from local businessmen and toward Javanese and Jakarta-based timber interests. Thus spurned, members of the Banjarese elite began to transfer their support from the governing party, Golkar, to its Muslim alternative, the Development Unity Party (PPP). This further undermined Sjahranie's position, based as it was on assuring Banjarese support for Golkar. Meanwhile other Banjarese cooperated directly and profitably with Golkar and national power brokers in Jakarta, bypassing Sjahranie.

When Sjahranie's governorship ended in 1978, Jakarta chose Ery Supardjan, a Javanese officer who had been the local Kodam commander, to replace him. There was still room for indigenous leadership in Samarinda, but it would have to be, and remain, beholden to the center. This was the route that Mohammad Ardans, a Banjarese civilian bureaucrat, followed in the 1970s and 1980s. Loyal to Golkar, he rose rapidly through the provincial administrative ranks and was appointed governor in 1988. He proved cooperative enough in Jakarta's eyes to earn a second five-year term in 1993.

The contrasting cases of West Sumatra and East Kalimantan show how the social bases of New Order authority and rule varied from one province to another, and how, across such differences, the center sought to achieve and retain control without precluding roles for provincial leaders. But those roles could not imply the makings of an independent base of power. Conversely, in return for continually accommodating the center, a provincial elite could try to enhance his position in local socioeconomic and political life. That accommodation rested on the clear understanding that PPP and PDI must be shunned—that Golkar was the sole route to power. However, Golkar's dominance did not put a stop to competition between contending elites, who still had recourse to allies outside Golkar's formal structure—in the Kodam, in Jakarta, in local social organizations, and in the provincial bureaucracy.

The potentially broad scope of such competition meant that, despite the highly centralized character of the system, struggles for local advantage could and did sometimes spill into public view in dramatic ways. Since one of the few formal roles of a regional legislature was to participate in the selection of the regional chief executive, who would serve simultaneously as governor, *bupati*, or mayor, and since the post conferred important patronage privileges on its holder, factional struggles in regional legislatures over such selection could and did become heated and public enough even to embarrass Jakarta. Brief case studies from Riau on Sumatra and from Central Kalimantan will illustrate such outcomes later in this chapter. Before noting the abnormal or "unscripted" elections for governor that occurred there, however, it will be helpful to specify the terms of the script itself.

Scripted Elections

Befitting a strongly centralized regime and its predilection for uniformity, the procedures for selecting regional executives were nearly identical for both level I and level II regions. The chief difference was that the Department of Home Affairs in Jakarta handled level I regional elections directly, but generally dealt with level II regional elections through its provincial representatives, mainly the head of its sociopolitical affairs office and the governor.

An incumbent regional head was required to submit a letter of resignation six months before the end of his term. (Female governors were unknown, and female *bupati* virtually unknown, in Suharto's Indonesia.) It was in the ensuing three or four months that local actors had the greatest chance to influence the selection of the next regional head. Typically for a month or so during this period the local legislature (DPRD) entertained nominations from social organizations, and interested groups began to lobby, often at the instigation of potential candidates. The armed forces and the central administration in Jakarta could recommend candidates at this time, but did not always choose to do so. The Department of Home Affairs expected to be involved in the nominating process, but in theory at least, DPRD leaders could at this early stage try to draw up a list of names without requesting or considering Jakarta's advice.

Once a set of potential candidates emerged, level I DPRD leaders consulted with their respective party leaders in Jakarta in order to narrow the set to five individuals; level II regional legislators needed to consult directly only with provincial officials. Since Golkar was almost always the majority party, most of the lobbying took place within it. Normally by the time a list was drawn up, one candidate was acknowledged to be the intended winner, but intense jockeying might continue, particularly if the military had not yet put forward a candidate.

When level I DPRD leaders finally had a list of five individuals, they took it to the minister of home affairs in Jakarta, who reduced the number of candidates to three. Level II DPRD leaders delivered their list to the governor, who trimmed it to three candidates as well. The DPRD leaders then took the shortened list back to their colleagues in the regional legislature for a vote on each of the three remaining candidates. Neither the minister nor the governor had any obligation to explain his reasons for rejecting the other two names, and there was no provision for disappointed candidates or legislators to challenge the actions of the minister or governor.

The legislative voting was a public event. Home Affairs officials from Jakarta (in the case of level I elections) or the provincial capital (in the case of level II elections) attended, along with top-ranking local civilian and military officials. The candidates themselves, however, did not have to be present. Normally the voting was rehearsed a day beforehand to ensure that the visitors from the national or provincial capital were not embarrassed. In the script and its performance the intended losers received some votes, since the election would have been considered invalid had one of the three listed candidates received all the votes. The names of the two candidates with the highest number of votes were then sent to the president (in the case of level I elections) or to the minister of home affairs (in the case of level II elections). The higher level executive selected one of the candidates—not necessarily the one who had received the most votes—and about a month later the winner was inaugurated.

Or so the story usually went, though not without a good measure of cynicism as to the degree of democracy involved. And such cynicism was not only expressed in private. "The election of the Bupati of Kediri [East Java] in the Kediri Kabupaten DPRD assembly hall Tuesday was truly relaxed," reported the *Surabaya Post* in 1995. "Everything went like a musical rhythm whose intonation is well known. ... Such an atmosphere certainly did not startle the invited guests who attended the session. Perhaps because the plot was easy to guess—who would be chosen and who would bow out—an atmosphere that should have been sacred instead was like a 'joke.' "[6]

A Westerner might think the *Post* reporter naive to have expected a "sacred" atmosphere to have surrounded an occasion as secular as an election. But many urbane *Post* readers in Surabaya, Indonesia's second largest city after Jakarta, would have taken "sacred" to be an ironic comment on the ritualistic nature of such events under the New Order. In any event, the victor in this instance was an army colonel. Most of the DPRD—thirty-seven members—voted for him. But true to the script, his civilian opponents received enough support—four votes and one vote, respectively—to make the balloting valid. The fact that the minority parties held as many seats in the Kediri legislature as Golkar did made no difference to the outcome—yet another indication to the public that such a vote was far more a ritual than an instrument of democratic change.

Journalistic resort to irony is hardly surprising given government officials' penchant for creating terms that belied their claims to support democratic processes. Informally, they employed two terms that spoke volumes about the true character of regional executive elections. A "dropped candidate" (*calon dropping*) was parachuted into regional office by higher authorities—usually Home Affairs, the armed forces, or both. An "escorting candidate" (*calon pendamping*) was not really in competition to become a regional head,

---

6. *Surabaya Post*, 10 August 1995, p. 5.

but served merely to flesh out the list accompanying the predetermined winner partway down the path to success.

Again, such arrangements did not entirely preclude local involvement in the nominating process. The military's opportunity to drop a candidate on the DPRD could lead legislators to debate whether local conditions "required" an officer to handle them or not. But although these discussions may have reflected genuine uncertainty during the New Order's early years, it became obvious to DPRD members that executive posts in their province or district were, in effect, allocated either to the military or the civilian side of the regime. Occasional grumbling could, however, still be heard. The Department of Home Affairs' ability to drop a favored bureaucrat into any region as a reward for long service elsewhere, for example, might cause local complaining that "native sons" (*putera daerah*) were not given a chance to lead their own people.

Refusal in Riau

Regional contests that deviated from the predetermined script were much less rare than one might think, especially at the district level where less was at stake. These exceptions neither curbed the ability nor weakened the resolve of the center to control its periphery. But they were instructive for what they revealed about the nature of center-region relations.

Consider what happened in Riau in 1985. On 2 September of that year some three hundred people filed into the provincial DPRD building in Pekanbaru to witness the reelection of a retired Javanese army officer, Major General Imam Munandar, to a second term as governor. In the six months since he had tendered his resignation, there had been no publicly known reason to think that he would not be reelected. In early August the national leaders of Golkar had called the leaders of Riau's DPRD to Jakarta to tell them that Munandar was the party's choice, and a few days later Golkar officials arrived in Pekanbaru to prepare for his reelection. At the end of August, emissaries from national military headquarters and the Department of Home Affairs in Jakarta also traveled to Pekanbaru. There they met with "their" military and Golkar leaders in the DPRD and presented them with the script: Each of the two escorting candidates would receive three votes, and the rest would go to Munandar.[7]

But on election day, 2 September, the legislators refused to perform their assigned roles. As the paper ballots were taken from the ballot box, read aloud in the legislative chambers, and tallied stroke by stroke on a board for all the DPRD members and their distinguished guests to see, the atmosphere grew tense. For the winner was not Munandar but one of his escorts, a mere *calon pendamping*,

---

7. A detailed Indonesian-language account of these events appeared in *Tempo*, 14 September 1985, pp. 12–18.

Ismail Suko, who received nineteen votes to Munandar's seventeen, with one vote going to the third candidate. Moreover, when the chairman of the session, following customary practice, asked the members of the DPRD whether they agreed with the result, they, along with most of the audience, shouted back, "Agreed!" and broke into loud applause.

In the light of this remarkable setback for the center it was no less remarkable that Munandar could be—and was—reappointed governor of Riau right on schedule, just one month later. In that month Suko was forced to renounce his own candidacy. And that left just two candidates' names to be forwarded to the president for his decision: those of Munandar, with seventeen votes, and the remaining escort, who had received the one vote needed to validate the election. As expected, Suharto chose Munandar.

Reasons had to be found to explain how such an unusual event could have occurred. Most of them involved Munandar himself, including alleged shortcomings in his leadership. The immediate cause, however, had nothing to do with the governor. Rather what had tilted the DPRD against Munandar was the heavy-handed approach that Golkar's national leaders from Jakarta had taken in dictating the script to Golkar's contingent in the Riau legislature, a group whose votes obviously were crucial to the outcome. Pressure tactics used in the run-up to the vote included hints to independent-minded local Golkar legislators that their lack of support for Munandar amounted to disloyalty, and threats to compel them to vote for the national party's choice.

In local Golkar eyes, Munandar had grown distant from the people of the province and their concerns. His less than harmonious relations with regional officialdom also hurt him with Riau's Golkar legislators, many of whose careers had unfolded within provincial administration. Officials in Pekanbaru complained that the governor bypassed them, preferring to rely on his own kitchen cabinet; that he was personally difficult to deal with; that sometimes he did not even recognize them. An example they often pointed to was Munandar's inclination to bypass the officials in the provincial administration's secretariat. That body had been led by Riau's highest ranking professional regional bureaucrat, Baharudin Jusuf, whom Munandar had defeated in the previous gubernatorial election. Not coincidentally, Jusuf headed Golkar's Riau branch.

Munandar was also thought to be arrogantly Javanese. He had a reputation for failing to show proper respect for local traditions and cultures. Much was made of one particularly egregious act involving the Riau heroes' statue described at the beginning of this chapter. Munandar had set an imprint of his foot into the concrete base of the monument. The footprint was supposed to imitate a custom of indigenous leaders from earlier eras. But it was seen in Riau as a symbol of how Munandar, an outsider, was trampling on local values, and how he, if not also those on Java whom he represented, were recolonizing the province. Munandar's footprint was later removed, but the memory remained. So did the already noted irony that a monument to homegrown heroes should stand at an intersection of streets named after two Javanese—one of them, Gadjah Mada, an architect of Java's earlier imperial expansion.

One may dismiss Munandar's initial rejection as an oddity, a curious but insignificant exception to the rule of central dominance that his quick reinstatement, after all, exemplified. Nevertheless, as the New Order grew older, the process of selecting regional executives in Indonesia became more complex, and this made the enactment of preplanned scenarios somewhat harder to assure.

Although still very far from provoking a crisis for the center, regional Golkar and military legislators increasingly strayed from the scripts sent to them from Jakarta. In large part this could be attributed to increasing competition between Golkar's bureaucratic and military components at the regional level touched off by a change in party rules in 1987. That year, Golkar's then general chairman Sudharmono, a retired army lieutenant general, reversed the chronological order of Golkar's national and regional congresses. He put the latter first, hoping to leverage his support at the regional level to ensure support for his reelection by the national party organization the following year.

Sudharmono did not retain the chairmanship. President Suharto named Sudharmono to be his vice president for 1988–93, and the general chairmanship of Golkar for the same period passed to Wahono, a retired army general and former governor of East Java (1983–88). But Sudharmono's rule change gave unprecedented national political significance to regional struggles within Golkar. Everyone understood that President Suharto retained ultimate authority to choose the head of Golkar, but this did not deter Golkar bureaucrats and their military counterparts from sparring with each other for control over Golkar branches in an effort to influence Suharto's decision.

Such conflicts became especially intense in the early 1990s. For the first time, party members in the center and the regions knew that, well in advance of changes in party leadership, regional-level outcomes could be used to influence the balance of power among party factions at the national level. By the time Golkar held its quinquennial party congress in 1993, the military had succeeded in gaining control of a majority of the party's regional boards. Yet the military was unable to translate its regional strength into national power. In 1993 Suharto named his longtime information minister, Harmoko, to succeed Wahono and become Golkar's first-ever civilian general chairman. That the president could do this over military objections showed how unassailably strong his position was.

Withdrawal in Central Kalimantan

Under the New Order, Indonesia's political temperature usually remained high during the year following a general election. In such a year, the People's Consultative Assembly held the only meeting of its five-year term, to elect the president and vice president, and Golkar held regional and national congresses to choose its own new leaders. A large proportion of regional executives were also appointed during roughly the same period. Between the general election in May 1992 and the end of 1993, for example, the five-year terms of twenty of Indonesia's twenty-seven governors expired. Typically, officials were reappointed or replaced without serious incident. But there were exceptions, and among them, the case of Central Kalimantan stands out.

In 1985 in Riau the governor's election had gone the "wrong" way and been reversed. But in the hotter political climate of 1993, participants in a gubernatorial selection in Central Kalimantan managed to invert this sequence: The DPRD first voted for the "right" candidate, but then the central government, without exactly reversing itself, pulled back from naming him governor.

On 18 December 1993 in Palangkaraya, the normally quiet capital of Central Kalimantan, about three hundred police officers stood on guard around the building housing the DPRD. They were there to protect a roughly equal number of people inside the building from the thousands of protesters who had been gathering on the streets outside since early morning. Yet the appearance of such a large demonstration was no surprise. Controversial from the start, the entire nomination process had been marked by such activities.

The demonstrators were protesting the effort by Home Affairs Minister Yogie S. Memed, a retired army lieutenant general, to drop a candidate from outside the province into the governorship. Having been himself a governor of West Java, home to the Sundanese ethnic group, Yogie wanted one of his former vice governors, a Sundanese named Karna Suwanda, to become governor of Central Kalimantan. Local leaders in Palangkaraya objected. They argued that the province had plenty of capable native sons who deserved a chance to head the provincial government, and that the people of Central Kalimantan—home to the Dayak among other ethnic groups—deserved to be governed by a *putera daerah* familiar with provincial conditions and aspirations.

In West Sumatra, advocates of customary law in a Minangkabau context had supported Jakarta and done well. Their counterparts in Central Kalimantan chose a different course. In Palangkaraya *adat* leaders, known as *demang,* joined with the Consultative Body for Dayak Society (Lembaga Musyawarah Masyarakat Dayak) and local branches of two national veterans' associations to protest Jakarta's plan to foist its candidate onto the provincial DPRD. With this support, the Central Kalimantan branch of Golkar managed to keep its favored candidate, D.J. Nihin, the *bupati* of North Barito district, on the list of candidates that the national government approved for the election. Although Golkar's central leadership supported Karna Suwanda and expected its members in Central Kalimantan to do so as well, the executive board of the regional Golkar branch privately ordered all thirty-one Golkar legislators to vote for Nihin.

The crowd and the police had gathered at the DPRD in Palangkaraya on 18 December 1993 because inside the building the legislators were due to vote on the three candidates who were still in the running to become governor. The crowd grew enraged when the results became known. The unpopular, centrally dropped candidate, Karna Suwanda, had won, but by a margin of only three votes: twenty-four for Karna Suwanda versus twenty-one for the *putera daerah,* D.J. Nihin. A third candidate had received no votes.

The ensuing uproar kept the legislators, the governor, and other officials trapped inside the building for several hours. In subsequent days, to protect themselves and their families from the protestors' wrath, ten Golkar members who had voted for Karna Suwanda had guards posted at their homes. While the presence of the police on election day showed that the authorities had feared some sort of outburst, they had not anticipated its intensity, which far outstripped anything seen at a gubernatorial election anywhere in Indonesia during the New Order. In order to reassert order, the government had to fly troops into Palangkaraya from neighboring East Kalimantan.

The twenty-one legislators who had voted for the local favorite, Nihin, were members neither of PPP nor PDI. They all belonged to Golkar. But this affiliation with the New Order and, by implication, Jakarta, did not prevent them from issuing an ultimatum: If Karna Suwanda were named governor, they would resign their seats in the DPRD.

Stunned by the strength of local reaction, Karna Suwanda and his backers in the central government retreated. The government did not want to provoke further unrest by appointing Suwanda governor, and it certainly did not want to name Nihin, who could have proved difficult to control given the strength of his local support. Instead, Jakarta brought pressure on both candidates to withdraw their names from contention. Within a week, this move had succeeded, although Nihin held out until he had been shown Karna Suwanda's written statement withdrawing from the race.

The carrot that the central government had extended to the candidates and their supporters to convince them to withdraw was the promise of a fresh round of nominations followed by elections within six months. Minister Yogie then selected Warsito Rasman to serve as a caretaker governor until new elections could be held. Warsito, a career bureaucrat, was the highest-ranking official in the Department of Home Affairs responsible for regional governance—a post he retained alongside his new appointment in Palangkaraya.

Yogie, to allay fears in Central Kalimantan that he was imposing another outsider on the region, promised in his speech appointing Warsito that a caretaker would not be eligible to be nominated for election to a permanent post. The caretaker's task was to oversee the new round of nominations and shepherd regional government until a new regional executive could be chosen. Consequently, opponents of Karna Suwanda did not oppose the appointment of Warsito, a Javanese who had never held a position in Central Kalimantan. (Nihin, Suwanda, and Warsito, unlike Minister Yogie, were all civilians.)

About a month before the promised second round of elections in June, Central Kalimantan political leaders learned that Minister Yogie intended to make Warsito a candidate for governor. Since Warsito was too high-ranking an official to be nominated without being guaranteed victory, regional leaders felt Yogie had betrayed them a second time. Warsito's appointment as acting regional executive and subsequent nomination for election, according to regional leaders, was as unfair as assigning a referee to a soccer match and then allowing him to join the game.

The central government insisted that Warsito's name remain on the list of candidates. The lateness of his nomination seriously hindered regional leaders' efforts to organize opposition to his nomination. Still, they did launch a series of vigorous protests. Veterans and *adat* groups went to Jakarta to complain to Home Affairs, Golkar's central leadership committee, and the national legislature (DPR). But the central government refused to budge: It would brook no more interference in its efforts to administer the province of Central Kalimantan, and Golkar members who failed a second time to follow instructions from Jakarta would be "disciplined."

At first glance, the second election, on 22 June 1994, followed Jakarta's scenario exactly: Warsito far outpolled his two rivals, receiving thirty-nine of the forty-four votes cast. Three votes were declared invalid, and his opponents received just one vote apiece. The small number of votes not cast for Warsito told an important story. With no way left to protest, other than by risking their careers, legislators who opposed Warsito had tried to subvert the process in one of those perverse ways that a system concerned more with the facade of democracy than its substance permits: Knowing that under New Order rules the election of a regional executive would be invalid if one candidate received all the votes and his rivals none, Warsito's opponents had decided to cast all of their votes for him.

The main stakes in the struggle to control Central Kalimantan's leadership were almost without doubt the province's extensive forest resources. Logging permits were granted by the central government. Large businesses with good connections in Jakarta were able easily to displace local timbermen, many of whom sought accommodations with officials in the region to allow them to log illegally. Central government officials wanted someone from outside the region to protect the interests of the big loggers linked to Jakarta. Regional officials wanted a *putera daerah* who might be able to defend the interests of local businessmen against the onslaught of wealthy, well-connected outsiders. The conflict between these interests, and the dismissive approach of the minister toward candidates proposed by the region's DPRD, aroused a strong local reaction, expressed in loud demands that the governor be a native son.

These differently problematic elections, in Riau in 1985 and in Central Kalimantan nearly a decade later, are instructive in several respects. First, contrary to the national orientation and Jakarta-centered focus of most observers of politics in Suharto's Indonesia, politics did also take place in the regions. Regional leadership posts, for example, were important enough for groups in and outside of Jakarta to want and contest them.

Second, the rules of the game were so heavily weighted in favor of the center that they enabled it to have its way without resolving the issues that caused it difficulty in the regions in the first place. The power that these rules conferred was backed up by the regime's capacity and willingness to exert political pressure on those who attempted to manipulate the rules to their own advantage. This preponderance of power amounted to a disincentive to compromise with regional interests. Rather than being resolved, center-regional tensions accumulated.

Third, ethnic identity remained an important mobilizing force in regional politics. More often than not, what was seen to be "regional" about such politics was their intersection with ethnic concerns and interests, motivated by a perceived ethnic imbalance in the distribution of economic resources and political power. Finally, departures from centrally written scenarios were caused by divisions within the government's own electoral vehicle, Golkar, not by the actions of the two nongovernmental parties, PPP or PDI. This suggests that pressures for decentralization arose as much from tensions inside regime institutions as from tensions between the regime and outside forces.

Political violence was another matter, as the next sections will show. They will consider three armed movements that sought separation not just from the New Order but from the Republic of Indonesia. These movements were active in Aceh in northwestern Sumatra and in two half-islands in eastern Indonesia, Irian Jaya and East Timor. Observers tended to treat them as distinctive, even *sui generis,* and each one did have unique roots. Jakarta, by contrast, treated them as if they were similar, even applying the same generic label—"security-disturbing movement"—to all of them.

The common treatment to which Jakarta subjected Aceh, Irian Jaya, and East Timor included an unwillingness to share returns from local economic resources with the inhabitants and a readiness to resort to harsh methods of repression. Similar treatments elicited similar results. New generations of Acehnese, Papuans, and Timorese grew up tending to mistrust the regime and to resist Jakarta's control. For these reasons, and in order to speculate on their meaning for the unity or disunity of Indonesia, I will treat these instances of political violence in the context of center-region relations.

Repression in Aceh

As Robert Cribb argues in his chapter, the regional rebellions that swept Indonesia in the 1950s were for the most part meant to change the nature of the republic, not secede from it. In contrast, rebellions during the New Order were intended to achieve independence for their territories. For example, in December 1976, just two months after announcing its existence, the Free Aceh Movement (Gerakan Aceh Merdeka, or GAM) declared that province's independence, a step never taken by the regionalist Acehnese leader Daud Beureueh in the 1950s. Retribution was swift. By the early 1980s the Indonesian army had captured, killed, or chased into exile most of GAM's leaders.

Aceh Merdeka's founder, Hasan di Tiro, traced his roots back to Cik di Tiro, an admired native hero of Aceh's struggle against the Dutch and a symbol of tenacious Acehnese opposition to outside rule. The Dutch had only managed to conquer Aceh in the early twentieth century, after more than three decades of war. In the minds of Acehnese and the Indonesian military alike, GAM's struggle was also linked to the House of Islam's (Darul Islam) movement to turn Indonesia into an Islamic state. In the 1950s Acehnese Muslim leaders had joined Darul Islam under the leadership of another highly regarded anticolonial leader, Daud Beureueh, from Pidie. (Later, the fact that Hasan di Tiro also came from Pidie would be used to strengthen the younger man's connection to Beureueh.) Beureueh could not bring Indonesia under explicitly Islamic rule. But he did win one concession from Jakarta: Aceh would be recognized as a "special region" with the right to make its own rules on religious and educational matters.

Although seemingly crushed by the early 1980s, Aceh Merdeka reemerged in 1988–89. By the following year, the central government had committed some 12,000 troops to defeat the movement a second time. By the accounts of Indonesian and international human rights organizations, the military campaign against the rebels was brutal, and resulted in an estimated 2,000 casualties, mostly civilians.[8] Using tactics developed in East Timor, the army forced local Acehnese to assist in operations against the rebels. Reportedly, homes and even whole villages suspected of aiding the movement were burned, and individuals thought to have been in contact with it were subject to arbitrary arrest, torture, rape, and execution. By 1993, the rebellion was effectively quashed.

Most insurgencies have many causes, and this one was no exception. Nevertheless, in Aceh in the late 1980s and early 1990s, if not beyond, the core problem seems to have been twofold: the central government's preferential treatment of one local group over another—"modern" Acehnese technocrats over "traditional" Islamic elites—and its failure to help develop Acehnese resources for the benefit of Acehnese.

Just as the Dutch had favored the traditional nobility over the religious leaders in their own governance of Aceh, so in the early years of the New Order did Jakarta forge ties with an emerging young technocratic elite in the provincial capital, Banda Aceh, while marginalizing local religious leaders. As in West Sumatra, educated and relatively secular Acehnese technocrats, among them economists associated with Syiah Kuala University in Banda Aceh, in effect sought to redefine the region's identity away from religion and toward ethnicity. They did this partly because they were by no means Islamists themselves and feared those who were, and partly to disconnect the province from its past association, in Jakarta's eyes, with the drive for an Islamic state. Also attractive to the

---

8. A detailed account of the counterinsurgency campaign may be found in *Indonesia: "Shock Therapy": Restoring Order in Aceh, 1989–1993* (New York: Amnesty International, 1993). Kell's monograph (see "Further Reading") is the best account of the rebellion.

center was the priority this new local elite gave to economic development rather than to social or religious issues.

By the late 1980s, however, many Acehnese had come to feel that the center's alliance with local technocrats had not yielded equitable development for the people of Aceh, but rather had opened the province to exploitation by outsiders. For evidence of the latter outcome, Acehnese generally and GAM especially focused on the town and hinterlands of Lhokseumawe, located in the district of North Aceh, on the eastern border of Cik and Hasan di Tiro's home district of Pidie (see Map 1).

On the outskirts of Lhokseumawe in the 1970s the central government had begun to develop a massive industrial area. The scheme took advantage of infrastructure already built to accommodate a major investment in natural-gas extraction and liquefaction for export to Northeast Asia. The liquid-gas facility, two fertilizer plants, and associated port facilities and housing in the Lhokseumawe area, along with a paper factory and other projects elsewhere in the province, rapidly transformed these few parts of Aceh.

Thousands of outsiders, mainly from Java, came to work on these projects and in related activities. Geared as they were to production for shipment abroad or to other parts of Indonesia, the projects seemed to benefit the center and foreigners far more than the Acehnese. Many Acehnese also worried that industrial pollution threatened their traditional farming and fishing pursuits. Poor rural dwellers in particular resented the influx of Javanese, including still poorer people who had come to re-settle with help from the Department of Transmigration in Jakarta.

Aceh Merdeka was able to organize mainly because of such grievances and the local climate of indifference, if not hostility, toward provincial government that they inspired. The rebels were helped as well by the persisting importance of Islamic authority within Acehnese society, despite decades of effort by the New Order to recruit an alternative elite with more technical training, fewer political ideas, and greater loyalty to the regime and its developmental goals. By challenging the very legitimacy of the New Order in Aceh, GAM invited and received a response whose brutality, while effective in defeating the rebels for the time being, appeared to feed local resentment.

If Jakarta's experience in Aceh during the New Order yields a general lesson for handling center-region relations, it is this: Limiting the democratic aspect of regional government so sharply that unfavored groups are excluded from the political process may permit the separation of politics from administration in the short run. But it tends to delegitimate the authority of those who are included, and it encourages the excluded to take violent measures outside the legal arena. So long as Jakarta does not address this issue, the quelling of unrest in Aceh may prove a temporary success. Attacks on a bank and government offices in early 1997 put the Indonesian military back on high alert and indicated that even on the eve of what would turn out to be the end of Suharto's long rule, the struggle simmered still.

Resistance in Irian Jaya

By 1997, about 5,000 kilometers east of Aceh, the Free Papua Movement (OPM) had been struggling for more than three decades to gain independence for the territory it called West Papua, but which Jakarta called Irian Jaya—physically by far the largest province in Indonesia. In 1962 the Netherlands had ceded the western half of the island of New Guinea to the United Nations. In 1963 the United Nations had transferred the territory to Indonesia under an agreement whereby, within five years, Jakarta would organize an "act of free choice" enabling the inhabitants to decide between independence and integration with Indonesia. In 1965, as Sukarno's Guided Democracy grew more unstable, but before Suharto's rise and repression, the OPM was born, and sporadic resistance to Jakarta's presence in the region ensued.

The "free choice" that finally occurred in 1969 was an operation by Indonesian military intelligence to ratify integration as a fait accompli. Slightly more than 1,000 tribal leaders were selected from the province's districts and brought together to agree, ostensibly by consensus, that the territory should indeed be the country's twenty-sixth province. The United Nations "noted" this ratification, but declined to "endorse" it.

The 1969 "act of free choice" was not free at all in the judgment of OPM's leaders. In 1971 they announced the formation of an independent Government of West Papua and stepped up the guerrilla resistance to Indonesian rule. The OPM managed to launch major attacks in 1977–78, including one against the operations of the copper-mining giant, Freeport. But the movement was internally divided and in 1984 suffered a serious defeat when the Indonesian military learned of a planned attack on the provincial capital, Jayapura. The resulting escalation in Jakarta's military campaign, which included bombing and strafing suspected rebel zones from the air, caused over 10,000 Papuan villagers to flee to neighboring Papua New Guinea. Often hampered as much by the mountainous terrain as by Indonesian troops, the rebels kept the armed struggle going intermittently into the 1990s.

Beginning in late 1994 the conflict reintensified. In July of that year Indonesian troops were reported to have rounded up and eventually killed four members of OPM leader Kelly Kwalik's clan. In November, following the death of a Freeport employee, apparently at the hands of OPM, the company turned to Jakarta for assistance. Military action against the rebels and their suspected helpers escalated and gained wide public attention after it was revealed that in May 1995 Indonesian soldiers had massacred eleven Papuans at a jungle site about 90 kilometers from Freeport's mine.

Significant unrest continued in 1996. In January the OPM kidnapped a group of foreign and Indonesian environmental researchers and held many of them for several months. After a team of negotiators from the International Committee of the Red Cross spent four futile months seeking a peaceful settlement, an army operation involving hundreds of troops managed to free the remaining hostages. Major riots broke out twice in March. The first occurred in the Freeport town of Timika when a company vehicle struck a local man, triggering attacks on Freeport installations. The firm's chief executive officer came to Timika from Jakarta for talks with the local people and Indonesian officials, and the mine itself was closed for a month.

The second incident flared up less than two weeks after the first, lit this time not by an accident but a funeral. Thomas Wanggai, once employed by Irian Jaya's provincial administration, had been jailed in the late 1980s for having proclaimed the territory's independence as "West Melanesia." While in prison in Jakarta, he had died, and his body had been returned to Irian Jaya for burial. Hundreds, perhaps thousands of people turned out for the occasion, including students from a university located along the road from Jayapura's airport to the city itself. When security forces prevented the crowd from escorting the body, the students rioted. Shouting pro-independence slogans, they burned down a local market dominated by non-Irianese Indonesians.

Located at opposite ends of the archipelago, Aceh and Irian Jaya differed in many respects. Yet local grievances and Jakarta's response to them in the two locales were similar enough to warrant parallel conclusions regarding center-region relations. The complaints of Papuans would have sounded familiar to the Acehnese, and vice versa. Irian Jaya was, and still is, rich in copper, gold, and petroleum, among other natural resources. As with natural gas in Lhokseumawe, the central government in tandem with a foreign corporation (Freeport) had been exploiting Irianese assets for the benefit more of outsiders than inhabitants.

In both provinces the resulting environmental damage significantly impaired traditional uses of land and water over wide areas. Also in both places, economic development attracted migrants, foreign and Indonesian (notably Javanese), who lived apart from, and more richly than, local society. In Irian Jaya hundreds of thousands of transmigrants from Java and other islands encroached on traditional lands, and certain key fields of employment such as government service and market trading came to be dominated by people from outside Irian Jaya.

Irianese evidence thus appears to confirm the lesson suggested by Jakarta's experience in Aceh: So long as regional government remains accountable upward and inward to the center rather than downward and outward to the indigenous population, local grievances are likely to go unaddressed and local unrest is likely to continue.

War in East Timor

Roughly halfway between Java and Irian Jaya lies the island of Timor, its eastern half the site of Indonesia's most widely known conflict. A coup d'état in Lisbon in April 1974 toppled Portugal's military dictatorship and set its colonies on their rocky roads to independence. Nearly a quarter century later, in 1997,

Indonesia was still embroiled in political and military conflicts in East Timor.[9]

As the Portuguese dictatorship crumbled, Timorese sought a new political format for the territory. Favoring independence were the two major political parties—the leftist Revolutionary Front for an Independent East Timor (Frente Revolucionária do Timor Leste Independente, or Fretilin) and the more conservative Timorese Democratic Union (Uniao Democrática Timorense, or UDT)— while the much smaller Timorese Popular Democratic Association (Associaçao Populár Democrática Timorense, or Apodeti) endorsed becoming a province within Indonesia. Within a year of the Portuguese coup, Fretilin had defeated its erstwhile ally UDT in local elections and on the battlefield. Members of UDT and Apodeti then escaped across the border to Indonesia.

After appearing initially to support East Timorese independence, the Indonesian government began to intervene aggressively on behalf of Apodeti and the increasing number of UDT leaders who favored integration into Indonesia following their defeat by Fretilin. As Fretilin grew stronger, Jakarta's zealously anticommunist generals grew ever more fearful of the establishment of a leftist state within the archipelago, a potential "Southeast Asian Cuba" on their back doorstep.

On 7 December 1975 Indonesia invaded. As many as 2,000 people in the capital, Dili, are thought to have died within the next few days. Fretilin forces retreated into the hills with Portuguese arms, and Indonesia was left to dominate a few urban areas. Many East Timorese fled behind Fretilin lines to escape persecution by Indonesian troops. In May 1976 Indonesia convened in Dili a carefully screened twenty-eight-member Representative Council of the People of East Timor to request that Indonesia accept the territory as a new province. In July in Jakarta, the DPR obligingly approved the request. In mid-1998 Indonesia still called East Timor its twenty-seventh province, while the United Nations continued to withhold formal recognition of this status, and the United States continued to acknowledge integration as a fact, although without endorsing how it had happened. Suharto seems to have believed, correctly, that Washington would acquiesce in his fait accompli.

For the first two years following the invasion, Indonesian and Fretilin troops were locked in a stalemate. But late in 1977 the Indonesian military launched a new campaign of attacks on Fretilin, destroying crops, water supplies, even whole villages, and finally encircling Fretilin forces, whom the Indonesians bombed into surrender in December 1978. On the last day of the year, Jakarta's troops captured and killed Fretilin's guerrilla leader, Nicolau Lobato. According to human rights groups, during this two-year campaign as much as a third of the territory's population perished in battle or as a result of war-induced famine and

---

9. More information on East Timor and its conflict with Indonesia since the mid-1970s may be found in the further readings, websites, and videos listed at the back of this book.

sickness. Fretilin itself estimated that it had lost 80 percent of its troops and 90 percent of its weapons.[10]

During the 1980s, Fretilin and its shattered military wing, the Armed Forces for the National Liberation of Timor (Forças Armadas de Libertação Nacional de Timor, or Falintil), reorganized and developed fresh political and military strategies under the new leadership of Jose Alexandre ("Xanana") Gusmao. Under his direction, Fretilin became less unilaterally leftist, and as a result was able to construct a broad alliance of nationalist groups inside and outside of East Timor under the umbrella of a National Council of Maubere Resistance (Conselho Nacional da Resistência Maubere, or CNRM) formed in 1986. (Maubere is a nationalist term for East Timorese.) Meanwhile, recognizing its diminished military capabilities and the increasing Indonesian presence in the region, Falintil reorganized itself as a guerrilla force. Henceforth, it would be divided into small and highly mobile units linked to clandestine networks of civilian resistance to Indonesian rule.

Indonesia kept up its military campaign against the guerrillas, and human rights violations continued. Hoping to Indonesianize the younger generation of East Timorese, Jakarta incorporated its new province into its system of national education and encouraged the local use of the Indonesian language. The Indonesian system of regional government was also extended to the East Timorese, who were to be administered in the same way as their fellow citizens in other provinces. As it had in Aceh and elsewhere, Jakarta found, trained, and promoted technocratic local leaders who were willing to define East Timor's problems mainly in economic terms. One such figure was Mário Viegas Carrascalao, a former UDT leader who served as governor of East Timor from 1982 to 1992.

But Indonesian occupation produced unintended effects. Forcibly resettling rural dwellers into camps during the military onslaught of the late 1970s brought Timorese speaking different languages into contact with each other. From such interactions the Tetum language developed as a common local medium and a symbol of East Timorese, or Maubere, identity. Partly because it had cared for the families of resistance fighters and the many women and children widowed and orphaned by the war, the Catholic church emerged as the most important social institution (On Tetum and Catholicism in the territory, see Maps 2 and 4, respectively).

As violence in East Timor declined, Indonesia became emboldened. Jakarta

---

10. For estimates by human rights groups, see *East Timor Violations of Human Rights: Extrajudicial Executions, "Disappearances," Torture and Political Imprisonment, 1975–1984* (London: Amnesty International, 1985), p. 6; and Amnesty International, *Power and Impunity: Human Rights under the New Order* (London: Amnesty International, 1994), p. 5. On Fretilin's losses, see Steve Cox and Peter Carey, *Generations of Resistance: East Timor* (London: Cassell, 1995), p. 35, which also contains extensive photographic evidence of the conflict.

decided to open the province to Indonesians from other islands as well as foreign visitors. The influx of Indonesians from elsewhere had the same effect as in Irian Jaya: It caused conflicts over land rights in areas where transmigrants were settled, and resentment when outsiders took over market activities and filled good jobs. In late 1989, Pope John Paul II visited East Timor, and the American ambassador followed in early 1990. For each visitor and his accompanying journalists, young activists organized pro-independence demonstrations.

A new generation of resistance was coming of age. As Indonesian-educated witnesses to New Order–style development and militarily enforced political stability, young East Timorese realized that their plight had not been forgotten by the outside world. But their activism attracted increased attention from the armed forces. When an eagerly awaited Portuguese visit was canceled in October 1991, it appeared that an opportunity to deliver another statement to the world had slipped away. Instead, in Dili on 12 November, hundreds of young activists used the occasion of a funeral for one of their number, who had been killed by the security forces, to stage a peaceful demonstration in favor of independence. As the marchers escorted the body into the Santa Cruz cemetery, hundreds of Indonesian troops opened fire, killing more than one hundred East Timorese.

More than any other event, the Santa Cruz massacre kept the issue of East Timor's status on the Indonesian and international agendas. On the third anniversary of the Dili massacre, when Jakarta's hotels were filled with foreign delegates and journalists attending or covering the annual summit meeting of the Asia Pacific Economic Cooperation forum, Timorese activists clambered over the American embassy's fence and requested political asylum. In Jakarta throughout 1995 activists continued to enter embassies and demand asylum abroad, usually granted by Portugal.

In East Timor itself, protests continued, while violent conflicts broke out between native Timorese and recent immigrants from other islands, especially Sulawesi. Although some incidents were sparked by perceived insults to the Roman Catholicism of most Timorese, many more stemmed from economic competition. In Dili in September 1995, unrest broke out after a Timorese trader was killed by a trader from Sulawesi. So serious was the ensuing violence that thousands of immigrants packed onto passenger ships for weeks afterward to return to Sulawesi and Java.

As of 1997 it could be argued that the struggle for Timorese independence was unwinnable—as long as Jakarta remained willing to continue fighting it. It was clear, however, that politically the conflict would not go away. Neither Indonesian-language schools, nor large budgets for economic development, nor punishments to enforce the status quo had prevented a new generation of Timorese, who had not even been born when Indonesia invaded in 1975, from keeping the hope of independence alive.

Barely heard during the widespread regional rebellions of the 1950s, the issue of separatism had come back to haunt the republic. Through much of its existence, the New Order had faced rebellions in Aceh, Irian Jaya, and East Timor, and it had responded to these movements in similar ways, despite their immense differences. The New Order had kept these regions under the same pattern of militarily enforced political control, and had subjected them to broadly similar policies of economic development—policies that often seemed to have less to do with improving local welfare than with enriching outsiders. These commonalities likely account for the intensification of separatist demands, backed by a readiness to take up arms against Indonesian rule, which occurred almost simultaneously in each of these regions in the early 1990s.

The people who took part in the regional rebellions of the 1950s still hoped to remain part of the single, united Indonesia for which they had struggled in the 1940s. The Irianese and East Timorese, however, were not part of that revolution. Few Irianese remember the Indonesian struggle to liberate their territory from Dutch rule in the 1950s and 1960s in the same way that most Indonesians recall the revolution of 1945. Acehnese, in contrast, can claim a central role in the fight to defend the nascent republic from recolonization. That may be a small part of the explanation why the movement against Suharto's Indonesia was, on the whole, less persistent in Aceh than in Irian Jaya or East Timor. Nevertheless, as of 1997, resistance if not outright rebellion seemed likely to endure in all three regions.

Issues, Pressures, Prospects

In this chapter I have argued that the New Order imposed a complex and highly centralized structure on relations between Jakarta and the regions. In sharp contrast to the 1950s, the military was under firm central control, and the state's bureaucratic reach extended farther and deeper than ever before. But even by the end of Suharto's regime some things had not changed. Chief among these were interregional economic inequality and a marked lack of regional political autonomy.

Reactions to the increasing centralization of power and the persistence of inequality under the New Order ranged from quiescence to military insurgency. The unscripted elections and separatist rebellions discussed above did little if anything to improve the lot of those who supported them and less still to remove the barriers placed by the regime between regional administration and regional politics. But these elections and rebellions illustrated how the institutions that the New Order created to contain and marginalize regional political life themselves elicited and shaped challenges to the regime.

In 1997–98 political and economic shifts were underway in Indonesia that portended growing pressures to revise the structure of center-region relations described in this chapter. Economically, the center of activity had been moving toward Java since the middle 1980s, a sharp break with a decades-old pattern. In the 1990s this was accompanied by increasing social unrest on Java and strong gains there by the minority political parties. In the future, however, diminished economic opportunities outside Java may arouse a different type of resentment toward Jakarta in these outer regions.

Traditionally, the sparsely populated provinces outside Java contributed the bulk of Indonesia's exports, while densely populated Java accounted for most of the country's imports. This imbalance was largely due to the far greater concentration of population and industrial and infrastructural development on Java compared to other islands. During the 1970s and early 1980s, the government attempted to redress this imbalance. But even though it channeled subsidies, as well as investments in several major natural resource developments, away from Java, industrialization continued to be concentrated on that island.

Beginning in the mid-1980s, the national government pursued economic reform policies that started a process of structural transformation of historic proportions. From the 1950s until the mid-1980s, Java had accounted for just 15–20 percent of the country's exports but around 70–75 percent of its imports. The rapid growth of manufacturing industries on Java caused the island's share of exports to rise above 40 percent by the mid-1990s—a level not recorded since the early twentieth century, when the exported goods were almost entirely agricultural commodities. At the same time, Java's share of imports rose only slightly to around 80 percent.

Trade figures are only the most dramatic indicators of this important regional shift. Java's total economic output, measured in terms of gross regional domestic product, rose from about 55 percent of the national total in the mid-1980s to around 60 percent a decade later. For the first time, the island of Java contributed a share of national economic activity as large as its share of the national population.

This shift of economic power is directly attributable to changes in New Order economic policies. Put most simply, efforts to deregulate and liberalize the country's economy succeeded in fostering the development of labor-intensive, export-oriented manufacturing. But because labor was most abundant on Java, industrialization was concentrated there. In only a few areas outside Java, such as Medan and Palembang in Sumatra and Ujungpandang in Sulawesi, were large numbers of new factories opened.

Economic policies that benefited Java more than other islands only partly explain Java's more rapid industrialization. Another, equally important part of the explanation lies in the reluctance of New Order governments to liberalize those sectors of the economy that were and remain vitally important to people in Sumatra, Sulawesi, and other islands.

In 1995 an economist from North Sulawesi, Lucky Sondakh, argued that a subtle form of discrimination had prevented the poorer eastern islands from attaining high, sustainable rates of growth. In particular, he contended that the national government had provided protection for the main agricultural crops produced on Java, including rice and sugar, while imposing restrictive regulations on agricultural commodities produced on other islands. Such policies had aimed to ensure social stability among the numerous peasant farmers on politically crucial Java, as well as among the consuming population of that island's cities.

Another goal had been to guarantee industry located mostly on Java a cheap supply of agricultural raw materials produced mostly outside the island.

In contrast to the complaints of economic exploitation in the 1950s, in the 1990s the critique came not from wealthy regions made poorer by government policy, but poor regions kept poor by national policymakers' disregard for their interests. Sondakh was not shy in calling attention to the potential consequences of continuing disregard: "The fact is that a further increase in regional inequality . . . [could] revive regional sentiments and possibly regional protests, as happened in North Sulawesi in 1957, West Sumatra and North Sumatra in 1957, and Aceh in 1990."[11] In 1992 a foreign economist, Anne Booth, argued that regional development "is the most serious of the problems facing Indonesia over the next decade," and that permitting at least one province to secede "paradoxically . . . may be essential in order to preserve and strengthen the Indonesian state."[12]

This chapter has been about the New Order. The economic and political shocks of 1997–98 are reviewed at the end of this book. These shocks appear to have weakened the center in its relations with the regions. Yet if Booth is right, allowing at least one province to secede might actually strengthen Indonesia. The political impact of economic changes will vary from region to region. But center-regional tensions may not subside even if, or when, the stalled Indonesian economy begins to grow again. Further processes of industrialization and urbanization on Java are likely to continue to produce protests against the sharp economic inequalities between rich and poor so visible in its cities.

Even under the New Order, Java was a problem for Golkar. In Suharto's Indonesia, Golkar consistently was more successful in obtaining rural than urban votes, and Java's higher level of urbanization made Golkar's position more precarious there than elsewhere. In the 1997 election, for example, Golkar posted its best performance ever, but its record 67 percent of all votes cast on Java was well below its national average of 74 percent, and far below the levels it achieved in Sulawesi (92 percent), Sumatra (84 percent), and the eastern provinces (88 percent).[13]

Although the twin processes of industrialization and urbanization proceeded

---

11. Lucky Sondakh, "Deregulation and Its Potential Impacts on Agriculture and Regional Disparity in Indonesia," a paper presented at "Building on Success: Maximizing the Gains from Deregulation," a conference hosted by the World Bank and the Indonesian Economists Association, Jakarta, 26–28 April 1995, p. 17.

12. The first quote is from her introduction to her edited volume, *The Oil Boom and After* (Singapore: Oxford University Press, 1992), p. 28; the second is from her "Can Indonesia Survive as a Unitary State?" *Indonesia Circle*, 58 (June 1992), p. 46. Also see her chapter in this book.

13. The eastern provinces include Bali, East and West Nusatenggara, East Timor, Maluku, and Irian Jaya. The comparable figure for Kalimantan was 73 percent—higher for Java but also below the national average.

rapidly in Suharto's Indonesia, urban industrial agglomerations remained the exception outside Java. On Java, their rapid growth meant a strengthening of urban-based political opposition, including, more than anywhere else, electoral challenges by minority parties. In the 1992 poll, when the government permitted freer competition among the parties than in 1997, the minority parties made large gains on Java. In 1992 in a few level II DPRDs in Central and East Java, the PPP won more seats than Golkar, and in more than two dozen others the PPP and the PDI together gained more seats than Golkar. Although the minority parties' strength in urban areas extended to islands other than Java, the lower levels of urbanization beyond Java limited such parties to just a few strongholds.

Outside Java, social and political responses to economic change were more likely to center on issues of inequality between outsiders and native members of regional societies. Although economic growth was generally as rapid outside Java as on Java, the nature of economic change was often much different. Timber and mining displaced local people from traditional lands and yielded greater economic benefits to outside investors than to local workers. The increasingly rapid spread of agricultural estates, especially oil palm on Sumatra and Kalimantan, had similar effects. The weaker role of minority political parties, as well as the subordination of regional Golkar branches to its central leadership, made political expression of such grievances more difficult than on Java.

As of 1997 not one of the movements for secession discussed in this chapter possessed the military resources to achieve it, and Suharto and the regime remained adamantly opposed to it. Leaders of Indonesia after Suharto may be more inclined, or more easily persuaded, to relax strong central control. Then again, if the military continues to influence the selection of such leaders, that could inhibit the willingness of Jakarta to loosen the reins substantially, let alone acquiesce in secession. Throughout the history of the republic, central military authorities have preferred to suppress instances of regional defiance rather than to accommodate them.

Resistance to disunity, however, is not purely military in nature. As this chapter has shown, the New Order created a complex structure of institutions whose chief aim was to centralize control over regional affairs. In the view of most central government officials, nearly any expression of regional difference, especially if it were made in ethnic and religious terms, threatened national unity. To limit the politically centrifugal effects of regional politics, the regime subordinated politics to administration in a system of control that placed regional government in the care of a department of the central bureaucracy—Home Affairs. The multiple elements of the resulting system—law, finance, recruitment, election, and organization, including the armed forces' key role—were woven into an inertial fabric that resisted change. Yet pressures to reform the system intensified over the New Order's final decade, and exploded into a variety of proposals for more or less radical changes in the wake of Suharto's fall.

One great obstacle to change in center-region relations in Suharto's Indonesia was the lesson that his regime drew from its official memory of the 1950s. The divisiveness of that earlier time continued in the 1990s to animate elite fears of the risks to national unity that freer political competition and expression could pose, including genuine political autonomy for the regions. From the standpoint of the New Order, unitary and federal forms of government were mutually exclusive packages, not variable aspects of a continuum of mixed solutions to the problem of balancing central and regional power and interests.

Looking back from 1997 to the mid- to late 1950s, I have noted that a democratic government in Indonesia was able to draft a legal framework for center-region relations—a framework that managed to acknowledge regional needs for autonomy and identity within the constitutional requirement of a unitary state. But the framework was stillborn. Events overtook it. Four decades later, the stewards of the New Order, having purposely built a system that would not suffer from the centrifugal pluralism that in their view had doomed the country in the 1950s, were still unwilling to return to such a tumultuous future.

The cost of enforcing national unity has been rising. For Suharto, the likely cost of democracy was even higher. The question is whether, and to what extent, his successors will reconsider his calculation, and with it the stigmatizing of Indonesia's historical experiment with democracy as an object lesson in what not to do. In the midst of Indonesia's transition beyond Suharto and on the eve of what could be far-reaching changes, I prefer nevertheless to close this chapter on a note of caution against expecting either that Indonesia's periphery will soon break up into countries, or that its relations with the center will soon be successfully reformed.

PART TWO: ECONOMY

Chapter 4

Development: Achievement and Weakness

Anne Booth

Events in the second half of 1997 made it a difficult year for the Indonesian economy. A rise in surface ocean temperatures east of the archipelago—a periodic phenomenon known as El Niño—contributed to a drought severe enough to cause hundreds of deaths in Irian Jaya while calling into question the ability of the national government to maintain stable prices for basic foodstuffs. Smoke from forest fires in Kalimantan created an atmospheric haze broad and dense enough to result in the closing of schools and airports and the cancellation of tourist visits. The fires and haze endangered the health of at least twenty million Indonesians and caused considerable damage to natural resources.

That was not all. Indonesia's currency, the rupiah, plunged in value in U.S. dollar terms—part of a regional cascade of devaluations that had begun in Thailand in early July. One could debate whether this loss of confidence in the rupiah rested on a realistic critique of the Indonesian economy or reflected the ignorance of currency speculators about differences between Indonesian and Thai conditions. But whatever the explanation, the rupiah's decline, a related wave of selling on the Jakarta stock market, and the resulting downward revisions in estimates of near-term economic growth all showed that not even three decades of success had made the Indonesian economy safe from further setbacks.

In the course of 1998, as told in chapter 10, these setbacks proved to be severe. Even toward the end of 1997, the full devastating shape of things to come remained unclear. But the turmoil already under way served to warn observers against excessive optimism. One could still entertain the idea that Indonesia might someday evolve into the economic superpower of Southeast Asia. But that would not happen soon. It will be well into the twenty-first century before this vast country can realize its full economic potential. By then, even its boundaries may have changed. In his historical chapter, Robert Cribb traces the making of a single nation—Indonesia. But how far into the future can one assume the continuing unification of diversity? The economic successes of the Suharto years could not be denied. But they could not be extrapolated into the future, as the shocks and reversals of 1997–98 showed. Whether and how the country survives as a unitary state will greatly depend on how Indonesian leaders respond, or fail to respond, to the formidable challenges of development in the twenty-first century.

The main goal of this chapter is to review and evaluate the record of development preceding the crisis of 1997–98 and to answer the question: How did Indonesians fare? Following a brief historical summary, I will assess the growth and transformation of the economy by focusing on key issues: the performance of agriculture and industry, manufacturing and exports, revenue and expenditure, and regional infrastructure. The focus will then shift to issues of performance and policy regarding population, education, and poverty and its alleviation. I will end with some thoughts about prospects for the Indonesian economy in the post-Suharto era.

Overview

At the beginning of 1997, after three remarkable decades of economic growth, it was hard to recall Indonesia's earlier, and at least equally long, record of economic decline. Yet in 1967 the archipelago's per capita gross domestic product (GDP) was lower, in real terms, than in 1940, before the Japanese invasion, and probably also lower than in 1913, before World War I.[1] Regarding Indonesia in the mid-1960s, the harsh verdict delivered by one economist with first-hand experience, Benjamin Higgins, portrayed the dismal picture that most economists with knowledge of the country drew at that time. Indonesia in 1966, wrote Higgins, "must surely be accounted the number one economic failure among the major underdeveloped countries."[2]

In the first half of the 1960s, exports declined, foreign currency reserves shrank to zero (in 1965), and inflation mounted to an almost 600 percent annual rate (in 1966). By mid-decade, over half of the people living in rural Java were "very

---

1. Pierre Van der Eng, "The Real Domestic Product of Indonesia, 1880–1989," *Explorations in Economic History,* 29 (1992), pp. 343–373.

2. Benjamin Higgins, *Economic Development: Problems, Principles, and Policies* (rev. ed., New York: W.W. Norton, 1968), p. 678. In the view of another economist, Heinz Arndt, the mismanagement of Indonesia's economy had brought about "a degree of economic breakdown with few parallels in modern history." Bruce Grant, *Indonesia* (3rd ed., Melbourne, Australia: Melbourne University Press, 1996), p. 110, quoting Arndt.

poor," leading demographer Nathan Keyfitz to portray the crowded island as "asphyxiating for want of land."[3] Nor were the signs of deterioration evident only to specialists. For lack of maintenance, let alone new investment, the country's infrastructure—ports and airports, roads and railways, factories and power plants—had become badly run down. Not even a casual visitor to a major Indonesian city in the 1960s could fail to notice the poverty, squalor, and dilapidation.

Policies soon changed. From 1965 to 1968, as Suharto succeeded the country's first president, Sukarno, the material neglect, fiscal recklessness, and revolutionary rhetoric of the so-called Old Order gave way to a "New Order" regime that found its highest priorities—indeed, its self-justification—in economic development and political stability.

The New Order's authoritarian character still tempts observers to assume that it must have been established in the mid-1960s by force alone. Admittedly, without the army behind it, the regime would not have been born. But Suharto and his colleagues also enjoyed substantial support among Muslims, students, and intellectuals, among other elements in society. By the same token, the impressiveness of their subsequent performance should not lead one to imagine that it was easy for Suharto's technocrats to restart the economy and make it productive again.

The willingness of major foreign and multilateral donors to lend a hand was crucial to success. To place the country on a stable growth path, Suharto realized that he would have to restore credibility with Western governments and companies. Accordingly, he recruited into his cabinet a so-called Berkeley Mafia of experts on economics and demography from the University of Indonesia, all trained in the West and several with degrees from the University of California at Berkeley. Radical Western critics accused the group, led by Professor Widjojo Nitisastro, of implementing an ultraliberal policy agenda based on dogmatic faith in free markets.

In fact, these technocrats were pragmatists and realists. They knew that economic—and political—liberalism had been treated with great suspicion in Indonesia ever since independence. They knew, too, that Suharto and the armed forces were no more willing to introduce a completely free-market economy than Sukarno had been. Far from mounting a hyperliberal campaign, the technocrats cautiously pressed for reform. (Markets and deregulation are explored by Richard Borsuk in the next chapter.)

The new regime's most immediate need was to stop the ruinously spiraling rate of inflation. Crucial to achieving this goal was balancing the government

---

3. Inflation figures are from H.W. Arndt, "Banking in Hyperinflation and Stabilization," in Bruce Glassburner, ed., *The Economy of Indonesia: Selected Readings* (Ithaca, NY: Cornell University Press, 1971), p. 388. Data on rural and urban poverty in 1964–65 are given in my *Agricultural Development in Indonesia* (Sydney: Allen and Unwin, 1988), p. 126. Keyfitz's image is from his "Indonesian Population and the European Industrial Revolution," *Asian Survey,* 5:10 (October 1965), p. 505.

budget, whose deficit had risen by 1965 to some 3,000 percent of revenues.[4] Crucial to balancing the budget, in turn, were Western and Japanese aid and investment, which Sukarno had scorned but Suharto and his technocrats now sought and obtained. At first mainly injected into the budget without being earmarked, foreign assistance was gradually redirected into support for specific development projects.

In 1967 a new foreign investment law was adopted to attract private capital into sectors such as mining and manufacturing. The inflow of public and private funds from abroad allowed the budgetary and the balance-of-payments deficits to be brought under control without triggering a major recession. Between 1966 and 1969, the rate of inflation was pared to a single digit, and most controls on transfers of capital into and out of the country were removed. By 1971 multiple rates of exchange were unified and pegged to the U.S. dollar.

All was not smooth sailing. In 1967 a poor harvest led to a sharp rise in domestic rice prices, which threatened to derail the recovery program. But the crisis showed regime leaders how acute the need to expand food-crop production was. Bad news encouraged good policy: In the New Order's first five-year development plan, which began in April 1969, agriculture received major attention, and by the mid-1980s the country had become, barring future surprises, self-sufficient in rice. Compared with other oil-and-gas-exporting nations, whose leaders used rising world energy prices as an opportunity to import food with earnings from exported hydrocarbons—oil and gas—Indonesia's attention to agricultural production was particularly impressive.

Between 1968 and 1981 the Indonesian economy grew more than 7 percent per year, a record unprecedented in the archipelago's modern history. During most of these years, and especially after 1974 when world oil prices began to increase rapidly, Indonesia enjoyed substantially improving commodity terms of trade—that is, export prices rose faster than import prices. As world oil prices fell in the early and mid-1980s, so did the rate of economic growth. But bad times again fostered good policies: Suharto and the technocrats used the decline in the price of the country's chief export, petroleum, as a reason to begin a wide-ranging program of structural reform, including two substantial devaluations of the rupiah, major taxation and banking reforms, and a series of measures aimed at improving incentives for exporters.

By the late 1980s, non-oil exports, especially of manufactured goods, were growing strongly, and GDP growth rates had revived to approximately 7 percent annually. From having been labeled by Higgins in the mid-1960s as a "chronic drop-out" from the economic development race,[5] Indonesia had gained the admiration of the international development establishment. In the turbulent wake of a

---

4. Grant, *Indonesia,* p. 110.
5. Higgins, *Economic Development,* p. 678.

boom-and-bust in world oil prices, Suharto and his technocrats had managed to reposition the Indonesian economy away from dependence on hydrocarbons and toward a more diversified export mix that could support broadly based industrialization. And they had accomplished this without neglecting agriculture. Such achievements would lead the World Bank in 1993 to place Indonesia in the select company of high-performing economies responsible for the "East Asian miracle" of "rapid growth *and* declining inequality."[6]

From "drop-out" to "miracle" in three decades? The next section explores in more detail the empirical basis for this seemingly extravagant claim.

Growth and Transformation

Until the crisis of 1997–98, Indonesia enjoyed remarkably rapid economic growth. Over the span of the New Order's first five five-year plans, from 1969 to 1994, GDP expanded on average 6.8 percent annually. Over the same quarter century, population grew on average 2 percent per year, leaving average annual gains in per capita GDP at 4.8 percent.[7] In effect, per capita GDP doubled every fifteen years.

The dire straits to which the economy had been reduced by the mid-1960s made even small absolute improvements look impressive. And much of the subsequent growth could be attributed to the oil boom of the 1970s. But if these were the only reasons for the economy's expansion, it should have lapsed by the 1990s. Instead, in the aftermath of declining hydrocarbon prices in the early 1980s, annual average GDP growth accelerated from 6.1 percent from 1980 to 1990 to 7.6 percent from 1990 to 1995, while population growth fell further to 1.8 percent per year on average from 1980 to 1995.[8]

Agriculture and Industry

These changes were accompanied by a striking proportional shift from agriculture to industry. As a share of GDP, from 1965 to 1995, agricultural output shrank from 56 to 17 percent while industrial output expanded from 13 to 42 percent. Industry's contribution to the economy burgeoned from less than a quarter to

6. *The East Asian Miracle: Economic Growth and Public Policy* (Washington, DC: World Bank, 1993), pp. 1–3. The other high performers identified by the Bank were Hong Kong, Japan, Malaysia, Singapore, South Korea, Taiwan, and Thailand.

7. The figure for economic growth is from my "Repelita VI and the Second Long-Term Development Plan," *Bulletin of Indonesian Economic Studies,* 30:3 (December 1994), p. 4. I have derived the demographic growth figure from official estimates of the size of Indonesia's population—115.0 million in 1968 and 189.1 million in 1993.

8. *World Development Indicators 1997* [henceforth *WDI97*] (Washington, DC: World Bank, 1997), pp. 35 [population], 131 [GDP].

more than twice that of agriculture. The proportion of working Indonesians employed in agriculture also fell, though less dramatically, from 71 to 44 percent over the same period.[9]

Yet this rapid growth of industry could not have been achieved without priority attention to agriculture. Agriculture accounted for almost 30 percent of the rapid economic growth achieved from 1967 to 1973, when annual gains in GDP averaged nearly 8 percent.[10] In these early years, for example, the government subsidized the introduction of higher-yielding rice seeds developed at the International Rice Research Institute in the Philippines. Rice harvest yields began to increase, especially on Java, laying a basis for future industrialization by feeding prospective factory workers in towns and cities, enlarging rural buying power to consume these factories' products, and reducing inflationary pressures by keeping the prices of key foodstuffs stable.

After 1973, revenues from oil company taxes were used to increase agricultural productivity further. New high-yielding and pest-resistant varieties of rice were developed and distributed. These efforts contributed to a burst of growth in rice production between 1979 and 1985, when total output of the crop increased by 49 percent. In 1985 the government proclaimed Indonesia's self-sufficiency in rice. In the meantime, the availability of rice to the population had increased from less than 100 kilograms per person annually in the mid-1960s to 146 kilograms in 1983, alongside rising production and consumption of meat, milk, vegetables, and other foodstuffs.[11]

The rate of increase in rice production decelerated markedly after 1985. From 1986 to 1995, output of this key crop grew by only 29 percent, or 2.5 percent per year compared with the 6.8 percent annual average increase achieved from 1979 to 1985. In 1997 most rice farmers on irrigated land were harvesting yields close to the technological maximum. The extent of such land on the outer islands had been expanding, but the yields achieved there tended to be lower than on Java. In addition, on Java many farmers found other crops such as vegetables to be more lucrative than rice, and began converting rice land to the cultivation of these other crops.

The drought of 1997 cut rice production for that year to 49.4 million tons of

---

9. World Bank, *World Development Report 1987* (New York: Oxford University Press, 1987), pp. 206, 264 [data for 1965]; *Results of the 1995 Inter-censal Population Survey, Series S2* (Jakarta: Central Bureau of Statistics [CBS], 1996), p. 318 [population data for 1995]; *WDI97,* p. 236 [other 1995 data].

10. R.M. Sundrum, "Indonesia's Rapid Growth, 1968–81," *Bulletin of Indonesian Economic Studies,* 22:3 (December 1986), p. 58.

11. *Indikator Ekonomi Mai 1990 [Economic Indicators May 1990]* (Jakarta: CBS, 1990), p. 69 [data for 1985]; Leon A. Mears, "Rice and Food Self-Sufficiency in Indonesia," *Bulletin of Indonesian Economic Studies,* 20:2 (August 1984), p. 126 [remaining data].

dry threshed paddy from the 51.1 million tons achieved in 1996,[12] forcing the authorities to import rice. The government's Food Supply Agency (Badan Urusan Logistik, or Bulog) was prepared to try to stabilize rice prices by running down its stocks of the commodity. But the rupiah's steep devaluation from August 1997 onward made domestic price rises inevitable, not only for rice but also for sugar, corn, and soybeans, among other staple foods. Ironically, by late 1997 the role of Bulog itself was under fire, and a substantial deregulation of the domestic food market was reported to be one of the conditions to which the International Monetary Fund was tying its financial assistance to Indonesia.

Manufacturing and Exports

By the mid-1990s, manufacturing had been the leading engine of growth in Indonesia for more than a decade, contributing nearly one-third of the increase in GDP from 1983 to 1995. The rapid expansion of manufacturing reflected in part the growth of industries based on processing petroleum and natural gas. But by 1995 these two activities accounted for less than one-tenth of total manufacturing ouput. The other nine-tenths comprised a diverse range of manufacturing industries. Some of these, such as motor vehicles, were oriented largely toward the domestic market; others, such as wood products, garments, footwear, and electronics, were also sold abroad. Agriculture contributed only 9 percent of the increase in GDP from 1983 to 1995, and tree crops—not annual food crops— were the most rapidly growing part of this sector. Mining also played a minor role, accounting for less than 7 percent of GDP growth during the period.[13]

The growth of manufacturing transformed the composition of exports. In the 1960s a few primary commodities had accounted for the bulk of goods shipped abroad—a common pattern among undeveloped economies. In 1965, for example, two products, rubber and petroleum, contributed almost 70 percent of Indonesia's officially recorded earnings from exports.[14] Inefficiency and corruption in the archipelago's ports, and an officially overvalued exchange rate that made Indonesian exports costly to foreign buyers, motivated many exporters to smuggle their cargoes to neighboring markets in Malaysia, Singapore, and the Philippines.

By the early 1970s supply and demand were allowed to determine the value of the rupiah in foreign currencies, so there was less incentive to smuggle, and export volume was growing rapidly. Furthermore, world prices for most of Indonesia's exported staples rose between 1968 and 1973, leading to an overall

---

12. *Indonesia in Crisis: A Macroeconomic Update* (Washington, DC: World Bank, 1998), Table 30.

13. *Indonesia: Sustaining High Growth with Equity* (Washington, DC: World Bank, 1997), p. 156.

14. *Statistical Pocketbook of Indonesia 1964–1967* (Jakarta: CBS), p. 213.

improvement in the commodity terms of trade. The ratio of export to import prices continued to rise from 1973 to 1981, mainly due to sharply climbing world oil prices. At the peak of the boom, oil, gas, and associated products accounted for more than four-fifths of Indonesia's total export earnings. The proportional value of total exports accounted for by hydrocarbons and related products then plunged, from 82 percent in 1981 to 24 percent in 1996, while nonhydrocarbon receipts rose over the same period from 18 to 76 percent of total export earnings.[15] The latter increase was driven mainly by rising exports of manufactured goods—processed wood products (especially plywood), textiles, garments, and footwear, among other manufactures—rather than traditionally exported staples such as rubber, coffee, and nonferrous metals. The rapidity of the growth of these "new exports" amazed many observers.

Several explanations for this success have been put forward.[16] Two large devaluations of the rupiah, in 1983 and 1986, and an ensuing policy of allowing it to float, within a band, downward relative to the dollar, led the exchange rate to decline steeply over time in real terms. Because of this policy, which lasted until the rate was freed in August 1997, Indonesian exports could be attractively priced in dollar terms on world markets. The policy enabled Indonesia to compete successfully with producers of labor-intensive manufactures from other parts of the region, including China, Thailand, and Malaysia.

Meanwhile the very steep appreciation of the currencies of Japan, South Korea, and Taiwan after 1985 led producers of exports in these countries to relocate their labor-intensive manufacturing processes to other parts of Asia where wage costs were lower. Indonesia, along with Thailand and Malaysia, benefited from the resulting flood of foreign investment from Northeast Asia, much of it in manufacturing for export.

Constructive, too, were the official steps taken to improve incentives for export makers. The finance ministry began administering a duty drawback scheme for exporters. Under the program, domestic manufacturers who produced largely for export could claim a refund of taxes paid on imported raw material. By thus lowering their costs, the scheme enabled these producers to price their exports more competitively in world markets.

Duty drawback arrangements are administratively cumbersome and prone to corruption. Nevertheless, to the surprise of many businesspeople, the finance ministry was quite efficient in making the necessary refunds. In addition, in 1985 the authority to inspect trade shipments was taken away from the notoriously corrupt Directorate General of Customs and Excise Taxes and contracted out to a

---

15. *Indikator Ekonomi Juni 1997* [*Economic Indicators June 1997*] (Jakarta: CBS, 1997), p. 101.

16. See Hal Hill, "Manufacturing Industry," in Anne Booth, ed., *The Oil Boom and After: Indonesian Economic Policy and Performance in the Soeharto Era* (Singapore: Oxford University Press, 1992), pp. 204–257.

Swiss firm, the Societé Generale de Surveillance. By reducing the time needed for imports and exports to reach their destinations, this reform considerably improved the efficiency of Indonesian ports. Steps were also taken partially to deregulate inter-island shipping.

Government Revenue and Spending

When the New Order's first five-year plan began in 1969, foreign aid and borrowing accounted for 27 percent of the government's budget revenue. Another 14 percent came from a tax on income earned from the foreign sale of crude oil and petroleum products. The rest was derived from a range of domestic taxes, most of them inefficiently administered and yielding little revenue. After 1973, however, revenues from taxing the oil companies expanded rapidly. Returns from this one source dominated budget revenue in the late 1970s and early 1980s. For much of the period from 1971 to 1990, income from the oil company tax, together with foreign aid and borrowing, contributed well over half of all budget revenue.

Because such "painless" sources of revenue were so readily available, there was little incentive to reform the domestic tax system. In the 1980s, as world oil prices fell and Indonesia's returns from exported oil and gas contracted, foreign aid and loans, especially the latter, gained prominence among sources of official revenue. The government also began to address the inefficiency of the country's low-yielding arrangements for collecting domestic taxes. A value-added tax was introduced, and the income tax was drastically reformed. As these measures took effect in the second half of the 1980s, domestic non-oil revenues also grew. By fiscal year (FY) 1996–97, domestic sources other than oil supplied 68 percent of all budgetary income—and 12 percent of GDP. In contrast, at the height of the oil boom in FY 1980–81, non-oil domestic revenues had accounted for merely 27 percent of the government's budget—and a mere 7 percent of GDP.

A fundamental tenet of New Order budgetary doctrine called for maintaining a "balanced budget" in the sense that total outlays would not be allowed to exceed income from all sources, including government borrowing. This definition may be criticized as insufficiently disciplined on the revenue side. But the government's long-standing commitment to such a policy did imply a readiness to reduce expenditure, whether for routine matters or for development, in response to reductions in income. When falling oil returns in the early and mid-1980s created such a situation, for example, the government sharply cut spending.

However, this "balanced budget" policy also allowed official borrowing from abroad to increase rapidly, especially in the early part of the 1980s. Much of this debt was denominated in Japanese yen. Accordingly, when the yen appreciated in 1985–86, the value of Indonesia's external debt-servicing obligations in rupiah increased greatly. The rupiah devaluation of September 1986 worsened this problem. By FY 1988–89, debt-service payments reached one-third of total government expenditure. The fifth five-year plan (1989–94) included an explicit commitment to lower the level of government indebtedness, and official debt-service obligations were indeed reduced to a quarter of government spending by FY 1996–97. But the growth in foreign debt incurred by the private sector kept total external debt-servicing obligations worrisomely high: over 30 percent of the value of exports.[17]

The point of such detail is to underscore the implications for foreign debt of the structural transformation of the Indonesian economy, including the growing role of the private sector. Government policies might be—generally they were—macroeconomically sound. But as the economy expanded under a basically market-oriented regime, the private sector grew even more rapidly, and businesses became more and more willing to borrow from abroad. Official fiscal discipline still mattered, but in the new context of the 1990s, decisions and actions by domestic private entrepreneurs began to affect the level of foreign debt in an increasingly obvious way. And these decisions and actions were not always salutary from the standpoint of the economy as a whole.

Reportedly by the end of the fifth five-year plan in 1994 almost three-quarters—73 percent—of all investment funding originated in the private sector. While this figure may be inflated, private investment does appear to have grown more rapidly than government investment since the latter part of the 1970s.[18] Nor did this new private investment come primarily from abroad. Although foreign direct investment (FDI) in Indonesia grew rapidly beginning in the mid-1980s, by the end of that decade its share of total investment was still quite modest. It has been estimated that from 1986 to1991 incoming FDI accounted for only 2.4 percent of gross domestic capital formation in Indonesia—compared with 6.3 percent in Thailand, 9.7 percent in Malaysia, and 29.4 percent in Singapore.[19] The transformation of the Indonesian economy that began in the 1980s can thus be seen as the result of three more or less simultaneous expansions: in manufacturing, in nontraditional exports, and in the participation of domestic (as well as foreign) private investors in these and other economic activities.

---

17. World Bank, *World Development Report 1997* [henceforth *WDR97*] (New York: Oxford University Press, 1997), p. 246.

18. According to estimates in John Chant and Mari Pangestu, "An Assessment of Financial Reform in Indonesia, 1983–90," in Gerard Caprio, Izak Atiyas, and James A. Hanson, eds., *Financial Reform: Theory and Experience* (Cambridge, UK: Cambridge University Press, 1994), from 1985 to 1989 private investment grew from 48 to 59 percent of total investment. The 73 percent figure for 1994 is from *Rencana Pembangunan Lima Tahun Keenam* [*Sixth Five-Year Development Plan*] *1994/95–1998/99* (Jakarta: Koperasi Pegawai Bappenas, 1994), Book 1, Table 4.5.

19. M. Yoshida, I. Akimune, M. Nohara, and K. Sato, "Regional Economic Integration in East Asia: Special Features and Policy Implications," in Vincent Cable and David Henderson, eds., *Trade Blocs? The Future of Regional Integration* (London: Royal Institute of International Affairs, 1994), pp. 72–73.

Infrastructure and the Regions

Consistently, through boom times and austerities, the government emphasized public spending on infrastructure, including power and roads, ports and airports, and water for irrigation and personal use. Such outlays were made through sectoral allocations to central government departments, grants by presidential authority (Inpres) to provincial and lower levels of government, and loans by state banks to state-owned firms such as the national electric company. Sectoral and Inpres spending rose rapidly in the 1970s, and all three methods together enabled the government to enlist all levels of administration, from national to local, in infrastucture development. In the 1980s, budget cutbacks in response to falling oil revenues and rising foreign debt-service obligations slowed the growth of spending on infrastructure, but this trend was reversed in the more buoyant economic climate of the early- to mid-1990s.

Overall, the results were impressive. Thirty-three times as much electricity was generated in 1995 as in 1968. By 1995 seven out of ten households had access to electricity for lighting. Kilometers of asphalt roads increased more than eightfold from 1968 to 1995. More and better roads combined with rising incomes to boost the number of motor vehicles twenty-one-fold to 13.2 million by the latter year. Repeat visitors to Indonesian cities were likely to notice the increasing numbers of cars, and the traffic jams they produced. But the number of buses increased more than three times as fast, and with far greater effect on the mobility of most Indonesians. Improved bus transportation and inter-island ferry services connected Java, Bali, and Sumatra in a network of intercity bus routes, enabling people to move easily and cheaply around much of the western portion of the country.[20]

The outer islands, however, lagged behind. In 1995 Java and Sumatra had 93, 83, and 68 percent of all the electricity, vehicles, and sealed-surface roads, respectively, in Indonesia.[21] And the relative abundance of infrastructure in the west corresponded, though much less starkly, to the greater regional incidence of poverty—the percentage of people in a given part of the country living below the official poverty line—on the archipelago's eastern and northern periphery.

As Table 4.1 shows, in 1996 the four provinces of West and East Nusatenggara, East Timor, and Maluku ("much of eastern Indonesia"), and three of the four

---

20. *Lampiran Pidato Kenegaraan* [*Appendix to the State of the Nation Speech*] *1994* [henceforth *LPK94*] (Jakarta: Departemen Penerangan, 1994), p. IX/53, and *Lampiran Pidato Kenegaraan 1996* [henceforth *LPK96*] (Jakarta: Departemen Penerangan, 1996), p. XIV/67 [electricity generated in 1968 and 1995, respectively]; *Results* (Jakarta: CBS, 1996), Table 72.3, p. 516 [access to electricity for lighting in 1995]; *Statistical Pocketbook of Indonesia 1968 and 1969* (Jakarta: CBS, 1971), pp. 270, 272 [roads and vehicles in 1968 and 1995].

21. *Statistical Yearbook of Indonesia 1995* (Jakarta: CBS, 1996), pp. 377–379, 390–391.

Table 4.1

Incidence and Distribution of Poverty (1996), Estimated by Region

Region	Incidence of poverty Poor people as a share of all people in a region (%)	Distribution of poverty Poor people in a region as a share of all poor people in Indonesia (%)
Much of eastern Indonesia	20.2	9.3
Most of Kalimantan	17.1	6.4
Java and Bali	11.5	56.1
Mining/oil/gas provinces	11.2	6.1
Most of Sumatra	10.3	15.6
Sulawesi	8.6	5.4
Jakarta	2.5	1.0
Indonesia	11.3	99.9

Notes: Poor people = members of households in a given urban or rural area who fell below the poverty line for that area in 1993 set by the Central Bureau of Statistics (CBS). Much of Eastern Indonesia = West and East Nusatenggara, East Timor, and Maluku. Most of Kalimantan = West, Central, and South Kalimantan. Mining/Oil/Gas Provinces = places more than 30 percent of whose GDPs came from mining, oil, and/or gas, namely, Aceh, Riau, East Kalimantan, and Irian Jaya. Most of Sumatra = Sumatra except for Aceh and Riau. Java includes the adjacent island of Madura. Percentages do not total 100.0 due to rounding.

Source: CBS, unpublished data from a 1996 Household Expenditure Survey conducted as part of the National Socioeconomic Survey (Susenas).

provinces on Kalimantan, had the highest regional incidence of poverty in Indonesia. At the same time, inside Indonesia as a whole, poverty remained heavily concentrated in the west—on Java, Bali, and Sumatra. For it was on the latter islands in 1996, on the eve of the crisis of 1997–98, that more than 70 percent of all Indonesians living below the official poverty line could be found.

The subject of poverty will be taken up in more detail later. Suffice it here to identify the choice for public policy that was posed in the mid-1990s by the difference between the high intraregional incidence of poverty in eastern and northern Indonesia and its concentration on a national scale in the west. If the goal was to reduce national poverty, arguably development spending should have focused largely on the west, especially Java, where most poor Indonesians still lived. But if the goal was to correct for seeming discrimination against the east and north in the allocation of infrastructural and other benefits—benefits that might have reduced the gap between living standards in these islands compared with standards to the west—then arguably the national government should have directed its resources disproportionately toward the eastern islands and parts of Kalimantan.

Not surprisingly perhaps, given the location of the national government in Jakarta on Java and the concentration of power in central, not regional, hands (as Michael Malley's chapter shows), actual policies tended to favor the west. To be sure, during the fifth development plan (1989–94), the eastern islands of West and East Nusatenggara, East Timor, and Maluku received 10.9 percent of Inpres spending, and that infusion did slightly exceed their 8.6 percent share of the national distribution of poverty in 1993. (West, Central, and South Kalimantan, too, received a higher proportion of Inpres outlays than one would have expected on the basis of their shares of national poverty.) But arguably 10.9 percent was still too low, given the high incidence of poverty on these eastern islands, as shown for 1996 in Table 4.1. Had Indonesia's outer islands had more political power than the New Order allowed them, other things being equal, one might have expected proportionately more fiscal attention to reducing poverty and improving infrastructure there.

Historically, the structural transformation of Indonesia involved several kinds of industrialization: the processing of agricultural products and natural resources, import substitution for the domestic market, and the labor-intensive exporting of manufactures. All three of these patterns tended to exacerbate the inequality between the western areas such as Java, where the bulk of Indonesians live, and those sparsely populated outer islands that lack exportable minerals or hydrocarbons. Provinces not well endowed with oil, gas, or minerals could hardly attract investments in resource processing. Initially, the concentration of import-substituting industries on Java, especially Jakarta and West Java, reflected an effort to serve the large domestic market located there. Later on, its superior infrastructure and abundant cheap labor favored Java in a new way by making it the preferred location of factories where workers made products for export.

The third-to-last column in Table 4.2 shows the results. That column groups eight of the nine provinces of eastern Indonesia, omitting only resource-rich Irian Jaya. The eight provinces are Sulawesi's four, Nusatenggara's two, East Timor, and Maluku. They accounted for 12.3 percent of the country's population in 1995, but only 6.5 percent of national GDP and a paltry 2.7 percent of its manufacturing component in 1994. The prospect of rapid industrial growth in these eastern provinces was not encouraging, given their few natural resources, poor infrastructure, and small and dispersed populations. And the same might have been said of other relatively isolated provinces, such as West, Central, and South Kalimantan. Relevant to Kalimantan's outlook in particular was the damage done to its forest resources by logging and burning.

In the late 1990s in such places, even leaving aside the effects of the crisis of 1997–98, prospects were poor for the sort of rapid agricultural growth that occurred to the west, on Java, Bali, and Sumatra, in the 1970s and 1980s. Much of eastern Indonesia suffers from unfavorable biophysical circumstances such as low rainfall and poor soils—endemic limitations long predating the drought of 1997—and a dearth of new agricultural technologies appropriate to such condi-

Table 4.2

Distribution of Gross Domestic Product (1994) by Sector and Region, and Population (1995) by Region

Sector	Jakarta (%)	Mining/oil/ gas provinces (%)	Most of Sumatra and most of Kalimantan (%)	Most of eastern Indonesia including Sulawesi (%)	Java and Bali (%)	Indonesia (%)
Finance	44.7	5.3	13.4	4.2	32.4	100.0
Construction	30.7	7.5	15.4	7.5	38.9	100.0
Utilities	22.7	3.6	11.5	3.9	58.4	100.1
Trade	19.4	5.7	18.3	5.2	51.5	100.1
Transport	18.9	11.6	22.5	7.6	39.4	100.0
Other services	16.5	5.5	17.4	10.3	50.4	100.1
Manufacturing	13.9	14.0	15.1	2.7	54.4	100.1
Agriculture	0.2	10.3	27.2	13.5	48.8	100.0
Mining	0.0	70.4	10.9	2.5	16.2	100.0
Total GDP	15.7	14.4	18.0	6.5	45.4	100.0
Population	4.7	6.2	21.1	12.3	55.7	100.0
Regional "productivity"	+11.0	+8.2	-3.1	-5.8	-10.3	

Source: *Gross Regional Domestic Product of Provinces in Indonesia by Industrial Origin 1993–95* (Jakarta: CBS, 1996), Table 106; *Results of the 1995 Inter-censal Population Survey, Series S2* (Jakarta: CBS, 1996), pp. 55–57.

Notes: Regions are defined in Table 4.1. Percentages do not always total 100.0 due to rounding. Regional "productivity" = the share of national GDP generated in a region minus the share of national population there.

tions. In the 1990s, for all the New Order's five-year plans, roads and irrigation on many eastern islands were still absent or inadequate. Agroindustries based, for example, on fish, livestock, or fruits and vegetables, held some promise of becoming commercially viable in selected places. But these pockets of opportunity were not likely to underpin a transformation of eastern Indonesia comparable to the impact on Java, Bali, and parts of Sumatra of the rapidly growing export-oriented manufacturing concentrated there, even assuming a recovery from the national economic setbacks of 1997–98.

In the 1990s, the central government increased the share of development funds going to the northern and eastern periphery of Indonesia. But this positive trend, even if it continues in the context of resumed growth, will not soon make up for the decades of neglect of infrastructural development there. Meanwhile, remittances from exported labor could become an increasing source of income for the most isolated and laggard among these parts of the archipelago, especially if their relatively high birth rates and the paucity of local opportunities persist.

In any case, as Table 4.1 indicates, in 1996 most of the poverty in Indonesia was still located on Java, despite the heavy concentration of infrastructure there. And as shown by Table 4.2, if "productivity" is defined as the difference between a region's contribution to national GDP and its share of total population, Java (with Bali) was even less "productive" than most of the eastern islands. That status is an incentive for the central authorities, already more sensitive to events and demands in their immediate hinterland than to what happens on the periphery, to focus attention and funds on Java.

Population and Education

Java is among the most densely settled parts of Asia. To the extent that governments under President Sukarno were concerned about overpopulation and poverty on Java, the preferred "solution" was transmigration—relocating people from the core to the outer islands—rather than family planning. Community leaders and women's groups recognized the need to encourage modern birth control practices on Java and elsewhere in Indonesia. But Sukarno was pronatalist, and family planning remained a taboo subject in most official circles. In 1968 Suharto changed previous policy by establishing a National Family Planning Institute. A year later it was given full responsibility for implementing a family planning program, beginning on Java and Bali. Support from foreign aid donors was solicited and obtained.

By the mid-1970s there were clear signs of fertility decline on Java and Bali, and on Sumatra as well, due mainly to increases in the average age of marrying couples and their use of birth control methods within marriage. These changes in behavior reflected the impact of modernization on aspirations for better living standards and upward social mobility, including the welfare of children.

Indonesian families have come to realize the value of education as a means to a better life, and the drain on household resources that education entails. Smaller families have come to be equated with better-educated—and healthier—families. Along with fertility, infant and child mortality also declined under the New Order, reflecting more widespread access to health facilities and a greater willingness on the part of parents to seek medical help when children fell ill. In the quarter-century following Suharto's rise to power, for Indonesia as a whole, infant mortality rates fell by nearly two-thirds (from 145 per thousand live births in 1967 to 51 in 1991), while life expectancy at birth lengthened by more than two-fifths (from 45 years to 64 years over the same period).[22]

These achievements look much less impressive, however, when compared with those of other Asian countries. In the 1990s infant and child mortality rates in Indonesia exceeded those in China, the Philippines, and Vietnam, even though per capita GDP was higher in Indonesia. Maternal mortality was of particular

---

22. *Welfare Indicators 1997* (Jakarta: CBS, 1997), p. 8.

concern. An estimated 650 Indonesian mothers died of pregnancy-related causes per 100,000 live births in 1990, reflecting inadequate access to proper health care before, during, and after childbirth. The only East Asian country on record with a higher figure for that year was Cambodia.[23] Even before the calamity of 1997–98 tore what social safety nets existed in Indonesia, much remained to be done to bring the benefits of modern medical care to all of the country's citizens.

The New Order had substantial success in making a basic education widely available: In 1968 merely 41.4 percent of the children aged between seven and twelve were in primary school. By 1993 proeducation policies and parents' rising ambitions for their children had more than doubled this rate—to 93.5 percent.[24] By 1988 the government had already decided that since the vast majority of the children in the relevant age group were enrolled in primary school, the focus of development spending should shift to secondary education. Given this new priority and the resources the authorities could commit to its implementation, one might have expected quick growth in matriculation, enrollment, and graduation at the secondary level.

But the results were disappointing. The total number of new pupils who entered junior or senior high school, whether for general or vocational education, in 1995 represented a mere 1 percent increase over the intake in 1989. Between the same two school years (1989–90 and 1995–96), total numbers of enrollees increased by only 4 percent, while numbers of graduates fell slightly. In the case of general (nonvocational) education, matriculation into junior and senior high schools actually declined by 3 percent over the period. In vocational secondary schools, matriculation and enrollment did improve, respectively, by 35 and 28 percent. But the magnitude of these gains reflected in part the small initial size of the contingents in vocational compared with general secondary education. Nor in the 1990s was the New Order able to lift rapidly the crude participation rate (CPR) at the secondary level—that is, the number of pupils of any age enrolled in secondary school expressed as a proportion of the relevant age group. The authors of the fifth development plan projected CPRs of 67 and 45 percent for junior and senior high school, respectively, by the final plan year (FY 1993–94). But performance fell short of these goals. The participation rates actually achieved by fiscal 1994 were, respectively, 43 and 30 percent.[25]

---

23. That same year Australian and American maternal mortality rates per 100,000 live births were 9 and 12, respectively, compared with Cambodia's 900 and—the worst rate—Sierra Leone's 1,800. United Nations Development Programme, *Human Development Report 1997* [henceforth *HDR97*] (New York: Oxford University Press, 1997), pp. 174–175 [Asia, Africa], 204 [Australia, the United States].

24. *LPK94* (Jakarta: Departemen Penerangan, 1994), p. XVI/11.

25. *LPK94*, pp. XVI/18, XVI/25 [FY 1988–89]; *Lampiran Pidato Kenegaraan 1996* (Jakarta: Departemen Penerangan, 1996), pp. XVII/53, XVII/55 [FY 1995–96]. The data exclude pupils enrolled in Islamic schools but include those enrolled in other religious and state schools.

It is difficult to know what relative weight to assign to each of the multiple likely reasons for these shortfalls. But economic considerations were important. Both the direct expense and the opportunity cost of secondary schooling limited demand for it. In particular, such reasons may have kept many young people in the 16–18-year age bracket out of senior high school classrooms. First, their parents may not have been able to afford the necessary expenses, including fees, transportation, and the cost of a uniform. Second, the income that these older children might have contributed to their parents' households by working may have been considerable, and certainly was higher than the earnings foregone by keeping younger children in school at lower levels. Third, the probability of a long period of unemployment appears to have been somewhat greater for those entering the job market upon graduation from senior high, compared with those leaving school at lower levels.

In 1992, sending these older children to senior high school cost their families on average the rupiah equivalent of about $140—more than a third of total per capita spending on consumption in Indonesia that year. Unemployment after senior high school was especially common among female graduates. In 1994 among male and female senior high graduates, respectively, 14 and 25 percent had not yet found jobs. Jobless rates for graduates of senior vocational high schools were lower: 9 percent among males and 15 percent among females. The better prospects of these more technically trained graduates may help to explain the already noted substantial increases in vocational secondary school intake and enrollment in the 1990s.[26] However, it is difficult to assess the effect of high unemployment rates for senior high school graduates on parental decision-making.

On balance, it is probably safe to conclude that, compared with a hypothetical net opportunity cost of sending one's children to and through senior high school, the direct cost of doing so may have been, and may remain, the more important barrier to expanding enrollments rapidly at this level. As for junior high, the intake-, enrollment-, and graduation-boosting effects of reducing direct costs should be even greater at that educational level. Increasingly in Indonesia, a certificate of graduation from junior high school has become a screening device used by factory managers in recruiting for low-skilled jobs. If the direct expense of such schooling were less, many lower-income parents would probably be willing to invest in their children by keeping them in the classroom for the three post-primary years of schooling needed to obtain this certificate. Meanwhile, the recession of 1998 and the resulting impoverishment of many Indonesian families has made them all the more sensitive to the cost of education.

The children's own desire for schooling is not in question. Sample survey data

---

26. *Statistik Pendidikan Survei Sosial Ekonomi Nasional* [*Educational Statistics from the National Socioeconomic Survey*] *1992* [henceforth *SPS92*] (Jakarta: CBS, March 1994), p. 39 [cost of education]; *Labor Force Situation in Indonesia 1994* (Jakarta: CBS, March 1995), pp. 35–36 [unemployment].

for 1992, for instance, show, respectively, 89 and 87 percent of boys and girls then enrolled in primary school wanting to go on to higher levels of education. At the junior high level, 92 percent of boys and 93 percent of girls expressed a desire to progress to higher levels. Other results in the same study strengthen the case for the greater relative importance of actual direct cost as a disincentive compared with hypothetical opportunity cost. Of a sample of people in the 5–29-year age range who had dropped out of school, nearly half gave financial reasons for having done so, compared with only 8 percent who reported having left the classroom in order to work.[27]

How could direct costs have been reduced? Partly by improving physical access to secondary education and thus reducing transportation costs, as was done at the primary level in the 1970s and 1980s. A particular priority should have been given to building, equipping, and staffing more junior high schools in rural areas, including improved training for more teachers. The authors of the sixth development plan (1994–99) emphasized just such goals. Indeed, a twenty-five-year plan (1994–2019) calls for universal compulsory education through junior high. According to this schedule, the CPR for the first nine years of a child's schooling—including three years in junior high—would rise to 66 percent by 1999 and 87 percent by 2004.[28] But will these plans become realities?

Certainly, progress toward such goals will be delayed by the shrinkage of the economy in 1998. But quite apart from that dramatic reversal, a careful look back at what the New Order managed to achieve for primary schooling cannot be altogether reassuring. Under Suharto, primary education was widely thought to have become universal. Strictly speaking, for this to have been true, in any given year all Indonesian children aged 7–12 would have had to be in primary school. That is, the refined participation rate (RPR) should have been 100 percent. For the 1988–89 school year, official data do indeed place the RPR at a remarkable 99.6 percent. But just two years later (1990–91) it had fallen to 90.1 percent—although three years later still (1993–94) it had recovered somewhat, to 93.5.[29]

These figures are national averages across regions. In the more isolated rural areas of the country, RPRs could have been rather lower than these percentages imply. And the volatility in these national figures over time suggests that while virtually all Indonesian children were for some period exposed to primary education, not all of them spent, or would have spent, all of the six relevant years, from age seven to age twelve, in school.

Measures to improve the situation were undertaken. Teachers were flown to and from remote communities and offered incentives to work there. Village halls were used for instruction where school buildings did not exist. Yet at some high proportion of the age-eligible cohort, the drive to push RPRs toward 100 percent

---

27. *SPS92*, pp. 9 [reasons for dropping out], 90 [desire to continue].
28. *Rencana*, vol. 4, p. 90.
29. *LPK94*, p. XVI/11.

may have sacrificed quality for quantity. As late as 1997, and even in some densely settled parts of Java, primary-school buildings needed repair, teaching materials were inadequate, and teachers lacked the motivation to devote full attention to their curricula, or even to attend classes regularly. As policymakers look beyond the austerities imposed by the crisis of 1997–98, they may wish to consider the case for improving the quality of primary education before, or at least while, embarking on yet another drive to achieve and maintain universal compulsory education through junior high school.

The sixth plan (1994–99) acknowledged the problem of poor quality but offered few solutions. An obvious response would have been to raise teachers' salaries. But because teachers account for nearly half of all four million civil servants in Indonesia, that reform probably could only have been addressed within the complicating context of reforming the structure of remuneration for the civil service as a whole. And toward the end of 1997, let alone by mid-1998, such reform seemed potentially very expensive, to the extent that drought, fires, and devaluations had ushered in a time of economic stringency and fiscal restraint.

According to available data for 1980, only one Southeast Asian country (Brunei) spent less on education as a proportion of gross national product (GNP) than Indonesia did. Given the New Order's commitment to education as an aspect of human development and a key means to economic growth, one might have expected Indonesia to have lifted this standing by the mid-1990s. In fact, the ranking fell. No Southeast Asian country is known to have spent less on education as a share of GNP in 1993–94 than Indonesia did.[30] If this trend in education is not reversed, it is hard to see how Indonesians, even as they recover from the recession of 1998, will be able to grow their economy rapidly enough to close the gap that still separates them from their better-off neighbors, such as Malaysia and Thailand, let alone approach the living standards of industrialized countries. Reinforcing this conclusion are, first, the already noted structural shifting of the Indonesian economy toward manufacturing, and second, the long-run likelihood that globalization and the attendant competition for productivity through technology will favor skilled over unskilled workers.

Poverty and Policy

Poverty is not readily measured. Should it be defined as an insufficiency of wealth? Of income? Or of expenditure? Wealth is very hard to ascertain; income is easier; and expenditure is easier still, especially if the unit of analysis is the household

---

30. The data for public spending on education as a percentage of GNP in 1993–94 are: Indonesia 1.3; Laos 2.3; Philippines 2.4; Singapore 3.3; Brunei 3.6; Thailand 3.8; Malaysia 5.3. Percentages for other countries include: South Korea 4.5; Japan 4.7; United States 5.5; Australia 6.0. No figure is available for Laos in 1980, for Burma (Myanmar) in 1993–94, or for Cambodia or Vietnam at either time. *HDR97,* pp. 180–181 [Southeast Asia, South Korea], 208 [the rest]. Indonesia also lagged behind its neighbors in educational spending as a share of the government's budget.

rather than the individual. "Wealthy" is more obviously the opposite of "poor" than "high-spending" is. Knowing the consumption of specific individuals rather than households would avoid the loss of information entailed by dividing household outlays by household members to yield an average. But in gathering data in most developing countries, exactitude and comprehensiveness must be balanced against cost. And the use of household expenditure is not only convenient; asking specific individuals to specify their wealth or income could yield even greater distortion. From the standpoint of an interviewee, knowledge of his or her actual receipts and assets could invite unwanted questions about sources and taxability—and pressures to share any surplus with less advantaged friends and neighbors.

The case against using expenditures to measure poverty includes arguments that: (1) an amount of money spent in a city cannot be considered equivalent to the same sum spent in a village, since the cost of living is almost sure to be higher in the urban case; (2) expenditure data overestimate poverty by omitting consumption in kind by poor people who may, for instance, consume food they grow themselves; and (3) expenditure data underestimate the extent of poverty defined as low income, because poor people consume a higher proportion of their incomes than rich people do. But official statistics on Indonesian poverty accommodate the first two of these objections—by adjusting for spatial differences in living costs and incorporating the estimated market value of self-produced consumption. As for the third criticism, the error avoided by measuring income rather than consumption could well, for the reasons already mentioned, be less than the error incurred by doing so. And precisely because higher-income or wealthier households tend to save more than poor people do, measuring income or wealth, even if it could be done more accurately than measuring consumption, would be less useful to policymakers wishing to help poor households raise their actual rather than their hypothetical future (that is, savings-based) standard of living.

A more trenchant criticism for official Indonesian data is that the poverty line—the average consumption by household members below which a given household is classified as poor—was originally set too low, resulting in a low estimate of the incidence of poverty and possibly an overestimation of the reduction in poverty over time. Indonesia's poverty line has indeed been rather low compared with those drawn by other Asian governments for their economies. For example, in 1991 in Manila, the capital of the Philippines, all households whose members averaged less than the equivalent of $82 in monthly spending per household member—the Philippine government's poverty line for that city—were considered poor. Had these "poor" households been located in Jakarta and reclassified by Indonesian standards, only those whose average monthly per capita spending fell below the equivalent of $64 per month would have been labeled "poor." And the disparity between thresholds was greater for rural areas where most such people lived: $61 in the Philippines compared with only $29 in Indonesia.

The issue is not that rural poverty lines are low compared with urban ones. Inside each country, rural living costs are less than those in the capital city, and this difference has been taken into account. Nor is there any particular reason to expect any two countries, even neighbors whose real per capita GNPs in 1995— $1,050 (Philippines) and $980 (Indonesia)—were only $70 apart, to define poverty the same way. Furthermore, governments in both countries regularly adjust poverty lines upward to control for inflation. All the same, lower starting points do tend to magnify ensuing gains. Thus, the official judgment that poverty in Indonesia declined more than fourfold from 1970 to 1993—that the share of the population below the poverty line fell from 60 to 14 percent over this period— may overstate the size of the actual decline.[31]

How, then, from an economic standpoint, did Indonesians fare under the New Order prior to the crisis of 1997–98? All things considered, the answer must be: Considerably better than before. Whatever its exact dimensions, a prolonged and broad-based improvement in living standards under the New Order did take place. Consumption of foodstuffs such as rice, meat, and dairy products, for example, rose continually since the late 1960s. Between 1968 and 1995, daily protein intake per Indonesian improved by more than 60 percent—from 43.3 to 70.0 grams. However difficult their specification in retrospect, increases in real purchasing power among the less well-off brought the ownership of goods such as televisions, refrigerators, and motorcycles—unattainable luxuries for the vast majority of Indonesians in the 1960s—within the reach of millions of households.[32]

Among the main domestic structural and policy explanations for this massive reduction in poverty, three stand out:

1. From the inception of the New Order onward, its leaders promoted agricultural productivity and rural development, which helped to boost rural incomes in many parts of the country but especially in the major rice-producing areas on Java and Bali.
2. In the early and mid-1980s the authorities responded to external shocks, including falling hydrocarbon prices, by encouraging economic diversification, facilitating the growth of the private sector, and reducing total public expenditure while preserving its poverty-focused component.
3. Facilitated by these policies and trends, the rapid expansion of manufacturing, construction, transportation, and trade in rural areas created employment for poor Indonesians formerly bound to agriculture, especially on Java and Bali.

---

31. *WDI97*, pp. 7–8 [per capita GNPs]; *Rencana,* vol. 2, p. 65 [poverty figure for 1970]: *Penduduk Miskin dan Desa Tertinggal 1993: Metodologi dan Analisis [Poor Population and Left-Behind Villages 1993: Methodology and Analysis]* (Jakarta: CBS, 1994), 21 [poverty figure for 1993].

32. CBS, food balance sheets, unpublished [intake in 1968]; *Statistical Yearbook of Indonesia 1995* (Jakarta: CBS), p. 519 [intake in 1995].

Notwithstanding the beneficial effect of these and other factors on the proportion of Indonesians who are poor, however, the absolute number behind that proportion remained quite large. In 1996 about 22.5 million people were in households classified below the poverty line. And this was on the eve of the setbacks of 1997–98.

Looking ahead, successful poverty alleviation in Indonesia will require a long-term commitment of talent, energy, and resources. These should be directed toward the poorest geographical regions and social strata. As a means to achieving further poverty reduction, rapid and sustained economic growth will be necessary, but it may not be sufficient. Consider the growing concentration of poor people in eastern Indonesia. They are not likely to advantage directly from the export-led industrialization of Java or Sumatra. Policies are needed that will transfer central resources to these least well-off areas. Such a regional focus could ensure the delivery or improvement of badly needed social and physical infrastructure—steps that would also help to create employment and stimulate demand. In this context, it is essential that poor but resource-rich provinces such as Irian Jaya be given greater control over revenues from their own natural assets.

The rationale for such a strategy is this: In 1996 some 56 percent of Indonesia's poor people lived on Java and Bali (Table 4.1). But the spatial distribution of poverty in Indonesia had been changing to the benefit of Java. Under the New Order, real per capita consumption expenditures rose—poverty decreased—more rapidly in rural Java than in other rural areas; more rapidly in the cities of Java that in other urban areas; and much more rapidly in Jakarta, which is of course located on Java, than in rural Indonesia.[33]

Inequalities in the distribution of expenditure within urban and rural Java, respectively, did not change greatly over the New Order's last decade or so. Over the same period, however, the faster growth in such spending by people on Java, compared with Indonesians in the regions, implied a long-term decline in the incidence of poverty on Java relative to those regions. It is not yet clear how the shocks and setbacks of 1997–98 will affect the distribution of poverty between Java and the rest of the country. When economic growth resumes, however, so too will the urbanization and industrialization of Java. Viewed in this future context, spatial disparities in the growth rates of consumption, and thus in the rates at which the incidence of poverty declines, are likely to reappear and persist. Speculating even further, one could argue that by the middle decades of the twenty-first century, if the redistribution of poverty away from Java continues, as many as three of four poor Indonesians could be located on other islands.

---

33. For details, see my "Income Distribution and Poverty" in Booth, ed., *Oil Boom,* p. 330.

This new phenomenon can be seen in part as a byproduct of the New Order's economic success. Of the three reasons already given as to why poverty was reduced, (1) and (3) are especially relevant: the earlier priority on agriculture productivity and rural development in the villages of Java and Bali; and the later rapid growth of wage-paying, off-the-farm jobs there. And these trends were linked: Expanded agricultural production not only fed the cities, it also led to the creation of rural employment in agricultural processing, transportation, and trade, and to rural and urban growth in construction and manufacturing jobs as well. Increased wage income augmented rural household incomes from more traditional sources such as farming—and thus reduced poverty on Java.

The lesson of this experience is that reducing poverty in rural areas outside Java in years to come will require comparable increases in agricultural output and nonfarm wage-paying jobs in these parts of the archipelago. But in those parts of the outer islands where poverty coexists with industry based on the extraction of natural resources, a rapid growth in mining activity, for example, may not create many jobs for local people. And much of the profit from such expansion, rather than being invested in the local or even the provincial economy, could be siphoned off to Jakarta (on Java) or abroad. As can be seen in Table 4.1, in 1993 the incidence of poverty in these ostensibly wealthy "mining/oil/gas" provinces was no lower than the national figure (or the figure for Java and Bali). (Also see, in this volume, Kathryn Robinson's account of Soroako, a mining town in Sulawesi.)

Noteworthy among these resource-rich regions is Irian Jaya. Among all Indonesian provinces in 1995, it had the fourth-largest per capita GDP. Yet the incidence of poverty in Irian Jaya in 1996 was the highest in the country after West Kalimantan and East Timor. The reason? Instead of being invested or consumed in Irian Jaya, much of the value of the GDP produced there was remitted to other parts of the country.[34] Per capita household consumption expenditures in the province were therefore very low, and the incidence of poverty correspondingly high.

East Kalimantan is another "mining/oil/gas" province. Immediately to the west lies the Malaysian state of Sarawak. The two jurisdictions are roughly similar in size and ecology, and have had similar per capita GDPs: $2,712 for East Kalimantan and $2,848 for Sarawak in 1993. Yet in that same year per capita consumption spending on the Indonesian side of this border was but one-third of the figure on the Malaysian side—$386 compared with $1,151, respectively. And if the Malaysian poverty line is applied to both places, the difference in living standards appears even greater. By that measure, 71 percent of households

---

34. *Gross Regional Domestic Product of Provinces in Indonesia by Expenditure 1993–1995* (Jakarta: CBS, 1996), p. 5 [provincial per capita GDP]; unpublished CBS tables [provincial poverty incidence].

in East Kalimantan were living in poverty in 1993 compared with only 19 percent in Sarawak.[35]

Seventy-one percent is far greater than the 13.8 percent incidence of poverty in East Kalimantan that results from applying the Indonesian poverty line for 1993.[36] One could argue that because Indonesia is so much poorer than Malaysia overall—in 1995 Indonesia's GNP per capita was a mere fourth of Malaysia's[37]—policymakers in Jakarta as compared with Kuala Lumpur should define poverty more restrictively, in order to focus limited resources on the truly abject. On the other hand, similarities between the economies of East Kalimantan and Sarawak, including their per capita GDPs, suggest that poverty in both places should be measured in roughly similar ways. And if using Sarawak's threshold enlarges the estimate of poverty in East Kalimantan so dramatically, one may wonder to what extent Indonesian definitions may understate poverty in other parts of the archipelago as well.

Statistics about poverty and inequality are one thing. Actual consciousness of them is quite another. If people on the resource-rich but less well-off outer islands of Indonesia had not known that "their" forests, minerals, and hydrocarbons were being taken away to benefit others, notably those at the center of economic and political power on Java, there might have been no political consequences. But economic growth under the New Order raised awareness. The increasing spatial mobility of Indonesians and their greater exposure to information about conditions elsewhere, including in neighboring countries, increased the potential for regional disparities and central exploitation to become controversial issues for policy. In 1991 a former governor of Irian Jaya went so far as to liken Indonesia to a village where "the people in the house called Irian Jaya feed those in the other houses but are themselves starving."[38]

It was a goal of the sixth five-year development plan (1994–99) to reduce the dwindling numbers of people below the (Indonesian) poverty line to 6 percent of the population (or 12 million people) by 1999, and to zero—the end of "absolute poverty"—by 2004. But, even before the recession of 1998, were these aims

---

35. *Gross Regional Domestic Product,* p. 5 [per capita GDP in East Kalimantan]; *Expenditure for Consumption of Indonesia per Province 1993* (Jakarta: CBS, 1994), pp. 30–31 [per capita consumption spending in East Kalimantan]; *Annual Statistical Bulletin: Sarawak 1996* (Kuching, Malaysia: Department of Statistics), p. 183 [per capita GDP in Sarawak]; *Mid-Term Review of the Sixth Malaysia Plan* (Kuala Lumpur: Government Printer, 1994), pp. 58–59 [poverty incidence and poverty line in Sarawak]. The Sarawak-derived incidence of poverty in East Kalimantan was calculated by converting Sarawak's official poverty line into Indonesian rupiah at the prevailing exchange rate and superimposing the resulting threshold on the distribution of East Kalimantan's population according to consumer spending there.

36. *Penduduk Miskin,* p. 23.

37. *WDI97,* pp. 7–8.

38. As quoted by Adam Schwarz, "Eastern Reproach," *Far Eastern Economic Review,* 11 July 1991, p. 24.

realistic? Already the annual rate of decline in the absolute size of the poor population in Indonesia had begun to slow. From 1990 to 1996, for example, the rate averaged only 3.1 percent, leaving 22.5 million people beneath the official poverty line in the latter year. Even by a generous calculation, shrinking the numbers of the poor to the sixth plan's goal of only 12 million by 1999 would have required an average annual reduction of almost 19 percent in 1997–99—a pace more than six times as rapid as the actual (3.1 percent) average rate in 1990–96. And this calculation does not take into account the national economic debacle of 1997–98 that made the sixth plan's targets for poverty reduction obsolete.[39]

As poverty in Indonesia decreased under the New Order, the marginal cost of further decreases rose. By 1997 it was doubtful that many of the people still below the official poverty line, especially those in remote areas, would be lifted above it by market forces alone. It seemed clear that if opportunities for such people were to be created, the government would need to focus on facilitating that process through, for example, targeted Inpres programs such as the one for "left-behind villages" (Inpres Desa Tertinggal, or IDT).

Unlike conventional Inpres programs, IDT tried to bring public and private entities together to undertake income-generating activities in the poorest parts of the country. The idea was to decentralize poverty alleviation efforts and root them as much as possible in local initiatives and entrepreneurship. But in 1997 it remained to be seen whether the experiment could thrive in a bureaucratic climate still dominated by more top-down approaches to poverty and its eradication. Then, in 1998, dramatic economic and political changes greatly enlarged the incidence of poverty while throwing into question who the country's future leaders would be, not to mention what they would or could do to revive the economy.

Whoever wins the competition to lead Indonesia into the twenty-first century, effective antipoverty policies will have to address the centralization of decision-making and the centripetal (Jakarta-ward) flow of benefits from aggregate economic growth, especially in provinces where widespread privation and natural resources coexist. Broad-based gains in welfare in these areas are not likely to be achieved without substantial transfers of authority to provincial and subprovincial levels of government. Only through such reforms are such regions likely to be able to retain a significantly greater share of the value generated by their physical resources and spend it on a range of local antipoverty priorities, including improved infrastructure and better education. In these as in other parts of the archipelago, prospects for alleviating poverty will depend in no small measure on chances for devolving political and economic power.

---

39. *Rencana*, vol. 2, p. 81 [poverty reduction goal]; *Penduduk Miskin*, p. 21; and unpublished CBS data [poor population and rate of reduction].

Development beyond Suharto

In 1950, having at last achieved their homeland's independence as one unified republic, Indonesian nationalists were optimistic. They attributed poverty to colonial
subjugation. Now that they were in charge, surely by exploiting their country's
abundant natural assets, they would be able to raise the living standards of the vast
majority of the population quickly enough to draw abreast of the advanced economies of the industrial West, or at least dramatically close the gap. Instead, development turned out to be a slow, difficult, and reversible process.

In 2020 Indonesia will have been a sovereign state for seven decades. But it will
still lag considerably behind the developed economies of Western Europe, North
America, and Northeast Asia. Nor is it likely that by 2020 Indonesia's living standards will have surpassed Malaysia's or Thailand's, let alone Singapore's. Even if
the ambitious goals of its development plans are somehow met—plans drawn up
before the crash of 1997–98—Indonesia in 2020 will remain what it was by World
Bank standards in 1997: a "lower middle-income" country.

In 1996 some observers were tempted to extrapolate Indonesia's past performance far into the future. Not so in the second half of 1997, as the economy
reeled from fires, drought, and the flight of capital from local currency and stocks.
As an open and indebted economy—in 1995 total trade and foreign debt were 52
and 57 percent of GDP and GNP, respectively—Indonesia certainly was vulnerable to fluctuations in the world economy.[40] Yet if overoptimism had characterized the boom years, in 1997 hyperpessimism seemed no more realistic.

Conditions worsened in 1998. Would Indonesia be able to export its way out
of that year's recession? In the 1980s and 1990s the country's exporters had been
able to sell a range of manufactured goods abroad without encountering major
barriers to access. Would such conditions continue to prevail? As long as a global
collapse in demand could be prevented, and momentum toward further trade
liberalization could be maintained, and provided Indonesia remained a competitive producer, manufacturing for export was still a viable long-run development
strategy. Debts denominated in dollars and yen posed a serious problem. Their
repayment had suddenly been made more expensive by the precipitously declining value of the rupiah. That same devaluation, on the other hand, had made
Indonesian exports more competitive.

External conditions—obstacles and incentives—will continue to affect the Indonesian economy. Yet in the long run the country's ability to recover, sustain, and
deepen its developmental momentum will depend at least as much, if not more, on
how it responds to challenges from within. This chapter has focused on two such
internal challenges: low educational standards (and a concomitantly underskilled
work force) and spatial disparities (between a rapidly industrializing core and a
lagging periphery). In 1997 the corruption-fostering restrictive practices that

---

40. *Indonesia: Sustaining High Growth,* p. 157 [trade]; *WDR97,* p. 246 [debt].

still prevailed in many sectors of the Indonesian economy were a third domestic obstacle to progress, despite signs that, in the wake of the rupiah's devaluation, some members of the government were trying to tackle these problems.

As Richard Borsuk shows in the next chapter, steps taken by the New Order toward deregulation and privatization did not always move Indonesia's euphemistically termed "high-cost" economy toward greater transparency and accountability. Too often the beneficiaries of such reforms were large conglomerates with close links to senior officials, and especially to President Suharto and his rent-seeking children. Nor did the channeling of soft loans from state banks into costly "strategic industries," such as aircraft manufacturing, improve the efficiency or transparency of the economy.

In 1997–98 such industries seemed highly unlikely to succeed in global markets. The rupiah's devaluation made Indonesian exports more competitive in terms of final prices. But the need to cut official spending and lending, along with the increased prices of imports, including imported inputs into high-technology products such as airplanes, dealt a major, and perhaps in the long run a constructive blow to these artificially "strategic" efforts to leap ahead in the development race. Or were they merely dormant and awaiting eventual revival by Suharto's successor, B.J. Habibie—the very man who had pursued them so enthusiastically?

In 1998 it was impossible to know who Indonesia's coming leaders would be, let alone how they might respond to these problems and trends. But after thirty years of generally impressive development prior to the crisis that began in 1997, development based on acknowledging and using market forces, many Indonesians outside and even inside the policy establishment remained fearful that measures to make the economy more open and internationally competitive would not reduce poverty. The fear was that such measures would instead further concentrate wealth in the hands—the disproportionately Chinese hands—of the richest citizens of Indonesia. Whichever set of leaders might be running the country when the twenty-first century began, such fears were likely to remain, and with them a certain reluctance to plunge Indonesia onward into an ever more open, globalizing, and capitalist future.

In 1967 the pessimists were wrong. In 2027 the pessimists of 1997 may turn out to have been wrong again. On the other hand, future historians may conclude that the range and complexity of the socioeconomic problems awaiting solution in Indonesia beyond Suharto made them less tractable than those faced by the general and his technocrats at the onset of the New Order. Recovering and sustaining rapid economic growth; improving the availability and quality of physical infrastructure, and of education beyond basic levels; reducing persistent poverty in hard-to-reach places; and resolving centripetal bias in the distribution of income and opportunity—all while curbing further damage to an already stressed natural environment. . . . The ability of Indonesians to handle such challenges may depend not only their chance for prosperity but also on their survival as one nation.

Chapter 5

Markets: The Limits of Reform

Richard Borsuk

Until the late 1980s, the floor of the Jakarta Stock Exchange (JSX) offered a serene escape from the Indonesian capital's chaotic and stressful traffic. The exchange had been quiet since its opening in 1977. Every weekday in the dingy government building some twenty traders were on duty, but they rarely had work. One might have expected transactions to have surged in the wake of the Wall Street crash of 19 October 1987. Instead, the next day, Jakarta newspapers ran photographs of traders asleep at their stations.

By the mid-1990s this picture had changed dramatically. On most days the trading floor was a beehive of activity. The noise level remained low despite the busyness, but that was because the JSX had computerized its trading system. The exchange had relocated to a state-of-the-art floor in a new skyscraper. Though still far from the international big leagues in trading volume, Jakarta's bourse was attracting global interest and money, as a steady flow of foreign fund managers pushed up the occupancy rates of Jakarta's five-star hotels.

The stock exchange was not the only place in town undergoing major changes in the early 1990s. Shopping malls were springing up and being thronged by consumers, worsening traffic. While some Jakarta residents still had to wait years to get telephone lines, the country's increasingly diverse economy was being plugged into world markets. By 1996 oil and gas accounted for less than a quarter of exports by value, down from well over half a decade before. Manufactures had taken up the slack, expanding over the same period from less than one-fifth to roughly one-half of all exports while exploding in value from $2.7 billion to $24.5 billion.[1] By the mid-1990s, for example, a mid-size Indonesian conglomerate, the Modern Group, was assembling millions of Fuji cameras near Jakarta for sale throughout the world. Such investments stemmed in part from changes in high-wage Japan and its neighboring "tiger" economies, relative to global markets, which "pushed" capital out of Northeast and into Southeast Asia. But "pull" factors inside Indonesia also played a role, including steps taken by the New Order to deregulate and privatize the Indonesian economy.

As noted by Anne Booth in the preceding chapter, General Suharto and his civilian advisers had started out in the 1960s by freeing the economy from the ruinous policies of President Sukarno. Yet by the mid-1980s, official favoritism and interference were taking their toll. In some sectors—plastics, for instance—the government had awarded import monopolies to well-connected individuals, including relatives of the president. In other sectors—banking comes to mind—the government had thwarted competition and efficiency by freezing the number of issued licenses to operate. Notwithstanding the commitment of economic policymakers to competitive markets in principle, actual markets in practice were seldom truly free. Corruption and rent-seeking further fueled Indonesia's reputation as a "high-cost economy."

In the mid-1980s plunging oil prices shocked the New Order into becoming more serious about economic reform. In the later 1980s and early 1990s various official restrictions on markets were reduced or removed in a series of reform packages. In key areas, competition replaced control. New banks were licensed and began to vie fiercely for customers by offering different rates and services. Strictures on foreign and domestic investment were eased. And trade was deregulated to an extent in various ways.

Any licensed trading firm or manufacturer, for example, could now bring into the country a lengthening list of commodities whose importation previously had been limited to a few officially approved traders drawing monopoly rents. The market for information was also made more competitive: The government licensed five private television channels to compete with state-owned Televisi Republik Indonesia (TVRI), a monopoly until 1989. The authorities allowed the new channels to make a profit by advertising—TVRI remained ad-free—but required a portion of the resulting revenues to be transferred to the state network as a subsidy.

Deregulation, however sporadic and incomplete, succeeded. It attracted trade and investment, sped economic growth, won plaudits from the World Bank, and encouraged Japan and other donor governments to raise their aid pledges in the

---

1. Calculated from data in the Indonesian government's *Monthly Statistical Bulletin: Economic Indicators June 1997* (Jakarta: Central Bureau of Statistics, 1997), pp. 101 [fractions], 103 [value].

annually convened Inter-Governmental Group on Indonesia (IGGI). Renamed the Consultative Group on Indonesia (CGI) in 1992, the consortium's yearly commitment to supporting the archipelago's economy had risen to some five billion dollars by the mid-1990s. But the picture was far from uniformly bright. Markets were far from being in command in scores of sectors. Many regulations that pinched consumers and kept prices up remained in place. Key industries were still stifled by decrees, controlled by a few players, or both at once.

Despite their lower per capita income compared with that of their immediate Southeast Asian neighbors, Indonesians were still paying more for chicken, flour, and sugar due to monopolies and market controls. Obliged to pay high prices for raw materials and components, not to mention the bribes needed to circumvent red tape, Indonesian exporters were struggling to stay competitive in foreign markets. In 1995, after more than a decade of deregulation packages, two World Bank economists concluded that insufficient competition was still making Indonesian firms pay billions of dollars more for their intermediate inputs than those goods should have cost at world-market prices. The economists estimated this overpayment as equivalent to one-tenth of the final value of sales in the manufacturing sector—"a huge amount to be passed down to consumers."[2]

Media markets further illustrated the limits of reform. Evenings at seven o'clock, television viewers could choose to watch the news on any of six channels—one public (TVRI) and five private. But the private channels were only permitted to show TVRI's carefully scripted, state-prepared newscasts, which gave no time to events and views that the authorities considered unwelcome. Nor could any of the hundreds of private radio stations carry its own news. Forty-year-old regulations limiting the number of pages in newspapers—rules written when Indonesia could not afford newsprint—remained in effect in the mid-1990s. In June 1994 the authorities tightened their grip on domestic information flows by closing the country's leading news weekly, *Tempo,* and two other publications.

Domestic media were among a number of sensitive fields that remained off-limits to foreign investors. In many other sectors, however, regulations that had restricted foreigners were significantly loosened, and capital quickly flowed into the country to take advantage of the improved climate. Rising investment, foreign and domestic, helped to lift the economy. Average annual economic growth topped 7 percent in the first half of the 1990s, while by 1995 per capita income, whose rate of increase had been hurt by falling oil prices in the 1980s, had risen to a level just shy of $1,000.

The combination of solid growth, rising incomes, and timely reforms further

---

2. Guozhong Xie and Oscar de Bruyn Kops, "Clogged Distribution Channels: Marketing Practices for Industrial Commodities in Indonesia," conference paper, "Building on Success: Maximizing the Gains for Deregulation," Jakarta, 26–28 April 1995 [henceforth "BOS95"], p. 3.

stimulated the interest of investors. In 1995 the government approved a record $70 billion worth of investment proposals—$40 billion from foreigners, $30 billion from Indonesians—and these figures rose higher still in 1996. Proposals are one thing, expenditures quite another. Projects may be cancelled or postponed, and even if they are implemented on schedule, spending on them may be spread over years. Yet the high and rising level of total approvals, up from merely $16 billion in 1989, shows that corruption, red tape, and other distortions did not discourage investors in those heady days. Nor did concerns over the presidential succession and what might happen to the economy "beyond Suharto." An executive with a European chemical company, for example, said that his board had put aside fears of political risk in deciding to build a factory in the mid-1990s. The opportunities in Indonesia were simply too great and the stakes too high. "With the economy growing well and our competitors here," he reasoned, "we also have to be here."[3]

Deregulation facilitated privatization. Economic reforms and growth stimulated not only direct investment, such as factory construction, they also buoyed portfolio investment by motivating foreigners and Indonesians to buy shares on the JSX. And a growing stock market encouraged the government to use it to sell shares in state-owned companies. Privatizing a portion of the economy's large and inefficient state sector, in turn, facilitated further growth, broadened the stock exchange, raised cash to help reduce the country's huge foreign debt, and in theory widened the opportunity for Indonesians to gain a stake in the economy by becoming shareholders. Global portfolio managers in particular were attracted to the JSX by the higher potential returns associated with emerging markets. An example: The proportionally tiny number of telephones in Indonesia in the mid-1990s—fewer than two per hundred residents—meant that an Indonesian phone company could be expected to grow far more rapidly than its counterparts in developed countries, assuming continued economic growth.

The economy's proliferating links to global capital markets strengthened it, but also made it potentially more vulnerable to a sudden change of heart by portfolio investors. In 1997–98 Indonesian equity and foreign-exchange markets collapsed under severe speculative blows. In the second quarter of 1997 Thai authorities had tried and failed to defend their currency, the baht, from a wave of selling by money traders convinced that it was overvalued relative to the dollar. Arbitragers soon reevaluated the Malaysian ringgit, the Philippine peso, and the Indonesian rupiah as well, and as these currencies were driven down in value, foreign and domestic owners of equity shares reconsidered their own positions. In the span of a few months—from July to November—the rupiah and the JSX each lost about two-fifths of its value. And the rout raged on through the first half

---

3. *Indonesia Source Book 1996* (Jakarta: National Development Information Office, 1996), p. 104 [investment]; conversation, Jakarta, 15 May 1995 [quote].

of 1998. The question was no longer whether the economy would shrink in 1998 but by how much—10 percent? 15? 20?

Deregulation and privatization had been expected to make markets work better. But in the permissive atmosphere created by rapid economic growth before 1997, not all reforms fulfilled this expectation. Not all privatizations, for example, were market-improving. Some public assets were not sold competitively to the highest bidder but to favored buyers with inside knowledge and connections. Instead of benefiting the state treasury, such transactions rewarded politically influential businesspeople, especially those with family or other ties to President Suharto. As long as the economy kept humming along, the president could dismiss complaints against such cozy arrangements as mere carping. It took the brutal reality check of 1997–98 and the austerities entailed by that prolonged crisis to reveal "crony capitalism" for what it was: a debilitating luxury Indonesia could not afford.

The ambiguity of market reforms prior to 1997 reflected a policy struggle inside the New Order regime. Understanding that contest should help to clarify why market freeing measures did not always succeed.

Technocrats and Nationalists

In her chapter, Anne Booth notes the important role in economic policy played by a set of reform-minded officials around Suharto known as the "technocrats." They were in some respects diverse, but they tended to advocate deregulating markets and privatizing assets. The views of the technocrats differed from those of another group, sometimes called the "nationalists," who were more inclined to use the state to limit and shape markets for the sake of national goals. Both camps vied for the president's ear.

The technocrats were not antinationalist. They wanted to strengthen the nation through economic growth. But they differed with the nationalists over the best way to develop the country: whether to free markets from state control for the sake of efficiency and productivity based on comparative advantage, or to use the state to shape—even to create—markets for the sake of technological progress and added value. Conversely, the nationalists were in some respects quite technocratic. They, too, had higher degrees, though typically in engineering not economics, and they also tended to favor decision-making by experts possessing technical knowledge. Nevertheless, if these qualifications are kept in mind, distinguishing the two groups is useful. From the 1980s to the late 1990s the two camps were not always in conflict, but they represented two broad sides in a crucial ongoing debate over the proper economic role of the state.

The technocrats argued for downsizing the public sector, leaving government to concentrate on helping private business exploit Indonesia's competitive advantage, notably its large supply of relatively low-wage labor. The nationalists disagreed. They argued that Indonesia was strong enough to put more, not fewer, resources into state enterprises, especially at the higher-tech end, including designing, building, and selling planes and ships "made in Indonesia."

The technocrats had been around since the so-called Berkeley Mafia had placed Indonesia on the road to development in the late 1960s. Their unofficial chairman and senior figure, Widjojo Nitisastro, was a Berkeley-trained economist who retained access to Suharto and influence over economic policy even after leaving the cabinet in 1983. Other technocrats included Ali Wardhana, a minister until 1988; Radius Prawiro and J.B. Sumarlin, in the cabinet until 1993; and Mar'ie Muhammad and Saleh Afiff, respectively finance minister and coordinating minister for the economy from 1993 to 1998.

At times, the technocrats had Suharto's ear. But sometimes he listened more intently to the dean of the nationalists, Research and Technology Minister B.J. Habibie. Like Widjojo, Habibie had a decades-long relationship with Suharto. In the early 1950s when Suharto, then a colonel, had served a tour of duty in South Sulawesi, he had been a regular guest at the Habibie household. Compared with Widjojo, the American-educated economist, Habibie, the German-trained engineer, was closer to the president. When Suharto chose Habibie to be his vice-president in March 1998, Widjojo was not even in the running.

Also more or less in the nationalists' camp was another politically ambitious engineer, Ginandjar Kartasasmita. In the cabinet reshuffle of 1993, Ginandjar was transferred from the ministry of mines and energy to become the first noneconomist to head the National Development Planning Agency (Badan Perencanaan Pembangunan Nasional, or Bappenas). Sometimes Ginandjar joined other nationalists in opposing the technocrats on a given issue. On the other hand, in the 1990s, he kept a certain distance between himself and Habibie. In March 1998 Suharto promoted Ginandjar to be his chief economic minister, a position he retained in the cabinet that Habibie announced upon replacing Suharto in May.

Other ministers who were important in economic policy could be viewed as straddling the fence between technocrats and nationalists. A prime example was Minister of Industry Tunky Ariwibowo, who in December 1995 was given responsibility for trade as well. Having previously labored to build up a government-owned enterprise, Krakatau Steel, Tunky was seen as favoring state industry. Although the firm remained highly inefficient, he won good marks from technocrats and entrepreneurs for trying to promote reform. He was a driving force behind a 1994 measure, discussed below, which permitted many foreign investors to start out with, and retain, sole ownership of their ventures. Still, he remained sensitive to the desires of Suharto's children as they strengthened and extended their positions in a variety of industries in the 1990s. And since Suharto would not take questions from the media, it fell to Tunky as trade and industry minister to defend the "national car" policy announced in February 1996, which bestowed overwhelming tariff and tax advantages on a company owned by Suharto's youngest son.

The nationalists were not necessarily against deregulation. But they did not want it to touch certain industries, or to liberalize the economy too quickly or too much. Speaking off the record, they worried that selling off state assets would simply enrich the ethnic-Chinese Indonesians who already dominated the private sector. So controversial were the connotations of the Indonesian word for privatization, *swastanisasi,* that for years after the government began promoting the activity, the technocrats who favored it were careful to use euphemisms when discussing it. When he was finance minister, for example, Sumarlin described the New Order not as championing privatization outright but rather as "inviting private-sector participation" in state activities.

Opponents of deregulation included bureaucrats whose traditional power and sources of income were threatened, business elites who feared the loss of favored positions, and politicians who resented a program they felt would mainly benefit the conglomerates run by Indonesians of Chinese descent and thus widen the divide between rich and poor. For Adi Sasono, for example, an economist who ran a think tank linked to Habibie, deregulation was a gift to big business. In his view, what was needed for small businesses was not cutting back on regulation but the opposite: issuing new regulations that could strengthen the ability of these weaker firms to compete with the conglomerates.[4]

If Adi at least acknowledged the value of competition, other Indonesians were less sure. They tended to quote the quasi-socialist language to be found in the 1945 constitution. According to that document, "social prosperity is the primary goal, not individual prosperity"; the economy shall be based on "the principles of the family system" as embodied in cooperatives (not corporations); and the state shall control key sectors of production including all natural resources, lest production "fall in the hands of powerful individuals who could exploit the people." Constitutionally, "only enterprises which do not affect the life of the general population may be left to private individuals."[5] Far from implementing these phrases, the technocrats' promarket policies contradicted them, for example, by shrinking the already marginal role of cooperatives. Nationalists, on the other hand, were likely to use the constitution as a rationale against further privatization.

Suharto was the final arbiter of these disputes. In the turbulent mid-1980s, when falling oil prices began to drag the economy down, Suharto favored the technocrats, and reforms surged ahead. By the prospering mid-1990s, however, the economy had again grown accustomed to fast growth. The technocrats worried lest nonchalance and "reform fatigue" postpone badly needed additional progrowth moves, while Suharto sent mixed signals as to just how rapidly he wanted to continue freeing up the country's markets.

---

4. Adi Sasono, conversation, Jakarta, 18 May 1995.
5. *The 1945 Constitution of the Republic of Indonesia* (Jakarta: Department of Information, 1995–96), Article 33 (p. 11) and its elucidation (pp. 30–31).

Then came the multiple shocks of 1997–98: waves of devaluation, stock market losses, and downgraded credit ratings and growth forecasts. Initially, Suharto tilted toward the technocrats. He brought Widjojo out of quasi-retirement to lead the Indonesian team that negotiated a large rescue package from the International Monetary Fund (IMF) conditional on further reform. Habibie's empire of "strategic" state industries languished because Indonesia could no longer afford to supply the public subsidies or import the parts-making machines and components on which his plans for national planes and ships depended.

But even before these setbacks, general prosperity in Indonesia was a long way off, as Anne Booth documents in this book. Although exports outside the oil and gas sector had grown rapidly since the mid-1980s, in 1994 they still amounted to less than the total value of exports from Ireland that same year. And while the JSX had matured, it still had not attracted the savings of more than a tiny proportion of the country's population of some 200 million. In 1995 securities analysts estimated that no more than 300,000 Indonesians had ever bought shares. The number of bank savings accounts, on the other hand, had roughly doubled to 43 million between 1989 and 1994.

Despite all the moves toward deregulation and privatization, Indonesia remained a difficult place to do business. Investors still faced endemic corruption, a lack of transparency and legal recourse, and hassles over land rights, among other obstacles. The urgent and ongoing need to create jobs for the millions of young Indonesians entering the labor force every year made continuing and deepening economic reform a critical priority. As Tunky put it in 1995, "We don't want our deregulation to fade. This we must avoid."[6] And that was before the shocks of 1997–98 had so painfully emphasized his point.

Deregulation

Indonesia's reputation as a "high-cost economy" reflected the endemic nature of corruption. But it also implied the effect of widespread overregulation—thick layers of needed permits and signatures—on the cost of doing business: the red tape that "justified" bribes as the equivalent of scissors. Where it succeeded, deregulation had been a comparable tool: cutting and removing layers of rules and requirements that had hobbled markets and prevented the private sector from efficiently mobilizing foreign and domestic resources to productive, job-creating, income-generating ends.

Broadly speaking, deregulation was most successful in opening capital markets. The sudden flight from the rupiah and the JSX in 1997 reminded Indonesians that not all capital was the same, and that openness could work both ways, facilitating outgo as well as influx. But had the authorities tried to prevent the

---

6. Conference speech, "BOS95," 26 April 1995.

mobility of capital, especially direct investment, the economy would not have grown nearly as fast as it did. The deregulation of industry, on the other hand, bore mixed results. Least successful of all was the record of steps to deregulate agriculture. The next sections review these outcomes by examining the effects of deregulation on five markets—in stocks, foreign direct investment, automobiles, soybeans, and cloves.

Stocks

The JSX opened long before it functioned. During its somnolent first decade (1977–87) it was not thought to be a place where companies could raise capital so much as a tool the government could use to promote "Indonesianization"—an official priority at the time. Under investment rules in place by 1970, companies owned mostly by foreigners had to increase Indonesian ownership to at least 51 percent within fifteen years. High-profile product-makers with little or no Indonesian equity, such as Unilever and British American Tobacco, used the otherwise dormant JSX to sell minority stakes in order to show progress toward divesting control. But there was no autonomous or permanent market for the shares of even big-name companies such as these. Usually the buyer was a securities firm, PT Danareksa, owned by the ministry of finance.[7]

For most of the 1970s and 1980s, banks paid high annual rates of interest on rupiah savings accounts—typically more than 20 percent. Ordinary Indonesians saw little reason to withdraw these deposits and buy stocks on the untried JSX. As for foreigners, until the late 1980s they were not allowed to acquire the shares listed by multinational corporations to boost Indonesian ownership. Late in 1988, before the rules changed, only twenty-four companies were listed on the exchange. And only shares in the seven that were not using the JSX to attract Indonesian buyers could be acquired by foreigners. In a market so small and illiquid, days could—and did—go by without a single trade taking place.

Indonesia needed a vibrant stock market to attract capital inflows and reduce the high borrowing costs faced by Indonesian firms. Knowing this, the technocrats sought and got Suharto's approval to make the JSX more accessible to foreigners. In 1990 he agreed to let foreigners purchase up to 49 percent of the listed shares of an Indonesian-owned company. Technocrats and nationalists alike could accept this limit. It was high enough to attract foreign investors—the JSX became more open than the stock markets in, for example, South Korea or Taiwan—but just low enough to ensure Indonesian control.

The impact of this among other reforms was immediate. From 1988 through 1995 the number of listed firms increased tenfold, from 24 to 238, while the volume of listed shares skyrocketed from 60 million to nearly 46 billion. At the

---

7. Comparable to "Inc." or "Ltd.," the initials PT (Perséroan Terbatas) denote a limited liability company.

start of 1996 the JSX was capitalized at $67 billion at the exchange rate then in effect.[8] The expansion was largely foreign-driven. Ordinary Indonesians were still hesitant to risk buying shares—a reluctance reinforced when the market plunged in 1991 and again in 1997.

Animating the dormant JSX not only brought needed capital and helped some companies raise funds more cheaply, it also fostered a more transparent corporate culture. Traditionally secretive firms were sometimes shocked to learn that, after collecting funds by selling shares, they needed to explain their plans and accounts to their new shareholders. Under the improving rules of the board that regulated the JSX—the Capital Markets Supervisory Agency (Badan Pengawas Pasar Modal, or Bapepam)—listed companies also had to learn how to court and assuage minority shareholders who previously had been taken for granted. In 1992, for example, following complaints that PT Indocement Tunggal Prakarsa, owned by the Salim Group, had steamrolled major acquisitions, Bapepam required that in the future such expansions by any listed company had to be approved by a majority of the firm's "independent" minority shareholders. The adjective singled out minority owners of stock who were not affiliated with the group that owned a majority of the firm's shares.

The JSX also became better known abroad. Typically, an Indonesian firm that had decided to "go public," that is, to list its shares on the exchange, would travel overseas in search of foreign buyers. These "road shows" were occasions to meet with and inform fund managers and analysts. The resulting circulation of information helped to put Indonesia more on the global financial map. Meanwhile, more and more Indonesians also bought stocks.

Rising confidence in the JSX was not always justified. In September 1990, for example, a scandal erupted when the nation's fifth-largest private bank, Bank Duta, announced that it had lost $420 million in high-risk foreign-exchange speculation. Only months earlier thousands of Indonesians had bought shares with no knowledge of this red ink because it had been hidden from them. The bank assured stockholders that its loss had been covered by three Suharto-chaired foundations that owned 72 percent of its shares. It was believed, however, that two extremely wealthy ethnic-Chinese businessmen close to the president, Liem Sioe Liong and Prajogo Pangestu, actually put up the funds.

For years optimists in Jakarta had expected the JSX to become the biggest stock market in Southeast Asia. In the mid-1990s such talk remained premature. At the beginning of 1996 the Jakarta exchange had risen more than eightfold in value since 1990. Yet that value had not reached even half the capitalization of the stock market in neighboring Singapore, a city-state with less than 2 percent of Indonesia's population. Nevertheless, the JSX had come a long way toward credibility—although not far enough to escape the debacle of 1997–98.

---

8. *Indonesia Source Book 1996*, p. 98.

Investment

When the New Order began in 1966, Suharto knew that he needed private capital from abroad to help lift the Indonesian economy from the desperate straits into which it had fallen under Sukarno. A year later the provisional legislature rubber-stamped the New Order's first and most generous guidelines for foreign investment. Two large mineral firms quickly arrived—Freeport from the United States to mine copper in Irian Jaya, and Canada's Inco to dig nickel in Sulawesi. (On the latter investment, see Kathryn Robinson's chapter in this book.) In 1996 these two firms were still the largest investors in Indonesia outside the oil and gas industry, and had been spending huge sums to increase production.

Windfalls from the world oil booms of 1973–74 and 1979–80 were taken to mean that Indonesia did not need to court foreign investors more than it already had. Steps to continue liberalizing the regulatory framework came to a halt. The priority shifted toward Indonesianization, while the state's already large economic role grew larger, almost literally fueled by oil. Lieutenant General Ibnu Sutowo, as head of the state petroleum enterprise (Perusahaan Tambang Minyak dan Gas Bumi Nasional, or Pertamina), embarked on a spending binge that took the government to the brink of bankruptcy in 1975. While it took years for the technocrats to repair the damage, the rich and flamboyant Ibnu got off lightly, merely losing his post.[9]

As these events suggest, Indonesia's oil highs were a distinctly mixed blessing. They paid government bills and put schools and clinics in remote parts of the country. But they also postponed reform and thereby deepened the pit that plunging oil prices would pull the economy into in the mid-1980s. And just as good times had fostered profligacy in the guise of nationalism, the shock of bad times encouraged reform, specifically deregulation, in the name of restoring rapid growth. No longer would factories have to obtain fresh permits whenever they wanted to add capacity. No longer would goods wait and wait, tied in red tape and vulnerable to theft, in the country's corrupt ports. Punitive duties on exports and imports would be reduced.

Following the shocks of the mid-1980s, more and more sectors were ruled open to foreign investment, and the rules themselves were simplified. Investors had struggled over thick and recondite books that stated what was allowed but left unclear the status of other activities. These "positive" rules were replaced by

---

9. Special treatment for the Sutowos was not a one-time thing. Twenty years later, Ibnu's eldest daughter, Endang Mokodompit, was president of PT Bank Pacific, which her family co-owned with the central bank. She quietly used PT Bank Pacific to guarantee hundreds of millions of dollars of offshore loans taken out by a finance company owned by the Sutowo family. When the loans proved unrecoverable, the state suffered a huge loss. Endang was never prosecuted. Richard Borsuk, "Indonesian Officials Grapple with Finance Firm's Debts," *Asian Wall Street Journal,* 18 April 1996, p. 1, contains details.

"negative" ones listing activities that were off-limits to all investors, such as importing wheat (a state monopoly), and those closed only to foreigners, such as retailing. The shrinking of forbidden activities and the expansion of allowed ones had made it more practical to list the former not the latter.

These reforms made Indonesian markets more competitive and the economy more productive—but still not competitive or productive enough. Every year the demand for employment grew, as another 2.3 million young Indonesians joined the labor force. Nor were Indonesia's Asian competitors standing still. In the early 1990s China became a particular favorite with investors; Malaysia and Thailand remained attractive; and all three economies grew substantially faster than Indonesia. Beginning about 1993, thanks partly to market-loosening moves, the traditionally protected and sluggish economies of the Philippines, Vietnam, and India also began to attract foreign capital and pick up speed.

Compared with Indonesia, a number of Asian countries had more liberal foreign-investment rules. Generally in Indonesia, for example, foreigners were not permitted to start out owning more than four-fifths of an enterprise, and even if they began with majority control, they were obliged to pare their stake to 49 percent or less after fifteen years. Prospective foreign investors who objected to these conditions could and did find more generous terms elsewhere in Asia.

In two bold moves, Suharto reversed this disadvantage. In March 1992 the government announced that it would allow foreign investors to start up enterprises fully under their control, subject only to a few limitations, notably that such firms be of a minimum size. In June 1994 this reform was extended with the issuing of Government Regulation (Peraturan Pemerintah, or PP) No. 20 of that year, which virtually eliminated the requirement to divest. Henceforth, in most sectors, foreigners could not only own 100 percent of a company from the start; they could expect to retain 99 percent control over time. Tunky as industry minister had these reforms in mind when he boasted in 1995 that in its toleration of foreign ownership Indonesia had become "better than China, Vietnam, India, all the others."[10] Whether he exaggerated or not, the results were quick to arrive: PP 20 triggered a new flood of foreign investment proposals and approvals.

Automobiles

In the 1970s, Indonesia used a combination of foreign investment and import substitution to incubate a domestic motor vehicle industry. Selective tariffs on imported components and an outright ban on importing finished cars created a captive market for domestic production and assembly. The automobile industry that grew up behind these walls amounted roughly to a duopoly. More than half of the country's vehicle market was taken by the Astra Group, led by an ethnic-

---

10. Conference speech, "BOS95," 26 April 1995.

Chinese Indonesian entrepreneur, William Soeryadjaya, and its Japanese part-
ners, Toyota, Daihatsu, and Isuzu. The Salim Group, chaired by another ethnic-
Chinese Indonesian tycoon, Liem Sioe Liong, and partnered with Datsun and
Mazda, took most of the rest of the market.

Indonesia had created an auto industry. But it was inefficient; its products
were pricey; and it continued to depend on foreigners for the components it
assembled. In 1993 tariffs replaced the ban on importing fully made cars. But the
duties were prohibitive—up to 300 percent. In May 1995 they were reduced to
200 percent. Although proportionally substantial, that cut was far from enough
to free the market.

In February 1996 President Suharto stunned the industry by announcing a
"national car" policy. At first the policy seemed likely to lower prices and foster
competition. An accompanying decree laid out criteria under which a vehicle
maker intending to produce a "national car" could be exempted from existing
duties—a 35 percent luxury tax, which roughly doubled the price of domestic
sedans—and stiff tariffs on imported parts. It appeared that the criteria would be
fairly easy for a variety of existing and prospective car companies to meet.

But then the president sent word through his trade and industry minister (Tunky)
that, initially, only *one* company would get the big breaks: PT Timor Putra
Nasional, a brand new firm owned by Suharto's youngest son, Hutomo ("Tommy")
Mandala Putra. Tommy's new company would work on the project with Kia
Motors of South Korea. Tommy said the new car, to be called the Timor, would
sell for 35 million rupiah—compared, for example, to the 70 million rupiah it
cost to buy a Toyota Corolla assembled by PT Astra without the exemptions. At
that difference in price, other things being equal, the Timor seemed destined to
leave its competitors—and any hope of deregulation—in the dust.

Economist Mari Pangestu (no relation to Prajogo) at the Centre for Strategic
and International Studies (CSIS), a Jakarta think tank, expected the Japanese to
"jump up and down" in anger over this protectionist discrimination against existing investors. And Japan did criticize the project, as did the United States and the
European Union. All three quickly threatened to seek a judgment against Indonesia in the World Trade Organization for violating WTO rules. Tunky replied on
the government's behalf by asserting that the policy was consistent with WTO
precepts and was, in any case, merely meant to give the domestic car industry the
ability to compete with the influx of fully made imports at low or no tariffs that
Indonesia's participation in world and regional free-trade agreements would eventually require. He had in mind not only imports from Japan and the West, but also
a prospective "flood" of Protons—neighboring Malaysia's national car.[11]

Ironically, in June 1996 it was Tunky who had to announce that the first "flood"

---

11. Interview, Jakarta, 28 February 1996 [Pangestu]; press conference, Jakarta, 18
March 1996 [Ariwibowo].

of imported fully built vehicles, from which the new policy was meant to protect the country, would soon arrive from South Korea—fleets of purportedly "national" Timors that had been wholly manufactured abroad. The inability of Tommy's newborn firm to organize itself quickly or well enough to assemble Kia's components in Indonesia had led Suharto to indulge his son: For one year, Tommy could bring up to 45,000 finished Timors into the country from South Korea for sale free of the stiff tariffs and luxury tax that other such imports would still have to face.

Tunky tried to soften the appearance of favoritism by announcing that other vehicles could eventually gain the same duty-free status as Tommy's Timor. But first they would have to achieve 60 percent local content, meaning that three-fifths of their components by value would have to be manufactured inside Indonesia. And in 1996 none of the Timor's potential competitors was even close to meeting that standard.

The blatant dispensation given by Suharto to his son made a farce of the "national car" policy and strengthened the case being made in Tokyo and elsewhere that it broke WTO rules. Even before the June decree allowing Tommy, and Tommy alone, to import his Korean-made Timors duty-free, the World Bank had characterized the protection of the proposed national car as "discriminatory," "non-transparent," and "out of step" with Indonesia's own "rules-based approach to trade reform."[12]

The waves of regional economic crisis that engulfed Indonesia after mid-1997 crushed Tommy's widely unpopular Timor scheme, but not before it had caused more damage. In July 1997, just as the crisis in Thailand was getting underway, Indonesia's biggest state and private banks were arm-twisted by the government to supply $650 million to Tommy to build a Timor factory east of Jakarta. It was not clear how much of this money was actually committed, but even a modest amount would have increased the bad debts of banks that were already shaky and becoming more so as the rupiah began to fall amid worsening financial conditions. In January 1998 Suharto complied with the terms of a revised IMF rescue program by ending tax breaks for the Timor. That agreement rendered moot WTO's verdict in March that the Timor's tax advantages violated international trade rules meant to give businesses equal treatment.

Soybeans

In November 1988 the government took what appeared to be an important step toward deregulation by ending lucrative monopolies on plastics imports that had benefited Suharto's children and their friends. Too sensitive for the technocrats to tackle in previous deregulation, these monopolies had been thought to lie

---

12. *Indonesia: Dimensions of Growth* (Washington, DC: World Bank, 1996), p. 43.

beyond the reach of reform. Their inclusion in the November package, in addition to helping plastics-using industries by making their inputs cheaper, boosted the credibility of the deregulation process as a whole.

While this was going on, however, an also crucial but politically less visible commodity, soybeans, was becoming the focus of a different and less publicized story. Processed into bean curd, soybeans are a major source of protein for Indonesians. Crushed to form soymeal, they are an important ingredient in animal feed. Indonesia grows soybeans, but not enough to meet these two needs.

Since the mid-1980s only one producer of soymeal had been permitted to operate—PT Sarpindo Soybean Industri—and only the state food distribution agency—Badan Urusan Logistik, or Bulog—had been allowed to import soybeans. In 1988 Sarpindo started up Indonesia's first and only licensed soybean-crushing facility. Nor was the company merely the sole authorized crusher. Bulog paid it a fee substantially higher than the world price for crushing soybeans. Sarpindo got a further bonus in the form of the soybean oil that crushing yielded, which Sarpindo was allowed to keep and sell at a handsome profit.

Not coincidentally, the owners of Sarpindo included two of Suharto's children—Tommy was one—and two of his wealthiest and oldest friends: Liem Sioe Liong of the Salim Group and the plywood magnate Mohamad ("Bob") Hasan (formerly The Kian Siang). The control over soybeans Suharto had given them greatly benefited these presidential offspring and cronies. The main immediate loser was the feed industry, which paid more for what in a freer market would have been among the least costly ingredients of food for animals. These arrangements also hurt the economy as a whole. Because of them, for example, Indonesia could not develop, as Thailand did, a booming business exporting frozen chicken to Japan.

Economists had a simple solution: End the monopoly. Early in 1992 the technocrats tried to do just that. A delegation of cabinet ministers with economic portfolios visited the president to press for trade reform that would have deregulated soybean imports. But when they made their request, the president replied, "If you want to kill Sarpindo, go ahead." The conditional first phrase effectively cancelled the permission granted in the second, leaving Suharto's true meaning clear: "Forget it." In June a trade reform package was unveiled, but it did not mention soybeans. And Suharto was right about Sarpindo. As a foreign economist later noted, genuine deregulation would indeed have created a suddenly price-competitive environment "too harsh" for "the domestic monopolist" to survive.[13]

While deregulators continued gingerly to nudge the soybean issue without result, money-makers who had profited from protection began to position them-

---

13. Adam Schwarz, *A Nation in Waiting: Indonesia in the 1990s* (Boulder, CO: Westview, 1994), p. 134 ["go ahead"], as recalled by someone who had been at the meeting; Jacqueline L. Pomeroy, "Measuring Costs and Benefits of Soymeal Deregulation in Indonesia, 1991–94," conference paper, "BOS95," 27 April 1995, p. 8 ["too harsh"].

selves to gain from future reform. In 1995 the Salim Group began building a large facility to make animal feed. Anticipating that controls on soybean trading would eventually end, Liem's conglomerate planned to establish itself downstream in time to benefit from the drastically reduced cost of soymeal that deregulation would bring.

Basically, that is what happened to Suharto's children when their monopolies on plastics imports were ended. They moved out of the newly risky—that is, competitive—business of importing plastics and into the domestic manufacture of products they had previously obtained abroad. In these new positions, the first children regained official protection. A case in point was the polyethylene factory partly owned by the president's eldest son, Sigit Harjojudanto, that opened in 1993. An effective external tariff of 40 percent crippled its competition.

Cloves

In the early 1980s the government tried to put a floor under the price that farmers got for selling cloves—the key ingredient in Indonesia's distinctive spice-flavored cigarettes known as *kretek*. The scheme failed and was abandoned. Officials lacked the massive funds and storage facilities needed to guarantee a minimum price.

After this blunder, some trading guidelines remained on the books. But they were largely ignored in a more or less decentralized system: Farmers in different provinces sold cloves to various traders who resold them to *kretek* manufacturers on Java. The arrangement was not tension-free. Farmers tended to believe that traders were colluding to buy low and sell high. But the cigarette makers' buying networks more or less competed for supply and retained the option of bypassing the traders by purchasing cloves directly from those who grew them. And in years when clove prices were especially high, farmers got rich. Compared with other farmers in North Sulawesi, the biggest cultivation area, many clove growers grew affluent. But their prosperity was precarious. Good prices tended to stimulate cultivation, triggering oversupply and causing prices to decline.

In the late 1980s, a group of spice traders tried to corner the market in home-grown cloves by outbidding buyers hired by the *kretek* factories. The traders acquired a large stock, but it was not large enough. Domestic production was too high, and the availability of cloves, including the stockpiles of the cigarette makers, too great. But after failing to control the market, the traders managed to persuade Suharto's son Tommy to help them unload their hoard at a profit. The traders proposed setting up a government-sanctioned monopoly that would force every *kretek* manufacturer downstream to buy only from them—using the state to ensure that their middleman's role could not by bypassed, and thereby making the market for cloves completely unfree. To distract attention from the true nature of the scheme—official collusion for the enrichment of a few—the plan was portrayed as helping impoverished clove farmers, who at the time were getting low prices due to oversupply.

Tommy's father, the president, made his son's project possible by designating cloves an "essential commodity" that would have to be regulated by the state. This decision was followed by the formation of a Clove Support and Marketing Agency (Badan Penyangga dan Pemasaran Cengkeh, or BPPC), with Tommy as chairman, which got underway early in 1991. Touted by then minister of trade Arifin Siregar as a way to "perfect" existing clove regulations,[14] the BPPC turned out to be a perfect disaster for almost everyone involved.

Upstream, clove farmers did not receive the high minimum price promised to them by the new monopoly. But downstream, *kretek* makers saw their clove costs soar. The companies raised cigarette prices. *Kretek* sales fell. In the new program's first full year (1991), declining sales caused the government's excise-tax revenue on the cigarettes to drop as well. To keep the monopoly going, Suharto ordered the central bank to give more than $350 million in subsidized credit to the BPPC. Thus did Tommy's scheme make losers of the farmers, the firms, the government, and the smoking and nonsmoking public. The only winners were Tommy himself and the BPPC—the middleman and his monopoly—who could and did at one time buy the spice from farmers at 4,000 rupiah per kilogram—less for raw cloves—and then sell it to the companies at triple that price.

The clove monopoly caught heavy flak from unhappy farmers and the feistier Indonesian media. But the president did not get, or did not want to get, the message that his son's monopoly was damaging farmers. Indonesian editors were even asked—in effect, told—by the government not to report critically on cloves. Criticisms continued, however, as did the unpopular monopoly, until finally, in January 1998, Suharto was forced to agree to its abolition by the toughened terms of a revised IMF-backed program of reform. The monopoly finally ended in May 1998. Clove farmers welcomed this outcome. Over the previous seven years, because of the monopoly, they had earned less than they had been promised, partly due to an oversupply of cloves that prevented the BPPC from disposing of its stocks. Yet the BPPC escaped being held publicly accountable for its actions. Indeed, long before its abolition, the agency had been able to shift much of its financial burden onto the ledgers of state-owned banks. Their new debts further weakened these institutions. And that weakness undermined the resilience of the financial system at the worst possible time—on the eve of the devastating economic shocks of 1997–98.

Speaking off the record in 1993, a former economic minister characterized Suharto's clove policy as a "complete disaster." The fiasco signaled the markets that whenever the president's children or other businesspeople close to him were involved in an activity, he might decide to regulate it to their benefit, whatever the cost. Foreign investors, actual or prospective, were not significantly affected

---

14. Siregar at a press briefing on the government's FY 1991–92 budget, Jakarta, 4 January 1991.

by the clove monopoly. But those who knew of it took it as a reason to doubt Suharto's commitment to deregulation. In that regard, too, the timing was bad. For in the crisis of 1997–98, few things would become more valuable to Indonesia than credibility abroad.

Privatization

If deregulation is meant to free markets by reducing the reach of the state, privatization should expand them by taking assets out of state hands. But even when these two sorts of reform work as intended, they may not be popular.

Under the New Order, as this chapter has already noted, public support for privatization in Indonesia was never strong. Most Indonesians who thought about it seem to have felt comfortable with the idea that government should play a major economic role. Especially suspicious of privatization were ethnically non-Chinese (*pribumi*) Indonesians unhappy over the dominance of the private sector by their Chinese-descended (*nonpribumi*) compatriots. The fear was that privatizing state assets would really mean turning them over to already wealthy *nonpribumi,* including the ethnic-Chinese business cronies of the president and his family.[15]

Despite the sorry historical record of state efforts to control markets, not to mention the principles of economics, the feeling lingered among many Indonesians that state-owned firms must be good for the country. A former cabinet minister put it this way: "Many people feel a good company is one that employs many people, not one that is efficient or has good service. By that criteria, state companies are good companies, no matter how inefficient they might be."[16]

In the 1980s and 1990s such sentiments collided with economic realities. The more Indonesia opened its economy to global markets, the more important the competitiveness of its firms became, and the less it could afford the luxury of allowing the state to own, run, and subsidize the typical state corporation—large, inefficient, and losing money. The resulting drag on the economy was rendered all the more acute by the quintupling of Indonesia's total external debt during 1980 to 1995, from $21 billion to $108 billion, and the doubling of the debt service ratio over the same period, from 14 to 31 percent of the value of exports. The last figure—31 percent—exceeded that of any other debt service ratio recorded in Asia by the World Bank for 1995.[17]

---

15. Insofar as *pribumi* means "native to the soil," Indonesian citizens descended from non-Chinese immigrants—Arabs and Indians, for example—also qualify as *nonpribumi.* In practice, however, the latter term refers to Chinese-Indonesians. Nor does the "immigrant" label take into account the possibly large number of ancestors such a person may have who were born, lived, and died in the archipelago.

16. Conversation, Jakarta, 29 April 1993.

17. *World Development Indicators 1997* (Washington DC: World Bank, 1997), pp. 219 [debt], 222–224 [debt service].

In such a context there was no economic justification for the state to keep on making paper, for example, not when private companies could do it more cheaply, or to retain large rubber and oil palm plantations where yields badly lagged those of private estates. In 1996 the state still ran businesses that could not remotely be considered "strategic." The ministry of finance, for example, still owned and operated a chain of pawn shops.

Beginning in the late 1980s, in line with the need to trim state spending, technocrats did begin promoting limited privatization. But its unpopularity made them cautious, and kept their initiatives modest. Nor was privatization limited merely by a general or traditional willingness to tolerate a large state sector. Privatization threatened specific interests and individuals. Among these were serving and retired generals and officials for whom privatization meant a loss of jobs—if not their own, then jobs they could use as patronage to reward their associates, relatives, and supporters. In 1989 Sumarlin, then finance minister, listed fifty-two state companies out of a total approaching two hundred, that were to become at least somewhat private in character within five years. By the time President Suharto finally resigned nine years later, this goal was still far from being met.

And privatization, when it did occur, did not always augur freer markets. Public cynicism in this regard rose each time another relative or friend of Suharto acquired this or that ailing state company, without competitive bidding and on undisclosed terms. In such cases state assets could be sold for much less than their true worth. As two economists noted in 1995, in some sectors privatization had merely transferred monopolies intact to businesspeople with the right connections.[18]

But while some instances of privatization did not go well, others did. Failure and success could even occur in the same sector. A case in point was telecommunications. In that field, efforts to ensure private-sector participation in three different firms, PT Satelindo, PT Indosat, and PT Telkom, yielded markedly different results.

Satelindo

The company known as PT Satelindo—an acronym for "Indonesian satellite" in Indonesian—grew from an effort to reconcile two priorities. In the early 1990s, the government was looking for ways to limit its mounting debts. But it was also making plans for an expensive new generation of telecommunication satellites capable of stitching together more closely the archipelago's far-flung provinces.

The first two generations of satellites, known as Palapa A and B, had been entirely state-owned. They were being used to provide telephone service by a

---

18. Anwar Nasution and William James, "Future Directions for Economic Policy Reform," conference paper, "BOS95," 28 April 1995.

state monopoly called PT Indosat—a contraction of "Indonesian satellite" in English. In 1992, under pressure to contain new state borrowing, the government decided to allow some private equity in the third satellite series, Palapa C. Throughout that year, behind closed doors, officials held meetings to work out the terms under which private businesses would be allowed to invest in Palapa C.

In January 1993 the minister in charge of telecommunications, Soesilo Soedarman, unveiled the decision: Palapa C would be handled by a new company, Satelindo, in which private investors would enjoy a majority stake. Since the venture could not be expected to become profitable soon, it would be given two lucrative dispensations to ensure its viability in the short run: For ten years Satelindo would be guaranteed its status as Indosat's sole competitor, public or private, in providing international telephone service. Satelindo would also be allowed to pioneer a mobile phone system in major cities around the country.

Those two licenses, plus the Palapa work, were extremely valuable. But these benefits were not auctioned off in a competitive bidding process. Instead, they were bestowed directly on Satelindo, despite the fact that the new firm had a paid-up capital of less than $50 million—a small sum in view of the considerable outlays the company would need to make. And who was fortunate enough to own such a favored new venture? One-tenth of Satelindo went to Indosat. Three-tenths went to PT Telkom, short for Telekomunikasi Indonesia, the state-owned domestic phone service company to which the earlier satellites, Palapa A and B, had belonged. But by far the largest stake—six-tenths—was given to PT Bimagraha Telekomindo, a company led by Bambang Trihatmodjo. Bambang was the chief executive of the Bimantara Group and, more to the point, Suharto's second son.

To obtain capital and capability, Satelindo in 1994 looked for a foreign partner. International phone companies badly wanted access to rapidly developing markets such as Indonesia. Satelindo found multiple suitors bearing attractive offers. After winning a bidding war with Britain's Cable & Wireless, Germany's Deutsche Telekom in March 1995 paid $586 million for a 25 percent stake. Nine months before the launching of its first (Palapa C) satellite, and only two years after it had been founded with less than $50 million in capital, Satelindo was valued at nearly $2.4 billion—a substantial gain for the two government shareholders, but an enormous windfall for Bambang's company through its 60 percent share.

The way the Palapa program was privatized upset the technocrats and those in the business world who opposed favoritism. Unhappy, too, were government officials who had expected the state at least to retain a majority of the new company. Indeed, that had been the plan. But it had been revoked, said one senior official, by none other than Suharto himself, who had been monitoring preparations for Satelindo's birth, just as he had played a role in all previous decisions to award major government contracts.

The creation of Satelindo showed just how anticompetitive privatization could be. Transferring public rights into privileged private hands without an open bidding process cost the government dearly in foregone revenue and damaged credibility. Ironically, had the government invited competing proposals to invest in Palapa, Bambang's company, Bimantara, probably would have won anyway. No other Indonesian firm had more experience in launching satellites. But at least the process would have been less suspect in the eyes of investors and more helpful to the public purse.

The World Bank may have had Satelindo's birth in mind when it urged transparency in privatization in its June 1995 annual economic report on Indonesia. The nontransparent placement of a state company in private hands, warned the Bank, could artificially lower the sale price, increase the concentration of ownership in the economy, and encourage impressions of unfair dealing and favoritism that could threaten privatization in particular and reform in general.[19]

Indosat and Telkom

A year after the controversial creation of Satelindo, the Indonesian government partially privatized its international phone company, Indosat, in a share sale that some business magazines called 1994's "deal of the year" for Asian equity markets. This time Finance Minister Mar'ie Muhammad, apparently unhappy over how Satelindo was set up, wanted to conduct a proper privatization by marketing shares openly to domestic and foreign buyers. Indosat was a natural choice because its shares were likely to prove attractive. Even though it was a state monopoly, the company was widely considered to be well run.

Mar'ie's ministry was Indosat's sole shareholder. In early 1994 he announced that shares in Indosat would be sold in Jakarta and on overseas exchanges later that year. The move promised several benefits: It would push ahead privatization, promote Indonesia's name in world financial markets, and raise money to pay off some of the government's large foreign debt. The timing for such an offering was also auspicious. Global fund managers were hungry for shares of phone companies in briskly growing economies with few phones in place and, therefore, potentially huge future sales.

In October 1994 Indosat successfully sold 10 percent of its shares on the JSX and 25 percent on the New York Stock Exchange (NYSE). The latter sale—the biggest initial public offering in New York that year by a non-American company—received an "enormously favorable reception" from investors.[20] The two offerings together raised more than $1.1 billion, about $750 million of which

---

19. *Indonesia: Improving Efficiency and Equity—Changing the Public Sector's Role* (Washington, DC: World Bank, 1995), p. 85.

20. NYSE President Richard Grasso, quoted in Richard Borsuk, "New York Bourse Seeks Listing from Southeast Asian Companies," *Asian Wall Street Journal,* 22 April 1995, p. 3.

was used to reduce government debt. Meanwhile, Indosat became a core holding in the portfolios of many international mutual funds. Fund managers were impressed by the company's commitment to transparency and competitiveness—a refreshing change from their experience with other Indonesian firms.

Following as it did the compromised birth of Satelindo, Indosat's success suggested that the government had learned from its earlier mistake. But the reality was more complex. There was little reason to believe that Suharto had come to believe in the virtue of open global offerings compared with opaque local placements—in privatization through markets rather than around them. More probably, he had been persuaded by his technocrats on narrower grounds: that selling a quarter of Indosat openly and globally would maximize revenue to pay down state debt.

A year later Indonesia had a third and still different experience with privatization in telecommunications. An offering by the previously mentioned state company in charge of domestic telephone service, PT Telkom, ran into trouble when it appeared that demand for its shares would be unexpectedly weak. Accordingly, at the last minute, amid bickering between domestic and foreign underwriters, the offering's size and price were slashed.

This disappointment seemed to shake whatever confidence Indosat's success had given to Suharto that Indonesia could make privatization work by attracting buyers on world equity markets. He removed two finance ministry officials who had pushed for global offerings by state companies, and indicated that future sales of shares should be done only on the JSX. Privatization would still be pursued, but with greatly reduced chances of retiring national debt, in view of the much greater buying power accessible through overseas compared with domestic equity markets.

Ironically, when it actually began to trade, the offering by PT Telkom, which had looked like a calamity in the making, did very well. In three months the price of stock in the company soared 70 percent. Stockbrokers and fund managers expected this success to set the stage for more offerings by Indonesian state companies.

Instead, in 1996, the pace of privatization slowed. Because the initial sale of Telkom had been scaled down in size and price, Suharto apparently still considered it a disappointment. And among the remaining state companies, candidates for lucrative privatization were scarce, if only because so few were professionally and competitively run, that is, attractive to global buyers. In contrast to Indosat, most state firms doubted their ability to compete freely on a level playing field, and Suharto was not naturally inclined to make them try.

Any lingering hopes that Suharto would foster professionally run, competitive privatizations were dashed at the end of 1996. In that year the government hastily arranged a controversial private placement of another 4 percent of PT Telkom. Several investment banks competing to underwrite the placement dropped out upon learning, at the last minute, that they would have to reserve a large block of shares for a "well-connected businessman," widely believed to be a Suharto child.[21] In the end, there was only one bid to underwrite the sale. The ensuing deal reduced the proceeds the government should have received and further damaged the credibility of the overall privatization process.

Packages

In the late 1980s an annual ritual was added to the calendars of Indonesian cabinet members. Several weeks before creditor governments and agencies in the IGGI (later CGI) gathered in Europe to announce their annual pledges of loans and aid, a battery of ministers would assemble in Jakarta to announce a package of deregulatory reforms. And every year there would be an official denial that the package had been timed to loosen the purse strings of foreigners who could again commend Indonesia for maintaining the pace of deregulation.

The denial was never convincing. At junctures when the pace of reform flagged, unwrapping a package of reforms was the government's way of showing that deregulation was alive and going forward. The bundles' contents varied, as did reactions to them. In some years, bold steps were taken to advance the process of reform. In other packages, the changes seemed timid, and observers were underwhelmed. Often, behind each annual announcement lay a cabinet-level struggle to win the president's approval for this or that step. Approval might be given, or it could be withheld, as in Suharto's previously noted refusal to deregulate soybean imports in 1992.

These sets of reforms won broad acclaim in the 1980s. But enthusiasm for them cooled in the 1990s. Initially, when barriers were higher and expectations lower, it had been relatively easy to select reforms that investors were sure to applaud. A red-tape-cutting measure in the 1988 package, for example, slashed from more than ten to two the number of permits needed to open a hotel. But as these early reforms boosted investments, exports, and growth, they created higher expectations—that the pace of reform, so obviously beneficial, would be not only maintained but also accelerated—especially in the light of rising regional competition for foreign capital.

At the same time, the success of reform seemed to breed complacence and even backsliding on Suharto's part. In the 1990s he unveiled a number of policies that entailed not deregulation but its opposite, reregulation, including the clove monopoly and the anticompetitive scheme to build a "national" car. These moves called into question the government's overall commitment to reform, and the private-sector criticism that greeted them tended to drown out the applause for more positive steps.

---

21. Richard Borsuk and Sara Webb, "Telkom Offer Angers Bankers in Indonesia," *Asian Wall Street Journal,* 21–27 December 1996, p. 9.

The deregulatory packages of May 1995 and June 1996 illustrated the "yes, but" character of market-opening reform. The May 1995 package was unwrapped roughly a decade after *deregulasi*—deregulation—had entered the policy lexicon. By 1995 the feeling had grown that the reform process was running out of steam. In 1994, to be sure, the government had scrapped requirements obliging foreign investors to divest after a certain period of time. But for years no meaningful initiatives to deregulate trade had been undertaken.

Prior to the announcement of the May 1995 package, promarket reformers were optimistic. A senior official told diplomats to expect a "strong" set of measures. The chairman of Bulog, the state agency mandated to intervene in commodity markets, acknowledged that his organization would have to accept deregulation.[22] Yet upon their disclosure, the new round of reforms provoked more public criticism than any previous package.

Not only had high initial hopes raised the threshold of what constituted meaningful reform. Despite the Bulog chair's stated receptivity to reform, the measures of 23 May left untouched all of that agency's monopolies, including its exclusive right to import wheat and sugar. Also still standing was the plywood cartel run by presidential crony Bob Hasan. One economist called the inaction on nontariff barriers "pretty pathetic."[23] Even the Chamber of Commerce and Industry (Kadin), which could be counted on to praise almost any government initiative, voiced disappointment over the package.

The changes of May 1995 did impressively address tariffs as impediments to trade. Most such levies were to be cut immediately, and a schedule would be set for paring others incrementally down to an average level of only 7 percent of the value of the affected item by 2003. The World Bank praised these moves as "going well beyond" the General Agreement on Tariffs and Trade, and expected them to unleash "strong pro-competitive forces." In fact, however, the May package leashed reform by limiting deregulation to tariffs while ignoring other barriers.[24]

The May 1995 package sent a mixed message: When Indonesia's overt regulation of trade could be shown to impede the economy's competitive position, Suharto would do the right thing, as the tariff cuts showed. But the more opaque doings of vested domestic interests, including those of Bulog, Bob Hasan, and Suharto's children, were still largely off-limits to reformers. At the same time, it would become harder for the president to shield such dealings from competition. By 1998, for example, Bulog would have to relinquish many of its monopoly trading rights if Indonesia were to implement the rules it had agreed to under the Uruguay Round of GATT.

---

22. Beddu Amang, conference speech, "BOS95," 27 April 1995.

23. Mari Pangestu, interview, Jakarta, 23 May 1995.

24. The quotes are from *Indonesia: Improving Efficiency*, p. 37. The Bank did acknowledge "significant pockets of monopoly and oligopoly in Indonesia," and expected nontariff barriers to "exert a growing drag on the economy" (p. 48).

The package announced in June 1996 was quickly criticized on the same grounds used against its predecessor: It was focused almost wholly on tariffs. Apparently recognizing that tariffs would have to come down worldwide, Suharto had decided to place Indonesia in the vanguard of developing economies in this regard, rather than resisting cuts until the last minute. Yet his double standard on deregulation remained in effect. On 4 June, the very same day the tariff cuts were announced, the government issued the infamous decree allowing Suharto's son Tommy to import from South Korea 45,000 units of Indonesia's so-called national car.

Later that day several economic ministers, who had not expected the car decision to be made public so soon, held a briefing for the media on the new deregulation package. But the apparently nepotistic decision on Tommy's car was more newsworthy, in the eyes of reporters, than the announcement of changes in the arcane tariff code. At the briefing, journalists kept changing the subject from the tariff cuts to the car's breaks. The senior economic minister, Saleh Afiff, angrily refused to comment on the car decree, saying it had apparently been "unofficially released" and had nothing to do with the package of reforms that were the topic of the briefing. But the impression could not be dispelled that Suharto was willing to show a degree of favoritism toward pet projects involving his close relatives and friends that no amount of deregulation could outweigh.

At the annual meeting of the CGI in Paris less than three weeks later, Indonesia's lenders and donors promised $5.3 billion, a nominal decline from the total amount they had pledged the year before. Their praise for deregulation was less fulsome than in previous years, but they remained bullish on Indonesia. Back in Jakarta, several ministers tried to reprogram the reform process away from opportunistically timed and showcased annual displays of reform and toward a continuous process of incremental steps to be announced routinely by government departments. But the dominant decision-maker, Suharto, was content to retain the package approach, which had served him well. Not only had it allowed him to deliver reminders to outsiders that deregulation was alive, but it had also enabled him to avoid having to institutionalize the opening of markets as an everyday goal.

Ambivalence

The most obvious supporters of reform were the technocrats, who lobbied Suharto to make key liberalizing moves. Most businesspeople, too, knew the value of freer markets for economic growth. Joining these groups on behalf of reforms was a small, but rapidly growing, middle class. Its members, who could afford more than daily necessities largely because of market-furnished opportunities and rewards, wanted the consumer choices that a more competitive environment could provide.

On the other side of the policy struggle over deregulation stood an unorganized collection of divergent individuals and interests, including economic nationalists such as B.J. Habibie. For Habibie, it was more important to use state resources to incubate a capital-intensive aircraft industry than to deregulate the economy to attract, say, foreign manufacturers of sports shoes, despite the foreign-exchange-earning and employment-creating benefits of the latter investments.

Also unhappy with some promarket policies were those in the business world who had succeeded because of political connections, not entrepreneurial skills. As noted earlier in this chapter, some political figures sought to score points by arguing that deregulation had disproportionally benefited Indonesia's conglomerates and its ethnic-Chinese minority, whose size and wealth had given them unfair advantages against smaller and ethnically indigenous businesses in need of state help and protection. Also lukewarm on deregulation were officials who resented the loss of their sometimes lucrative authority to issue permits and licenses.

No strict consensus existed inside either of these two loose camps. The technocrats, for example, differed as to just how free Indonesia's markets should be. Nor were these differences necessarily consequential. What mattered in the end was what the president decided. Indeed, over time, the president grew less open to advice and came to rely more heavily on his own counsel as the sole and final arbiter of the course of reform.

In the realm of policy, as in politics, Suharto's strategy was to balance competing interests and opinions and not let any camp or individual become too strong. For example, as the 1990s unfolded, the technocrats' influence waned, but this did not necessarily translate into policy victories for Habibie. Tommy's Timor was a case in point. The project greatly distressed the technocrats, who failed to talk Suharto out of pursuing it. But the president's decision did not favor Habibie, who had his own plans for a state-produced national car, to be called the "Maleo," after a bird from his native Sulawesi. These plans were shelved when the president chose instead to favor his son's venture.

Suharto's inclination, in the mid-1990s, to listen less and less to the technocrats probably had several reasons. The economy was sailing along fairly smoothly. Foreign investors were beating a path to his country. Foreign governments and agencies were showering loans on Indonesia and praising his management of the economy. Seen in this light, the technocrats' warnings and sense of urgency regarding reform must have seemed unpersuasive. And sometimes his economists told the president things he did not want to hear. He particularly did not want to hear even muted criticism of his children and the market-hampering effects of their many preferences and monopolies, not just because they were family, but because as their business empires grew, Suharto argued, the economy as a whole did too.

Beyond his personal confidence that he and the country were on the right course, the president may have been attracted to the idea that Indonesia was finally becoming ready to assume a position in the world economy commensurate with its rank as the fourth most populous nation. He did not explicitly state this view, but he appeared to feel that Indonesia's economic success could be measured by the number of products it did not have to import but could make for itself. This philosophy of self-sufficiency seems to have reflected Suharto's child-hood roots in subsistence-based farming more than his adult years of tutoring by foreign-trained economists. Whatever the reason, he sincerely believed that it was better for Indonesia to build its own aircraft, rather than have to buy them abroad, however burdensome his economists believed the higher cost of domes-tic production to be.

Suharto did authorize deregulation as a priority and a process. His personal intervention was crucial to the commitment made by the summit of the Asia Pacific Economic Cooperation forum—which met in Indonesia in 1994—to achieve free trade in the Pacific Rim by 2020. Yet, to the end of his rule, he remained ambivalent about the value of free markets.

The effect of many of Suharto's policies was to liberalize the Indonesian economy. Yet to him the Indonesian word *liberal* meant having leftist, opposi-tional politics, or behaving in an inappropriately selfish, individualistic way. He opened his country to private businesses, foreign and domestic. Yet he believed in cooperatives as forms of endeavor that were ethically superior to firms. And, at least rhetorically, he was uncomfortable with the extreme pursuit of self-inter-est in unfettered markets, which he disparaged as "free-fight capitalism."

Economic liberalism in this sense appears to have contradicted Suharto's own self-image as a father providing for his people, not to mention the constitution's comparably familial portrayal of the economy and its resources. Opponents of privatization and deregulation especially liked to cite those parts of the charter that declared state control over vital branches of production and named coopera-tives as a third pillar of the Indonesian economy, along with the state and the private sector.

In 1990 Suharto startled Indonesia's wealthiest ethnic-Chinese businessmen by asking them to share their wealth with the larger society by selling up to a quarter of their companies' shares to cooperatives. That goal was conveniently forgotten after the executives had transferred a token one percent of some of their listed firms—a minute fraction of the total worth of the businesses involved. The president's proposal seemed to have been a mere public-relations exercise. Yet he probably did believe that the wealth created by private corporations should someday be channeled into public welfare through cooperatives, fulfilling the socialistic hopes of the republic's founders in 1945. "Ultimately," he once said, "cooperatives must be the main pillar of the economy."[25]

Most of the technocrats have never liked cooperatives, seeing them as eco-nomic dead-ends requiring expensive care by the state. Knowing Suharto's fond-ness for talking up cooperatives, however, the technocrats refrained from

---

25. *Soeharto: My Thought, Words and Deeds—An Autobiography,* as told to G. Dwipayana and Ramadhan K.H. (English ed., Jakarta: PT Citra Lamtoro Gung Persada, 1991), p. 304.

criticizing them, and tried instead to ignore the subject. After Suharto had urged companies to sell their shares to cooperatives in his January 1991 budget speech, for example, then-Finance Minister Sumarlin chose not to hold his traditional post-speech briefing for journalists rather than face all the questions he knew reporters would ask about the cooperatives initiative.

Market-minded technocrats were irked as well by Suharto's affection for expensive, state-owned, high-tech businesses—the ten designated "strategic industries" overseen by Habibie, including the aircraft factory he had built in Bandung and a shipyard in Surabaya. While he did not give his research and technology minister carte blanche, the president obviously was attracted to Habibie's vision. And with Suharto's backing, Habibie could find funding even as the technocrats were able to keep state budgets austere.

In 1994, in a move unsuccessfully challenged by environmentalist groups in a Jakarta court, Suharto in effect raided the government's reforestation fund to give Habibie $183 million to finish making the controversial N-250 passenger aircraft. Then, on the day of the N-250's inaugural flight in August 1995, Suharto announced that he wanted Habibie to build a 130-seat jet, the N-2130, by the year 2003. Anticipating criticism that Indonesia could not afford such a scheme, the president assured his listeners that the $2 billion needed for the project would not come from the state budget. Mystery about where the money would come from was cleared up in February 1996 when Suharto made himself chairman of a private company that planned to raise the $2 billion by selling shares to firms and individuals. This sparked grumbles—Indonesian executives knew they would be expected to chip in—and jokes, including one about the number 2130 in the plane's name standing for the year when the new company might begin paying dividends.

Fifteen years younger than Suharto, Habibie became a man to watch in the 1990s. While formally denying ambition for higher office, the peripatetic minister shrewdly increased his political influence by heading up a state-approved institute of Islamic intellectuals and by chairing his own think tank, the Center for Information and Development Studies (CIDES). The Center made no bones about being at odds with the technocrats over the proper role of markets.

The head of CIDES, Adi Sasono, said he supported deregulation and wanted more of it. He lamented the fact that investment approvals still took "much longer" in Indonesia than in other countries. But Adi also argued that deregulation had been badly managed in that it had unfairly helped large enterprises at the expense of small ones. As a result, he said, "you can't say small is beautiful" in Indonesia.

Adi claimed to favor reform. But the "dark side of the market" was that it could not "guarantee social justice." Indonesia needed regulations tailored to help small businesses. Without such new rules, similar to antitrust laws in the United States, he warned, resentments could lead to "radicalization" and "extremism." Indeed, if Indonesia failed to "make corrections" in economic policy, a "social upheaval" could destroy the New Order's material achievements. He gave this warning in an interview in Jakarta on 18 May 1995, almost exactly three years before mobs of poor people would burn and loot shopping malls around the city in the violent prelude to Suharto's resignation on 21 May 1998— and Adi himself would be named minister of cooperatives in the Development Reform Cabinet appointed by President Habibie one day later.

The CIDES also had links to Ginandjar Kartasasmita, another rising star. As minister of national planning in the 1993–98 cabinet, Ginandjar had been allied with a group of ethnically indigenous—*pribumi*—entrepreneurs who were dismayed to see so many contracts and benefits accruing to their Chinese-descended—*nonpribumi*—rivals and to Suharto's family. Although as planning minister he had worked closely with the technocrats, Ginandjar differed from most of them in being a polished political operator who felt comfortable promoting himself. He also adroitly distanced himself from the technocrats in policy terms. Like Adi, he regretted that the reforms had not done more to reduce poverty, and advocated state intervention to help smaller (often *pribumi*) firms compete with bigger (mostly *nonpribumi*) ones. In May 1998 President Habibie made Ginandjar his top economic minister, while observers speculated that Ginandjar might someday become president himself.

Conclusions

From the foregoing review of the record of market-opening reform in Suharto's Indonesia, several conclusions follow.

First, despite the growth of an entrepreneurial class that might be expected to champion deregulation, the base of support for free markets was never deep enough to institutionalize the effort to achieve them. The shallowness of proreform sentiment throughout the New Order period matched widely shared doubts that free markets were really good for Indonesia—doubts evident in the views of Indonesians from Suharto on down.

The failure to institutionalize reform also reflected, of course, the New Order's top-down nature. Whether a policy had a constituency mattered less than whether Suharto supported it. In the mid-1990s, for example, then Finance Minister Mar'ie Muhammad won popularity by living simply and talking straight. But a clean image was not enough. In a loan scam revealed in 1994, the state-owned Indonesian Development Bank (Bank Pembangunan Indonesia, or Bapindo) lost twice its capital. Mar'ie wanted to liquidate the bank, but he needed Suharto's approval to do so. Bapindo employed thousands of employees. Had the bank been closed, they would have lost their jobs. Suharto refused to allow it. Bapindo became a "zombie bank"—not dead, but hardly alive.

Suharto's ambivalence toward privatization and deregulation continued to jeopardize the process of reform. Alongside the market-enhancing annual packages, their unwrapping timed to impress foreign creditors, officially facilitated rent-seeking flourished. The clove and car monopolies were instances of a general phenomenon that came to be called "KKN," for *kolusi, korupsi, nepotisme*—collusion, corruption, nepotism. Within the Suharto family, KKN spanned three generations, including the president's eldest grandson, Ari Sigit Haryo Wibowo, who was given a lucrative license to stick labels on all imported Chinese medicines.

Second, and following from the limited character of domestic support for privatization and deregulation, the pace and scope of these reforms often depended on the pressure of circumstances. In the 1980s, for example, plunging world oil prices turned stimulating the economy and raising new revenue into urgent goals, and warranted reform as a means to achieve them. In the 1990s, Indonesia's commitment to help achieve effectively tariff-free commerce within the Association of Southeast Asian Nations by 2003 reminded policymakers that trade deregulation was only a matter of time.

In a lecture on Indonesia's reforms, an architect of deregulation, Ali Wardhana, put it this way: "Economic reform is rarely if ever undertaken for its own sake. Pressures for reform generally emerge from some crisis."[26] In this context, the Indonesian economy was relatively tranquil in the decade from the fall of oil prices in the mid-1980s to the fall of the rupiah in 1997–98. Reform-fostering crises were rare. That may help to explain why Indonesia did not make more headway in making its economy more competitive. Reforms did take place, and some markets flourished. But on the eve of the devastating economic debacle of the late 1990s, when (in retrospect) the economy could least afford them, antimarket practices—KKN—were still common.

Third, for the process of reform, the dominant role of Suharto was an asset, but also a liability, and the balance of this evaluation turned increasingly negative as time went on. Whatever the ups and downs of economic reform, political deregulation was not on Suharto's agenda. Parliament was compliant. Never in the course of the New Order did its members initiate legislation. They merely approved the government's own draft laws, which were far outnumbered by presidential decrees, especially in the 1990s. Lacking autonomy, the legal system could not restrain the president. Nor did the 1945 constitution authorize significant checks and balances against executive writ.

This concentration of power in Suharto's hands was an asset to the extent that it permitted quick remedial action on the economy. Legislators, lobbyists, and judges could not, for example, stop the president from stripping the country's corrupt and dilatory customs officials of their authority to inspect shipments. And when he hired a Swiss firm in 1985 to do the job instead, he did not have to worry about a nationalist outcry against replacing Indonesians with foreigners.

---

26. Ali Wardhana, "Structural Adjustment in Indonesia," speech, Bangkok, Thailand, 25 January 1989, as cited in John Bresnan, *Managing Indonesia: The Modern Political Economy* (New York: Columbia University Press, 1993), p. 260.

But autocratic rule was also a liability that worsened over time. As the years passed, there were fewer and fewer advisers who could give the president bad news or speak frankly to him about the need for reform, especially when it came to curbing favors and subsidies enjoyed by his children's schemes, or Habibie's. In early 1996, when the president agreed to halt a plan by his grandson Ari to collect a tax on beer in Bali, some Indonesians thought Suharto had finally decided to curtail rent-seeking by his relatives. But within weeks that hope was proven forlorn when the president showed his determination to assure state backing for his son Tommy's "national" car. Presidential micromanagement was another problem. Even the fees motorists paid for using the toll roads operated by his daughter, Tutut, were approved by Suharto.

The agenda of promarket reforms was not erased. They continued to be made. It was the reforms that were not on the agenda that caused concern. Especially glaring was the near-absence of the legal and institutional improvements needed to secure, implement, and expand market-opening moves. Even if the business environment were favorable today, it could change unpredictably tomorrow. General Motors executives learned this lesson the hard way. They invested $110 million to assemble vehicles in Indonesia only to have Suharto tilt the market against them by privileging Tommy's car.

In the absence of clear and consistently applied guidelines for doing business, Indonesian-style "crony capitalism" made a kind of sense. As already noted, for example, in 1994, to attract foreign investors, the portion of a new venture that they could own was enlarged to the maximum—100 percent. Yet many prospective investors from abroad declined this chance for exclusive control. They knew the value of having a savvy and influential domestic counterpart with good connections who could navigate the still unreformed bureaucracy. It was the ability of Suharto's children to sail through this maze on the strength of their links to the most powerful Indonesian of all, their father, that made them so attractive as partners in joint ventures with foreign firms.

Since the 1970s Indonesian cabinets had included a minister for administrative reform. But not enough headway was made. Eliminating some permits to investment made the remaining ones more valuable, and hence sometimes harder and more costly to obtain. And many civil servants either ignored or undermined reforms. The president might issue a decree, but its implementation was a different and often delayed affair, especially in the regions. Suharto was concerned about such policy lags and distortions. But he cared more for political stability and political control.

It is not the goal of this chapter to speculate about the fate of market reforms inside post-Suharto Indonesia. But it may be appropriate to end on a note of caution.

It is possible that the backlash against Suharto-style "crony capitalism" will propel the reform process toward the achievement of markets that are more transparent, efficient, and impartial—productive—than before. Unfortunately, however, it is also possible that the association of market freedom with personal greed, skewed wealth, capital flight, and ethnic-Chinese dominance of the economy will be used to justify populist interventions by the state on behalf of this or that preferred group.

Certainly the calamity of 1997–98 has discredited Suharto. In mid-1998 it remained to be seen whether the crisis had undermined as well the prospect of further and more far-reaching promarket reforms that Indonesians badly needed to implement, if their economy were ever to stop shrinking and begin growing again.

Chapter 6

Conglomerates: All in the Family?

Ahmad D. Habir

When the Dutch came to the Indonesian archipelago in the seventeenth century to trade and eventually to colonize, they competed with Malay princes and merchants who had for centuries been using monsoon winds to fashion a vast network of maritime commerce. At its greatest extension, that concourse ran from the eastern shores of Africa to the China coast. Yet it could not withstand the Dutch, who made short shrift of the competition. Dutch success reflected superior technology—guns and ships—but also an unrivaled ability to accumulate and concentrate capital.

As a long-term association of people who shared in the proceeds of trade according to the amount of capital they invested in it, the Dutch United East India Company prefigured the modern limited liability corporation. In contrast, Indonesian trading contracts were one-voyage business deals between individual merchants and the captain of a cargo vessel. No joint capital formation was involved. Could these short-term arrangements have developed into an effective indigenous form of business organization? The Dutch made the question moot as they reduced once-flourishing local trading principalities to little more than pirate dens on the fringes of what would become the Netherlands Indies.

During the colonial era, the Dutch impeded the rise of indigenous entrepreneurs. Immigrant Chinese traders were encouraged to form a commercial stratum that could serve as a buffer between the Dutch ruling class at the top of colonial society and the mass of Indonesians at the bottom. In 1886 the Chinese, among other "foreign orientals," were brought under the jurisdiction of commercial laws that had previously applied only to Europeans. Being made subject to such exclusive laws raised the status of the Chinese economically and socially.

Efforts were made to modernize Chinese business practices. To facilitate debt recovery by creditors, the colonial judiciary encouraged Chinese entrepreneurs to modify and codify their traditional form of commercial association, called *kongsi*. Realizing the advantage to be gained by operating within Dutch laws, many Chinese preferred not to turn their *kongsi* into hybrids, but rushed instead to form limited liability partnerships (*naamloze vennootschappen*) along fully Dutch lines.

But in what would become a recurring pattern, a modern legal form cloaked but did not replace a customary way of doing business based on family connections and personal access to resources and information. The typical Chinese family firm remained undercapitalized. If it needed large amounts of cash, such a firm would not rely on impersonal capital markets, which were in any case undeveloped, but would seek loans from trusted shareholders who were themselves often family members. Relatives would also be appointed directors. Outsiders would be denied accurate data on profits and assets. Such practices, if they did not erase the line between company and family business, certainly blurred it.

Engines of Growth or Greed?

In the 1990s, variations on these personalistic themes could still be found in the culture of business in Indonesia, especially in press accounts of corporate scandals. Such exposés reinforced a widely held image of big firms in particular as patrimonial, corrupt, and rent-seeking. Not to mention imprudent, as chronicled in news of company failures and losses—in 1992, for example, at Bentoel, a major producer of clove cigarettes, and Mantrust, a large food enterprise.

That same year the collapse of Summa Bank, attributed largely to mismanagement appeared to endanger what was then the second biggest business group in Indonesia, Astra International. The ensuing corporate drama ended in January 1993 when the Soeryadjaya family lost control of Astra to a consortium led by Prajogo Pangestu of the timber-based Barito Pacific Group. Prajogo was one of a coterie of entrepreneurs with business connections to the family of President Suharto.

This series of spectacular corporate mishaps continued in 1994. The large, state-owned Indonesian Development Bank (Bapindo) lost $436 million when one of its clients, Eddy Tansil of the Golden Key Group, misused credits allegedly obtained with the help of government officials. The resulting trials left Tansil facing twenty years in prison. Four Bapindo directors were given jail terms ranging from four to eight years. Tansil added to his notoriety by escaping from prison and fleeing the country in 1996. A year later his whereabouts were still officially unknown.

Tansil's behavior came to symbolize the negative stereotype of ethnically Chinese businesspeople as untrustworthy, opportunistic, and even disloyal. Meanwhile, also in 1994, another Chinese-Indonesian, Robby Tjahjadi of the Kanindo Group, lost Kanindotex, a large textile maker, when he defaulted on loans totalling $380 million. Kanindotex was taken over in 1995 by a consortium headed by Johannes Kotjo, a former top executive in the largest Indonesian business empire of all, the Salim Group, led by members of the Chinese-Indonesian Salim family in tandem with Bambang Trihatmodjo, the president's middle son.

Despite such corporate misadventures, the Indonesian economy continued to grow at a rapid rate until 1997. And just as genuinely value-adding entrepreneurship facilitated that growth, so did the mismanagement and overextension illustrated by these scandals contribute to the loss of confidence that drove the rupiah and the stock market down so steeply in the latter half of that year. In this chapter I will consider these two contrasting—productive and destructive—facets of business in Indonesia.

I will focus on large-scale business groups and leaders. Major attention will not be paid to official efforts to encourage medium-sized and small enterprises—efforts already noted by Richard Borsuk in his chapter. Compared with smaller firms, the largest business groups, or conglomerates (*konglomerat*), have had far more—and more controversial—influence on economic and political conditions and trends. What these larger firms do or fail to do will also vitally affect the success or failure of efforts to overcome the managerial weaknesses implicated in the shocks of 1997–98—whether and how "crony capitalism" is reformed. Because, unlike smaller enterprises, the conglomerates mainly belong to ethnic-Chinese Indonesians, illuminating them here should also, if indirectly, shed light on the contested role of this economically key minority.

A large business group, or conglomerate, is an association of various firms operating in many sectors. Typically, such a group is owned, if not also operated, by related individuals whose cooperation is more or less based on personal trust. Observers are divided as to whether conglomerates are, in principle or in practice, good or bad for the economic betterment of poor countries such as Indonesia.

The argument in favor of such groups holds that they are well suited by structure and leadership to play constructively entrepreneurial roles: The size of the conglomerate allows its leaders to marshal and focus large sums to maximum advantage. Intersectoral flows of information between member firms improve awareness of opportunities in linked markets. Compared with smaller enterprises, business groups are more likely to be headed by aggressive empire-builders capable of daring moves, yet they are also more able to afford professional management and advice. Also, compared with smaller-firm executives, large business group leaders are in a better position to cultivate and use official connections to achieve company goals. In this positive view, much of the rapid economic growth of South Korea and Japan can be attributed to the success of the large business groups that have operated there—the *chaebol* and the *keiretsu*, respectively.

Critics of conglomerates paint a different picture: Far from representing or encouraging entrepreneurship, business groups inhibit it by dominating industries, monopolizing markets, and using political connections to forestall or defeat competition. The families that control business groups place unqualified relatives in top managerial positions, preventing skilled individuals from gaining the experience necessary to become successful entrepreneurs. Meanwhile, the conglomerates' preferential access to government contracts and licenses worsens the distribution of wealth to the detriment of efforts to reduce poverty.

These are opposing arguments. But they are linked and contained within a third view: that the development of the business group as a structure is a strategic response to an environment rife with political, economic, and legal uncertainties. From this third standpoint, if and when conditions become more certain and stable, the business group will evolve into a more professional and less personalistically managed organization. "Crony capitalism" in this light amounts to a rational response to conditions that already inhibit efficient investment and production—conditions whose diminution could allow conglomerates to play more constructive roles.

The goal of this chapter is to review and illustrate, in the context of these arguments, the nature of conglomerates in Indonesia. Particular attention will be paid to patrimonialism and professionalism as competing influences on the Indonesian business environment, historically and in relation to more recent events and trends, including the crisis of 1997–98.

Ironies of Favoritism

Entrepreneurship in Indonesia has been particularly affected by three distinct but related phenomena: nationalism, race, and patronage. In the eyes of Indonesian nationalists, the Dutch had deliberately restricted the archipelago's indigenous inhabitants to manual labor in a plantation economy, while enabling a rising inflow of Chinese immigrants and their descendants to profit, as middlemen and overseers, from colonial exploitation. The stewards of independent Indonesia were determined to reverse this legacy through industrialization sponsored by the state. Dutch businesses were nationalized. Non-Chinese (*pribumi*) Indonesians were favored with cheap credit in hopes of enlarging their economic role. Enlarged, too, were the number and size of the state-owned companies to which *pribumi* citizens could be appointed.

These strategies of nationalist "reverse discrimination" both fostered and reflected traditions of patronage in which economic and political calculations were intertwined. During the struggle for independence, and afterward, Indonesian army officers had been expected to provision their troops by raising outside revenue. To this end senior officers and businessmen, the latter often of Chinese (*nonpribumi*) descent, had formed potentially enduring partnerships.

Under the New Order the best known and most controversial of these relationships was the one between President Suharto and Liem Sioe Liong. Just as Liem, the wealthiest Indonesian of Chinese origin in the country in the 1990s, benefited economically from Suharto's political patronage, so was the president able to tap his *nonpribumi* friend's economic resources for political ends. In 1997 Liem's Salim Group was still by far the largest conglomerate in Indonesia (see Table 6.1 on pages 176–177).

References to Liem and his empire will recur in this chapter. Suffice it here to note how his relationship with Suharto illustrates the race-mediated tension between nationalism and patronage in Indonesia. Suharto's objective was never to nationalize the wealth of the Salim Group, or even to transfer a significant portion of that wealth into *pribumi* hands. For the president, it was easier and politically more productive to tap into Liem's resources without restricting his operations. One might conceivably argue that such payments served the national interest by augmenting scarce public funds, as suggested by Liem's original help in supplying Suharto's troops back in the 1950s. But the opacity of the ties between the two men, and the impression of elite-level corruption it encouraged, stoked criticism of the president for colluding with an ethnic-Chinese tycoon.

Such relationships implicated larger questions: How should the state treat its *nonpribumi* citizens? Should it discriminate in favor of the vast, poor, and mainly *pribumi* majority at the expense of this small and relatively wealthy ethnic-Chinese minority? Or should all of the nation's citizens be treated equally, regardless of racial origin? Indonesians differed as to which was the more nationalist course of action.

Arguable, too, in this context was the relationship between the nation and its largest conglomerate. If the Salim Group fit the positive case for business groups as necessary engines of market-based economic growth, then it followed that Liem was helping to make the country, at least in the aggregate, better off. But if the Salim Group illustrated the symptoms listed in the case against conglomerates—growth-hampering nepotism and corruption under inefficient and unprofessional management—then Liem and his privileged access to the president belonged at least as much to the problem of underdevelopment as to its solution.

As the New Order wore on, public sentiment seemed increasingly to weigh against the favoritism shown by the president toward particular firms, especially the Salim Group and the notoriously expanding business empires of Suharto's own children. Criticisms were seldom expressed openly, however, for fear of retribution. Initially, there was some tolerance of the success of the presidential children's undertakings, defended as evidence of desirable *pribumi* control over the economy. The force of this justification waned, however, the more blatant the favoritism toward the children's businesses became.

Meanwhile, on the larger question of how to treat *nonpribumi* Indonesians, a separate argument developed: between economic "nationalists" who wanted to lift the *pribumi* majority through positive discrimination—in American parlance, affirmative action—and the mainly neoclassical economists, called "technocrats," who preferred to grow the economy as a whole through race-blind policies geared to open competition on international markets.[1] Over the life of Suharto's regime, a consensus developed among politically minded Indonesians against the president's ties to his "cronies," including Liem among other wealthy ethnic Chinese. But the broader conflict over how to treat the *nonpribumi* minority was never resolved.

Intensifying these moral uncertainties was the practical difficulty of using the state to incubate *pribumi* capitalists who could later withstand market competition. Policies intended to provide entrepreneurial opportunities to racially "indigenous" Indonesians have backfired time and again since the achievement of unitary independence in 1950. Before that year was even over, the new republic's leaders had launched such a program. It was aimed at reversing the "double monopoly" of the colonial years whereby Dutch trading houses and ethnic-Chinese merchants had respectively controlled importing from beyond and marketing within the Indies.

The Indonesian word for fortress—*benteng*—was given to the new policy to underscore its goal of building *pribumi* entrepreneurship into an economic bastion that would allow the new nation to compete with the West and the overseas Chinese alike. The program gave selected domestic but non-Chinese businessmen exclusive rights to import certain categories of goods, along with access to start-up capital on favorable terms. However, largely because the recipients of this largesse were chosen not for their skills or experience, but rather for their personal or political links to those in charge of the program, it failed.

Indeed, more than a few of these favored would-be *pribumi* firms, upon receiving their exclusive import licenses, turned around and sold them to Indonesians of Chinese descent while pretending to retain control. Though legally owned by *pribumi,* such businesses were in fact run by *nonpribumi,* from whom the former were content to collect periodic rents in return for the political cover represented by the appearance of their usefully "indigenous" names, and signatures, on company documents.

Whose Fortress?

In these instances the so-called fortress policy wound up entrenching some of the very people it was meant to circumvent. Indeed, a few of the non-Chinese businessmen helped by the program did remain active. Among these, the Bakrie business group, owned and run by *pribumi* Indonesians, became by the 1990s the most visible example of large-scale, private-sector, domestic but non-Chinese enterprise in the country—apart from the vast business empires associated with President Suharto's children, if indeed the latter could be fairly classified as

---

1. For convenience, I will refer to these two groups without using quotation marks, but as Borsuk notes in his chapter, the terms are problematic. The nationalists' advice was not necessarily good for the nation, and the technocrats' focus was not always narrow.

Table 6.1

Twenty-five Largest Conglomerates in Indonesia (1996) by Ownership, Field, and Size

Conglomerate	Owner(s) Main	Field(s) Main	Approximate size, by		
			Sales (bl Rp)	Firms	Employees (1995)
Salim	Liem Sioe Liong F	Cem Fin Aut Foo	53,117	600	200,000
Astra International	PT Delta Mustika(Prajogo Pangestu), PT Nusamba (Bob Hasan)	Aut Agr	20,202	125	51,000
Sinar Mas	Eka Tjipta Widjaja F	Agr Woo Fin	20,191	200	75,000
Gudang Garam	Rachman Halim F	Cig	9,440	39	60,000
Lippo	Mochtar Riady F	Fin Rea	9,032	70	21,000
Bimantara P	Bambang Trihatmodjo S, Indra Rukmana S	Tra Rea	4,292	50	11,000
Gajah Tunggal	Sjamsul Nursalim F	Tir Rea Fin	4,196	80	31,000
Ongko	Kaharuddin Ongko	Rea Fin	4,183	55	8,500
Djarum	Robert and Michael Hartono F	Cig	4,032	25	51,000
Rodamas	Tan Siong Kie F	Che	3,969	40	26,000
Nusamba	Bob Hasan, Sigit Harjojudanto S	Woo Agr	3,893	90	27,500
Kalbe	F. Bing Haryanto	Pha Rea	3,660	60	7,400
Dharmala	Soehargo Gondokusumo	Agr Rea	3,426	130	1,200
Argo Manunggal	The Ning King	Tex	3,360	54	22,000

Company	Owner	Business			
Barito Pacific	Prajogo Pangestu	Woo	92	2,869	34,750
Maspion	Alim Husein	Hou	35	2,458	14,500
Bakrie P	Bakrie F	Ste Agr	76	2,449	7,800
Humpuss P	Hutomo Mandala Putra S	Oil Ton Che	40	2,324	1,625
Danamon	Usman Admadjaja	Fin	33	2,323	1,200
Cipta Cakra Murdaya	Murdaya Widyawimarta Foo	Ele Ecs	32	2,254	25,000
Panin	Mu'min Ali Gunawan	Fin	50	2,225	48,000
Jan Darmadi	Jan Darmadi	Rea	12	2,115	11,540
Pembangunan Jaya	Jakarta Gov't, Ciputra, Sukrisman, E. Samolo	Rea	37	2,091	4,600
Sampurna	Putera Sampurna	Cig	14	1,969	19,470
Raja Garuda Mas	Sukanto Tanoto	Woo Tex Fin	33	1,783	14,900
Totals			2,072	171,853	775,985

Notes: bl RP = billions of rupiah; F = family-owned business; p = business wholly or mainly owned by *pribumi* (rather than ethnic Chinese) Indonesians; S = person related to then-president Suharto by blood or marriage; Agr = agroindustry/plantations; Aut = automotive (excl. tires); Cem = cement; Che = chemicals; Cig = cigarettes; Ele = electricity; Ecs = electronics; Fin = finance; Foo = food; Hou = household goods; Oil = oil/oil products; Pha = pharmaceuticals; Rea = real estate/construction; Ste = steel; Tex = textiles; Tir = tires; Ton = transportation/ shipping; Tra = trading; Wood = wood/wood products.

Source: Warta Ekonomi (Economic Report), 9:27 (24 November 1997), p. 32; Warta Ekonomi, 7:25 (25 November 1996), pp. 36–37 [employees].

belonging to the private sector. On balance, however, the *benteng* policy entrenched the system it was meant to change.

There was irony, too, in the results of the nationalization of Dutch businesses in 1958. For the first time a sizeable chunk of the economy was in the *pribumi* hands of the state. But again the experiment largely failed. Not only did many of these enterprises fall victim to combinations of unskilled managers, rent-seeking officials, and the economic turbulence and decline that beset the economy in the early-to-mid-1960s. It was also the *nonpribumi* entrepreneurs who were best positioned, by talent, experience, and resources, to fill the economic void created when the Dutch were expelled, and later to take advantage of the opportunities created by the New Order.

Many of these opportunities flowed from the adoption of liberal foreign and domestic investment laws in 1967 and 1968, respectively. Foreign firms in joint ventures with domestic partners, along with strictly domestic companies, began producing a wide range of consumer goods for home consumption or export. Most of these domestic partners and firms were owned and run by Chinese Indonesians. Low tax rates and easy access to credit, along with still high tariffs against competing imports, encouraged *nonpribumi* companies to move beyond their traditional focus on trade and explore opportunities in manufacturing—a trend that the national shift from hydrocarbons to light industry in the 1980s would accelerate.

The typical foreign investors seeking local partners preferred ethnic-Chinese businessmen for several reasons. *Nonpribumi* entrepreneurs were intimately familiar with Indonesian conditions, knew how to operate within them, and brought to the relationship up-and-running networks of funding and distribution to which they were connected by ties of kinship, friendship, and experience. Of particular value among such connections were those that converged on the first family: President Suharto, his late wife Siti Hartini, and their children, as the latter grew older and began establishing themselves as key business players.

It was during these early years of the new regime—the late 1960s and early 1970s—that Suharto's long-standing Chinese-Indonesian business partner, Liem Sioe Liong, began the ascent that would lead to the formation of the Salim Group.[2] Business relationships strengthened during this period also sped the rise of another *nonpribumi* magnate, William Soeryadjaya, the founder of another prominent conglomerate, Astra. In return for facilitating the growth of

---

2. The precursor of the Salim Group was PT Waringin, a trading company that had been granted lucrative official licenses to export primary commodities. Liem Sioe Liong, Liem Oen Kian (also known by his "Indonesianized" name, Djuhar Sutanto), Sudwikatmono (Suharto's cousin), and Ibrahim Risyad had incorporated the firm in 1968. They became the core owners of a growing collection of companies that would eventually be called the Salim Group. Yuri Sato, "The Salim Group in Indonesia: The Development and Behavior of the Largest Conglomerate in Southeast Asia," *The Developing Economies,* 31:4 (December 1993), pp. 428–429.

such enterprises, President Suharto and his family felt free to exact informal rents. Many of these payments were channeled into "foundations" where they could be put to a range of uses, from coopting potential opponents to making charitable contributions.

Chinese-Indonesian tycoons were by no means the only source of extra-budgetary income available to the New Order. State enterprises and trade barriers, for example, were also used to generate such funds. Accessible, in principle, were portions of the revenues of state companies—firms whose boards were reserved for non-Chinese Indonesians to showcase *pribumi* achievement—while impediments to commerce could be selectively removed in return for a share of the resulting rents.

The Enterprising State

In the 1970s the state oil and gas company, Pertamina, became the regime's most prominent source of off-budget funds. At its zenith early in 1975, having benefited from soaring global oil prices, Pertamina was said to be the largest Asian corporation outside Japan. The company's operations at the time included 7 oil refineries, a network of 2,680 domestic gasoline stations, and 29 joint-ventures and subsidiaries. Buoyant oil prices had led the company well beyond hydrocarbons into a wide variety of activities. These ranged from providing insurance to buying or building if not also operating infrastructure—from tanker fleets, an airline, hotels, and roads to high-tech hospitals and fertilizer plants.[3]

It is not possible to know for certain the sizes and destinations of informal transfers from Pertamina's coffers into the hands of the state. One may surmise, nevertheless, that the armed forces ranked high among the recipients of such payments. Such informal funding would have lessened the effect of formal cutbacks in military spending that were needed to persuade foreign donors of the New Order's commitment to development.

During its heyday, Pertamina was held up as a model of indigenous entrepreneurship. It was said to illustrate an Indonesian adaptation of large-scale enterprise as practiced in Japan, whose business groups had expanded beyond any one sector and thus enlarged their contribution to national welfare. Officials pointed to Pertamina as evidence for the case in favor of using the state to accumulate capital for economic growth. As a counterweight to ethnic-Chinese family firms on the one hand and Western-held multinational corporations on the other, Pertamina satisfied the self-styled nationalists among *pribumi* Indonesians.

Their satisfaction was short-lived. Later in 1975, under the weight of unpayable debts, Pertamina's viability and standing crumbled. So did the plausibility

---

3. John Bresnan, *Managing Indonesia: The Modern Political Economy* (New York: Columbia University Press, 1993), p. 171.

of the argument that Indonesia could be lifted from poverty by an expansionary state. But it was not until the collapse of world oil and gas prices in the early 1980s that deregulation began in earnest. And before that precipitous fall in hydrocarbon prices, oil and gas revenues continue to buoy the economy, keeping the nationalist—state-expansionist—option alive.

Having quadrupled in the mid-1970s, hydrocarbon prices doubled again toward the end of the decade. The resulting windfalls to the state encouraged the government to establish and protect state-owned or state-influenced enterprises in the hope that they could produce for domestic consumption goods that were still being bought from abroad. A maze of regulations kept this strategy in place. The executives who benefited most from these conditions were not economic entrepreneurs. They were people with political and personal influence and skills. The use of such informal assets enabled these elites to comply only with those regulations that served their own interests, while ignoring those that did not—or lobbying the bureaucracy for dispensations.

The logic of import substitution led to the formation of state enterprises that could stake out upstream positions in a variety of production sequences and thus capture the costs of inputs and components previously bought abroad. Industrial activities chosen for such treatment ranged from processing natural resources to making machines. A few high-technology industries, such as aircraft, were also targeted. Capital-intensive state companies such as Krakatau Steel and the petrochemical plants of Pertamina, it was hoped, would use their state funding to wrest control of the upstream from foreigners and take over the business of supplying intermediate goods downstream to the mostly private companies—domestic firms operating alone or in joint ventures with foreigners—that would make finished products for distribution and sale.

The enlarged state sector spawned by this strategy was seen by nationalistic Indonesians as evidence of the prowess of the vast *pribumi* majority. But, as already noted, the actual performance of these state-funded entrepreneurs sorely disappointed such expectations. Bad management and red tape, arrogance and corruption, and a lack of capital available for productive use combined to erode faith in the state as the locomotive of economic growth. If the Pertamina crisis began this process of disillusion in the mid-1970s, the collapse of hydrocarbon prices in the early 1980s finally brought it to fruition in the incremental deregulation of the economy that got underway in the latter decade.

Not all of the beneficiaries of the oil years failed to survive. Just as Liem and Soeryadjaya had been able to parlay their associations with the regime in the late 1960s and early 1970s into successful ongoing positions, so did the oil boom leave its own business legacy in the form of entrepreneurs and companies that had managed to use state access and protection to establish themselves. Cases in point were the textile and automobile-assembly industries, including firms such as Argo Manunggal, Sinar Sahabat, and Texmaco in textiles, and Astra, Indomobil, and Krama Yudha in automobiles. Of these six companies, the ownership of only one was unquestionably *pribumi*. That was Krama Yudha, which assembled and distributed Japanese (Mitsubishi) cars. Of the other five firms, Texmaco was owned by an Indonesian of Indian ancestry, Marimutu Sinivasan, while the rest belonged to ethnically Chinese entrepreneurs, namely, Soeryadjaya (Astra), Liem (Indomobil), The Ning King (Argo Manunggal), and Sukanta Tanudjaja (Sinar Sahabat).

These were, of course, not the only Chinese-Indonesian figures and firms to have been strengthened by boom-time patronage. Others included long-time Suharto confidante Mohamad ("Bob") Hasan and the Dharmala Group. To the extent that there were far fewer *pribumi* companies rising to prominence during this period, as an experiment in affirmative action the import substitution strategy did not succeed.

Professionals in Demand

In the 1980s, declining oil prices and the accompanying recession stimulated the professionalization of business management in Indonesia. The government was forced to begin a deregulatory drive that would make the economy less dependent on hydrocarbons and more competitive in the global marketplace. Budgetary constraints, the proven inefficiency of the public sector, and the reformist advice of the technocrats, described by Anne Booth and Richard Borsuk in this book, combined to reorient the state toward relying on private-sector entrepreneurs to lead the new export drive. As Booth and Borsuk also recount, steps were taken to lessen the protection and regulation that had previously hampered market-minded, but poorly connected, entrepreneurs.

As they moved into their new roles in the less indulgent climate they faced "after oil," private-sector companies felt the need to professionalize their management and operations. Professionalization meant recruiting, promoting, and relying more on executives with market-based expertise and skills who could be used to improve firm efficiency. And that meant relying less on an older generation of well-connected moguls whose success had involved using personal or family ties to obtain state favors. Indonesians themselves sometimes distinguished these types as "market-minded" and "patronage-minded businesspeople"—respectively, *pengusaha pasar* and *pengusaha fasilitas*.

But if market-sensitive executives were to be hired, they would have to be trained, and if professional expertise were to be used, it would have to be acquired. Accordingly, in the wake of the oil bust, a number of more or less private entrepreneurs supported the establishment of institutes where management as a professional discipline could be taught and researched. Indonesia's first master's degree in business administration (MBA) was offered by the "Noble Vow" Management Institute (Institut Manajemen Prasetya Mulya, or IMPM) in 1982. And competing MBA degrees were soon available—at the Indonesian Institute for Management Development (Institut Pengembangan Manajemen Indonesia, or IPMI) in 1984, and the Institute for Management Education and Development (Institut Pendidikan dan Pembinaan Manajemen, or IPPM) a year later.

While much of the impetus and financing of these bodies came from the private sector, their founders were by no means all market-minded professionals. *Pengusaha pasar* and *pengusaha fasilitas* were overlapping and porous categories. Men who had succeeded, thanks to political patrons such as Suharto, were hardly insensitive to market opportunities and risks. When budget austerities made the shift to more professional management more rational, many of these entrepreneurs were willing and able to reposition themselves. Nor were state officials ignorant of the need for professionalization; support for IMPM, IPMI, and IPPM, therefore, was diverse.

Indeed, taken together, these institutes formed a virtual microcosm of Indonesian political economy. The oldest of the three, IMPM, reflected the dominant presence of *nonpribumi* Indonesians in the private sector. Behind IMPM stood the "Noble Vow" Foundation (Yayasan Prasetya Mulya, or YPM), which used the new body to strengthen the philanthropic, nation-benefiting image that it wished to project to the larger community—an image implicit in the reference to a "noble vow."

Its desire to be seen as altruistic did not, however, keep YPM from wheeling and dealing. In the 1990s, for example, following the collapse of Summa Bank, YPM helped a consortium of prominent businessmen, led by Prajogo Pangestu of the Barito Pacific Group, gain control of Astra. The foundation's benefactors included many of the wealthiest Chinese Indonesian entrepreneurs: men such as Liem Sioe Liong, William Soeryadjaya, The Ning King, and Sofyan Wanandi. Sofyan (previously known as Liem Bian Koen) headed the Gemala Group, while his brother Jusuf Wanandi (once Liem Bian Kie) led an influential think tank, the Centre for Strategic and International Studies (CSIS). In 1997 both men retained these affiliations while continuing to serve on the boards of IMPM.

The second management institute to offer an MBA was IPMI. Its founders were *pribumi* entrepreneurs with backgrounds in academic and public service: Siswanto Sudomo, an academic-turned-businessman, and Bustanil Arifin, junior minister for cooperatives at the time. Sumitro Djojohadikusumo chaired IPMI's board of advisers. A prominent economist, businessman, and former cabinet member, Sumitro was sometimes called "the father of the technocrats" for having founded the faculty of economics at the University of Indonesia back in the 1960s. (Of Sumitro's sons, Hashim Djojohadikusumo went into business, while Prabowo Subianto married President Suharto's middle daughter Siti ["Titiek"] Hediati Harijadi and became a high-ranking army officer.) Other prominent figures on IPMI's advisory board included Aburizal ("Ical") Bakrie of the Bakrie Group; Tanri Abeng, who in the 1980s headed Multi Bintang, a joint venture with the Heineken brewing company; and the chief executive officers of Mobil Oil, British Petroleum, and several other foreign firms. Its willingness to involve a mix of public figures and domestic and foreign entrepreneurs distinguished IPMI from the other two management institutes.

The oldest of the three institutes was IPPM, born under a different name at the very beginning of the New Order in 1967, and it, too, was distinctive in composition and outlook. It was founded by A.M. Kadarman, a Jesuit priest and dean of the economics faculty at the Sanata Dharma Teacher Training College in Yogyakarta. T.B. Simatupang, formerly chief of staff of Indonesia's armed forces and in 1967 chairman of the Indonesian Council of Churches, served as the first chairman of IPPM's Foundation.

Just as, later, the *nonpribumi* YPM and IPMI would stress their commitment to helping the Indonesian nation by encouraging professional management, so did its association with another influential minority, Indonesian Christians, lead IPPM self-consciously to develop its identity as a national institution serving a national clientele. By the same token, but in reverse, the racially and religiously majoritarian origins and make-up of IPMI—in effect, the security of its national identity—made it somewhat easier for its leaders to commit the institute to an international outlook, by enlisting the help of foreigners, including multinational corporations, and by using English as the medium of instruction. The last was considered a radical step, since the New Order did not allow anything but the national language (*bahasa Indonesia*) to be used as a vehicle of instruction in public education.

Despite initial skepticism, the three institutes quickly earned good reputations and stimulated further demand for professional training. To meet that demand, other management schools were started, public as well as private. Even then, the demand for MBAs exceeded the supply, as the economy's "post-oil" recovery was driven increasingly by export-manufacturing industries whose owners knew they had to improve efficiency and productivity to survive, let alone prosper, in the less forgiving new world of globalized trade.

Deregulation and the Rise of Conglomerates

Steps to deregulate the economy in the 1980s were meant to invigorate the private sector and help its companies mobilize funds for productive use. The lifting of restrictions on the Jakarta Stock Exchange (JSX) galvanized that moribund institution. Other reforms stimulated a proliferation of new banks, many of them sponsored by large business groups. Established banks were encouraged to open new branches. Heightened competition for deposits enlarged the pool of funds available for investment. But the going was not smooth. Domestic companies confronted a widening range of bottlenecks and risks, including weak infrastucture, especially in electricity and telecommunications, and stock market volatility.

In 1991, for example, the JSX fell proportionally lower than any major exchange in the world. In that year the government shifted to a tight money policy to cool down the overheating economy. Businesses that had overexpanded during the boom times of the late 1980s suddenly faced very different conditions.

In the business community, these trends and events reinforced the need for qualified, market-minded executives. To become more efficient while managing their rapid expansion in periods of faster economic growth, business groups needed the ability to decentralize authority without inhibiting coordination. They also needed professionals who could make the tough decisions needed to survive capital shortages and market downturns. Family-run firms were ill suited to such tasks. Increasing competition on a wider, even global scale, together with a gradually shrinking role for the state under deregulation, called for strategies of management beyond merely lobbying the bureaucracy. Finally, as capital-hungry firms "went public," that is, made their shares available for purchase and sale on the JSX, disclosure requirements associated with being listed subjected such companies to unprecedented public scrutiny. And that, too, furthered professionalization.

But the upsurge in private business activity and the number of companies engaged in it were not merely a response to deregulation, as if the economy were a faucet and removing the stopper of government had released a pent-up stream of entrepreneurship. The state was also in part proactively responsible for the flourishing of private business. Many of the new firms that arose in the 1980s and 1990s dated their inception from the promise of a concession or a project obtained from the government or with the help of an official patron. With that commitment in hand, the new entrepreneur could establish a limited liability company, a legal step required of bidders on government contracts and needed to obtain bank loans. At least until the crisis of 1997–98, the government was still the largest purchaser of goods and services in Indonesia, and government contracts remained an important stimulus to enterprise.

Government regulation spurred the private sector in other ways as well. To illustrate: According to Indonesian law, a company's articles of incorporation must state the nature of its business, and separate companies must be established for different business activities. Consider the hypothetical case of a company whose founder had, at the time of its incorporation, stated narrowly its field of operation. Should he or his (rarely she or her) successors have decided to expand into an entirely different field, they would have had to form a brand-new company focused on that new activity. This applied even to closely related fields. Within a single overarching timber business, for instance, one firm would be responsible for felling trees, another for processing them, and a third for marketing the resulting wood products.

By discouraging vertical integration within a single company, government regulations encouraged the formation of many companies and their association in large business groups. In 1996, for example, as Table 6.1 shows, the 25 largest *konglomerat* accounted for more than 2,000 different firms. Whatever its managerial benefits for the companies themselves, the resulting dispersion of authority made it harder to implicate the heads of conglomerates in incidents that resulted in damage to public welfare. While a more concentrated pattern might have opened business groups to even greater criticism on antitrust grounds, the practice of spinning off companies for particular niches made it easier, for example, for timber business group owners to avoid responsibility for the land-clearing fires that caused the vast pall of smoke that blighted Singapore and parts of Indonesia and Malaysia in 1997.

As shown, Indonesia's conglomerates had antecedents dating back to the 1950s. Yet it was not until the late 1980s that business groups became a topic of intense and widespread public discussion. The media played a key role in making them more visible. Major press attention was paid, for instance, to an official list of 150 Indonesians who were given awards for paying the most in taxes. The authorities had released the list of awardees to promote faith in the fairness of a new economic reform whereby individuals would be required to assess their own tax liability. But the reading public apparently was more impressed with the identity and sheer wealth of these tycoons than with their compliance with the law. And the list was dominated by owners of conglomerates: Liem of the Salim Group, Soeryadjaya of Astra, Rachman Halim of the clove cigarette manufacturer Gudang Garam, and many others. In 1989 the leading Indonesian business weekly, *Warta Ekonomi* (*Economic Report*), further stimulated public discussion of business groups by ranking and reviewing forty of the biggest ones.[4] Soon expanded to 200 such groups and issued annually, the list helped to keep conglomerates in the public eye.

Much of the discourse that resulted from such publicity was critical of the *konglomerat* because of the official favors that had enabled them to grow so large. An especially frequent target was the flour-milling monopoly enjoyed by PT Bogasari Flour Mill. Part of the Salim Group, Bogasari had been established in 1970 by Liem Sioe Liong in partnership with President Suharto's cousin and adoptive brother, Sudwikatmono, to whose parents' care Suharto had been entrusted as a child. Bogasari's articles of incorporation provided, in effect, that 26 percent of the company's profit—amended to 20 percent in 1977—would be channeled into two ostensibly charitable bodies: the "Our Hope" and "Princely Duty" Foundations (Yayasan Harapan Kita and Yayasan Dharma Putra), respectively headed by Mrs. Suharto and belonging to the Army Strategic Reserve Command.[5]

Many in the country's emerging middle class felt that Bogasari's monopoly was unfair. Some wanted antitrust legislation to level the playing field for smaller firms. There was a perception that conglomerates such as the Salim Group had grown and prospered not because of their ingenuity in exploring new markets and meeting consumer demand, but thanks to political backing and favoritism. Such skepticism was intensified by the close association that several of these conglomerates enjoyed with the first family. *Warta Ekonomi* was careful to acknowledge that President Suharto had defended business groups as a national

---

4. "40 Konglomerat Indonesia" ["40 Indonesian Conglomerates"], *Warta Ekonomi*, 5:5 (31 July 1989).

5. *Berita Tambahan Negara Perseroan Terbatas* [*Supplementary State Gazette Register of Limited Liability Companies*] No. 258 (1970), as cited and updated by Sato, "Salim Group," p. 437.

resource available for use in the national interest.[6] But more than a few of the magazine's readers must have wondered whether conglomerates belonged more to the problem of Indonesia's "high-cost economy" than to its solution.

That said, these business empires were diverse in nature. Many of them were family-owned, but a number of them had already begun to sell minority shares in Indonesia's emerging capital market. Others had family ties but were run collegially by unrelated persons. An example of the latter was the Bimantara Group, led by the president's second son, Bambang Trihatmodjo. Bambang's brother-in-law Indra Rukmana, who had married the eldest Suharto daughter Tutut, was among the group's owners. But they also included two of Bambang's friends from school days, Aling Tachril and Rosano Barack, both of whom were actively involved in running the group, and even a professional manager, Peter Gontha, who had worked for American Express in Jakarta.

If relationships within *konglomerat* were often complex, so were the connections between them. Sometimes, for example, a pair of groups would collaborate in forming new ventures, even new groups, and the same group might be involved with different partners in several such launchings. Illustrations of this pattern included Sinar Mas Inti Perkasa, a venture between the Sinar Mas and Humpuss Groups—Suharto's youngest son, Hutomo ("Tommy") Mandala Putra, headed Humpuss—and the Sadang Mas Group, also created by Sinar Mas but this time in collaboration with the Salim Group.[7]

Finally, a number of these business groups had begun to expand their activities overseas by making investments in other countries. Examples of these included the Salim, Sinar Mas, and Dharmala Groups. This made it possible for Indonesians to feel proud that Indonesian companies had grown strong enough to take on the world, leaving aside their *nonpribumi* character. But such expansion was also grist for the mill of self-described nationalist critics who interpreted outward investment as capital flight and concluded that for all the time they had spent in the archipelago and the profits they had gained there, Liem and his fellow ethnic-Chinese tycoons were still not loyal to Indonesia.

It may be helpful now to discuss some of the characteristics and activities of the *konglomerat* in the 1990s, using the annual ranking and review of such groups in *Warta Ekonomi* since 1990.[8]

---

6. "40 Konglomerat," p. 71.

7. The often florid or acronymic names of conglomerates are not easily translated. Sinar Mas Inti Perkasa, for instance, might be rendered "The Golden-Gleaming Essence of Bravery." Salim is the "indigenously Indonesian"-sounding family name taken by Liem Sioe Liong.

8. In issues dated 11 February 1991, 27 April 1992, 3 May 1993, 25 April 1994, 24 April 1995, 25 November 1996, and 24 November 1997, *Warta Ekonomi* ranked the two hundred largest groups by size based on gross revenue in the previous year. While questions of reliability make it advisable to treat these data as inexact, they can be used, as in the next section, to suggest the rough sizes and relative positions of different firms.

Conglomerates in 1990–96

The many dimensions along which business groups in New Order Indonesia may be compared include their relative size, the sectors where they were active, their debts and roles in banking, the extent to which they were owned or run by families, and their attraction to markets overseas.

Sizes and Sectors

Taken as a whole, the largest business groups were a massive presence in the Indonesian economy prior to the crash of 1997–98. Indonesia's national budget for FY 1991–92 amounted to about half of the gross revenues from sales earned by the top two hundred firms in 1990, and exceeded by only a third the sales of the top ten.

The conglomerates were thus doubly concentrated: They did not just represent a major clustering of capital within the larger economy. Compared with each other, the very biggest groups were much bigger than those lower down on *Warta Ekonomi*'s list. The largest conglomerate of all, the Salim Group, epitomized this second inequality. In 1996 the Salim Group's estimated sales of 53 trillion rupiah (Rp) more than doubled the Rp 20 trillion reportedly taken in by the second largest group, Astra—and amounted to nearly a third of the total Rp 172 trillion in sales that the largest twenty-five business groups together were thought to have earned that year. In contrast, in the same year the twenty-fifth largest conglomerate, Raja Garuda Mas, had sales merely 3 percent of those achieved by Liem Sioe Liong's top-ranked conglomerate (see Table 6.1).

The typically multisectoral character of large business groups makes categorizing their activities difficult. Instructive nonetheless are *Warta Ekonomi*'s annual classification of conglomerates by the fields in which they conducted most of their operations. In 1996, for example, the twenty-five largest groups were active in a major way in up to four different fields, and the inclusion of lesser specializations would have made this diversity even more striking. Also worth noting is the fact that despite the shifting of the economy in the 1980s from extracting oil and gas to making products, the highest concentrations of the largest businesses in 1996 occurred in sectors that did not directly involve manufacturing at all.

These fields were real estate (including construction), with eight conglomerates, and finance with seven (see Table 6.1). Most of the multisectoral conglomerates had major positions in one or both of these two services. Looking back with the advantage of hindsight, one could interpret this pattern as an omen of misfortune to come. For arguably compared with most of the seventeen other major fields represented among the top conglomerates in 1996, real estate and finance were more likely to attract manipulation and speculation—that is, to help swell the bubble of favoritism and borrowing that would burst so devastatingly in 1997.

Debts and Banks

If the severity of the 1997–98 crisis was unprecedented, the bad loans and excessive debts that contributed to it were not. These earlier mishaps implicated more than a few conglomerates. The reckless overextension of Bentoel and Mantrust in the early 1990s has already been noted, and they were not the only large firms with unsustainably high ratios of debt to equity. Other victims of financial imprudence included, for example, the Asia Permai and Tigamas Groups under Mohammad Amid and Soebagio Wirjoatmodjo, respectively.

Except for Tigamas, these were Chinese Indonesian groups. Clearly their penchant for overexpansion got them into trouble. But the sheer frequency of ethnic-Chinese-owned conglomerates in the rankings of conglomerates also made it more likely that they, rather than *pribumi* groups, would become associated with imprudence. Entrepreneurs of "indigenous" descent were far from immune to the temptations of easy growth. Soebagio Wirjoatmodjo, for example, had made a name for himself as one of the top *pribumi* professional managers in the Astra Group. But when he struck out on his own, he could not maintain that reputation.

Reference has already been made to the Summa-Astra and Bapindo-Golden Key scandals, whose extensive coverage in the media built public support for the argument that conglomerates were more a cause of underdevelopment in Indonesia than a way to overcome it. Borrowers and lenders, protection and corruption, and officials and families were all in various ways implicated in these fiascos.

The core business of Astra was its joint venture with Toyota. This arrangement was hardly exposed to market forces, protected as it was by high tariffs against imported cars. Yet Astra under William Soeryadjaya was reputed to be one of the most professionally managed business groups. Astra had become strong enough, and willing enough, to provide information about itself—to go public. The fact that it was known as a nurturing ground for *pribumi* professional managers spoke well of its nondiscriminatory recruitment policy.

What brought down William Soeryadjaya was the collapse of the Summa Bank, owned and mismanaged by his eldest son, Edward. In the end, selling his shares in Astra became the only way that the elder Soeryadjaya could bail out the younger one. All the same, the father was left with enough to start a new business group, Suryaraya. And because of the buffering layers of professional managers that the elder Soeryadjaya had developed in Astra, that group was not particularly affected by the change in shareholding. As already discussed, mismanagement including collusion and corruption brought down Golden Key, whose founder Eddy Tansil had decided to extend his conglomerate from its retailing base into petrochemicals.

Conglomerates enjoyed access to state funds much more than smaller businesses. Reportedly in 1994 some four-fifths of all bank credit, most of it from state banks, went to business groups.[9] Many of these loans were intended to fund megaprojects, whether to improve the country's infrastructure or to facilitate the conglomerates' expansion upstream into the production of various industrial inputs. Among such megaprojects in 1988–94, 146 were domestic while 57 entailed joint ventures with foreigners. These two sets of endeavors absorbed 29 and 41 percent of all domestic and foreign investment, respectively, over the period. Conglomerates accounted for a striking 79 percent of all 203 such projects. And among these favored groups, family-owned enterprises were especially common. The Salim business dynasty, for example, had the largest investment, in 23 projects, followed by groups controlled by the sons and daughters of President Suharto.

Nor had all of these loans been made using purely economic criteria. Conglomerates bore at least partial responsibility for an estimated 80 to 85 percent of the officially recorded Rp 87.9 trillion worth of bad loans outstanding in 1994. And such firms continued to borrow from Indonesia's developing capital market, not only to retire debt or strengthen equity, but also to obtain collateral that could be used to obtain more loans for a variety of purposes. At the same time, compared with state banks, private banks and financial instruments, including bonds of varying quality and floating-rate notes, became increasingly important sources of capital. Again, with hindsight's advantage, one could argue that this frenzy of financing, whose participants tended to assume exchange-rate stability, or at least a predictably gradual depreciation of the rupiah, helped set the larger economy up for the precipitous fall it would experience when confidence in the rupiah evaporated in 1997.

Families and Markets

Not all families are equal in the world of Indonesian business. It was not just the tendency for conglomerates to be owned by Chinese Indonesian families that made such enterprises so controversial. It was also, and particularly, the proliferation and expansion of businesses owned by the families of current and former high government officials. On *Warta Ekonomi*'s annual listing of conglomerates in 1996, for example, elite families were common. In the eyes of a growing number of Indonesians, this trend seemed unfair. It appeared to reinforce political with economic power and vice versa, at the expense of ordinary firms and people.

Among the most controversial of these cases were the five business groups owned by the president's children. In 1997, these conglomerates and the Suhartos to whom they belonged were: Bimantara (Bambang Trihatmodjo), Citra Lamtoro Gung (Siti Hardiyanti ["Tutut"] Rukmana), Humpuss (Hutomo ["Tommy"]

---

9. "Mari Mengaudit Konglomerat Kita" ["Let's Audit Our Conglomerates"], *Swasembada* [*Self-Supporting*], 10:12 (March 1995), p. 14.

Mandala Putra), Arseto (Sigit Harjojudanto) and Datam/Maharani (Siti Hediati Harijadi ["Titiek"] Prabowo).

But these were by no means the only instances of official families-in-business. Other such business groups with family ties to the state in 1997 included: Timsco under Sujatim Abdurachman Habibie, younger brother of State Minister of Research and Technology B.J. Habibie (who would replace Suharto as president the following year); Ifas under Isfan Fajar Satrio, son of Vice President Try Sutrisno; Garama under the children of Coordinating Minister for Production and Distribution Hartarto; Manggala under Tantyo Sudharmono, son of former vice president Soedharmono; Perwira Panagan Ratu under the children of former coordinating minister for welfare Alamsjah Ratuprawiranegara; Citra Sari Makmur under the children of former minister of cooperatives Bustanil Arifin; Nugra Santana under Pontjo Sutowo and Aditarina under Endang Utari Mokodompit, respectively, son and daughter of former head of Pertamina Ibnu Sutowo; Era Persada and Tirtamas Majutama under Hashim Djojohadikusumo, son of the economist and former minister Sumitro Djojohadikusumo; Kariza under the children of another technocrat and former minister, Radius Prawiro; Kresna under Bambang Riady Soegomo, son of a former chief of state intelligence; and Kuningan Persada under Bambang Atmanto Wiyogo, son of a former governor of Jakarta, in partnership with several other men including Suharto's cousin Sudwikatmono.

According to *Warta Ekonomi,* families owned and managed most of the top two hundred business groups in Indonesia in 1992. But as the decade wore on, three kinds of restructuring altered somewhat the roles of families in business groups: the separation of ownership from management, the consolidation of similar or overlapping subunits, and the selling of shares on the JSX. Most of the largest firms initiated at least one of these reforms, and many tried all of them.

These steps were not unique to *nonpribumi* firms. Bakrie, for example, adopted all three reform measures. By their nature, separation, consolidation, and capitalization were mutually inducing. In the 1990s, among all family-owned firms, those listed on the JSX were much less likely to be family-managed as well. This was so in part because the reporting and other requirements of being listed were best met by professionals, including trained accountants. And those same professionals, given managerial responsibility, were more likely to press for consolidation of subunits that might originally have been created as sinecures for family members.

Historically in Indonesia, a family's control over a large business has tended to weaken over time as the firm's assets have been thinned out over successive generations of heirs. In the 1990s conglomerates handled this difficulty in different ways. Some founders ignored the problem and divided their businesses among their children anyway, or at least saw to it that each child had a company to run. Examples of these included Eka Tjipta Widjaja (Sinar Mas) and Chandra Djojonegoro (ABC). Some divided the business among their children but ensured that its assets would stay together by precluding their sale to outsiders. Mangaraja Haolanan Hutagulung did this for his firm, Arion Paranita. Another pattern was to choose only one son to head the entire group. The Gobel and Krama Yudha Groups took this route. Among firms that went public, some avoided losing control by making only a small portion of their shares available for sale to strangers on the JSX. These illustrations occurred in 1994, but their range was typical for most of the decade prior to 1997.

Internationalization

A final noteworthy trend in the mid-1990s was internationalization. This occurred in an outward direction, as Lippo, Salim, and Sinar Mas and a growing number of other conglomerates invested in assets abroad. It also took place inwardly, as Indosat, Raja Garuda Mas, and Sinar Mas, for example, were listed on the New York Stock Exchange. Also listed there, beginning in 1995, was Tri Polyta Indonesia, a chemical firm owned jointly by Bimantara, Barito, Napan, and Sudwikatmono.

However, internationalization in the sense of producing goods and services for export was not so high on the agendas of the conglomerates as one might have thought. As already noted, in the mid-1990s the largest business groups were less likely to be making goods for sale abroad than dealing in real estate or making loans inside Indonesia. The retailers Hero and Matahari—chains of supermarkets and department stores, respectively—were just two of the many firms catering to domestic markets. It was encouraging that Indonesia had developed a middle class large enough to warrant such businesses. Yet the extent to which conglomerates were not in world markets selling goods, and thus competing for needed foreign exchange, was one more reason to question their contribution to the country as a whole.

By the mid-1990s conglomerates in Indonesia were receiving deservedly mixed reviews. The public could take pride in the size of these groups and the scope of their operations, including the goods, services, and jobs they provided. But their scandals, their often excessive debts, and the incomplete nature of their professionalization were causes for concern. Such concern intensified, at least in retrospect, when the economy nose-dived in 1997.

Reform and Retrenchment

Notwithstanding the focus of this chapter on large conglomerates in the private sector, as late as the mid-1990s state enterprises still accounted for an even larger portion of the Indonesian economy. The total assets of the top three hundred business groups burgeoned from 1988 to 1995, both absolutely and as a percentage of the total assets of state firms. Yet in the latter year state-enterprise assets still slightly exceeded in total value those of the conglomerates.[10]

---

10. Based on a survey by the Indonesian Center for Business Data reported in "Mari Mengaudit," p. 15.

And if business groups were controversial, so were their counterparts in the public sector. Similar charges were directed toward both sorts of firms. But if conglomerates were especially vulnerable to charges of corruption, notably by profiting from official favors, state enterprises were more likely to be criticized for inefficiency—or squandering public funds by failing to become profitable at all. And if the first critique was popular among nationalists, including those—often Muslims—who resented the *nonpribumi* ownership of many conglomerates, the second was more likely to come from the technocrats and other believers in efficiency and in smaller, or at any rate more responsive, government.

A case in point was the judgment reached by one technocrat, then-finance minister Johannes Sumarlin, a Christian, in 1989. A two-year evaluation of 189 state companies, he reported, had reached damning conclusions: Merely a third of these firms, entrusted with the use of public funds, were "very healthy" or "healthy." Two-thirds were "less healthy" or "not healthy." And the last category was by far the most crowded: Nearly half—49 percent—of all 189 firms were judged "not healthy."[11]

Sumarlin went on to announce that a substantial number of nonperforming state firms would be "restructured" in either of two ways: if not by privatization, then by liquidation. The choice appeared clear-cut, even stark. In fact, however, it left ample discretion to the authorities to deal with ailing state companies in dissimilar ways. As noted in a subsequent official clarification, "privatizing" an unhealthy public enterprise could mean one or more of several rather different things: reorganizing the state firm as a limited liability company (PT); linking it to an existing PT in a joint venture; selling shares in it on the JSX, assuming certain requirements could be met, such as previously audited accounts; selling it less transparently, but with the approval of the finance minister, if the requirements for flotation on the JSX could not be met; and allowing its directors to contract the management of the enterprise to an outside party on a probationary basis for a year or, with the finance minister's approval, longer. Sumarlin's package of reforms also obliged every state-owned company to draw up and submit a five-year corporate plan for the finance minister's approval. The concentration of regulatory power in a cabinet portfolio normally held by a technocrat—finance—was ironic in a measure meant to reduce the economic scope of government, and typical of the swinging of the policy pendulum away from the nationalists during times of reform.

In an Indonesian context, Sumarlin's steps seemed radical. Yet over the course of the New Order, not one of these periodic shifts toward the market-based views of the economists ever fully renounced the nationalist preferences of the engi-

---

11. *Suara Karya* [*Vocation's Voice*], 7 October 1989. Of the 213 state enterprises in Indonesia at the time, 24 were not evaluated. One may speculate that the inclusion of these two dozen additional firms might well have swollen the "not healthy" category above 50 percent.

neers. And 1989 was no exception to this rule. When, that October, he unveiled the plans to reform state enterprises, Sumarlin also announced that they would receive no new equity funding from public coffers during the following (1990–91) fiscal year—with one signal exception. Explicitly exempted from this suspension of government largesse were ten so-called strategic industries.[12]

Under the terms of Presidential Decision No. 44 of 1989, issued the previous August, these ten state enterprises had been assigned to a Strategic Industries Management Agency (Badan Pengelola Industri Strategis, or BPIS). And the head of BPIS was the minister, not of finance, but of research and technology, B.J. Habibie—a big-vision, market-making engineer famously impatient with what he perceived to be the incremental, market-following advice of the technocrats. The clustering and apparent sheltering of these ten state firms under yet another government agency surprised many by seeming to contradict the privatizing tenor of the rest of the reform package. Nor was the BPIS just a late-hour gesture to the nationalists' inclination to treat the state as a motor for development. A team to set up such an agency had begun working five years before, in 1984.

The ten firms assigned to BPIS were in industries associated with heavy machinery, advanced technology, and/or national defense. The companies (and what they made or did) were: PT IPTN (aircraft), PT PAL Indonesia (ships), PT Pindad (small arms and ammunition), Perum Dahana (explosives), PT Krakatau Steel, PT Barata Indonesia (heavy engineering), PT Boma Bisma Indra (heavy equipment), PT INKA (railway rolling stock), PT Inti (electronic and telecommunications equipment), and Lembaga Elektronika Nasional (electronics research).[13] All planning and supervisory functions relating to these firms were assigned to Habibie.

Consolidating these "strategic industries" under Habibie's control was officially explained as a way of making them more efficient and competitive in the global marketplace. But their exemption from the other 1989 reforms suggested the opposite: that under Habibie, an enthusiast of state-led growth, they would be shielded from competition and ensured public subsidies. Establishing BPIS also reflected persisting high-level support for the ambitious idea, an anathema to the technocrats, that the state should create a new comparative advantage for Indonesia in heavy industry and high technology—an advantage intended to propel the archipelago into the ranks of the advanced economies.

To borrow the phrase used by Robert Cribb in this book, Indonesia's official

---

12. *Suara Karya,* 7 October 1989.

13. The availability of PT (limited liability company) status is not limited to private firms. Indeed, most public enterprises are PTs, meaning that their capital is held (by the ministry of finance) in the form of shares, and that they are expected to turn a profit. State enterprises with PT status can be, and have been, privatized through the sale of these shares. In contrast, a Perum (or Perusahaan Umum, meaning Public Corporation) is a non-share-issuing state enterprise wholly owned and managed by the government.

"search for modernity" under the New Order continued to imply hopes of state-based progress on a large scale. This was notwithstanding Suharto's decision to open the country to global market forces while seeking incremental gains based on existing comparative advantages in lower-tech, labor-intensive production. In this sense, Habibie and BPIS in the early 1990s could be said to have reanimated the options that Ibnu and Pertamina had pursued so extravagantly twenty years before.

The Importance of Performance

In 1986 a debate broke out in Indonesia over the desirability of privatization: the relative worth of the public and private sectors of the economy, and what balance to strike between them. The main issue was not the narrowly economic efficacy of one sector relative to the other. The case for strengthening the state sector rested instead on a political argument that Indonesia needed public enterprises to counterbalance the private sector's domination by ethnic-Chinese and foreign firms. In comparably political terms, Indonesians hoping to shrink the state's economic role tended to argue that it skewed the distribution of resources and opportunities in favor of already wealthy and well-connected elites, including relatives of the president and his officials.

While the two sides in this debate were at loggerheads over what should be done, they were alike in giving precedence to questions of race, family, and fairness over questions of efficiency, productivity, and performance. Evident, too, in this discourse were arguments against conglomerates and in favor of cooperatives as a less exploitative, more "Indonesian" way of organizing economic life. And these logics, too, tended to bypass questions of strictly material effectiveness.

In the 1990s this pattern gradually changed. The increasing immersion of Indonesia in the global economy, the accompanying validation of relatively unfettered markets as necessary means to economic growth, and the prolonged fact of such growth under the New Order prior to the debacle of 1997, combined to raise the legitimacy of entrepreneurship and the importance of judging businesses by performance criteria such as efficiency and profitability. Antipathy to capitalism was diluted as more and more—and more attractive—opportunities for jobs in private enterprise opened up relative to civil service employment, and the state sector lost increasing numbers of skilled personnel to more lucrative careers in business.

Until 1997 not even the controversy surrounding the commercial activities of the children of President Suharto and other officials could scuttle the general belief that entrepreneurship was good for the economy. Criticism focused not on the Suhartos' right to be active in business but rather on their zealous materialism and the privileged treatment they received—matters of modesty and fairness. In the eyes of a few of the most ethnically minded nationalists, such assertiveness and favoritism may even have made capitalism less suspect. From this standpoint, the *pribumi* character of the new state-linked, elite-family businesses that the Suhartos' holdings exemplified seemed to signal the formation of a racially less Chinese-Indonesian entrepreneurial class. Certainly the members of this new *pribumi* elite drew this inference in their own defense. Also involved was a generational change: away from old rhetorics of revolution and self-restraint, and toward the belief that efficiently run firms could make their owners wealthy while at the same time meeting social needs, including the needs of consumers and workers for goods and jobs.

Alongside their coverage of scandals involving corruption and mismanagement, the proliferating business media—newspapers such as *Bisnis Indonesia* (*Indonesian Business*) and *Neraca* (*Balance Sheet*) and magazines such as *Eksekutif* (*Executive*) and *Swasembada* (*Self-Supporting*), not to mention *Warta Ekonomi*—also circulated positive images of the private sector, notably by profiling creative and self-reliant entrepreneurs, *pribumi* and *nonpribumi* alike. By training their spotlights on venality and privilege—including, for example, the Suharto children's clove and citrus monopolies and television-service fee-collection schemes—these and other media, in effect, reinforced the legitimacy of performance norms, including hard work, efficiency, and transparency, from which such arrangements were seen to deviate. By the same token, news coverage of what appeared at that time to be the relatively clean and effective operation of Sempati Airlines, a private carrier partly owned by Tommy Suharto and professionally managed by Hasan Soedjono, reinforced performance norms.

Most important of all in explaining this growing acceptance of the private sector, however, was the sheer buoyancy of the sector itself.

Professionalization?

As noted earlier in this chapter, the controversy over conglomerates revolved in part around the extent to which, compared with smaller firms, they were professionalized. Leadership recruitment was a key dimension along which professionalization did or did not occur. Other things being equal, recruiting managers because they were relatives of the owners of a company was less likely to foster good practices than hiring managers with at least some professional training or experience.

A list of the four hundred best-paid managers of companies in Indonesia published by *Warta Ekonomi* for 1996 is an imperfect but useful source of light on the question of how professionalized conglomerates became during the New Order.[14] Apart from a few foreign multinationals with Indonesians in high positions, such as Freeport, Unilever, S.C. Johnson, Citibank, and IBM, domestic business

---

14. "Peringkat 400 Gaji Eksekutif 1996" ["1996 Ranking of 400 Executive Salaries"], *Warta Ekonomi,* 9:14 (25 August 1997), pp. 44–52.

groups dominated the list. Of the top—highest-paid—twenty-five executives named, twenty-three were employed by Indonesian conglomerates. Of these twenty-three, the Salim Group had the most names (eight), followed by Astra (six), and Lippo (three). But the reasons for these showings varied from group to group. If Astra's total was in keeping with its reputation for professionalism, Salim's reflected in part its sheer size and wealth.

And that introduced a complication: Did the preponderance of conglomerates on the list reflect their professionalization, or merely their greater economic clout, and hence their ability to hire expensive managers who might or might not be professional, or even effective? Generous wages could not be assumed to reward merit. Certainly the high frequency of bankers among these best-paid managers did not reflect the weakness of that industry—weakness that the crisis of 1997–98 would soon make so evident. On the other hand, many of these best-paid managers could command such high salaries not simply because of a firm's ability to pay. Also relevant in determining their pay were the managers' own records of education, experience, and success.

As expected, the conglomerates represented on the list were disproportionally owned by ethnic-Chinese Indonesians. But the rankings also showed that some Chinese-Indonesian conglomerates had recruited *pribumi* professionals into top management. This had long been true of the Astra companies, as suggested by the seventh-place ranking of Astra International's finance director at the time, Rini Soewandi.[15] But she was not the only *pribumi* to be hired and promoted to the top by an ethnic-Chinese firm. On the list of best-paid managers, those at the highest job level—"president director" in Indonesian parlance—also included *pribumi* such as eleventh-ranked Abdullah Ali of Bank Central Asia (Salim Group), twentieth-ranked Soebronto Laras of Indomobil Utama (another Salim company), and twenty-first-ranked Markus Parmadi of Lippo Bank (Lippo Group).

Such evidence may usefully be supplemented with a brief but closer look at a few prominent managers and, through them, the evolving relationship of ownership to management in corporate Indonesia. Of the many business groups one could focus on, I have chosen three because of their diversity: Bakrie, the most prominent *pribumi* group not owned by the relatives of officials; Humpuss, a *pribumi* conglomerate founded by a son of Suharto; and Salim, a *nonpribumi* complex that in 1997 was still the largest business group in the country.

Bakrie

Most of the conglomerates in operation in Indonesia in 1997 had been formed during the New Order, not before. In contrast, the origins of the Bakrie Group date back to the Japanese occupation of the Indies. In 1942 Achmad Bakrie es-

---

15. Rini Soewandi was not the highest-salaried female manager on the list. Eva Rianti Hutapea of Indofood (Salim Group) ranked sixth. Female executives were nevertheless still a minority among the 400.

tablished a company trading in coffee, cloves, and pepper. The business that evolved from this beginning, having survived the turbulence of the Old Order, would become one of the largest of only a few *pribumi* conglomerates in Indonesia in the 1990s.

Before his death in 1988, Achmad Bakrie turned over the firm's reins to his children. Led by the eldest son, Aburizal ("Ical") Bakrie, the group expanded and eventually restructured itself under three flagship companies distributed across seven functional divisions: industry, agrobusiness, property, finance, mining, trading, and engineering. One of the three core firms, PT Bakrie & Brothers, went public in 1989 as a business group in its own right. More and more young professional managers were trained and hired.

One such professional, Tanri Abeng, was appointed the group's managing director in 1991. A year later Ical and his brothers withdrew from day-to-day administration and became board members. By 1997, in effect, Abeng was administering the Bakrie Group as the chief executive officer, leaving Ical as chairman to concentrate on the entrepreneurial side of the business, scouting out new ventures. Ical also found time to become a spokesman of Indonesian business through his position as head of the high-profile Chamber of Commerce and Industry (Kadin). As for Abeng, in 1998 his professional reputation impressed President Habibie enough to be named a cabinet minister charged with overseeing the management and reform of state enterprises.

Humpuss

The Humpuss Group was established by President Suharto's youngest son Tommy in 1984. Tommy's business dealings, like those of his five brothers and sisters, were marked by controversy. What had propelled Humpuss so rapidly up the ranks of corporate Indonesia was not talent but patronage, or so it was widely believed. Compared with the Bakrie Group, or even with Tommy's older brother Bambang's Bimantara Group, Humpuss was not known for professionalism, either in its ethos or its behavior.

The one hundred best-paid executives on *Warta Ekonomi*'s list for 1996 did include three of Tommy's top managers. One of them was Hasan Soedjono, a man who had appeared regularly in the salary rankings and enjoyed a reputation for both professionalism and success. His high-profile performance appeared to have hurt him in the eyes of Tommy, however, who released Soedjono from Humpuss in December 1996.

A graduate of Harvard Business School, Soedjono was the president director of Sempati Air, the first private airline allowed to operate jet aircraft in Indonesia. Sempati had been established in 1971 by PT Tri Usaha Bhakti, a military-controlled business group. In 1989 two new shareholders bought into the airline. PT Nusamba, a group controlled by President Suharto's confidante Bob Hasan, obtained 35 percent, while Humpuss got 25 percent. Soedjono, then director of operations at Humpuss, was appointed to manage Sempati.

Soedjono did so effectively. The airline prospered and grew, both domestically and in the Asian region. In 1992 the Asian Institute of Management, a prestigious business school based in Manila, gave Sempati an award for excellence in marketing. Behind this managerial success, however, lay an overdependence on short-term borrowings to finance expansion—an all-too-common trait of Indonesian companies that, in retrospect, augured the general crisis to come. The downgrading of Sempati's commercial paper by the Indonesian Finance Rating Agency (PT Pemeringkat Efek Indonesia, or Pefindo) and the subsequent postponement of the planned listing of Sempati on the JSX led to Soedjono's downfall and his release as the airline's CEO.

In 1997 Sempati was only one among the many holdings of the Humpuss Group. Yet the airline's relatively impressive operations, its short-term debts notwithstanding, illustrated the risk of characterizing all of the Suharto family's firms as always or entirely unprofessional. On the other hand, had the government not granted Sempati the right to fly jets—a right previously monopolized by the state carrier, Garuda—would it have done so well? And why was Humpuss so favored if not at least partly because of who Tommy was—or, rather, who his father was? In any event, neither its monopoly right nor its highly regarded CEO could insulate the company from the crisis of 1997–98. And as Soedjono discovered when Tommy let him go, in the culture of Indonesian business under Suharto, professionals still served at the pleasure—and displeasure—of owners.

Salim

Liem Sioe Liong (Sudono Salim) was not locally born. In 1937, at the age of 21, he migrated from China's Fujian province to central Java to seek his fortune. He began his commercial career in the Indies as a petty trader selling odds and ends, often on credit. In the 1940s he helped supply Indonesian nationalist forces, a military connection that deepened in the 1950s when he began to provision the Indonesian army's Diponegoro division, headquartered in the north-central Javanese city of Semarang. A lieutenant-colonel named Suharto was in charge of supplying the division. In these early dealings between the immigrant Chinese and the *pribumi* officer lay the seeds of a lifelong connection.

Liem founded the Salim Group in 1968. He used official monopolies and concessions—fruits of his ties to Suharto—to build the group into a huge business empire. In his seventies, Liem gradually handed control over the complex to the youngest of his three sons, Anthony Salim, who became its president and chief executive. By the 1990s the Salim Group was said to have become the largest conglomerate not only in Indonesia but also in Southeast Asia.[16]

---

16. Adam Schwarz, "Empire of the Son," *Far Eastern Economic Review,* 14 March 1991, pp. 46–53.

Not surprisingly, Salim executives figured prominently in the annual listings of best-paid managers compiled by *Warta Ekonomi.* In 1993, for example, Salim directors Johannes Kotjo and Judiono Tosin ranked first and second, respectively. But they left the Salim Group soon afterward—Kotjo to fashion various firms he had bought into a conglomerate of his own, Tosin to start a securities company. (Despite their departure from Salim, as of 1996 the group's representation on the list had actually increased.)

In its early years the Salim Group grew, through acquisitions, into a congeries of diverse individual PTs. These ranged from a flour-milling monopoly (Bogasari) and a cement firm that would later go public (Indocement) to Indonesia's biggest private bank (Bank Central Asia). By 1989 the conglomerate's businesses had been consolidated into eleven strategic divisions, each with a steering committee to supervise operations. Executives of the firms within a particular division reported to its head, while the divisions themselves were coordinated by a group-wide board of directors.

Between professionalism and patrimonialism, the natures and roles of Bakrie, Humpuss, and Salim were ambiguous. Inside Humpuss and Salim one found a mixture of managers by profession and by connection. "Market-minded" *pengusaha pasar* coexisted with "patronage-minded" *pengusaha fasilitas.* Bakrie, too, had benefited from state patronage, notably as a supplier to Pertamina in the oil-driven days of state-sector expansion.

To the extent that these three otherwise diverse firms can be made to stand for big business generally under the New Order, their experience suggests this conclusion:

Organizational and other reforms meant to professionalize large firms had not so much replaced as taken their places alongside ongoing patrimonial ties and behavior. Rather than appearing as mutually exclusive alternatives, the two styles of management might even be said to have complemented each other. Market-based expertise and professional experience might be needed, for example, to implement successfully a contract originally won through personal or political influence.

This mixed picture will be revisited at the end of this chapter. First, however, attention must be paid to the extraordinary events of 1997 as they affected, and were affected by, Indonesia's conglomerates.

The Crisis of 1997–98

In mid-1997 there was reason to be optimistic about the Indonesian economy. It had been growing rapidly for three decades, and the country's business groups had grown along with it. It was not difficult to argue that the conglomerates had simultaneously benefited from and contributed to this record of aggregate success. The evidence of corruption, overborrowing, and overexpansion, reviewed in this chapter and periodically exposed to Indonesians in media coverage of the latest scandal, showed that under the surface all was not well. Yet the macroeconomic picture looked good. Fiscal deficits were safely within 1 or 2 percent of GDP, and foreign reserves appeared sufficient to cover imports and short-term debt.

The shocks that struck the economy in the wake of the fall of the Thai baht in July 1997 destroyed this sanguine outlook, but not immediately. Guarded optimism persisted through the early months of the crisis, only to collapse as foreign and domestic investors lost all confidence in the rupiah. Observers pointed to many reasons for this loss of confidence, including weak microeconomic policies, unsustainable investment in property, excessive foreign borrowing, and unsound banks. Other sources of investor reluctance included "KKN," for collusion, corruption, and nepotism, and the prospect of instability so long as the question of succession—who would replace the president, when, and how—remained unresolved.

But these issues had been around for a long time in Suharto's Indonesia. Unprecedented, to be sure, was the combination of events that accompanied them and made them so volatile. Notable among such catalysts were a severe and prolonged drought, a national election, and, once the crisis got under way, a series of intrusively conditional agreements struck with the International Monetary Fund (IMF) amid rising unrest. Nor did the results of the reselection of national leaders in March 1998—Suharto as president yet again, his long-time admirer Habibie as vice president, another reshuffled cabinet—inspire confidence in the regime's capacity for reform. But while business groups reacted and adapted to political instability, they were not themselves the main actors in bringing it about.

What distinguished the contribution of Indonesian business groups to the crisis of 1997 was the extent of their unhedged borrowing in foreign currency. They were motivated to contract such debts for reasons that included: the gap between higher domestic and lower overseas interest rates that made borrowing abroad look cheap; the assumption that the government would continue to manage the gradual depreciation of the exchange rate to facilitate reconvertibility; and the perception that Indonesia's foreign-exchange reserves were ample enough to deter attacks on the rupiah.

The Thai currency crisis forced a reassessment of risk in Indonesia. Conglomerates and their bankers, the latter often part of the same business group, became even more controversial than before. Eventually it became known that conglomerates had collectively borrowed abroad some $80 billion to $100 billion. They would face extreme difficulties paying back the loans as the rupiah weakened in value. The banks in turn would find their solvency threatened by vast amounts of bad debt.

The Indonesian stock market turned downward as investors sold shares of companies thought to be vulnerable to exchange-rate risk. Foreign investors used the rupiah proceeds from these sales of stock to buy foreign currencies. Many domestic investors did the same, because holding foreign currency looked more attractive than buying shares or making bank deposits in rupiah, or to pay back their overseas loans and cut their risks of further exchange-rate losses. The resulting demand for foreign exchange escalated into a rush when the government decided, on 14 August 1997, to float the rupiah in order to protect its own foreign currency reserves. The value of Indonesia's currency plunged.

Most observers had not realized the extent of private-sector foreign debt. Many Indonesian firms and financial institutions previously thought healthy were effectively bankrupted by their inability to service their large foreign debts from their rupiah earnings at the increasingly unfavorable exchange rate. Losing their confidence in Indonesian banks, the international financial community refused to accept letters of credit. The lack of credit drastically contracted Indonesian exports and imports, further undercutting the rupiah and spreading the damage into the real economy. In the five months after it was floated in August, the rupiah depreciated an astonishing 85 percent. Stock market prices also shrank—down at one point to half their previous value. By early 1998 companies were laying off thousands of workers and inflation was accelerating.

The government reacted to these disasters by tightening liquidity in the hope that high interest rates would attract capital back into the country and prevent further depreciation. Instead, the resulting surge in domestic borrowing costs almost shut down the economy. The authorities turned to the IMF for help. In the package announced on 31 October the IMF promised financial assistance in return for a three-year program of policy reforms. These included strengthening the financial sector, tightening fiscal policy, and undertaking structural adjustments.

But the government did not follow through on these commitments enough to overturn the pessimism of the market. Indeed, the authorities were seen as lacking any coherent strategy for coping with the crisis. In mid-January in Jakarta, IMF chief Michel Camdessus and President Suharto agreed to a package of assistance conditional on more far-reaching reforms, including steps to remove monopolies and cut spending on state enterprises. But Suharto soon showed his ambivalence toward these new commitments. Rather than concentrate on implementing them, he flirted with the idea of pegging the rupiah to the dollar through a currency board. By automatically satisfying buyers and sellers of the rupiah at a fixed and guaranteed rate, such a board would have operated, at least in principle, free of government intervention.

In the eyes of some observers, valuable time was wasted considering this option—time that might have been spent trying to prevent the further worsening of the economy. That deterioration, along with spiraling violence, Sinophobia, and calls for Suharto's resignation, including riots in Jakarta in mid-May that took more than a thousand lives, furnished the circumstances in which the president's long rule finally came to an end. On 21 May 1998, Suharto stepped down and was replaced by his vice president, Habibie.

Obviously, imprudent borrowing by Indonesian business groups did not cause Suharto's fall, at least not in any direct sense. On the other hand, private-sector debts, notably those that the country's conglomerates had incurred, were centrally implicated in the economic breakdown that was, if not a sufficient condition for Suharto's political exit, at least a necessary contribution to that result.

Overview and Conclusion

This chapter began by recalling the maritime weaponry and the limited liability company—the physical technology and the capitalist institution—that were used by Westerners to colonize the islands that are now Indonesia. Indonesians understand the need to acquire modern physical technology—the hardware of development—if their country is to industrialize. Its industrialization, they hope, will enable the republic, if not to rival the formerly colonial powers of the West, then at least to gain their respect.

Unappreciated by comparison are the organizational and legal underpinnings of capitalism, including well-run firms, banks, stock exchanges, and labor unions. These organizational forms have been thought by many Indonesians to imply a brawling kind of economy in which the rich and strong trample the poor and weak. Stereotypically, the ethnic Chinese are pictured among the rich and strong, lording it over the deprived and defenseless *pribumi*. This simplification and the related idea that market freedoms unfairly benefit the *nonpribumi* who can take advantage of them, help to explain why liberalizing economic reforms have been controversial in Indonesia.

The sluggishness of Indonesia's response to the crisis of 1997–98 was not unrelated to this enduring gap—between, on the one hand, eagerness for the hardware of industrialization, and on the other, ambivalence toward the market-regarding institutional software needed to industrialize efficiently. If, over the life of the New Order, the gap narrowed as markets delivered, one may wonder whether collapsing markets in 1997–98 may have widened it again. Whatever happens, suspicions of racially skewed capitalism will continue to tinge perceptions of business, including big business, in post-Suharto Indonesia.

In the absence of adequate legal and institutional safeguards to protect various freedoms and rights, including property rights, entrepreneurs will tend to seek refuge in potentially collusive arrangements based on family, friendship, and favored access to the state. As in the past, those who benefit from such patterns will be disinclined to reform them. Indeed such ways of doing business may be justified as necessary to accumulate capital, acquire technology, and close the racial distance between rich and poor. Far from altering this mindset, the crisis of 1997–98 may have reinforced it.

In contrast, this chapter has implied a very different view: that greater recognition and use of professional managerial skills in Indonesia could have made the crash less likely and, afterward, enhanced the chance and strength of a recovery. Nor is this judgment as unrealistic as it may appear. A thin but real stratum of professional managers did develop under the New Order, stimulated by economic opportunity, political stability, and openness to the outside world. Members of this new breed of market-minded entrepreneurs were able to build careers based more on the practice of managerial skills—experience and performance—than on family ties or strategies of access to authority.

Under less than ideal conditions, the establishment of Western-type business schools, public and private, did take place. Their success opened additional routes to executive positions, allowing members of an older generation of entrepreneurs accustomed to working in patrimonial settings, such as Liem Sioe Liong, to entrust their businesses to a younger, better educated, and more cosmopolitan generation of managers who were themselves more willing to encourage their own eventual replacement by professionals. Meanwhile, a shift in employment preferences from the bureaucracy and the military to the private sector helped to enlarge the ranks of *pribumi* managers—a desirable consequence given the prevailing nationalist mood. Seen from the outside, many large Indonesian firms began to look more and more like modern businesses anywhere in the world.

And yet, while the private sector became more valued as a place to pursue a career, and while more Indonesians were running organizations beyond the reach of government officials, modern management practices remained for the most part ancillary to patrimonial ones. One could argue that, with few exceptions, it was the owners and not the managers who made the decisions that created the burden of private-sector debt that crushed the currency in 1997–98—though one may wonder whether the managers would have acted differently, had they been empowered to decide.

At any rate, in the world of Indonesian business, managers will not soon displace owners. Indonesian managers, while they have been growing in number, remain in short supply. Only when the economy begins to grow again will professionally minded employees have the security they will need in order to develop and exert their influence in the workplace. As long as the legal and organizational underpinnings of business remain weak, personal trust will continue to matter more than managerial skill. Despite initial signs that the roles of owner and manager are being separated, the personalistic sort of capitalism long practiced in Indonesia will persist.

Will Indonesian businesses wean themselves from dependence on patronage? Will they be able to professionalize enough to ensure their survival once their founders and patrons have passed from the scene? The answer will greatly depend on how the state responds to the pressures for more competition and transparency, on the one hand, and for even more patrimonialism on the other—whether the authorities will choose, in the apt phrase of the politically active economist, Emil Salim, "the rule of law or the law of rulers."

In 1997–98, the debate over the best way to overcome the crisis illustrated these opposing choices. On one side were those who insisted that the crisis had resulted from systemic corruption and lack of transparency inside Indonesia. They placed their hope for change in the implementation of the reforms negotiated with the IMF. Some of those reforms, including steps to establish or strengthen laws and institutions enabling bankruptcy and preventing monopoly, carried wide implications for business. Politically, this liberalizing camp saw in such reforms a chance to achieve a more equitable and autonomous society that could dispense with race as a guiding criterion for allocating value.

On the other side, against liberalization, another group viewed the reforms as an attempt by the West to impose an unsuitable capitalist system that would once again prevent *pribumi* Indonesians from taking their rightful place at the economic table. In this camp, the crisis bolstered the conviction that full integration with the world economy was an intrinsically harmful course for the country to follow, and strengthened the preference for a more closed and protected system. This nationalist camp was unconvinced, or had not considered the possibility, that strong legal and institutional foundations could, in the long run, benefit the *pribumi* more than a mere redivision of existing spoils.

As the archipelago enters the twenty-first century, pressures for rationalization are likely to increase, from abroad and from within, as foreign companies and organizations join with professionally disposed elements in Indonesian society to make the case for more openness and predictibility. Nevertheless, for the foreseeable future, because of the ambivalence and disagreement described above, emerging professionalism is less likely to replace patrimonialism than coexist alongside it.

To return once more to my starting point, the early thriving Malay kingdoms and traders did not develop the institutional framework they needed to improve their chances of successfully confronting the power of the colonizing West. As this century ends, Indonesians face a comparable challenge: to reform the institutional framework in which they do business, and thereby facilitate their economy's recovery and further growth. Implicated as they are in the debacle of 1997–98, the conglomerates cannot afford to fail again. Nor can the country afford to let them remain "all in the family"—the family of Suharto, of Habibie, or of anyone else. Failure to reform the way they do business will only further delay the hopes of Indonesians, already interrupted and postponed, to become a strong nation.

PART THREE: SOCIETY

Chapter 7

Religion: Evolving Pluralism

Robert W. Hefner

The island of Bali is world-famous for its graceful Hindu temples, exquisite dances, and colorful cremations. Kalimantan (Indonesian Borneo) has achieved international renown for its small population of Punan Dayaks, who are celebrated for their supposedly religious concern for the rainforest. Tourist brochures regularly juxtapose images of Java's majestic Hindu-Buddhist edifices alongside photographs of bloody animal sacrifices and quaint ancestral effigies from among the Torajans of Sulawesi. In cities across Indonesia, travelers can encounter gaudy Chinese temples not far from stately Christian churches. With its several hundred ethnic groups residing on some 6,000 inhabited islands, there seems to be no end to the diversity of Indonesian religions and cultures.

As representatives from Indonesia's Department of Religion are quick to point out, however, the most remarkable feature of religion in Indonesia is that some 87 percent of the country's more than 200 million people officially profess Islam. This fact makes Indonesia the largest majority-Muslim society in the world. Toward the end of the New Order regime, a few activist intellectuals developed an interest in the political ideas of Iranian Shi'ism, but the great majority of Indonesian Muslims are officially Sunnis of the Shafi'i school of jurisprudence.[1] Despite differences of custom (*adat*), piety, theological interpretation, and organizational affiliation, the archipelago's Muslims are heirs to a remarkably uniform great tradition. That Indonesian tradition deserves a place alongside its

---

1. Some 85 percent of the world's Muslims adhere to the Sunni branch of Islam; Shi'i form the other major branch. Within Sunni Islam there are four recognized traditions of jurisprudence, of which the Shafi'i is one.

Arabic, Persian, and Turkish counterparts as a key stream within Islamic civilization.

Protestants account for 6 percent of all Indonesian citizens, Roman Catholics 3 percent, Hindus 2 percent, and Buddhists 1 percent.[2] Although their numbers are rapidly declining, several hundred thousand people adhere to local or tribal patterns of belief and ritual, while a substantially larger number uphold elements of such patterns while officially professing a world religion. Under Indonesian law, all citizens must profess a government-recognized faith, and in government eyes tribal traditions do not qualify as "religions" (*agama*).[3] Practitioners of tribal systems are encouraged, normally without being physically coerced, to affiliate with one of the five official *agama*: Islam, Protestantism, Roman Catholicism, Hinduism, or Buddhism.

Religion in Indonesia is thus not only a matter of personal conviction or choice. It is also a public, even a governmental, affair. In principle the Indonesian polity is nonconfessional—not based on any one religion. Yet Indonesia is not a secular state in the Western sense. As noted by Cribb and Liddle in this book, the first of the five principles in Pancasila, the nation's ideological charter, bases the state on monotheism—belief in one God. Under the New Order, citizens could not choose to be atheists, and the authorities actively promoted religion through public schools, media, and the Department of Religion. Citizens were required to possess identification cards listing the bearer's faith.

These circumstances—the diversity of religious traditions alongside the numerical predominance of Muslims, and extensive state support for religious affairs despite official nonconfessionalism—made religion in New Order Indonesia diverse and distinctive. What follows is an explanation of how these conditions came to be and how they were shaped during Suharto's long presidency, by political and social trends.

Foremost among the latter was the religious revival that swept large segments of the Muslim community beginning in the mid-1980s. The revival had features unlike those conventionally associated in Westerners' minds with resurgent Muslims—not least of all because many of its leaders were trying not to curtail but to deepen Islamic traditions of pluralism and tolerance. At the same time, however,

---

2. These figures, and the one previously cited for Muslims, are rounded official estimates as of 1985 from *Statistik Indonesia 1987/Statistical Yearbook of Indonesia 1987* (Jakarta: CBS, [1988]), pp. 172–173. Earlier estimates are given and sourced in Robert Cribb's *Historical Dictionary of Indonesia* (Metuchen, NJ: Scarecrow Press, 1992), p. 401.

3. *Agama* is a Sanskrit-derived term that originally referred to divine precept or command. In contemporary official discourse in Indonesia, however, the word's meaning has been colored by Islamic notions of religion or *din*. Thus, to qualify as an *agama,* a religion must acknowledge a unitary, monotheistic divinity, and have a tradition of prophecy, sacred scripture, and devotional rituals—all of which exist in Islam. On the challenges such an understanding of religion poses for minorities with local beliefs, see Janet

the rising interest in Islam seriously challenged nominal Muslims and followers of other faiths, and posed difficult questions about the role of religion in state and society.

Although it is not their main theme, other authors of this book discuss religion, notably Islam, in relation to Indonesian history (Cribb), politics (Liddle), and arts (Hooker). Because Muslims are far more numerous among Indonesians of so-called indigenous descent than among those of Chinese origin, the coverage of ethnic identities in markets (Borsuk) and business (Habir) also implicates religion. Religion surfaces, too, at the end of this book in the context of the transition from President Suharto to President Habibie and beyond (Emmerson). In contrast, the aim here is to situate and understand the archipelago's religions in social context as part of a distinctive pattern of evolving pluralism.

Hinduism and Buddhism

For many years it was customary in Western academic circles to think of Indonesian Islam in terms of a geological metaphor. Islam in this image was a thin layer of belief and practice covering a much thicker cultural sediment that was essentially non-Islamic. The metaphor assumed that Islam had appeared in the archipelago long after kingdoms throughout the islands had adopted Hinduism or Buddhism. Although eventually the majority of the inhabitants converted to Islam, it was said, the new religion never really displaced the pre-Islamic culture, but merely covered it over or (to shift metaphors) mixed it into a syncretic whole. Indonesia's Hindu-Buddhist heritage retained influence in modern times, it was argued, in areas as diverse as the classical arts, architecture, social etiquette, and notions of power and rule.

This view of Islam as a superficial veneer is simplistic. Certain elements of Malayo-Indonesian civilization[4] do owe much to pre-Islamic traditions. But to understand why this is so, and what it means for religion in modern Indonesia, we must dig more deeply into the history and meaning of Islamization and the impact of that process on Indonesia's other streams of religious meaning.

Hinduism and Buddhism diffused from India to court centers of the Indone-

---

Hoskins, "Entering the Bitter House: Spirit Worship and Conversion in West Sumba," in Rita Smith Kipp and Susan Rodgers, eds., *Indonesian Religions in Transition* (Tucson: University of Arizona Press, 1987), pp. 136–160. See also Jane Monnig Atkinson, "Religions in Dialogue: The Construction of an Indonesian Minority Religion," *American Ethnologist,* 10:4 (November 1983), pp. 684–696.

4. From a cultural-historical perspective, the territories now included in the country known as Malaysia were part of the same archipelagic world as Indonesia until their respective subjection to British and Dutch rule. When referring to precolonial cultural history, then, I include what is now Malaysia in "Indonesian" civilization. I am also using the term "Indonesian" anachronistically to label an area whose sovereignty within borders was not declared until 1945.

sian archipelago in the early centuries of the common era (c.e.).[5] The new religions came on the heels of an expanding Asian commerce that linked India, China, and the Indonesian archipelago in one of the world's most prosperous trading arcs. A few Hindu and Buddhist clerics migrated from India to the islands at this time. But the primary support for the diffusion of "Indic"—loosely, India-derived—religion into the archipelago came from the efforts of local rulers to clothe themselves in the garb of high civilization. While trying to imitate the ways of their sophisticated trading partners, these overlords wished to use "Indic" forms to legitimize their own rule.

A favorite activity of such sovereigns was the erection of temple-like structures known today as *candi*. At first these massive stone complexes incorporated religious images almost indistinguishable from those of India, as may be seen in monuments from the ninth-century c.e. in Central Java. As the tradition evolved, however, especially after the twelfth and thirteenth centuries, religious art and architecture underwent a process of indigenization, incorporating distinctly Indonesian religious motifs.

The great majority of these religious structures were built for political, as well as religious, reasons. They were not designed to be centers of regular congregational worship, as with churches in Christian Europe. Nor were they intended to serve as temples for the worship of a specific Hindu or Buddhist deity, as was the case with religious shrines in India. Instead, they served as centers for venerating the spirits of deceased royal ancestors. Typically, these human spirits were identified as incarnations of Hindu or Buddhist deities—or both at once—and were treated in ceremonies as guardians of the realm. If the royal spirits' descendants fell from power, however, the cult itself often declined, as the new rulers elevated a new set of ancestral deities. As this illustration shows, high religion in the pre-Islamic era was closely tied to dynastic politics and legitimization.

Islam and Christianity

It has been suggested, on the basis of such evidence, that Hindu-Buddhism in Indonesia was first and foremost a state cult, not a popular religion, and therefore unusually vulnerable to disruption when later rulers converted to Islam. It is true that Indonesian rulers were among the biggest sponsors of Hindu-Buddhist institutions. And some of these institutions declined when their parent kingdoms fell, by conquest or otherwise, under Muslim influence. However, on the evidence of contemporary Bali—which has remained Hindu to this day—and also pre-Islamic Java, it is equally apparent that in some parts of the archipelago, Buddhism and, most especially, Hinduism were able to extend their roots beyond the

---

5. "c.e." ("common era") is used here because it is more neutral than "a.d." ("Year of Our Lord"), which covers the same period of time.

royal courts into the surrounding society. In addition to state-sponsored religious hubs, pre-Muslim Java, for instance, had monasteries, hermitages, spirit shrines, and cult centers that depended less directly on the court.[6] In addition, there were diffuse Hindu-Buddhist influences in the arts, law, and politics, and in folk traditions of healing and mediumship.

Sustained by these influences, Hindu-Buddhist elements in court ritual, the arts, and folk traditions tended to survive, in nominally Muslim form, the initial Islamization of these kingdoms. The persistence of Indic traditions was especially pronounced in central and eastern Java. In other parts of what would eventually become Indonesia, such as coastal Sumatra, coastal Borneo, and several of the eastern islands involved in the spice trade, local culture appears early on to have been more decisively Islamized.

Archeological evidence indicates that the first Muslims to reach the archipelago arrived in or around the eighth century, when Arab traders established themselves in southern China with an eye toward joining the booming commerce in spices and textiles in the islands farther south. Alongside these newcomers to the archipelago, a few native Indonesians may have converted to Islam, but it was not until much later that entire local communities adopted the new faith. The first known case of society-wide Islamization occurred in the thirteenth century in the kingdom of Aceh on the northern tip of Sumatra, historically Indonesia's gateway to India and the Middle East. The timing and location of this change of religion were not accidental. By the twelfth century, most of India's great Hindu kingdoms had been conquered by invading Muslim armies. As a result, Muslim merchants came to dominate the Indian trade with the "lands below the winds," as island Southeast Asia was known.[7]

The new religion quickly spread to other local trading centers. By the fifteenth century, there were significant Muslim settlements in coastal Java and the adjoining Malay peninsula. The Islamic advance reached a decisive turning point in 1525 with the collapse of Majapahit, the last of Java's powerful Hindu-Buddhist states. Over the next one hundred years, most of the port kingdoms of Sulawesi and the spice islands northeast of Java converted on their own initiative or were conquered by their Muslim neighbors. By the end of the eighteenth century, of the dozens of patently Hindu-Buddhist kingdoms once found throughout the archipelago, only those on the small island of Bali survived.

Although Hindu-Buddhism declined, not all of the archipelago was drawn into this process of Islamization. Large areas of eastern Indonesia, upland Sumatra, and interior Kalimantan lay off the main trade routes, isolated from extensive

---

6. On the varied institutions of Hindu-Buddhism in pre-Islamic Java, see Theodore G.T. Pigeaud, *Java in the 14th Century: A Study in Cultural History,* vol. 4 (The Hague, Netherlands: Martinus Nijhoff, 1962), pp. 251–266.

7. See Anthony Reid, *Southeast Asia in the Age of Commerce 1450–1680,* vol. 1: *The Lands below the Winds* (New Haven, CT: Yale University Press, 1988).

intercourse with outsiders. Having been only marginally influenced by Hindu-Buddhist religion, people in these zones were little affected by the new winds of Islam, and some managed to preserve their indigenous religions well into the twentieth century. Long before then, however, others among the archipelago's inhabitants had encountered a new and startlingly powerful challenge to local lifeways: Christianity.

The maritime kingdom of Portugal began to send missionaries to eastern Indonesia in the 1540s. To the north, in the 1570s, Spain began colonizing and "missionizing" the islands that would ultimately become the Philippines. Although at times they were willing to trade with local and itinerant Muslims, the Iberians brought with them a crusading ideology forged in centuries of Christian holy war against the Islamization of Spain. That crusade had ended just a few years prior to the Iberian voyages to Southeast Asia, when in 1492 the Spanish completed their campaign to expel Muslim rulers from southwestern Europe. Eager to seize the riches of the Indonesian trade for themselves, the Portuguese and Spanish wasted no time in attacking Muslim-held trading centers throughout the archipelago.

The ferocity of the Iberian attack appears to have strengthened Muslim resolve to resist Christian proselytizing and press ahead with their own campaign to Islamize central and western Indonesia. It was only in animist eastern Indonesia that the Iberians succeeded in introducing some of the local population to the Christian faith. To this day, Christianity remains the dominant religion among the peoples residing in the dry and impoverished islands of southeastern Indonesia (see Map 4).

Renaissance and Retreat

The new faith made its greatest gains from the fifteenth to the seventeenth centuries, in what the historian Anthony Reid has referred to as Southeast Asia's "age of commerce." This was an era of intense commercial activity and cultural innovation, comparable in many ways to the beginning of the Renaissance in Mediterranean Europe. As in Renaissance Europe, Southeast Asia's age of commerce saw an expansion in commercial wealth, increases in social and geographic mobility, and a thirst in urban centers for new ways of thought. It was in this context that Islam spread. What had been the religion of a few traders became the religion of state and society.

Southeast Asia's age of commerce also unleashed demands for greater social participation, at the very least on the part of the urban middle class. In port kingdoms in the archipelago, merchants began to demand limits on the power of rulers, and a greater say in their own affairs. In a few port-states, representative councils brought together rulers, merchants, and Muslim notables to discuss matters of government. Such participatory institutions had no counterpart in the Hindu era.

As the age of commerce evolved, however, there were less democratic developments, ones that would have a lasting effect on Indonesian Islam. In the seventeenth century in particular, a new kind of absolutist ruler appeared on the scene, intent on reimposing centralized control over commerce and the urban population. In Aceh and Java these despots checked the power of the merchants, suppressed independent Muslim institutions, and subordinated religion to the needs of the state. Seeing the merchant class as a threatening rival, some rulers even crippled the overseas trade rather than allow merchants to acquire independent wealth and power.

Not coincidentally, the efforts of these autocrats coincided with the local rise of European power. Europeans often found it more convenient to arrange their commercial dealings through one ruler rather than a host of independent merchants. In the seventeenth century, with native traders marginalized, the Europeans moved to seize outright the lucrative commerce in spices. The resulting expansion of European control dealt a final blow to the Muslim merchant class, and hampered communication between Indonesian Muslims and those in India and the Middle East.

By the time European colonialism was fully underway, therefore, Muslim Indonesia had lost much of its earlier social dynamic. The optimistic, outward-looking profile of Islam during the age of commerce gave way to an inward-looking and bureaucratically managed conservatism. Initially, European penetration and rule reinforced this shift. However, as we shall later see, colonialism also fostered conditions that eventually facilitated an extensive and burgeoning movement for Islamic revival and reform.

A Muslim Civilization

This brief historical overview shows how oversimplified the image of Islam is as a thin veneer over essentially non-Muslim cultures. In many parts of the archipelago, Islam helped to integrate previously separate peoples into a regional culture quite different from that of pre-Islamic times.

This is not to say that all social institutions were equally influenced by the new religion, nor even that much of the population was, in modern terms, deeply Islamic. As in the interiors of Sulawesi and Kalimantan in the early twentieth century, for example, it seems that many inland peoples at this much earlier time were, if Muslim at all, then only nominally so. Nor was there much formal unity among the states of the archipelago that did consider themselves Muslim. These kingdoms regularly quarreled, and would later demonstrate a notable inability to unite in the face of the European threat.

Nevertheless, at a less formal political level, adherence to Islam provided a civilizational framework that strongly influenced the subsequent local evolution of religion and culture. The social characteristics of this civilization included the movement of religious ideas and scholars across borders, a more or less common body of religious law and literature, and an array of related customs in every-thing from mysticism and mosque construction to dress and cuisine. Critical, too, was the growth of a diffuse consensus on the importance of defending the faith against infidels from outside and apostates from within the Muslim com-munity. The precise manner in which these traits were elaborated varied from one ethnic group to another. But the overall repertoire bore striking testimony to a distinctly Indonesian Muslim civilization.

In playing this regional role, Islam served as a kind of "imagined commu-nity"—a way of thinking about and enacting a sense of shared identity and des-tiny beyond the confines of face-to-face interaction.[8] Unlike a dynastic kingdom or a nation-state, the reality of this imagined community was not dependent on its realization within demarcated territorial space. It was a civilization, and as such it influenced culture and behavior across great spatial expanses and periods of time.

As with Christianity in Europe, however, it was not only in religious terms that a community could be projected beyond local worlds. Among other refer-ents, language and ethnicity could also be used to express and enact popular identity. And ethnolinguistic and religious references often overlapped. For ex-ample, among those who held it, Malay identity was so closely linked to being Muslim that when non-Muslims in neighboring populations converted to Islam they were said to "enter Malayness" or "become Malay" (*masuk Melayu*).[9] Simi-larly, in pre-nineteenth-century Java, to be or become Javanese was associated with being or becoming Muslim, although there were Hindu Javanese in the eastern portion of the island who insisted otherwise.

Such correspondences were not static, however. The precise sense of what it meant to be or behave like a "Javanese"—or a "Malay" or a "Buginese"—changed over time. Beyond the profession of the faith and a commitment to a minimal array of beliefs, the social content of what it meant to be "Muslim" also changed. Different groups in the same society might disagree over the exact content of these various identities, creating a potential for conflict whenever one group sought to defend its preferred meanings against those of another.

Religion and Culture

For Muslim Indonesians the most consistent way of discussing the relationship between religion and local culture lay in the contrast between divinely revealed religion (*agama* or *din*) and humanly generated custom or tradition (*adat*). As this difference suggests, for orthodox Muslims there can never be absolute equality

---

8. Benedict Anderson, *Imagined Communities: Reflections on the Origin and Spread of Nationalism* (London: Verso, 1983).

9. Rita Smith Kipp, *Dissociated Identities: Ethnicity, Religion, and Class in an Indo-nesian Society* (Ann Arbor: University of Michigan Press, 1993), p. 31.

between religion on the one hand and mere ethnolocal custom on the other. The Qur'an acknowledges the reality of human diversity and affirms the importance of respecting other people's lifeways. But it also stipulates that for Muslims themselves, divinely revealed religion must always take precedence over anything made by human beings. As Islam has diffused to and through diverse societies, a primary task of Muslim scholars and rulers has been to ensure that local customs as practiced by Muslims do not violate God's commands. Again, however, what some people regard as practices consistent with divine requirement, others may consider forbidden.[10]

This point allows us to understand some of the tensions that have animated Indonesian religion from early times to today. Historical evidence indicates that, in the first days of Indonesian Islam, many pre-Islamic customs and beliefs were simply carried over into the new religion. As the process of Islamization advanced, however, some in the Muslim community objected to some of these older ways as violations of the true spirit of Islam.

The first Javanese mosques, for example, were built without the idols and offering towers that had figured so prominently in Indonesian Hindu temples. Mosque builders also opened interior space in such a way as to allow for mass prayer, replacing the priestly presentation of offerings to invoked spirits that had characterized Hindu temples. At the same time, however, these early mosques lacked the domed structure that we associate today with their counterparts in the Middle East. These early Indonesian Muslim structures instead preserved the peaked and multiple tiered roofs that had characterized earlier local architecture including pre-Islamic temples. Later on, as more Indonesians made the pilgrimage to Mecca in Arabia and returned familiar with cultural styles there, some of the islands' Muslims concluded that indigenously styled roofs were not properly Islamic. What had long been regarded as an appropriate model for building mosques was now criticized as Hindu or heathen. Others, however, irritated by what they regarded as a tendency to confuse merely "Arab" culture with Islam as a universal religion, defended local traditional architecture as entirely consistent with Muslim faith.

This illustration, and the ones that follow, show how dynamically Islam has interacted with its environs, from its arrival in the islands up to now. The Abrahamic world religions—Judaism, Christianity, Islam—require exclusive allegiance from their followers. Anything that contradicts the central tenets of such a religion must be eliminated or reformed. In practice, of course, not everyone who confesses one of these religions need hold such an orthodox view. But if there are people in society who do, and if they exercise significant political influence, they will powerfully affect the development and interaction of religion and culture. Then again, the politics of culture are complex, and the power of those who

---

10. See John R. Bowen, *Muslims through Discourse: Religion and Ritual in Gayo Society* (Princeton, NJ: Princeton University Press, 1993), pp. 245–250.

cleave to such a strict view of religion, once having waxed, may also wane. The consensus among followers of a religion as to what is essential within it may also change, obliging a reassessment of what is and is not compatible with what they have come to believe.

Example: When the Malay and Javanese courts adopted Islam, most of the clergy associated with the Hindu-Buddhist temple system were jettisoned, as the institutions with which they had been associated were now regarded as incompatible with the new religion. This straightforward disappearance contradicts the emphasis on syncretism in many Western accounts: that as Islam spread in Indonesia it did not displace existing cultural traditions but blended with them. On the contrary, Islamization in Indonesia—as opposed to, say, the spread of Islam through much of India—was remarkable for the way in which it led to the rapid and total collapse of the non-Islamic temple system. Not one Hindu temple in any Muslim kingdom survived into modern times as a functioning Hindu shrine.

A variety of magical and ritual specialists less explicitly identifiable as Hindu or Buddhist, however, survived the Islamization of states. Among these figures were shadow-play puppeteers, curers, midwives, spirit mediums, and specialists in certain political and agricultural rituals. Some of these specialists, like the shadow-puppeteer, were associated with popular institutions cherished as key features of ethnic cultures. Not infrequently were these traditions defended from Islamic criticism by mythical narratives that identified them as having been created by Muslim saints, or as being otherwise compatible with Islam. Yet early on there were Muslim reformists who attacked shadow-play puppetry, healing cults, and mediumship as heretical. What these purists found objectionably inconsistent with Islam was that these ritual specialists invoked guardian spirits to gain access to supposedly magical powers. And references to non-Islamic deities did often pepper the prayers of puppeteers, healers, and midwives, whose ritual supplications often included offerings to guardian spirits.

Example: The varied Muslim mystical and ascetic traditions known as "Sufism" facilitated the dissemination of Islam.[11] No doubt this was so in part because the Sufi temperament—more contemplative than legalistic—seemed consonant with aspects of pre-Muslim religion. Yet even in its first centuries in Indonesia, some in the Islamic community objected to Sufi practices. Even at this early time there were scholars familiar with the literature and doctrine of Islamic law. Some of these more legalistically inclined Muslims opposed Sufi mysticism on the grounds that by emphasizing the struggle to achieve union with God, it blasphemously confused what was divine with what was human. At the very least, they charged, Sufism distracted Muslims from the rules and rituals that lay, in the legalist view, at the heart of Islam.

---

11. Anthony Johns, "Islamization in Southeast Asia: Reflections and Reconsiderations with Special Reference to the Role of Sufism," *Southeast Asian Studies* [Tokyo], 31:1 (1993), pp. 43–61.

These instances reflect a long history of disagreement among Indonesian Muslims over what was most vital in their religion and, therefore, least admissible in ethnic culture. The disagreement was itself related to a broader social tension, between those who took a legalistic-cum-purist approach to Islam and those who preferred a more casually eclectic or esoteric view of the divine. Like alchemists and mystics in Medieval Europe, people with the latter attitude were willing to appeal to mysterious beings and powers that were not explicitly authorized in the texts of high religion. Although, today, many people associate such eclecticism with Javanese Islam, in fact it was once widespread throughout the Indonesian Muslim world.

Kings and Ritualists

Conflicts between different understandings of Islam were also influenced by political intrigues and the demands of the state. While at times there were pious rulers committed to implementation of Islamic law, many preferred to background the law in favor of hierarchical institutions that identified the ruler as the defender of the faithful and the shadow of God on earth. Although quite different from the law-centered Islam of jurists, such imperial or ruler-centered Islam was common in the Muslim world. It could be found in Muslim kingdoms as far from Indonesia as Morocco, Turkey, Iran, and India.[12]

In Indonesia, the tendency for premodern Islam to become ruler-centered was reinforced by aspects of local politics and culture. Most of the states in premodern Indonesia were "agrarian" states: Agriculture was the main productive activity, peasants were the great majority of the population, and social mobility between classes was rare. As with Christianity in the Middle Ages, Islam in the era of agrarian states was characterized by low levels of popular participation in the literary or "great traditions" of Islam.

Most Indonesian Muslims were illiterate and, by modern standards, poor. They had few chances to immerse themselves in the details of Islamic law or literature—activities that required, at the very least, training in classical Arabic. In the course of a day these ordinary Muslims were able, at best, to perform the required worship and utter a few petitionary prayers or magical spells. They did sponsor life-cycle rituals and help celebrate Islamic holidays. But when the spiritual task at hand required more specialized skills, they quickly deferred to religious experts. Thus, at a child's birth, circumcision, or marriage, or at times of illness, harvest, or death, Muslim villagers would turn to a local man or woman versed in religious ways.

---

12. Compare, for example, A.C. Milner, "Islam and the Muslim State," in M.B. Hooker, ed., *Islam in South-East Asia* (Leiden, Netherlands: E.J. Brill, 1993), pp. 23–49; and Henry Munson, Jr., *Religion and Power in Morocco* (New Haven, CT: Yale University Press, 1993).

Typically such ritual experts claimed a special spiritual pedigree. Their training had equipped them with the formulas required to appeal to God, the Prophet, archangels, and local deities and earth sprites, as the case might require. In the archipelago's more hierarchical states, the highest of such ritual experts were appointed or otherwise licensed by the ruler in his capacity as the spiritual and temporal guardian of the realm.

From a strictly Qur'anic perspective, Islam was and is a religion without priests. Nevertheless, as these examples show, traditional Indonesia, like many other parts of the premodern Muslim world, had an array of ritual specialists who looked a good deal like full-time clerics. Often they claimed descent from some once-renowned "man of God," and asserted an exclusive right to perform certain public ceremonies. Many of these specialists gave offerings to deities of dubious authority from the standpoint of scriptural Islam. Among the more popular deities of this sort in Indonesia were spirits of the four cardinal directions, the god and goddess of sky and earth, mountain divinities, and the goddess of the southern sea. Not surprisingly, many of these guardian beings bore a striking resemblance to those that had been invoked in pre-Islamic times.

The Muslim officials involved in these activities justified them on the grounds that these apparent divinities were really just species of *jin,* a type of spirit acknowledged by the Qur'an as having been created, by God, along with Adam and Eve. For legal-minded Muslims, however, such rituals smacked of polytheism, a grievous sin in Islam. From the earliest period of Islam's growth in Indonesia, such activities were criticized. Their abolition would become a main aim of Muslim reform movements in the nineteenth and twentieth centuries. It still is today.

This, then, was the typical social organization of Indonesian Islam in the premodern era. The great majority of people, while professing Islam and participating in its public rituals, had at best an indirect familiarity with its scripture. Ordinary Muslims relied on religious mediators for ritual services and guidance.

As the colonial era unfolded, contacts greatly increased between Indonesia and the Middle East. At the same time, European colonialism shook the confidence of Muslims in their way of life. If Islam were the last and the greatest of God's revelations, why were Muslims being conquered by Christians? In the Middle East and in Indonesia, many Muslims concluded that they had fallen from grace in part because they had failed to implement Islam in a manner consistent with God's directives. And therein lay inspiration for the modern project of Islamic reform.

Modernizing Reform

It is sometimes said that, in contrast to Western Christianity, the Muslim world has experienced not one big Reformation but a recurring series of smaller and less conclusive equivalents. This argument, while not quite accurate, is apt in one limited sense. Most of the Muslim world lacked a centralized church administration similar to that of the pope and bishops in Roman Catholicism. (Shi'i Islam, with its institutionalized hierarchy among religious scholars, differs from Sunni tradition in this regard.) When reformist Muslim movements arose, their efforts were usually directed not against a centralized ecclesiastical hierarchy— no such free-standing church existed—but against specific rulers and their appointed religious stewards.

Reformations of this sort have occurred throughout Islamic history. Understandably, purification was often followed by periods of laxity, eclecticism, or decline—conditions propitious to the eventual rise of another movement to reform religion, which might lead in time to another relaxation, and so on, perpetuating the cycle.[13]

This oscillating pattern typified Indonesian Islam from the sixteenth to the nineteenth centuries. Occasionally a ruler would become conscientious about the implementation of Islamic law or some other religious duty, and much of society, especially in urban areas, would fall in line. Other rulers were more lax, had a different understanding of Islamic piety, or preferred to focus on ethnic or dynastic glories rather than religion as the basis of their authority.

The nineteenth and twentieth centuries ushered in a new kind of reformation process. Its scope was much more vast, affecting not only individual kingdoms but also whole portions of the Muslim world. This powerfully coordinated striving for renewal would have an enduring impact on popular religion. Contributing to the emergence of this movement for more thoroughgoing reform were: the expansion of pilgrimages to centers of learning and worship in the Middle East, especially Arabia; the triumph of a radically literalist reform movement known as Wahhabism in the Arabian peninsula at the end of the eighteenth century; and, crucially, the destabilizing influences of Western rule in Muslim lands.

Western colonialism provoked crises of authority in all the Islamic kingdoms of the archipelago. Many rulers mounted stiff resistance to the Western advance. In the end, however, all were subjugated, and saw their administrations abolished or incorporated into a new, European-run bureaucracy. Although the precise manner in which indigenous polities were transformed varied, the long-term consequences were the same everywhere: The native population felt estranged from its rulers. Some of these indigenes urgently began seeking new leaders and ideals to help overcome the crisis of colonization.

Movements for Islamic reform in Arabia, Egypt, and South Asia eventually influenced this search. Reformist projects in Indonesia, while varying from region to region, shared and stressed these core beliefs: Scripture is complete and self-sufficient; the individual must assume responsibility for his or her moral

---

13. Schematic but useful on this topic is Ernest Gellner's "Flux and Reflux in the Faith of Men," in his *Muslim Society* (Cambridge, UK: Cambridge University Press, 1981), pp. 1–85.

conduct; and all improper innovations must be purged from Islamic tradition. These appeals, in effect, challenged the authority of traditional Muslim scholars (*ulama*) and indigenous government officials. Both were accused of compromising the faith by tolerating political injustice and unacceptable deviations from God's commands. Emphasizing the need for all believers to master the Qur'an and the commentaries on the life and sayings of the Prophet Muhammad (*hadith*), reformers denounced the religious texts that scholars traditionally had relied on when interpreting the Qur'an or training students. Many of these criticisms remain central to reformist discourse in Indonesia today.

In some parts of the archipelago—for example, among the Minangkabaus of western Sumatra—the struggle between reformers and traditionalists took place before the advent of full-scale European rule. Elsewhere, efforts for religious reform coincided with or followed colonial expansion. In the wake of advancing European authority, in towns established to support the European trade in coffee, tea, and other products, Muslim reformers set up mosques, schools, and publishing houses. By the beginning of the twentieth century, local initiatives of this sort were springing up all over Indonesia. In 1912 reformers greatly strengthened their movement by creating Muhammadiyah. This organization, from its base in the central Javanese city of Yogyakarta, would promote and coordinate Islamic reform across the archipelago.

Traditionalism Revised

Reform-seeking Muslims were not the only religious grouping to take advantage of the turmoil of the late colonial era. The *ulama* were active, too, partly in reaction to their reformist rivals' critiques, but also in response to the challenges and opportunities introduced by European rule. In east and central Java, for example, traditionalist scholars took advantage of the roads and the peace afforded by Dutch administration to extend a network of Muslim boarding schools (*pesantren*) in rural areas that had lacked facilities for Muslim education.

By building and staffing mosques, training pupils, and even, in their own manner, by reforming village rituals, the traditionalists provided resources and cadres to deepen and spread devoutly Muslim ways. The resulting culture of piety, later termed *santri* after the word for a *pesantren* graduate, spread through nominally Muslim areas whose inhabitants had been so more in name than in practice. Occurring as it did in the aftermath of Dutch conquest, this expansion of *santri* culture was attractive to the many Javanese who were looking for alternatives to the compromised authority of court-based elites.

In 1926 traditionalist Javanese Muslims again demonstrated their nontraditional organizational skills when they founded a national association known as the Revival of Islamic Scholars (Nahdlatul Ulama, or NU). Responding to reformist charges, the *ulama* argued that the meanings of God's scripture were complex. Understanding them required special training, including the prolonged study of religious texts. In matters of Islamic law, traditionalists also argued, Muslims should consult existing and recognized legal commentaries rather than presuming to interpret scripture anew on their own. Downplaying independent religious authority, of course, meant defending the role of Muslim scholars such as themselves.

While they fended off the reformers, the *ulama* quietly implemented reforms of their own. In the nineteenth and early twentieth centuries, for example, traditionalist religious schools renewed their curricula by replacing most of the Malay and Javanese writings on which they had long relied with texts of recognized Middle Eastern origin.[14] By the end of the nineteenth century, most leading traditionalist scholars had spent some time studying in the Middle East, and had been exposed to reformist ideas. During the first decades of the twentieth century, their religious schools began covering secular topics. Equally important, despite their long-standing tolerance of folk rituals, the *ulama* began to suppress overtly heterodox practices, such as the presentation of offerings to spirits.[15]

Western observers still tend to portray Indonesia's traditionalist Muslims as "conservative" and, especially on Java, tolerant of heterodoxy. In fact the *ulama* pioneered their own kind of reformation. The NU continues to be a case in point. Its leaders, who still defend the value of traditional learning, include some of the most daring and innovative Muslim thinkers in Indonesia.

Colonialism and Christianity

The winds of social change in the colonial era buffeted non-Islamic religion, too. The European advance opened the interior of Sumatra, Kalimantan, Sulawesi, and eastern Indonesia to outside influence, in some regions undermining long-established ethnic religions. In contrast to their missionizing Iberian predecessors, the Calvinist Dutch were less than zealous about promoting Christianity during the early colonial period. From the mid-nineteenth century onward, however, the Dutch tolerated a heightened missionary role, especially in non-Muslim areas still lacking a local colonial administration, where missions would at least ensure a European presence.

The record of such evangelism was mixed. Take the situation in the highlands of north Sumatra, home to the Karo Batak ethnic group (see Map 2). Here, conversion in the final decades of the nineteenth-century proceeded slowly, despite a sizeable investment of Protestant mission resources. The problem appears to have been that, in Karo eyes, Christianity was identified with European culture and colonial oppression, not least because Europeans excluded the Karo from

---

14. Mark R. Woodward, *Islam in Java: Normative Piety and Mysticism in the Sultanate of Yogyakarta* (Tucson: University of Arizona Press, 1989), p. 135.

15. See Bowen, *Muslims,* p. 32; and my "Islamizing Java? Religion and Politics in Rural East Java," in *The Journal of Asian Studies,* 46:3 (August 1987), pp. 533–554.

positions of authority in the church. Much later, when Indonesians became independent and the Dutch departed, the church expanded rapidly as native Karo assumed leadership positions within it.

On Java the progress of Christianity was still more uneven. Fearing unrest that might have jeopardized their economic schemes, the Dutch officially discouraged Christian evangelism among the Javanese until the 1840s. In 1831, for example, when copies of the first Javanese-language translation of the New Testament arrived at a central Javanese port, the Dutch confiscated them and let them rot, undistributed, in a warehouse.

Also for security reasons, the Dutch were reluctant to allow the Christian missions to take advantage of local religious cleavages. One such rift appeared in east-central Java in the 1830s. Tensions were growing among Muslims—legalistic *santri* on the one hand, eclectic "Javanists" on the other. A few of the more mystically inclined in the latter group had even begun wondering whether they were really Muslim at all. In this volatile context, some peasants in the area converted to Christianity under the guidance of a mixed-blood Javanese aristocrat.

When Dutch authorities learned of the conversion in 1842, they reacted not with delight but with instructions to curb the autonomy of these new native Christians. Independent-minded Javanese pastors were subjected to Dutch clerical authority. Local cultural habits, such as Javanese dress, hair styles, and gamelan music, which native leaders had tolerated, were forbidden. Christianity once again became identified with European domination, and Western missionary progress ground to a halt. As in the Karo highlands, Christianity on Java would experience its most dramatic expansion only after Indonesian independence and the exit of the Dutch.

Among Muslims as well, the penetration of colonial institutions into native society caused a crisis of confidence in indigenous authorities, including religious ones. One response to this crisis, evident in the actions of Muslim reformers, was to distance religion from the compromised political establishment and work for a purification of the faith. Thus did Muslim purifiers, in effect, turn colonialism to their advantage.

The growing thirst for education also benefited reformers. They were not narrow-minded zealots. Their schools adopted elements of Western education, including the study of science and mathematics. Such changes, though meant to defend religion, opened Muslim culture to an array of new intellectual influences, and worked to "secularize" areas of knowledge that many Muslims had once thought sacral. Traditionally religion-based views of authority and leadership, for example, became vulnerable to revision. Reforms introduced an important measure of pluralism into the Muslim community and fostered a new spirit of criticism and public debate.

A similar process of secularization and pluralization took place in the non-Muslim parts of the archipelago. Among the Karo of north Sumatra, for example, those who had converted to Christianity considered themselves no less "Karo" than the traditionalists who, in the converts' eyes, were still clinging to the animism of their ancestors. To justify this claim, the Christian Karo interpreted "Karo" as an ethnic identity, and argued that the Karo traditions they, too, revered were matters of custom not religion. Inasmuch as other Karo eventually accepted this redefinition, the Christian Karo worked to secularize aspects of the group's tradition previously regarded as religious—and thus contributed to the pluralization of Karo society. Such reconceptualizations of religion and ethnicity would characterize religious change in Indonesia throughout the modern era.

Religion and the State

Upon gaining its independence from the Dutch, Indonesia had a Muslim majority whose proportion of the total population was broadly equivalent to that of the Muslim community in Egypt or Syria. Indonesia's non-Muslims, however, compared with their Middle Eastern counterparts, were more concentrated in a few regions of the country. This pattern gave non-Muslims in the islands considerable influence locally and, therefore, in negotiations with national authorities. Having benefited from mission schooling under the Dutch, Christian-minority Indonesians were also "overrepresented" in the ranks of government, including the military, and in professions requiring Western education.

Further complicating religious politics in the new nation-state was the fact that a significant portion of the Muslim population—a majority in the 1950s—preferred a nonconfessional government to an Islamic state. The independence struggle had imbued many Indonesians with nationalist, democratic, and socialist ideals that were often decidedly secular. Secular nationalism was particularly influential among Muslim members of the largest ethnic group, the Javanese. For these reasons, throughout the period since independence, the influence of Muslim political parties has never matched the high proportion of Muslims in the population as a whole.

Political battles deeply influenced religious change in the new nation. From 1945 to 1957, Indonesia witnessed a steady escalation in political and ideological conflict. The history and politics of the period are covered elsewhere in this book. Instead, the focus here is on the role of Islam in the new nation-state—a central issue in political debates in the 1950s, when Indonesia had one of the freest parliamentary democracies in Asia.

The issue of Islam-state relations had long divided Indonesian politicians. In the weeks prior to the declaration of independence on 17 August 1945, the nationalist leader Sukarno had appealed to Muslims and secular nationalists to come up with a formula for balancing their respective interests. Among Muslim figures, many wanted to establish a full Islamic state. Christians, Hindus, and secular nationalists warned that an effort formally to link Islam with government would only provoke unrest in eastern Indonesia and other non-Muslim regions. Eventually a compromise was hammered out in an agreement known as the Jakarta Charter.

According to the charter, the state would remain officially nonconfessional, and freedom of religion would be guaranteed, but the state would also work to "implement" Islamic law within the Muslim community. As independence neared, however, Christian, Hindu, and nationalist leaders balked at even this compromise formulation, fearing it might be a first step toward an Islamic polity. Rather than risk disunity on the eve of statehood, the charter was quietly dropped from the declaration of independence and the preamble to the constitution.

Despite this failure to formalize a role for Islam in governance, the issue did not disappear, but remained a topic of bitter controversy over the ensuing decade. From 1950 on, the Indonesian government operated under what was supposed to be an interim constitution. The plan was that, after national elections in 1955, a constitutional assembly would convene to begin work on a constitution that would, among other things, definitively resolve the question of Islam and the state. The elections were bitterly contested, since it was expected that whoever won them would critically influence the shaping of a new constitution. All players knew that the future of the nation was at stake.

To the surprise of many observers, Muslim politicians not least among them, the 1955 elections failed to give a decisive majority to the Muslim parties. Illustrating the depth of division in Indonesian society were the roughly equal numbers of votes earned by the four most successful contenders—two Muslim parties, the modernist Masyumi and the traditionalist NU; and two secular organizations, the Indonesian National Party (PNI) and the Indonesian Communist Party (PKI). Neither the Muslims nor their secular-nationalist opponents emerged from the contest strong enough to impose their own view of religion and the state.

Controversies plagued the constitutional assembly. Although it achieved consensus on some matters, such as human rights, it seemed unable to settle the question of relations between Islam and the state. Citing this failure, along with the worsening situation in the country as a whole, President Sukarno dissolved the assembly in July of 1959 and returned the country to the 1945 constitution. Not coincidentally, that document accorded far more power to the president than to parliament.

The political crisis was aggravated by regional rebellions mainly led by Muslims. These leaders' motivations were complex, and included grievances unrelated to religion. But among Muslim rebels in Sumatra, West Java, and Sulawesi, many wanted an Islamic state. Although by the early 1960s these uprisings had all been quelled, the military campaign against them left a lasting mark on Indonesian politics, strengthening the role of the armed forces in national life and deepening their mistrust of political Islam.

Another fierce struggle pitted Muslims together with the military against the PKI. By the late 1950s, the economy was in deep crisis. In the face of steep economic decline, the communists mobilized the poor, especially among Java's nominal Muslims, and built the PKI into the largest party in the country. The PKI continued its advance even after President Sukarno's suspension of the assembly in 1959. In 1960, when the rebellions in Sumatra and Sulawesi flared up again, Sukarno banned Masyumi, ostensibly because some of its leaders had gone over to the rebel side. The abolition of Masyumi, an influential promoter of the idea of an Islamic state, left the modernist movement rudderless. Modernist Muslims would not recover from this disaster for three decades.

Masyumi's prohibition notwithstanding, the traditionalist NU continued to work within Sukarno's "Guided Democracy" regime. The president tried in his own way to stabilize the country by forging an unlikely alliance of nationalists, communists, and (traditionalist) Muslims. Yet his policies embittered many in the Islamic community, including many in NU. For Muslim leaders, it seemed that the president had taken a sharp leftward turn and now openly favored the communist party. Many Muslims were convinced that a violent showdown with the PKI had become inevitable. Even within NU, a Sukarno ally, several branches of the party's youth organization were quietly being given tactical training by members of the armed forces.

In the aftermath of a failed leftist officers' coup on the night of 30 September 1965, many in the Muslim community feared that the long-awaited showdown had arrived. Lacking coordinated support, however, the coup collapsed within a few days. Sensing their rivals' vulnerability, Muslim leaders accused the communists of staging the conspiracy, and called for the PKI's abolition. With covert military support, several Muslim youth groups organized violent attacks on PKI headquarters—opening actions in a fiercely anticommunist campaign that would consume the country. By the middle of 1966, hundreds of thousands of real or suspected communists had been slaughtered and the party leadership had been liquidated.[16] Although associations representing Indonesia's minority religions took part in the killings in some locations, Muslim youth groups working in cooperation with the armed forces were often at the forefront of the campaign.

In 1967, with the PKI gone, the man who had coordinated its destruction, Major General Suharto, was elevated to the position of acting president. Indonesia had entered a New Order and, with it, a new era in Muslim-state relations.

Hope and Disappointment

Because of their cooperation in the anti-PKI campaign, Muslim leaders expected the new government to make major concessions to Islamic political organizations. At the very least, Muslim politicians looked forward to the rehabilitation of Masyumi, the modernist Muslim party, and the holding of national elections. This time around, they believed, in contrast to the inconclusive 1995 poll, they would win a decisive majority of the vote. After all, their strongest competitor,

---

16. For details, see Robert Cribb, ed., *The Indonesia Killings, 1965–1966: Studies from Java and Bali* (Clayton, Victoria, Australia: Centre of Southeast Asian Studies, Monash University, 1990).

the PKI, had been destroyed, and their other secular rival, PNI, had been discredited. Muslim leaders also hoped that, in the aftermath of their expected electoral victory, the unfinished business of the constitutional assembly could be taken up, including the unresolved question of whether and how to link Islam more formally to the state.

Hopeful Muslims were thus taken aback when, in December 1966, the military named Masyumi, among other groups, as having deviated from Pancasila, thus ruling out its rehabilitation. Shortly thereafter, the authorities appeared to soften this blow by indicating that they would allow the formation of a new Islamic party, Parmusi. No sooner had this concession been made, however, than the government went on to announce that Masyumi officials would be barred from leadership positions in the new party. Many Muslim leaders began to feel that the New Order saw them not as allies but as rivals.

Muslim disappointment soon deepened. In 1971 the long-anticipated election was held and won by Golkar, the regime's vote-harvesting vehicle, with more than three-fifths of the ballots cast. In the wake of this resounding victory, the authorities announced that the nine still extant parties would be melded into two formations. One of these two groupings, Partai Persatuan Pembangunan (Development Unity Party or PPP), was supposed to represent the interests of Muslims; the other, Partai Demokrasi Indonesia (Indonesian Democratic Party or PDI), was an unwieldy amalgam of secular nationalists, Catholics, Protestants, and Hindus. These amalgams would compete in future elections with the government's Golkar. Generous official support tilted the electoral playing field in favor of Golkar, which went on to win all of the national elections held under the New Order, while backstage manipulation of the PPP by regime leaders further curtailed Muslim political influence.[17]

The New Order strategist most responsible for winning the 1971 election and consolidating the party system was Major General Ali Murtopo. Head of a powerful intelligence-and-covert-action unit within the army, Murtopo was among President Suharto's closest aides during the regime's first years. A man known for his close ties to the Chinese and Catholic communities, Murtopo was considered a technocrat with secular-nationalist views. His stated objective in restricting Muslim influence and the role of parties was to prevent a recurrence of the fiercely destabilizing political rivalries of the 1950s. Murtopo and other regime leaders were convinced that Indonesia would become stable only if politics were organized to express "rational" interests, rather than emotional ones based on "primordial" religion or ethnicity.[18] Implementing this conviction, the New Or-

---

17. On the 1971 election and its aftermath, see Ken E. Ward, *The 1971 Election in Indonesia* (Clayton, Victoria, Australia: Monash University Centre for Southeast Asian Studies, 1974).

18. On Ali Murtopo, see Richard Robison, *Indonesia: The Rise of Capital* (Sydney: Allen and Unwin, 1986), pp. 97, 107, 148–152.

der strictly limited the political activities of Muslims and other nongovernmental actors in the 1970s and 1980s.

The pessimism of Muslim leaders about their prospects was further confirmed in 1973, when government factions in the People's Consultative Assembly (MPR) proposed giving mystical beliefs (*kepercayaan*) equal standing with the scripturally based religions (*agama*) already recognized by the state. Muslim leaders felt directly challenged. Most of the people associated with mystical groups, they knew, were Javanese whose backgrounds and outlooks were only nominally Muslim. If the state were to accord mystical beliefs and actual religions equal status, would that not invite thousands of superficially Muslim Javanists to leave Islam?

These fears were exacerbated by the fact that the ranks of Indonesian Muslims had already been depleted by mass conversions in the wake of the violence of 1965–66: An estimated two million nominal Muslims had repudiated their faith by becoming Christians, while a smaller number had converted to Hinduism.[19] This was the largest conversion of Muslims to Christianity anywhere in the world in modern times. The great majority of these converts were from communist families who had suffered the horrors of 1965–66. For many of them, Christianity amounted to a safe refuge from association with suddenly dangerous atheism—a refuge made more accessible by their already fragile ties to Islamic belief and practice.

However intelligible such motives were, Muslim leaders resented the fact that, after 1966, the government had allowed Christian and Hindu proselytizers into communities where the PKI had been strong. The authorities had hoped to combat communism through religious education. They had wanted to appear evenhanded in allowing non-Muslim as well as Muslim access to the villages. But Muslim figures regarded the policy as further proof of anti-Islamic bias in the ruling elite. In this context, the subsequent suggestion that the state grant equal status to *kepercayaan* alongside *agama* was seen as one more blow against Islam. In the end, the intensity of Muslim protest led the government to rescind the latter proposal.

In the eyes of some Muslim leaders, the final blow to Muslim autonomy and aspirations came in 1984. In that year the government drafted a law requiring all sociopolitical organizations to accept the national ideology of Pancasila as their sole foundation and outlook. The leaders of Christian associations objected to the legislation as official interference in matters of religion. But Muslim leaders felt themselves and their organizations to be the real targets of the proposal, and

---

19. See my *Hindu Javanese: Tengger Tradition and Islam* (Princeton, NJ: Princeton University Press, 1985), pp. 239–265; and Margaret L. Lyon's "Politics and Religious Identity: Genesis of a Javanese-Hindu Movement in Rural Central Java," doctoral dissertation, University of California-Berkeley Department of Anthropology, Berkeley, CA, 1979.

it was thought that many of them would refuse to go along. In the end, all but one Muslim group—a small association of modernist students—relented and accepted the sole-foundation proposal, which became law. But in the eyes of many Muslim leaders, the Pancasila-only rule amounted to a final nail in the coffin of Muslim politics.

Cultural Revival

Not all Muslims of prominence shared these fears and resentments. One could always find Muslim intellectuals who were less pessimistic about the prospects for their religion under the New Order. Already in Islamic circles in the late 1960s, some young intellectuals had begun to question the longstanding preoccupation of senior leaders with party politics. The strategy of party-based mobilization, these critics said, had failed to win an electoral majority in 1955. The political campaigns and later violence, they argued, had merely divided the Muslim community. Arguably, in the 1960s, political conflict had even led some Muslims to become Christians. By putting political goals above religious ones, Muslim politicians had confused what was worldly and secular with what was essential in Islam. So ran the critique.

As an alternative to this failed policy of furthering "political" Islam, these intellectuals advocated a strategy focused on "cultural" Islam. What they meant was not that Muslims should ignore politics, or that Islam was apolitical, but that the priority for Muslims should be on deepening the faith of fellow believers. If this cultural or spiritual goal could be achieved, political change would follow in good order.

Not all of those who advised or pursued this strategy saw it the same way. Young intellectuals in and around the Islamic Students' Organization (Himpunan Mahasiswa Islam, or HMI) and several other moderate groupings, for example, who had never depended on party politics, urged fellow believers to look beyond the interplay of parties and government for paths toward Muslim renewal—spiritual, intellectual, and also economic. In the judgment of this group, the struggle for an Islamic state was not required in Islam and should be set aside forever.[20]

Others who spoke of a cultural strategy, however, saw it as a necessary detour in what to them was still a valid long-term struggle for control of the state. This view was particularly widespread among activists formerly associated with Masyumi, the modernist party whose 1960 banning the New Order had reaffirmed. In the 1950s, Masyumi had been a powerful political movement with an

---

20. For a fuller discussion, see my "Islam, State, and Civil Society: ICMI and the Struggle for the Indonesian Middle Class," *Indonesia*, 56 (October 1993), pp. 1–35; and Bahtiar Effendy, "Islam and the State in Indonesia: Munawir Sjadzali and the Development of a New Theological Underpinning of Political Islam," *Studia Islamika* [Jakarta], 2:2 (1995), pp. 97–122.

array of social and educational organizations. While wanting to Islamize the state, Masyumi had been neither authoritarian nor "fundamentalist" in outlook. In fact, most of its leaders had ardently supported the notion of constitutional government.

Since Sukarno had outlawed their party because of their unceasing criticisms of his policies, Masyumi's leaders felt that it was unjust for Suharto to continue denying them a political platform. Faced with the overwhelming power of the New Order, Masyumi leaders resigned themselves to not reconstituting their party. But they did so from compulsion not principle. For them, the turn to cultural Islam meant suspending, but not relinquishing, the goal of Islamic governance.

Given their rather desperate situation, the "cultural turn" of these former Masyumi Muslims tended to be more strident and less accommodating compared with the activities for nonpolitical renewal sponsored by the younger intellectuals linked to HMI. A case in point was the Council for Indonesian Muslim Proselytization (Dewan Dakwah Islamiyah Indonesia, or DDII), an organization closely identified with Masyumi's legacy. In the 1970s and early 1980s, DDII was an uncompromising critic of government policies toward gambling, sexual morality, and, most consistently, Christianity. Leaders of DDII also favored stridently anti-Western positions on matters of foreign policy.

Many observers dismissed DDII and its mouthpiece, the newsmagazine *Media Dakwah,* as fundamentalist.[21] Publications by DDII did sometimes stoop to fear-mongering and diatribe. The tone of their comments aside, however, most of the positions they took were consistent with theologically conservative, but still mainstream, views in the larger Muslim world. Nor were DDII followers uniformly harsh. They included a more moderate faction, and the two camps often disagreed, although rarely in public. As long as the once-proud leaders of Masyumi were treated as pariahs by the New Order, the resentment inside DDII ranks made it hard for moderate voices to prevail. As relations with the government improved in the early 1990s, however, the moderate faction grew more influential, and DDII statements softened accordingly.[22]

Détente?

In 1978 and 1979, the Departments of Religion and Home Affairs announced regulations severely restricting the freedom of missionaries to proselytize among citizens who already identified, however casually, with another religion. Issued

---

21. R. William Liddle, "*Media Dakwah* Scripturalism: One Form of Islamic Political Thought and Action in New Order Indonesia," in Mark R. Woodward, ed., *Towards a New Paradigm: Recent Developments in Indonesian Islamic Thought* (Tempe: Arizona State University Center for Southeast Asian Studies, 1996), pp. 323–356.

22. Following the death of Muhammad Natsir in 1993, the leadership of DDII passed to Anwar Haryono. A man of gentle if firm intelligence who had long played a moderating role within DDII, Haryono was well regarded even by liberal Muslims.

without warning, the new rules astonished and upset Christian leaders, who had in effect been barred from cultivating certain groups, such as Javanist Muslims, with whom they had been working since the 1960s.

The new rules were not unwelcome from the standpoint of Muslim suspicion toward Christian designs on Indonesians with at least some connection to Islam. And just as the shielding of the already affiliated from conversion was a turning point in the Christian missions' relations with the state, so did it reflect a willingness on the government's part to encourage cultural, though not political, Islam.

In the late 1960s, the government had already begun to expand its network of Muslim universities, known as State Institutes [for Higher Education] in Islamic Religion (Institut Agama Islam Negeri, or IAIN). By the early 1980s these colleges were graduating large numbers of students trained in Islamic law, theology, arts, and education. Many of these graduates found employment in the private sector, where they contributed to a heightened sensitivity in business circles toward Islamic devotion. But IAIN alumni were also well represented in government employment and public education.

In principle, religious instruction had long been mandatory for all schoolchildren. But the principle had been implemented consistently only since the late 1960s with the growth of a pool of qualified teachers. On entering primary school, every student was required to identify his or her religion, selected by the child's parents from among the five officially recognized alternatives: Buddhist, Catholic, Hindu, Muslim, or Protestant. Agnosticism, mysticism, and tribal beliefs were not options. For the rest of his or her educational career, the student received a few hours of instruction each week in the history and doctrines of the relevant religion. Such policies led, in the 1980s and 1990s, to the coming of age of a generation of Indonesians equipped with a basic knowledge of their respective faiths—at least as these had been presented in government-authorized textbooks.

Meanwhile the ministry of religion, long regarded by secular nationalists as a bastion of Islam, worked to build more mosques and prayer houses around the archipelago, especially in places where the piety of Muslims seemed insufficient or physical facilities for its expression were lacking. The results were impressive: In East and Central Java, two of the provinces targeted by the ministry, the number of mosques almost doubled, from about 27,000 to some 49,000.

The department also mounted a campaign to send Muslim proselytizers and preachers into communities regarded as lax in their observance of Islam, including places where Javanese had converted to Christianity or Hinduism in the wake of the upheaval of 1965–66. Combined with the new restrictions on Christian missions, these programs effectively halted new Christian and Hindu recruitment on Java. By the mid-1980s, the proportions of these minority affiliations among Javanese had stabilized. Indeed, in a few communities, there were reports of Christian and Hindu converts "backsliding" to Islam.

Other gestures during these years extended this evidence of rising official sympathy for Islamic culture, if not Islamic politics. In the late 1980s, Muslim missionaries began working in eastern Indonesia, Irian Jaya, and several other areas that had been the exclusive preserve of Christian missions. Rules for religious education in the schools were strengthened in 1988. In 1989 the jurisdiction of the nation's Islamic courts was expanded and unified, despite vigorous objections by advocates of secular law. A year later, responding to Muslim protests, the government allowed Muslim schoolgirls to wear religious head coverings in school. In 1991 an Islamic bank, previously illegal under the terms of Indonesia's banking laws, was established at the urging of the president himself. That same year Suharto and his family made the pilgrimage to Mecca, fulfilling one of the most esteemed among Muslim religious duties. Finally, in 1990, 1993, and 1995, the country was rocked by court cases in which the government accused public figures of slandering Islam.

ICMI and the Military

One event more than any other illustrates the complex motives and political interests at work in the New Order's rapprochement with Islam. This was the December 1990 establishment of the Indonesian Muslim Intellectuals' Association, known by its acronym, ICMI. Strong government and military opposition had thwarted several previous attempts by independent intellectuals to organize such an association. Yet President Suharto himself inaugurated ICMI at its founding meeting in 1990. High-ranking government officials also attended the meeting, which ended by electing one of Suharto's closest advisers, B.J. Habibie, to head the new organization.

The foreign and domestic press speculated on the president's motives in personally approving the birth of ICMI and what the association's impact on Indonesian politics might be. Many Muslim leaders spoke warmly of a new era in Islam-state relations. A few intellectuals expected governance to be further Islamized in tandem with the rising piety of Indonesian Muslims. They pointed to the popularity of Islamic magazines, the proliferation of prayer rooms in fancy hotels, and the rising frequency of religious pilgrimage among members of the elite as signs that Indonesia was becoming a more Muslim society. As Indonesia became more devout, they hoped, pressure would build to formalize the role of Islam in government.

In retrospect it is clear that beginning in the early 1980s Indonesians experienced an Islamic revival of major proportions. However, its political implications were not easily drawn. The community of Muslims across the archipelago was—and remains—diverse. So one could not—and cannot—speak of the rise of a single "Islamic" kind of politics.

Responses to ICMI illustrate the point. Muslims outside the new body criticized it as a tool of the regime's desire to coopt Muslims and deflect demands for democratizing change. This argument was voiced with particular consistency by Abdurrahman Wahid, the head of NU and a leading figure in the growing prodemocracy movement. Other democratist Muslims joined him, decrying what they saw as the sacrifice of democratic ideals in the name of a government-controlled Islam.

Meanwhile, inside ICMI, a clear divide opened between members with close ties to the New Order and those with a history of independence and criticism. Some of the former were nominal Muslims who had been encouraged or pressured to become members of ICMI to enhance official influence within the organization. Most of the people in this group showed a measure of genuine piety and supported programs designed to increase Muslim representation in governance and business. But they did not publicly criticize broader political conditions and were especially unwilling to join the calls for more democracy.

Many of the independent activists in ICMI, on the other hand, were tied into the prodemocracy community and its (nongovernmental) organizations. A few of these Muslims were known for their criticisms of corruption, the military, and economic inequality. Compared with their government-connected counterparts, these critics were less influential within the association. But the existence of a prodemocracy wing belied the idea that ICMI was a uniformly willing accomplice of the regime.

Suharto himself seemed keenly aware of these differences within ICMI and the larger Muslim community. From the start, he was careful to ensure that leaders of the organization were recruited from the governmental group. Particularly favored in this regard were individuals with a proven history of loyalty to him. But independent-minded Muslims in ICMI also benefited from the government's policy of rapprochement. They were able to travel and speak more freely than before. Few, however, were given positions of influence in the organization, and fewer still were named to important posts in the government itself.

Interesting in this respect was President Suharto's choice of cabinet ministers in 1993. In light of the new policy on Islam, many observers had expected an influx of ICMI supporters into the cabinet. Several ICMI members were named ministers, and the number of Christians in the cabinet shrank from six to three. But all of the ICMI ministers were drawn from the ranks of the government-linked group within the association, and most of them had ties to Suharto's confidante and minister, Habibie. Later on, several of ICMI's more outspoken prodemocratic members were subjected to legal harassment. However, ICMI leaders resisted demands to expel members who had criticized the regime.

The story of ICMI activist Sri Bintang Pamungkas illustrates the diversity inside the association and how risky such criticism could be. Sri Bintang was elected to parliament as a member of the PPP in 1993. But his bold castigations of corruption in government and military interference in politics quickly got him into trouble. Accused of slandering President Suharto in a speech in Germany, he was stripped of his parliamentary seat. His defenders insisted that he had said nothing slanderous, and accused the military of trying to silence him for speaking up. But the authorities eventually prevailed. (One of Habibie's first acts as president in 1998 was to release Sri Bintang from jail.)

Suharto, Habibie, and ICMI's own members aside, military officers also shaped the politics of the association's rise. From the start of the New Order, the military had been the president's most crucial and consistent supporter. Leading military figures had been rewarded with appointments to important posts in the bureaucracy, foreign service, and state enterprise. Yet in the months prior to ICMI's formation, high-ranking officers strongly advised the government not to allow it to become a legal organization.

Some took the fact that they were overruled as evidence of serious intra-elite disagreement—perhaps even a dangerous rift between the president and his military leaders. In retrospect, however, such alarm was premature, and the power of the anti-ICMI officers overrated. After naming a fresh cabinet in 1993, Suharto replaced the most vocal military critics of ICMI with officers who were loyal to him and neutral or supportive of his opening toward Islam. Beneath the surface, however, tensions remained between ICMI on the one hand, and on the other, certain military and civilian factions in government, including some ministers close to Suharto.

Responses and Adaptations

The circumstances of minority believers and once nominally Muslim or Javanist communities further complicated the dynamics of religion and public life in late-New Order Indonesia. The founding of ICMI in 1990 and its subsequent growth disquieted Hindu, Buddhist, and especially Christian notables almost to the verge of panic. Owing to their education, wealth, and prominent role in the military, Christians had long exercised influence far beyond their modest share of the country's population. Some Muslims saw in this disproportion two decades of deliberate bias on the part of the New Order. To whatever extent such a bias existed, however, it is also clear that historical and structural conditions had engendered Christian prominence.

In any case, in what would prove to be the final years of Suharto's Indonesia, elite and middle-class Christians were obliged to adjust their expectations. Christian influence in government and the media diminished, though much less than some militant Muslims might have wished. At the same time, however, the deregulatory steps, reviewed by Richard Borsuk in this book, probably strengthened the economic position of the largely Christian Chinese business community.

The latter possibility triggered calls for the state to protect and assist "indigenous" (*pribumi*) Muslim entrepreneurs and the public sector of the economy where Christian-Chinese influence was notably weak. And ICMI's close association with Habibie, in effect, united both aspects of this view: the Muslims' desire for compensatory opportunities and preferences in light of what they saw as the previous skewing of benefits toward Christian and Chinese Indonesians; and the minister's anti-laissez-faire enthusiasm for using the state as a platform for high-tech ventures on behalf of national strength and growth.

Elite concerns aside, the late New Order period was a disquieting time for Christians generally in Indonesia. Even in such remote corners of the archipelago as Flores and Roti, Christians took note of the changing tone of what the central government was saying about Islam. Some complained of feeling like second-class citizens in their own country. In the meantime, however, Christian leaders responded to the Muslim revival by consolidating and strengthening their educational and outreach programs within legal limits (including the ban on proselytizing Indonesians already identified with another religion). At least prior to the crisis of 1997–98, their anxieties notwithstanding, most Christian intellectuals remained optimistic that governmental respect for religious pluralism would survive the changes in Islam-state relations that cultural revival and official rapprochement had brought about.

The Hindu community replied to these changes by consolidating and deepening a process of reform long visible at its religious headquarters on the island of Bali. Not recognized as a formal religion during the first fifteen years of Indonesian independence, Hindu-Balinese reformers had struggled since the late 1950s to develop administrative and educational institutions capable of strengthening the knowledge and practice of the Hindu religion by its adherents. In this process, the reformers developed and disseminated a "modularized" version of the faith to interested non-Balinese. They standardized Hindu ritual practices, singled out a delimited body of Hindu "scripture" for popular study, and wrote textbooks introducing schoolchildren to these clearly delineated parts of the religion.

By recasting what had been distinctively Balinese Hinduism in a more communicable form, including a clear delineation and linking of its elements, the reformers gave the religion a modular coherence and appeal beyond the local status groups and village organizations on which it had been based. Traditionalist critics, including not a few Western anthropologists, charged the reformists with re-creating Balinese religion in the formally scriptural image of Indonesian Islam. Yet the Balinese middle class rallied to the reforms as a necessary response to the challenge of integration into a majority-Muslim nation.

At the onset of Indonesian independence Hinduism had been confined to Bali and a small pocket of Javanese believers not far to the west, in eastern Java. The development of a coherently unified or modular Hinduism allowed the religion to take hold among some non-Balinese on Java and other islands. Prominent among such converts were members of ethnic minorities whose ties to local beliefs had weakened, but who were not attracted to Christianity or Islam. Beyond Bali and Java, the most notable centers of Hindu affiliation during the New Order were among some Dayaks in Kalimantan, certain upland peoples in Sulawesi, and the Karo Bataks of Sumatra.

Longer-Term Prospects

In Indonesia beyond Suharto—for that matter, beyond Habibie as well—the out-look for Christians and other non-Muslims will be shaped by issues over which they exercise, at best, only indirect influence. These issues include the vexed question of official policy regarding Islam, and what is likely to be an ongoing struggle among Muslim leaders for the hearts and minds of the Islamic majority. Developments in the Muslim community will be shaped not only by activists, but also and more quietly by less organized and more "private Muslims" (*Muslim pribadi*)—the latter a label sometimes used by such persons to describe themselves.

A significant number of Javanese Muslims are of this "private" type, as are many Muslims in the middle class. Compared with their counterparts at the start of the New Order, these people are far more likely to pray, read the Qur'an, and perform the annual fast. Yet most of them are reluctant to associate with Islamic social or political organizations, have little interest in the scholasticism of Is-lamic law, and prefer nonconfessional governance to an Islamic state. It may seem paradoxical, but this segment of the Muslim community appears to have grown more confident in the face of the Islamic revival—confident that one can be a good Muslim without supporting a formally Islamic state. For them, the essence of Islam lies neither in government nor in thousand-year-old law, but in an ethics of justice and devotion to a God who is merciful as well as powerful.

What is perhaps most remarkable in this context about the Muslim commu-nity in Indonesia is that so many of its leading intellectuals, including some from quite orthodox backgrounds, whose counterparts elsewhere in the Muslim world might be expected to reject such "unorganized" views, basically accept them. In talking with individuals of this "privately" Muslim sort, one is also struck by the strength of their commitment to nationalist ideals. Often they voice the hope that, even as it provides a moral foundation for national development, Islam should not be a divisive force in the nation as a whole. If this occurs, they say, it is the fault not of Islam but of those who misuse it by confusing their personal interests and preferences with Islam's universal values. For these "private" Mus-lims, Islam is a deeply humanistic religion, entirely consistent with the modern values of civility and pluralism, and thus well suited to meet—not reject—the moral needs of a nonconfessional state.

Whether this view of Islam and the polity predominates in the long run will depend on more than the inventiveness of Muslim intellectuals. Also influential will be the nature of the political system that emerges in the aftermath of Suharto's rule. If, as many hope, the political system opens up and becomes more partici-patory, new coalitions will develop. With them may well come a new interest in Islam-state relations.

Some in the Muslim community may take advantage of freer conditions to press again for a formalization of the role of Islam in government. The greater their success in mobilizing a significant constituency to this end, however, the greater the chance of military intervention to defend the transconfessional Pancasila state. In such polarized circumstances, non-Muslim and "private" Muslim supporters of democratization could throw their cards in with the armed forces to avoid the risks of radical political change.

But such a drastic scenario is unduly pessimistic. This chapter attempts to show that Indonesian Islam has a rich tradition of pluralism and organizational independence. The New Order, to the extent that it reminded Muslim leaders of the dangers of concentrating power in state hands, reinforced this tradition. It is no coincidence that in the transition to post-Suharto times, Muslim intellectuals have been among the most ardent exponents of constitutional government and civil society.

The shocks and setbacks of 1997–98 have interrupted, but not ended, the process of economic growth. When growth resumes, as eventually it will, so will the country's search for modernity (to cite the terms used by Robert Cribb in his opening chapter). And if that search successfully incorporates respect for the power of markets and the worth of persons, a familiar social process should again be visible.

If such a pattern of development gets underway in Indonesia beyond Suharto, it will foster choice. Opportunities will stimulate people to realize their own potentials and make their own decisions. Especially in the growing ranks of the middle class, Indonesians are likely to want the freedom to determine not just their careers but their lives as well. There is a remarkable contagiousness to this experience of what Western philosophers have long referred to as modern freedom or liberty. But this moral appetite, this desire to be oneself and make one's own way, is not uniquely or necessarily Western. It is not unfamiliar to Islam or Muslims.[23] And it is more than a mere by-product of a certain kind of economic growth. Looking to the future—beyond Suharto, Habibie, and the crisis of 1997–98—one may guess that this idea of freedom will powerfully shape the interplay of religion and politics in Indonesia.

Conclusion

Unlike much of the Middle East or the premodern West, Indonesia has a history of pluralism in many realms, including the religious, ethnic, and political spheres on which this chapter has focused. It is the polycentric character of this tradition,

---

23. On ideals of individual autonomy and precedents for civil society within Islam, see Ellis Goldberg, "Private Goods, Public Wrongs, and Civil Society in Some Medieval Arab Theory and Practice," in Ellis Goldberg, Resat Kasaba, and Joel S. Migdal, eds., *Rules and Rights in the Middle East: Democracy, Law, and Society* (Seattle: University of Washington Press, 1993), pp. 248–271; and Ahmad S. Moussalli, "Modern Islamic

its complex and evolving pluralism, and not religious mixing or syncretism that distinguishes Indonesian Islam within the Muslim world.

The archipelago experienced periods of absolutist rule, and European colonialism reinforced authoritarian politics on some islands, notably Java. Violence with ethnic or religious overtones flared from time to time, as in the partly anti-Chinese rioting that swept Jakarta in May 1998. Yet looking back over the history of Indonesia, and keeping in mind how profoundly pluralistic its society has been, the most striking and persistent general feature of religious life on these islands is their inhabitants' sense of obligation to live, and learn to live, with one another.

This is not a trivial precedent. Sociologists of religion have observed that the most serious challenge in the contemporary era is not economic dynamism or modern rationalism, but the willingness of people from varied backgrounds to live and let live within the same nation-state.[24] As has often been noted by Nurcholish Madjid—a respected figure among the Muslim intellectuals who sought to renew and deepen cultural Islam during the New Order—compared with Indonesians Westerners, historically, have had far fewer degrees of cultural pluralism to deal with. Nor have the politics of Western societies always accommodated cultural differences, as national socialism in Germany and ethnic cleansing in Bosnia remind us.

The point is not to measure Indonesia's performance against that of Europe. Rather, it is to highlight what is neglected by the media's emphasis on crisis and strife: the existence in Indonesia's past of a remarkable precedent for the civility needed to achieve and sustain democratic politics and social peace in radically multicultural conditions.

This chapter has argued that one source of this precedent lies within the Muslim community. Historically in the islands, neither Islamic courts nor Muslim scholars exercised a clear monopoly of power over the social and intellectual life of this community. If there were always different views of what it meant to be a good Muslim, so did custom and behavior vary within and across different religions, ethnicities, and regions. The sheer diversity and overlapping or criss-crossing character of such differences invited the archipelago's peoples, including Muslims, to learn and practice toleration.

By itself, of course, this precedent guarantees nothing for the future. In the modern era, the central challenge for religious thinkers everywhere is to sift through the debris of tradition, locate elements relevant for contemporary life,

Fundamentalist Discourses on Civil Society, Pluralism, and Democracy," in Augustus Richard Norton, ed., *Civil Society in the Middle East* (Leiden. Netherlands: E.J. Brill. 1995), pp. 79–119.

24. See, for example, Peter L. Berger and Thomas Luckmann, *Modernity, Pluralism and the Crisis of Meaning: The Orientation of Modern Man* (Gütersloh, Germany: Bertelsmann Foundation, 1995).

and elaborate them in new ways that respond to modernity's demands. It is just such a process that facilitated the development of pluralist traditions in the West, to the degree that they have taken hold. And it is just such a process that is unfolding in Indonesia.

The future of that process cannot be known. Propitious traditions, as discussed, are no assurance of the future peaceful coexistence of religions. Among a host of other factors, political leadership and simple luck, good or bad, will also shape the outcome. However, at a time when reports of violence by Musilms tempt Western observers to conclude that Islam is inherently anti-democratic, it is helpful to be reminded that the world's fourth most populous country is involved in an experiment that holds real promise, not only for Indonesia but for the rest of the Muslim world as well. It is even conceivable that, in the twenty-first century, the creativity of Indonesians in managing evolving pluralism may offer insights for the leaders of Western countries in their own efforts to address the shifting balance of tension and opportunity that multicultural citizenship implies.

Chapter 8

Women: Difference Versus Diversity

Kathryn Robinson

The New Order promoted gender differences. Officially sponsored images of femininity portrayed Indonesian women as subordinate to men, within the family and the state. This chapter places such policies in social context, reviews their implications for women, and explores the gender-differentiated impact of the New Order's approach to development.

The main argument may be summarized as follows: Through the policies that it directed at women, the New Order tried to impose a homogenizing view of female social roles on the diversity of gender relations actually found throughout the archipelago. The material gains that Indonesians achieved under the regime, at least up to the crash of 1997–98, were reflected in many improvements in women's lives. Often, however, the New Order's ideological project with regard to gender contradicted the changes in gender roles and relations that arose from the regime's own manner of promoting development. Thus, in broadcasting an essentialized image of the ideal Indonesian woman as loyal wife and dutiful mother, the regime denied the transformation and diversification of women's roles that its own relentless campaign for material expansion had helped to bring about.

I begin with an overview of socioeconomic and political indicators relating to Indonesian women. Then I contrast the diversity of gender systems in the archipelago with the homogeneous definition of women's roles in a patriarchal family system advanced by New Order programs for women. Highlighted next are how two regime projects, family planning and industrialization, affected gender relations in ways that contradicted the apparent intent of specific state programs for women. Finally, I show how accelerating global flows of capital and culture further complicated the meanings of being a woman (or a man) in Indonesia.

The New Order's outlook on gender was not static. Beginning in 1993, the regime circulated a new rhetorical formulation featuring commitment to gender equity defined in Indonesian as *kemitrasejajaran*—literally "companions on the same level," although officially glossed as "harmonious gender partnership." This ideal was to be achieved by subjecting government policy to "gender analysis" (*analisa jender*), as if to acknowledge the need to address inequalities of power between women and men. The new language seemed to imply a radical widening of the regime's orientation toward women, away from the previous practice of dealing with the participation of women in Indonesian society through policies aimed specifically at them.

A few years later the economic and political shocks of 1997–98, which are not dealt with here, ended Suharto's rule. Also ended was the possibility of knowing whether this change in official rhetoric heralded a change in regime practice, or that it was just a symbolic gesture. Nevertheless, the shift in official language, and the public debate over gender relations that accompanied it, did underscore the instability of what it meant—and means—to be a woman (or a man) in contemporary Indonesia.

Achievements and Limitations

Under the New Order, despite the dominance of official images of women as wives and mothers, women were relatively active outside the domestic sphere. In 1995, for instance, 40 percent of Indonesia's labor force were women, compared with averages of 42 percent in "high-income" countries, 38 percent in "middle-income" countries (including Indonesia), 33 percent in South Asia, and 26 percent in the Middle East and North Africa. Figures for 1993 show that no Asian country for which data were available had a higher proportion of its economically active women working as employers or on their own.[1] In 1990 a substantial majority of all Indonesians employed in services—58 percent—were women. Comparable average rates for developing countries at "high" and "medium" levels of human development (the latter including Indonesia) were 56 and 48 percent, respectively, and for South Asia, 26 percent. Service employment was far more accessible to women in Indonesia than in other majority-Muslim countries, and Indonesia scored well, too, on this dimension compared with some industrial countries.[2]

---

1. *World Development Indicators 1997* [henceforth *WDI97*] (Washington, DC: World Bank, 1997), pp. 43–44 [labor force], 46–48 [employing or own-account workers]. In Indonesia employers and workers on their own account made up 11 and 28 percent of the female and male labor forces, respectively.

2. United Nations Development Programme [UNDP], *Human Development Report 1996* [henceforth *HDR96*] (New York: Oxford University Press, 1996), pp. 156 [developing countries], 197 [industrial countries], 210 [South Asia]. Percentage figures for comparison by country include: United States 60; *Indonesia 58*; Canada 57; Turkey 10; Egypt 8; Iran 7. The World Bank's method of distinguishing "high-" from "middle-income"

While these figures indicate high rates of economic participation, in the 1990s Indonesian women were disadvantaged relative to Indonesian men in key respects. Women earned only 32 percent of national income, compared with the 68 percent share earned by men. Female rates of adult literacy (77 percent) and educational enrollment (58 percent) were lower than those of male rates (at 89 and 64 percent, respectively). And as late as the 1980s, returns to labor were higher for men than for women in all sectors of the Indonesian economy.[3]

In 1990 only 7 percent of administrators and managers in Indonesia were women. By that indicator of elite professional achievement, Indonesia lagged behind developing countries at high and medium development levels alike (with average rates of 18 and 13 percent, respectively), although not behind South Asia (at 3 percent). Compared with their scarcity in top-level jobs, Indonesian women did somewhat better in professional and technical fields, and better still in less prestigious occupations such as clerical work and sales.[4]

The 1945 constitution, continuously in effect since 1959, states that "all citizens have equal status before the law" (Article 27).[5] Indonesia ratified the UN Convention to Eliminate Discrimination Against Women (in 1980) and the International Labor Organization's Convention No. 100 pledging equal pay for equal work. In 1978, for the first time, the quinquennially drafted guidelines of state policy included a chapter specifically addressing the role of women in national development. That same year, responding to the agenda for the UN-sponsored Decade for Women, the New Order created a junior ministry for women's affairs; five years later it became a full department. As for specific legislative and administrative provisions to implement gender equality, these were slow in coming.

In the early 1990s, women held roughly a third of the positions in the civil service. Few of these women were at the highest levels of government. But they were well represented in the middle ranks, particularly in public education and public health. Just over half of all primary school teachers and nearly a fourth of government doctors, for example, were women. Their prominence in government-sponsored education and health, activities that were centrally managed and

---

countries differs from that used by the UNDP to assign countries to a "high" or "medium" level of human development.

3. *HDR96*, p. 139 [income, literacy, enrollment]; *Indikator Sosial Wanita* [henceforth *ISW*] [*Social Indicators about Women*] (Jakarta: CBS, 1991), p. 79 [returns to labor]. The data in *HDR96* are for 1993. Enrollment refers to female (or male) students, regardless of age, at all educational levels.

4. *HDR96*, pp. 156 [administrators and managers], 210 [South Asia]. "Administrators and managers" includes senior government officials and members of parliament; executives and managers of corporations; and traditional chiefs and village heads.

5. *The 1945 Constitution of the Republic of Indonesia* (Jakarta: Department of Information, 1995–96), p. 9.

staffed, helps explain why women were more strongly represented in national than in regional administration.[6]

In the early 1990s, a mere 1.4 percent of the heads of the country's 67,000 villages were women. Over the course of the New Order, female membership rose slightly in the People's Consultative Assembly (MPR) and the People's Representative Council (DPR), constitutionally the country's highest deliberative bodies: from 5.5 percent in 1971 to 10.1 percent in 1992 in the MPR, and from 6.3 to 12.6 percent in the DPR over the same period. Women did somewhat better in the national judiciary, where they accounted for a quarter of the judges and more than a tenth of the Supreme Court.[7]

In 1995 Indonesia had proportionally more women in parliament than did any other member of the Association of Southeast Asian Nations (ASEAN), or any other majority-Muslim country, and slightly more than the United States (10.4 percent).[8] But is this evidence of empowerment? As described by William Liddle in this book, the New Order's representative bodies were not autonomous. Nevertheless, for Indonesian women legislators (and activists), greater female representation in national and provincial legislatures was an important goal, symbolically and also as a chance for greater influence over how government policies affected women.

Economic improvements under the New Order were reflected in improved health for all Indonesians. Average life expectancy increased from 59.2 years in 1986 to 61.5 for men and 65.3 for women in 1995. But the maternal mortality rate remained high: 425 deaths per 100,000 births in 1995—a steep rate relative to countries of similar income levels. In 1996 the authorities launched a campaign called "Cherish the Mothers" (Sayang Ibu) to address the problem. By then, however, continued high maternal mortality had become for many Indonesian women a sign of fundamental gender inequality in their country.[9]

Complexity and Diversity

Southeast Asian women often are held to be independent and have a "high status" relative to women in other Asian societies. Facts such as the strong presence of women in commerce are cited to support these claims. Such a view may arise,

---

6. *ISW,* pp. 52 [all civil servants], 53 [teachers, doctors], 55 [national versus regional administration].

7. *Profil Kedudukan dan Peranan Wanita Indonesia Tahun 1995* [henceforth *PKP95*] [*Profile of the Status and Role of Indonesian Women 1995*] (Jakarta: Kantor Menteri Negara Urusan Peranan Wanita/CBS, 1996), p. 133 [members of DPR, MPR]; *ISW,* pp. 53 [judges], 144 [village heads, legislators, Supreme Court justices].

8. *HDR96,* pp. 141–143.

9. These national data (*PKP95,* p. 66) conceal wide interprovincial variations, which reflect the distinctiveness of one region compared with another.

as Shelly Errington suggests, because observers have been "struck by the complementarity of men's and women's work and the relative lack of economic differentiation." Noting that the symbolic expression of gender differences in Southeast Asia is relatively uncommon, Errington argues that important, if subtle, distinctions may not have been seen because they did not fit the observers' assumptions about gender difference.[10]

The idea of "women's status" as an unproblematically singular dimension along which vastly different societies, economies, and polities can be ranked cannot, in any case, be sustained. "Status" is a synthetic construct that encompasses a range of variables, from economic and political to cultural and social. Nor should gender, as the cultural construction of sexual difference, be seen as an autonomous aspect of social life operating independently from other processes of social differentiation, such as kinship, ethnicity, and class. Such a view would ignore the extent to which these forms of social difference are mutually influencing, and even constitutive of each other.

Class differences, for instance, are entwined with gender differences in the exploitation of women as lower-paid wage laborers and the exclusion of women from productive work. In a now-classic paper, Ann Stoler argued that the degree of autonomy exercised by Javanese rural women depended on the amount of land available to them and their families, rather than deriving automatically from their social position as women.[11] And while prostitution has been understood as a form of gender oppression caused by patriarchy, it is also a form of class oppression into which particular women may be recruited on the basis of their membership in an ethnic group as well. The aim here is to locate differences in gender relations in this context, and within a socially and culturally heterogeneous archipelago.

Take the community in Soroako, South Sulawesi, where I conducted fieldwork for twenty months between 1977 and 1979, and for several shorter periods in 1981 and 1984–85 (see Map 1). There marriage is followed by uxorilocal residence: Until such time as they can establish a separate dwelling for themselves, the new couple lives in the home of the bride's parents. The matrilineal Minangkabaus of West Sumatra also follow this custom. In contrast, among the patrilineal Balinese, usually a new wife resides with her husband in the compound that houses his relatives. There she lives with other in-marrying women

---

10. Anthony Reid, *Southeast Asia in the Age of Commerce 1450–1680*, vol. 1: *The Lands below the Winds* (New Haven, CT: Yale University Press, 1988), pp. 6, 146–172 [high status]; Shelly Errington, "Recasting Sex, Gender, and Power: A Theoretical and Regional Overview," in Jane Monnig Atkinson and Shelly Errington, eds., *Power and Difference: Gender in Island Southeast Asia* (Stanford, CA: Stanford University Press, 1990), pp. 5 [symbolic expression], 10 [complementarity].

11. Ann Stoler, "Class Structure and Female Autonomy in Rural Java," *Signs: A Journal of Women in Culture and Society,* 3 (1977), pp. 74–89.

who may be strangers to her. Should the new couple have children, they will belong to the husband's local group, so if the marriage should fail, the wife may have to relinquish them.

This diversity of ways in which gender and kinship intersect has implications for everyday behavior. In Soroako the uxorilocally dwelling husband is likely to reorient at least some of his economic activity toward his wife's relatives and their resources, for example, by working his parents-in-law's land. Typically, after the wedding, it is he who is the stranger, who creeps around self-consciously, while the wife, in the dwelling that has always been her home, lives life almost as before. Young women in Soroako, on the morning after their wedding, have been seen doing the family laundry in the lake with the same group of women they associated with prior to marriage, as if nothing had changed.

Kinship is bilateral in Soroako, as in most of the rest of South Sulawesi. Kinship is also bilateral among the Javanese, who form the most numerous ethnic group in Indonesia. Typically in such societies, male and female lines of descent are of equal importance in reckoning relatedness, and usually also inheritance. In bilateral societies there tends not to be a marked preference for sons over daughters. In Soroako, the ideal family is thought to include at least one child of each sex, and usually the youngest daughter will inherit her parents' house, on the understanding that together with her husband she will live in it with her parents and care for them as they age. Among the bilateral Javanese, unlike the patrilineal Balinese, when marriages break up, typically the children stay with the mother.

The forms of gender relations found in the archipelago have been responsive to historical and contemporary changes, for example, in religion and rule, as discussed by Robert Hefner in his chapter. In predominantly Muslim South Sulawesi, Islamic principles of inheritance, which favor male rights, have been encroaching on bilateral principles of inheritance that recognize the entitlement of both sexes. In contested cases, a sharp difference of economic interest can pit male proponents of Muslim rules against women championing traditional norms. A similar dynamic has been observed in Minangkabau society. In that region, matrilineal principles of inheritance, which give women inheritance rights, are being challenged on Islamic grounds, while the commodification of land creates opportunities for men to pass property in land to their sons. In these cases, as elsewhere, religious as well as economic variables are reshaping the economic rights of women.

Particular representations of gender relations are also embedded in the ways ethnic groups define themselves. The Bugis, or Buginese, are the dominant ethnic group in South Sulawesi (see Map 2). They are stereotyped as being deeply concerned with *sirih,* a local concept translatable as "honor and shame." Bugis men are assumed by others—and they themselves proudly claim—to be passionate, impulsive, and preoccupied with *sirih.* Greatly valued are the sexual virtue of women and the role of men in protecting that virtue.

In 1984 in Ujungpandang, the capital of South Sulawesi, I witnessed an example: A young Bugis man, a student with a modern lifestyle, wished to marry his girlfriend despite parental opposition to the match. So he pretended to kidnap her at gunpoint—thus enacting the stereotype of Bugis males as hot-headed. He intended to run off with her by ship to Jakarta. But her brothers caught them together on the vessel before it left port. In defense of honor and to prevent shame, that is, by the code of *sirih,* the brothers had no choice but to insist that the couple marry. The couple had every reason to comply, since the alternative under the code would have been for the brothers to kill the young man. The couple thus "gave in" and were wed, neatly achieving their original goal of marriage over parental objection while restoring the bride's virtue in accord with *sirih.*

Such behavior might be viewed as simply a case of the perpetuation of male control over female sexuality. But this explanation does not fully account for the significance of *sirih* in social practice, including the constitution of ethnic difference. *Sirih* is fundamental to how the Bugis see themselves, how they contrast themselves to others, and how others see them. That is why it takes on significance in everyday interactions involving Bugis in contemporary, multiethnic Indonesia.

Another illustration of how gender relations are used to express ethnicity may be drawn from the Minangkabau region. It is common to hear Minangkabaus describe themselves to outsiders as a matriarchal society (*matriarki*). From the anthropologist's point of view, they conflate the idea of matriarchy—the exercise of public authority by women over men—with matriliny—the reckoning of descent through the female line. Minangkabau society is in no sense matriarchal; public office and familial authority are exercised by men. During the New Order, nevertheless, Minangkabaus felt proud to express their distinctiveness in terms of an ideology of gender relations that varied sharply from the typically patriarchal assumptions of the central government.

Rarely in Suharto's Indonesia were the dynamism and variety of gender relations in everyday social practice reflected in government documents and policies. Official programs assumed, for example, that household heads were men. This often resulted in the collection of official statistics that misrepresented social reality. In Soroako there were households where, on issues such as disposing of land or considering a proposed marriage, a widow was the principal decision-maker. Yet these households were classified in official documents as being headed by a man, someone who lived there, usually a son, even though he was young, unmarried, and without domestic authority.

I encountered the same bias in Lombok in 1989 during a review of an Australian-funded water supply project. The main users of the water were women, yet on official lists the members of the water-user groups were all men. The user groups were critical to the functioning of the project. They were responsible for the maintenance of wells and standpipes on a daily basis. The work on these facilities was carried out on an organized basis by the women who used them.

Yet the official lists assumed that only its male head could represent a household in public institutions—that is, in the user groups.

The next section further explores the official construction of gender roles in contrast to the actual participation of women in society.

Official Ideology

The calendar of nationally commemorated days in Indonesia includes two occasions for celebrating women: Mother's Day and Kartini Day. Mother's Day falls on 22 December in honor of the first national congress of Indonesian women, held on that date in 1928. This meeting proclaimed the goals of Indonesian feminists in the preindependence period: equality between men and women within a liberal discourse of equal social rights for all. A principal concern of these women was gender equality within the family, including equal rights to choose or divorce a spouse.

Kartini Day recalls the struggles of Raden Adjeng Kartini (1879–1904), a colonial-era Javanese woman who sought to expand her life's possibilities beyond the strictures of Javanese court culture. Kartini expressed her hopes for autonomy in marriage and the right to pursue her education, as well as her dream of establishing a government schools for girls, in a series of letters to Dutch correspondents, most of them women. Kartini's letters were published in 1911 following her tragically early death in childbirth.[12]

In New Order Indonesia, rather than providing an occasion for the promotion of equality between men and women, these two national days were observed in ways that marked women's differences, their distinctiveness as mothers and wives. Typical modes of celebration included healthy-baby competitions and quizzes testing women's knowledge of how to be good mothers and wives. Officials gave speeches urging women to honor the memory of national heroines such as Kartini by supporting government programs for women—programs stressing motherly and wifely duties and skills.

Not all Indonesian women endorsed this official construction of women's citizenship. The prospect of another such Mother's Day made the Indonesian feminist scholar Julia Suryakusuma feel "allergic—an allergy to witnessing all sorts of empty ceremonies [and] listening to speeches burdened with empty flattery of women as mothers."[13] In effect, the official celebration of such occasions sent a

---

12. Raden Adjeng Kartini, *Letters of a Javanese Princess*, Hildred Geertz, ed., and trans. Agnes Symmers (reprint, Lanham, MD: University Press of America, 1985). Commentaries on her life and thought include Ailsa G. Thomson Zainu'ddin, "What Should a Girl Become?': Further Reflections on the Letters of R.A. Kartini," in David P. Chandler and M.C. Ricklefs, eds., *Nineteenth and Twentieth Century Indonesia: Essays in Honour of Professor J.D. Legge* (Clayton, Victoria, Australia: Monash University Centre of Southeast Asian Studies, 1986), pp. 243–279.

13. Julia I. Suryakusuma, "Salah Kaprah Hari Ibu" ["Mother's Day Misunderstood"], *Kompas* [Jakarta], 5 January 1994.

message that the ideal of equal citizenship originally pursued by the nationalist movement had been set aside for a stereotype of women based on difference, especially the uniqueness of motherhood. In sanctifying Kartini on her epony-mous day, the New Order seemed to show not support for her championing of women's freedoms, but sympathy for her suffering as a mother.

Among the irritants that triggered Suryakusuma's "allergic" response to these national rituals were the *kain* and *kebaya* that Indonesian women had to wear at such times. This modern version of the wrapped batik cloth (*kain*) and fitted blouse (*kebaya*) worn by Javanese and Balinese women confined the wearer within an image of domesticated femininity. The *kain* was worn with a corset, and wrapped so tightly that the wearer could hardly walk, let alone go to the bath-room. High-heeled slippers and an artificial bun affixed to the back of the head completed the impracticality of this transformation of what was originally a peas-ant woman's garb into a highly stylized symbol of the well-off wife and mother. The corresponding dress for men was not an urbanized version of the sarongs of village men, but an adaptation of Western dress—trousers and a (batik) shirt—that did not sacrifice freedom of movement. In symbolic representations of gen-der on public occasions over the long life of the New Order, notwithstanding references to "partnership" toward the end of the regime, difference prevailed over equality.

The marriage law of 1974, and enabling statutes adopted in 1975, provided for a minimum age at marriage, protected women from marriage against their will, and gave wives rights to divorce equal to those of husbands. This was a triumph for Indonesian women's rights organizations, which had urged mar-riage law reform ever since the 1928 congress. That the marriage law was adopted so late after women begin advocating it shows, however, that it was more than a response to women's aspirations. Regime leaders were committed to slowing the rapid rate of population growth, and knew that higher minimum ages for marriage would assist in that campaign. In this sense marriage reform was not undertaken merely for its own sake, but to facilitate another official priority: family planning.

Marriage law reform and the family planning program brought personal as-pects of women's lives under official purview, as the state challenged the author-ity of religions (particularly Islam) and local traditions to regulate personal and family relations. These initiatives, together with the close association of women with wifehood and motherhood in official rituals and rhetoric, suggested an ef-fort to subsume the diversity of gender constructions around the archipelago under a single national definition of the feminine: being wifely in a monoga-mous union while mothering a few well-spaced children inside the home, leav-ing the husband free to take on roles beyond the family, including pursuing productive work in a career and participating in public life.

The implications of this familist ideology ran beyond relations between men and women. It provided a naturalized model of hierarchy and authority. It showcased the patriarchal family as a model for social behavior, and for the unequal exercise of political power. Thus it validated not only the exclusion of women from public life, but also the absolute authority of Suharto's regime.

Official Organizations

The New Order's constraining vision of female roles took institutional form in two officially sponsored organizations. The first of these was called Dharma Wanita (DW), a Sanskrit-derived name that implied a preordained role for women and carried the sense in English of a "ladies' auxiliary." Dharma Wanita organized elite women, in particular the wives of civil servants. Indeed, membership in DW was compulsory for government officials' wives. In DW these women were mobilized to participate in official functions and carry out charitable work in the service of national development. They were expected to subordinate their other interests to the furtherance of their husbands' careers. So thoroughly was DW subsumed under masculinized public power that leadership within the organization was determined not by comparing the talents and achievements of candidates, or democratically by voting, but mechanically according to the women's husbands' positions in the hierarchy of government. When a man was inaugurated governor of a province, for example, his wife would simultaneously be installed to head DW in the same province.

Women who were themselves civil servants were anomalous in the ideology of gender difference underlying DW. If wives were assumed to have free time for volunteer work, a female public official also felt pressure to find time to participate in DW—on her own account or, if she were married to another civil servant, in the chapter of DW associated with his department. Relevant in this context is a conversation once had with a high-ranking female civil servant. She had been passed over for professional promotion and transfer in favor of a man who in her view was less qualified and less experienced than she. Her male superior at work explained the decision thus: Had she been promoted and transferred, it would have left his wife "lonely" inside DW. Such reasoning engendered the public sphere as a male domain.

New Order familism was manifest as well in the nomenclature used inside such state-sponsored organizations, where women were called "Ibu X." *Ibu* is the Indonesian word for "mother," but "Ibu X" meant "Wife of X" not "Mother of X." This amounted to a radical change from the teknonymy common to patterns of address in much of rural Indonesia. A teknonym is a reference to someone as "the mother of X" or "the father of X" where X is the name of that someone's first-born child. Teknonymy, the custom of using teknonyms, emphasizes parenthood as the basis of adult social identity.

In contrast, address usage under the New Order implied a gendered hierarchy. And patriarchal references—knowing a woman by her husband's name—were not just an alternative to teknonymy. They also replaced the terminology of

Indonesia's radical-nationalist period, when adults had favored the gender-omitting egalitarianism of the term *saudara,* a form of address that could as well mean "sister" as "brother." More broadly, the idealized exclusion of women from independent participation in the public life of the New Order, and the related economic dependence and vulnerability of elite civil servants' wives, recalled the "golden cages" of the wives of higher-level Dutch officials late in the colonial era.

This is not to impute passivity to the women who belonged to DW. On the contrary, DW members and leaders tried to use the organization and its official cachet to reduce their risk of unfair treatment by the husbands on whom they depended. Thus, in 1981, the association asked President Suharto for a special law to protect the civil servants' wives from polygamy and divorce.

Suharto responded with Presidential Decree No. 10 of 1983, promulgated for symbolic effect on 21 April—Kartini Day. Under this regulation, a male civil servant would have to seek permission from his superiors before he could divorce his first wife or acquire a second one. (According to the 1974 law on marriage, a husband could not take a second wife without the permission of the first, but in practice consent often was coerced.) The new rule enabled an aggrieved wife to submit a complaint through the head of DW in the husband's office, that is, through the wife of the complainant's husband's superior, who could then bring the matter to the attention of her own husband, that is, the superior male official.

By entitling this superior in principle, if he chose, to overrule civil and religious law, the decree legitimated the intrusion of state officials into the private lives of their subordinates. A husband who refused to abide by his superior's decision could be punished, for example, by being denied career advancement. Decree No. 10 also articulated the right of women to special state protection in their capacity as wives and mothers. While it gave them some power in their relations with husbands, the new edict also reinforced a restrictive understanding of women's role.[14]

If DW organized the wives of civil servants, village women in Indonesia were required to join the chapters of a second association, the nationwide Pembinaan Kesejahteraan Keluarga (PKK), usually rendered in English as the Family Welfare Movement.[15] Like DW, PKK was governmental, being synonymous at the base of society with one of the ten sections of village administration, the one

---

14. See Julia I. Suryakusuma, "The State and Sexuality in New Order Indonesia," in Laurie J. Sears, ed., *Fantasizing the Feminine in Indonesia* (Durham, NC: Duke University Press, 1996), pp. 92–119.

15. Norma Sullivan, *Masters and Managers: A Study of Gender Relations in Urban Java* (St. Leonards, NSW, Australia: Allen and Unwin, 1994), includes a comprehensive account of the functioning of PKK.

dealing with women's affairs. In PKK, as in DW, wifehood determined leadership. Nationally, for example, PKK was housed in the Department of Home Affairs, and led at that level by whoever the minister's wife happened to be. The same criterion operated at lesser levels of government down to the village, where the local PKK chapter was entrusted to the wife of the village head.

These village-level chapters had multiple functions. One was to disseminate official gender ideology among rural women, emphasizing their responsibilities as custodians of the household and for bearing and nurturing the next generation of Indonesians. This normative definition of their role contradicted how these women really lived their lives, which were not limited to housewifery. These nonelite women had to work outside the home to help their families meet basic needs. As for the growing middle class, there was increasing evidence that at that level as well two-income families were becoming the norm, reflecting the career aspirations of educated women and the level of income needed to support expectations raised by economic growth.

PKK was also designed to enroll village women in official programs for maternal and child health. Women were encouraged to pay regular visits to integrated health-service stations for mothers and children known as *pos pelayanan terpadu,* or *posyandu.* At these sites infants were weighed, vaccinated, and charted; pregnant women were examined and vaccinated; and mothers were instructed in infant nutrition and health. The importance of these stations in instilling the virtues of motherhood was made evident to me while visiting a *posyandu* in a poor neighborhood of Ujungpandang in 1990. Sometimes, if she were too busy earning money or performing domestic chores to accompany her children herself, a mother would delegate the task to a sibling caretaker or other female relative. Yet the health-care providers at the station criticized the fact that the children who came were not always brought by their birth mothers.

The criticism indicated that it was not just the children's health that was under surveillance. It was the women's parenting as well. The critics themselves were women, and many of them were also mothers who could not have been working at the *posyandu* but for the help of a caretaker who was looking after their own children at home. Routinely in Indonesia poor households allocate their labor for the sake of collective economic goals. This often involves entrusting the care of a child who is no longer breast-feeding to someone other that the birth mother, who is thereby freed to work in the rice-fields or elsewhere outside the house. Households may even recruit temporary members to permit this to occur. What the *posyandu* staff in Ujungpandang assumed, that women should privilege tasks directly associated with mothering over all other activities, was a luxury many poor women and their families could not afford.

The criticism I heard in Ujungpandang was symptomatic of a larger anomaly. The PKK priorities and activities tended to promote a construction of the feminine that had more to do with elite urban lifestyles, or with a romanticization of housewives as guardians of domesticity, than with the lives of poor Indonesian women trying to make ends meet within local economies centered on seasonal agriculture and petty trade. In one instance, women in rural Java whose families could not afford chairs or tables—they used woven floor mats instead—were advised by PKK personnel to move the furniture around regularly "so husbands wouldn't get bored."[16] At about the same time, the author of a letter that appeared in the Jakarta daily *Kompas* complained of a PKK-sponsored event in which poor village women had been taught to make black forest cake using imported cans of cherries and whipped cream from a city supermarket.

Family Planning

Suharto made family planning a major official priority. He reversed the pronatalist rhetoric of his predecessor, Sukarno, for whom Indonesia's large and growing population had been an asset not a liability. The ensuing deceleration of Indonesia's rate of population growth was seen by commentators as a major success of the New Order.

The priority was established early. In 1968, the first year of his first term as full president, Suharto saw to the formation of a National Family Planning Institute. Two years later he upgraded it to a coordinating body reporting directly to him. By 1976 contraceptive services were being provided free of charge through some 2,700 government clinics and 20,000 village centers, and child-bearing rates had begun to register significant declines, especially on densely populated Bali and parts of Java. According to World Bank data, a steep long-term reduction in the average annual increase in population size was underway—from 2.4 percent in 1970–75 to 1.8 percent in 1980–95 down to a projected 1.3 percent in 1995–2010. From an average of more than six children per mother in the 1960s, total fertility fell to less than three children per mother in the 1990s.[17]

The rhetoric of the family planing program firmly located fertility within families. Formally the program's clients—"targets" in the military-sounding term used by its officials—were "couples of child-bearing age" (*pasangan usia subur*). In everyday usage by family planning workers, however, the phrase referred to married women. In addition, the campaign's methods were overwhelmingly centered on women—the pill, intrauterine devices (IUDs), injectables, and implants.

---

16. Barbara Schiller, personal communication, 1984.

17. World Bank, *Social Indicators of Development 1996* (Baltimore, MD: Johns Hopkins University Press, 1996), p. 159 [2.4]; *World Development Indicators 1996* (Washington, DC: World Bank, 1996), p. 35 [1.8, 1.3]; Terence H. Hull, "Fertility Decline in the New Order Period: The Evolution of Population Policy 1965–90," in Hal Hill, ed., *Indonesia's New Order: The Dynamics of Socio-economic Transformation* (Honolulu: University of Hawaii Press, 1994), p. 124 [1960s]; *WDI97*, p. 39 [1990s]. The total fertility rate is the number of children a woman would expect to bear were she to live to the end of her child-bearing years and give birth at a frequency matching the age-specific rates of fertility prevalent at the time.

On radio and television and in posters and pamphlets, motivational messages associated spacing children and limiting family size with responsible citizenship. The program thus reinforced the New Order's basing of women's citizenship on their uniqueness as mothers. The program vested reproductive responsibility in women, rather than in women and men as equal participants in conception. Premodern methods of fertility regulation used throughout the archipelago, such as abstinence and noncoital sex, had made men accountable, as well as women. The family planning program tended to replace these practices with modern contraceptive techniques. The increasingly widespread use of such techniques contributed, in turn, to a reworking of ideas about female sexuality: the woman as ever ready for sexual relations and as wholly responsible for controlling her own fertility.

In 1991 married women were asked to report the birth control method they and their husbands used. Of the nine techniques cited, the top five were all female-centered: pills, IUDs, injections, implants, and tubectomies, in that order. Next in frequency came the one method requiring cooperation by both partners: periodic abstinence. Least often mentioned were three male-focused methods: condoms, withdrawal, and vasectomies, in that order.[18]

Prior to an initiative in the mid-1990s to privatize family planning in Indonesia, most contraceptives were available only through the state-sponsored program. Despite the pill's popularity, the program emphasized injections, implants, and IUDs as preferable for new consumers—methods that gave control to the service provider. As the role of private-sector providers expands, the range of choices available to women who can afford to pay for conception—a serious potential constraint in light of the economic crisis of 1997–98—should widen as well.

Formally, the state promoted the idea that a wife and her husband should jointly discuss and decide how to plan their family. Yet the woman was the real "target," and she could "accept" modern contraceptive techniques without involving her husband. Knowing this, and feeling the pressure to achieve high rates of participation, more than a few program officials were tempted to encourage wives to enroll without their husbands' knowledge or approval.

In a mass family planning drive that was held in Ujungpandang in 1990, a potential "acceptor" who had previously consented to be fitted with an IUD changed her mind when her husband disagreed with her decision. The female doctor who was ready to fit the IUD tried to persuade the woman to go ahead, arguing that her husband need not know about it. In another case in the same area, a wife was beaten by her husband when he learned that she had secretly been fitted with an IUD. What prompted his discovery was her unwillingness to have sex with him in the period of abstinence required after insertion of the device.

---

18. Hull, "Fertility Decline," p. 142, citing CBS data. Comparable surveys in 1976 and 1987 had yielded roughly similar rankings.

Both the official principle, that family planing was a conjugal decision, and the actual practice in some cases, where women were exhorted to take decisions on their own, were potentially in conflict with existing social values regarding fertility control. A population as diverse as Indonesia's did not necessarily agree, for example, that spouses should jointly decide whether to use modern contraception. In 1984 in South Sulawesi, an extraordinary 85 percent of eligible women in the original village of Soroako were using modern, and therefore mostly female-centered, methods of preventing pregnancy. High, too, was the 43 percent of these users who reported having first taken this step on their own, without consulting their husbands. One woman summed up this attitude by remarking that it was the wives who should be able to decide, since pregnancy after all happened to them.[19] Nor were Indonesians equally amenable to state regulation of their personal behavior.

In the early 1990s, according to government data, half of all married women of child-bearing age in Indonesia were using some form of contraception.[20] Explanations of this success by admirers of the family planning program featured the program itself: Its ability to recruit large numbers of auxiliary workers—including volunteers, for example—and the imaginative and flexible methods it used to deliver supplies to the villages. The demographer Terry Hull questioned such reasoning. For him, it was crucial to understand the social and cultural phenomena underlying fertility decline, in particular the genesis of a "felt need" for fertility limitation in the light of broader socioeconomic and cultural change.[21] The following research illustrates Hull's point: that family planning succeeded not just because of the efficiency of the program but also due to basic changes in economic and social life that led parents to revalue the implications of having children.

Soroako, South Sulawesi, is a mining town. It was established at the site of a facility for mineral extraction and processing run by the International Nickel Company (Inco) of Canada. Beginning in 1984, using its medical services, Inco set up its own version of the state's family planning program. The initiative yielded extremely high contraceptive prevalence rates: more than 80 percent among the indigenous inhabitants of the original village of Soroako, and well above 50 percent in the town as a whole. Company fieldworkers were extremely proactive, seeking out the wives of employees in their homes to offer supplies, incentives, and advice.

---

19. Kathryn Robinson, "Choosing Contraception: Cultural Change and the Indonesian Family Planning Programme," in Paul Alexander, ed., *Creating Indonesian Cultures* (Sydney: Oceania Publications, 1989), pp. 27 [prevalence], 36 [decision].

20. *ISW,* p. 109, reporting a prevalence of 49.7 percent. Claims of prevalence in Indonesia varied with differences in the data used to estimate acceptance rates. Typically, compared with user surveys and census calculations, family planning program records yielded higher results. "Half" is modal in this context.

21. Terence H. Hull, "Fertility Decline in Indonesia: An Institutionalist Perspective," *International Family Planning Perspectives,* 13:3 (September 1987), pp. 90–95.

Soon after giving birth, for example, a woman would be visited by project staff. Often the visit would result in her being injected with a long-lasting contraceptive called Deproprovera, deemed appropriate for women who breast feed. Deproprovera users would be visited at home when injections were due. Couples who had chosen condoms were also visited, and urged to "upgrade" to a more reliable—but also more invasive—method. Women reported being questioned regarding contraceptive use when they sought medical treatment for themselves or their children at the company clinic. Were such women forced by clinic staff to accept contraception? Answered one man, "Well, not forced, but obliged [diharuskan]."

Yet the zealous pursuit of project goals alone cannot explain Soroako's extremely high rates of acceptance. A female informant agreed that company policy had influenced her use of contraception and its use by other wives. However, she added, "it also fits with our way of thinking." Her comment jibes with Hull's argument that high prevalence in Indonesia reflected a desire, independent of program activities, to limit births.

What explains this desire in Soroako? In the agricultural economy of the past, the household had been the unit of production, and the labor of young children had held economic value. But mining had transformed Soroako. Wage labor had become the main type of productive work, and it was only available to adult men. In such an economy, with only limited niches for child labor, high fertility no longer brought economic advantage.

Reproductive behavior in Soroako was embedded in strongly held notions of responsible parenthood. The great majority of local residents understood that the economic transformations associated with the mine and its development necessitated lower fertility. To their "way of thinking," limiting fertility meant exercising one's parental responsibility to provide for a better future for one's children, especially through education. Once, land had sustained livelihood through agricultural labor. But the land was gone, taken over by the company. In the new setting, education was the key to a better life.

A woman commented to me that in the past people had assumed that all children would find some work, such as hoeing or collecting firewood. "Many children, much fortune" had been the common saying. People had not cared much about modern education. But now, she said, "we think about school for our children." A man reinforced her point from a different angle: Economic conditions, he said, were tight. Working for Inco was the only hope, and opportunities there were limited. He complained of losing out to others in the company who were better off than he, including immigrant bosses, mainly from Java, who had been given more authority and higher pay. Why? "Because," he replied, "they have education and we don't."

The new reliance on wage labor in Soroako separated work from domestic life. Most women were dependent spouses who did not have an income of their own. Indigenous Soroakan women keenly felt this limitation, exacerbated as it was by rapid socioeconomic change. Typically their older children, who might have helped care for younger siblings, were away at work all day, or had left Soroako to pursue the new goal of post-primary education. These women's responsibility for child care had increased accordingly, and they were feeling it as a burden. That feeling reinforced the rationality of spacing births—"so you are not harrassed," as one woman put it. Thus did Inco's family planning activities in Soroako succeed in part because of economic changes that had restructured social relations, between genders and between generations.

As a mining town hosting a foreign firm, Soroako was not typical of towns elsewhere in Indonesia. Across the archipelago, economic change did not affect fertility decisions in only one way. Of greater importance in some densely populated rural areas was the impetus to family planning provided by the loss of economic niches that parents could rely on to absorb child labor. Elsewhere in the islands, and especially in eastern Indonesia, people were still convinced of the economic utility of large families. In Soroako, an important aspect of the economic changes set in motion by foreign investment in mining was the erosion of space for women to participate in remunerative activity outside the home. As noted in the next section, government policies, too, had contrasting effects in different places.

Work and Wages

In the economic history of the New Order, the 1970s are chiefly remembered for the oil boom and the related opening of the country to foreign investment in natural-resource extraction. But the decade also saw the beginnings of an influx of foreign and domestic capital into light manufacturing. When world oil prices fell in the 1980s, raising the need for new sources of revenue, this shift toward manufacturing became a national priority. Beginning in 1983, a series of decrees incrementally deregulated the environment for investors.

As Anne Booth argues in this book, the changing composition of exports, away from primary materials such as oil and rubber toward manufactured goods such as garments and appliances, crucially shifted the structure of the Indonesian economy. Two aspects of this change were especially consequential for women: the opening of factories in the countryside and the hiring of women to work in them. The employment of women in manufacturing reversed the tendency of the earlier foreign investment in extractive industries to employ mainly men.

Economic planners in Jakarta might have tried to sequester foreign capital in special economic zones removed from the cities whose infrastructure and services were already overloaded. The government did prohibit the building of additional factories in urban areas. But rather than concentrate foreign investment in special zones, the authorities directed it outward into rural areas, notably on Java. The intention was to reduce demographic pressure on the cities by keeping rural dwellers in place while spreading nonfarm rural employment, thereby inducting the broad mass of the population into a modern economy. National policymakers who first encouraged it saw in the shift to light manufacturing a way of reducing unemployment and underemployment among men Yet young women in their teens or twenties came to constitute the majority of this new work force.

From the standpoint of the companies that opened factories in rural areas, weaknesses in infrastructure could be outweighed by the cheaper cost of land and labor, especially young female labor. Not needing to migrate to seek employment, these women could turn to their families in the village for food and housing. Indeed, this subsidization of formal-sector employment by the informal-sector activities of other family members was necessary whenever the low wages paid to these women did not cover their full living costs.[22]

The entry of women into manufacturing employment could not be seen as a harbinger of gender equity. Typically women's incomes were much lower than men's, with women earning 60–70 percent of the wages earned by men for comparable work. In the hinterland of Jakarta, women might earn as little as half of what men did. Private and state firms avoided the legal requirement to pay equal wages for equal work by, for instance, concentrating women in particular sections of the enterprise, where they could more easily be paid lower wages. And young women were preferred not only because they were cheaper, but they were also assumed to be more docile. Thus did the companies use gender stereotypes in seeking control over the workforce.[23]

The New Order legislated minimum wages. But studies of the manufacturing sector show that women did not receive them. Legally, women workers were entitled to two days of paid menstruation leave monthly, maternity leave with pay, and breast-feeding breaks. Seldom were such benefits granted in practice, however. Owners and managers could avoid compliance with regulations concerning benefits to permanent employees by hiring women on a daily basis. Far from assuring leave with pay, pregnancy might result in dismissal. Compared with men, women workers were less likely to be unionized or go on strike, and so were less able to change conditions on the factory floor—long hours in cramped, dirty, poorly ventilated workplaces with inadequate access to water and food.[24]

Late in the New Order many strikes were reported to have broken out in these

---

22. Diane Lauren Wolf, *Factory Daughters: Gender, Household Dynamics, and Rural Industrialization in Java* (Berkeley: University of California Press, 1992), p. 216.

23. Celia E. Mather, "Industrialization in the Tangerang Regency of West Java: Women Workers and the Islamic Patriarchy," *Bulletin of Concerned Asian Scholars,* 15:2 (1983), pp. 13, 15.

24. For evidence of such conditions in West Java, see the chapters in Mies Grijns, Ines Smyth, Anita van Velzen, Sugiah Machfud, and Pudjiwati Sayogyo, eds., *Different Women, Different Work: Gender and Industrialisation in Indonesia* (Aldershot, UK: Avebury, 1994), by Sayogyo and Ekawati Sri Wahyuni, "An Introduction to the Economy and People of

factories. Organizations representing women workers were active as well in protests against the draft legislation on labor presented to parliament in 1997. Of particular concern were proposals to eradicate certain special privileges of women workers, as well as provisions thought to limit the right to strike. Such activities showed that, although factories hired women partly because of their presumed passivity, it was not a necessary attribute. And to the extent that women had seemed passive, the perception was subject to change once they began living the lives of industrial workers.

What motivated these young women to seek industrial employment? Despite the low wages, such jobs could provide a much-needed regular source of income to households whose alternative earnings were irregular. The extra income enabled the families of female factory workers to pay the school fees of younger family members, or even to buy expensive consumer items such as furniture or motor cycles on installment. According to one researcher, Diane Wolf, young female Javanese factory workers from poor rural families felt they had acquired more freedom to make life choices than they would otherwise have had. They were unwilling to relinquish these new jobs for work in the informal sector, in farming, or in domestic service. The latter sorts of employment were not just considered more arduous. The women also knew that going back to such work meant going back to the village, "where they would be controlled more by parents or other villagers, would have to work longer, and would earn much less" than in the factory.[25]

The young female workers whom Wolf interviewed felt privileged to have factory jobs. These women had a sense of independence. Many were determined to choose their own marriage partners and enjoyed being able to purchase their own clothes and cosmetics. Some of the women joined rotating savings clubs (*arisan*), to which each member contributed the same fixed amount every month. The monthly jackpot thereby created would be won by a member chosen randomly from among those who had not yet won. Participating women were thus assured periodic access to a lump sum of disposable capital, although such winnings were more often used to pay off personal debts or buy goods for the women's parents back in the village than to make a bank deposit or invest in income-yielding property.[26] Not all women were equally positioned to enter the paid work force, however. Wolf found that factory workers were not only single, they

West Java," p. 57 [avoiding the law]; and by Nurmala Hutagulung, Grijns, and Benjamin White, "Women as Wage Workers," pp. 158 [responses to pregnancy], 162 [less unionization], 171 [unhealthy conditions].

25. Wolf, *Factory Daughters,* pp. 255–256.

26. Diane L. Wolf, "Making the Bread and Bringing It Home: Female Factory Workers and the Family Economy in Rural Java," in Gavin Jones, ed., *Women in the Urban and Industrial Workforce* (Canberra: Australian National University Press, 1984), p. 230 [independence]; Wolf, *Factory Daughters,* pp. 188–189 [savings].

were also from households with other adult female members, who could take over and continue the domestic and farming tasks that the factory-bound women had performed.

In the cities, meanwhile, street-vending and other informal-sector activities that tended to yield relatively high returns to female labor became less available. As part of the New Order's pursuit of modernity—Robert Cribb's theme in this volume—streets were cleared of hawkers. Street markets were relocated to shopping complexes where space was expensive to rent. Some of the people in lower-income urban neighborhoods who were moved into modern apartment buildings found it hard to continue home-based informal-sector businesses in flats that were smaller than their former dwellings had been and that were less accessible from the street. Poor women who saw their options reduced might be displaced toward less remunerative work in offices and factories, or be driven to prostitution.[27]

Adding to the difficulties faced by women in the informal sector, government programs to assist small businesses may have benefited men more than women[28]—despite the income-generating purpose of many state initiatives for women. Such disparity again reflected the policy bias implied by the assumption that household heads must be men.

Sexuality and Freedom

The changes in Indonesian society brought on by the New Order's development strategy and the related opening of the archipelago to global markets and culture affected not only the economic participation of women, but also the expression of their femininity. Their new economic roles and the differing images and norms of female behavior circulating in the mass media contributed to the ability of women to make choices for themselves. At the same time, however, the media's commercially driven emphasis on sexual attractiveness and the growth of prostitution created new opportunities for women's exploitation.

The family planning program exemplified the contradictory impacts of socioeconomic change on constructions of masculinity and femininity. The program had the consequence, intended or not, of separating sexuality from reproduction. Increasing numbers of women were using contraception, which enabled them to

27. See Lea Jellinek, *The Wheel of Fortune: The History of a Poor Community in Jakarta* (Sydney: Allen and Unwin, 1990); Alison J. Murray, *No Money, No Honey: A Study of Street Traders and Prostitutes in Jakarta* (Singapore: Oxford University Press, 1991).

28. Artien Utrecht and Pudjawati Sayogyo, "Policies and Interventions," in Grijns et al., eds., *Different Women,* pp. 49–56. Utrecht and Sayogyo (p. 55) did identify one small pilot project—a cheap-credit scheme modeled after the Grameen Bank in Bangladesh—that as of mid-1990 had helped slightly more women than men.

have intercourse without having to worry about pregnancy. The mainly female-focused character of the techniques they used made it easier for these women to make reproductive decisions without consulting male partners. One study, for example, found Balinese women increasingly likely to view their sexuality not within the context of family and motherhood but as an expression of their own personal freedom—an outlook attributed by the author of the study to decades of widespread contraceptive use.[29]

At the same time, to an extent, family planning replaced one set of controls for another, trading older constraints based on power derived from kinship for newer ones originating from the state. Meanwhile, the opening of Indonesia to global capitalism promoted a sexualization of culture and femininity whose implications for women were potentially confining. Evidence to this effect could be found, for example, in the women's magazines and romance novels discussed by Virginia Hooker in the next chapter.

Another manifestation of both the socioeconomic change and the cultural sexualization that accompanied modernity was the growing importance of prostitution. Life in Soroako illustrated this result. Typically in natural resource exporting economies, minerals are extracted in remote locations requiring the mining enterprise to import materials and provisions to house and feed its workers. To reduce costs, the company recruits workers on "single status," that is, without taking responsibility for housing their families. The resulting concentration of single men creates markets for bars and brothels. Preferential employment of male laborers also means that employment opportunities for women are limited.

In mining towns as well as in the cities of Indonesia a woman could be drawn into a commercial sexual arrangement as a "contract wife" who would live with an expatriate man for the duration of his stay in Indonesia. The official view was that prostitution was a pathological deviancy.[30] But just as a woman might choose factory work to escape the economic and social constraints of village life, so might she choose sex work as preferable to toiling in a rural factory. Or there might be no alternative—a condition whose likelihood rose as opportunities for employment in the informal sector declined under official pressure to modernize petty commerce.

But the implications of sex work for Indonesian women were not unambiguously beneficial. Elite, high-income prostitutes were a small minority of all the women involved in the sex trade. Most sex workers faced substantial dangers to

---

29. Lynette Parker, "Fecundity and the Fertility Decline in Bali," written for a conference on "The State, Sexuality, and Reproduction in Asia and the Pacific," Australian National University Gender Relations Project, Canberra, 1993. Bali has had the highest contraceptive prevalence rate—71.9 percent in 1991—of any province in Indonesia; *ISW*, p. 109.

30. Murray, *No Money, No Honey*, p. 107.

their health—from sexually transmitted diseases, including a growing risk of AIDS, and from abusing alcohol and drugs. The clients and ostensible "protectors" of these women were potential sources of violence and intimidation. Requests for clients to use condoms for health reasons often triggered such abuse. As the case of prostitution shows, in opening Indonesian economy and society to global commercial and cultural flows, the New Order also opened men-women relations to incentives and images that contradicted official norms of femininity.

The ambiguity of modernity could also be seen in Soroako in the implications of freer choice in marriage. Wedlock had once been a family affair, arranged by the new couple's kin, who had taken careful account of the need to establish a harmonious and economically viable household. Sexual passion had been considered an outcome of marriage, not its requisite. Over the course of the New Order, however, among young people in the town, a growing desire for romantic love arose, reflecting a new kind of sexualized culture. These young people were able to exercise their preference for free choice in marriage based on romantic love because the older generation no longer controlled the material resources needed to arrange a union. And that shift could, in turn, be attributed to the occupational changes that the New Order had fostered in Soroako by opening it to the global economy.

One could read this outcome as an advance in personal autonomy—the freeing of sexuality from kin-based forms of power and control. But the shift to free-choice marriages based on romantic love could also be taken as a kind of self-subjugation—an enslaving of young women and men to the consumerist values of the market. For the market had fostered and disseminated, in print and visual media, a new model of sexualized femininity.

The risks of free-choice marriage were all too clear to older women in Soroako. In their youth they might have entertained the idea of a love match, but they had settled for the partner of their parents' choice. Their argument, as they explained it, ran as follows: If you accepted your parents' decision and the man turned out to be a bad husband—if, for example, he did not support you and your children—the two sets of parents, as instigators of the match, had a responsibility to look after you. If you married according to your own will, the consequences were different, and you had to live with them.

In Soroako, women had lost independent access to land as a means of production, and hence as a source of self-support. In this sense, the introduction of industrial capitalism had increased the material risk to women of exercising free choice in marriage. If conditions of modernity had increasingly freed women from ties to the family and its reproduction, such conditions had brought new forms of subordination and exploitation as well.

Difference versus Diversity

The state policy guidelines approved by the MPR in 1993 correctly stressed the importance of the contribution made by women, as human resources, to national development. More and more women were working outside the home—proportionally more than in other Asian or Muslim societies. In the light-manufacturing industries that were coming to dominate the Indonesian economy, most of the employees were women. Large numbers of Indonesian women were employed abroad as unskilled domestic help. But while New Order policies had opened Indonesia to the imperatives of the world economy, those imperatives were themselves endangering the regime's own familist ideology and agenda.

Under the New Order, prior to the collapse of 1997–98, Indonesian women made gains in literacy, education, longevity, and political participation, among other spheres. Yet they still lagged behind men in crucial respects. As Anne Booth notes in her chapter, for example, maternal mortality persisted at high rates—higher than those in comparable countries. Nationally aggregated data homogenized the diverse conditions actually encountered by women around the archipelago. And the gender bias in much official data collection—noted by the assumed masculinity of household heads—probably made slight the extent of women's social and economic participation, that is, their actual contribution to the country's welfare.

Government programs were homogenizing, too, in the way they located femininity and the female role within the family. Construed as a patriarchical unit, the family became a recurrent metaphor in efforts by the state to naturalize its possession of authority and exercise of power. In this chapter, this lofty image of uniformity has been contrasted with illustrations for the variety of gender systems in actual operation on the ground: the matrilineal Minangkabaus, the bilateral peoples of Java and South Sulawesi, and the patrilineal Balinese. None of these systems was timelessly traditional. All were experiencing change and would continue to do so.

The official rhetoric and rituals occasioned by national holidays focused on women also flattened the diversity of female roles and experiences under symbolic constructions stressing how women as a group were supposed to differ from men. Wifehood and motherhood were the hallmarks of that differentiation—stereotypes that enclosed and subordinated women within an idealized version of the family. In this familist ideology, gender-neutral teknonymy was replaced with gender-dependent forms of address that identified women in relation to their husbands. Meanwhile, official organizations—DW and PKK—were used to promote domesticated femininity as a norm for women to live up to.

During the New Order the national rate of fertility in Indonesia fell roughly in half. This steep decline reflected changing socioeconomic conditions and the efficiency of the official program to distribute birth control methods and information. But some of the program's effects undermined the regime's familist ideology. Female-centered techniques allowed women to make reproductive choices unilaterally, contrary to the formally conjugal model of such decisions promoted by the state.

This engagement of women in contraceptive practice also altered their perceptions of sexuality and fertility. More and more young women came to view reproductive choice as an expression of personal autonomy—and not, as the regime would have had it, within an idealized (male-headed) family exercising responsible citizenship. Late in the New Order, the prospect of deregulating family planning by turning the program over to the private sector suggested an acceleration of this trend toward personal autonomy, insofar as privatization would further remove reproductive decisions from direct scrutiny by government officials.

The opening of the Indonesian economy to a massive intake of foreign and domestic investment had ambiguous effects on women. Sexualized images of femininity in the media delinked intercourse from reproduction, empowering young women with autonomy from familial authority but also advertising new standards of attraction and seduction that amounted, in effect, to new forms of control. Capitalism brought large numbers of putatively docile young females into factories in rural Java. This shift challenged the confinement of women within patriarchal families and the equation of femininity with domesticity, but it also entrenched gender inequality in the workplace in violation of Indonesian laws.

These changes affected women in complex ways. Wolf found Java's "factory daughters" unwilling to trade the socioeconomic autonomy their new jobs had given them for the limitations of their former lives. In the cities, many women who had once worked in the informal sector were displaced by urban renewal into less remunerative employment or joblessness. A third outcome, prostitution, may have represented for some women a preferred alternative to less well-paid labor, but it carried high risks of violence and disease. As for government programs to encourage entrepreneurship in the informal sector, these were skewed toward male beneficiaries by the failure of policymakers to recognize the ubiquity and importance of women's involvement in paid work.

Again, these were not static conditions. Signs of change were particularly evident in the New Order's final years. Beginning in 1993 the regime's own agenda began to make at least rhetorical room for "gender analysis" of official policy using "partnership" as a standard. Nongovernmental organizations were also having an impact on public discourse about gender. Increasingly vocal in this context were feminist associations such as Kalyanamitra (Women's Friend) and Solidaritas Perempuan (Women's Solidarity). And while the proportions of women in positions of power remained low, in 1997 for the first time women's issues were debated in a national election campaign.

The changing policy language of the New Order in the latter half of the 1990s reflected the influence of middle-class women in the Department of Women's Affairs. Their success in gaining official legitimation of at least the rhetoric of gender equity, including support for *kemitrasejajaran*—gender partnership—cannot be dismissed. The new vocabulary seemed to imply a more radical rhetoric of rights than the New Order had been able to accept for other sectors of the polity, for example, regarding workers' rights.

A key unanswered question in 1998 was how such progress would be affected by the economic and political crisis that led to Suharto's replacement by his vice president, Habibie—and what further transitions would follow. But one could wonder as well about the converse: what impact events and trends regarding gender might have on broader conditions. For just as the influence of familist ideology ran beyond gender to underpin state power, so could the burgeoning of official and nonofficial discourse about women's rights toward the end of the New Order be seen to carry wider political implications. In this context, the question for the future was not only what democracy might have to offer to Indonesian women,[31] but it was also what the women might offer democracy.

31. As asked by Susan Blackburn, "Gender Interests and Indonesian Democracy," in David Bourchier and John Legge, eds., *Democracy in Indonesia: 1950s and 1990s* (Clayton, Victoria, Australia: Monash University Centre of Southeast Asian Studies, 1994), pp. 168–181.

Chapter 9

Expression: Creativity Despite Constraint

Virginia Matheson Hooker

Indonesia is a work in progress. Crucial to the changing character of that work is the ongoing reimplementation of the national motto, "Unity in Diversity" (*Bhinneka Tunggal Ika*): how to ensure the unity of the country for all its diversity, while at the same time respecting diversity as an authentic and therefore necessary complement to national unity.

To the extent that it tried to limit the variety of expression in Indonesia—in the media, literature, the arts—and to foster a uniform national political culture, the New Order championed, from the ramparts of the state, the first priority: unity. Meanwhile, however, from the walks of society, journalists, novelists, painters, and other creative Indonesians, many of them critics of official orthodoxy, contested this priority by exploring the second, less centripetal reading of *Bhinneka Tunggal Ika*: diversity.

This chapter will review and evaluate these two efforts in Suharto's Indonesia—the one to order and contain expression, the other creatively to enrich it and expand it beyond official models and limits.[1]

---

1. It has not been possible for me to write about all aspects of such a broad topic from first-hand knowledge. I have drawn freely on the work of other scholars, especially Greg Acciaioli, Keith Foulcher, Barbara Hatley, David Hill, Brett Hough, Krishna Sen, and Astri Wright. The interpretation of their writings herein remains mine alone. I am also grateful to Michael Laffan of the Menzies Library at the Australian National University for providing me with material from the Indonesian press, and to Anthony Milner and M.B. Hooker for advice and criticism.

Authority and Culture

The 1945 constitution, which the New Order claimed to embody, implicitly acknowledges the tension between culture as an official project and culture as popular creativity. According to Article 32, "the Government will advance Indonesian national culture." Yet "national culture" is defined as something that results from "the creative efforts of the entire Indonesian people." The constitution also implicitly recognizes two other tensions: between past and present, and between nation and world. Thus, national culture is said to include "old and indigenous culture" comprising "the highest achievements of the regional cultures throughout Indonesia." Indonesia should not, however, reject "new material from foreign cultures" that can "develop" or "enrich" national culture. Finally, "cultural endeavors" must be oriented not only toward advancing national unity but also toward civilizational progress and raising the level of Indonesians as human beings.[2]

How did the New Order interpret its mandate to advance the national culture? How did the regime position itself between culture as an official project and the creativity of Indonesians?

The New Order's own rhetoric points to the answer. The Sixth Five-Year Development Plan (1994–99) broadened "culture" to include "values" and linked both concepts to the project explored by Anne Booth in her chapter in this book: development. According to the plan, "cultural endeavors" should support development, while foreign values that threaten development should be rejected. The plan also called for: strengthening individual and national identity and unity; cultivating progressive and self-reliant attitudes through an understanding of information technology; culling negative influences from the mass media; and promoting cultural discourse nationally, regionally, and internationally.[3]

By linking culture to officially sponsored betterment, the five-year plan slanted the understanding of culture away from popular inspiration and toward state policy. That bias, in turn, invited conformity and control. Unfettered expression and creativity were muted in the plan, while "a sense of solidarity" and "social responsibility and discipline" were stressed. "National culture" itself was redefined, away from artistic experimentation and toward collective hopes and goals, to become "the totality of values and behavior" reflecting "the desires and wishes

---

2. Except for the initial definition from Article 32, all quotes are from a clarification of the meaning of the constitution appended to the document by its authors. *Undang-Undang Dasar* [*The Constitution*] (Jakarta: 2d ed., Department of Information, 1981), pp. 8 [Article 32], 20 [clarification]. My rendering differs only slightly from the official translations of these passages in, for example, *The 1945 Constitution of the Republic of Indonesia* (Jakarta: Department of Information, 1995–96), pp. 11, 40.

3. *Buku Repelita VI* [*Book of the Sixth Five-Year Development Plan*] (*1994–95–1998–99*) (Jakarta: Koperasi Pegawai Bappenas, 1994), ch. 33, pp. 149–181, esp. p. 165.

of Indonesian society" to accomplish "national development." The plan embedded development in the regime's other main motif, the five principles of Pancasila, by identifying the latter as development's "basis, goal, and guide."[4] Specific provisions mandated the Department of Education and Culture, for example, to promote language, literature, and the arts, and administer libraries, monuments, and museums. Such language gave notice of the government's intention to exercise its legal right to control and interpret cultural diversity, and to foster that interpretation.

Yet, as this chapter will show, the New Order's efforts to manage culture from the top down and the center out were only part of the story of expression in New Order Indonesia. For the regime, the management of culture was easier to propose in a plan than to implement in society. Before addressing some of the ways in which the New Order tried to shape expression in society, it will be helpful to illustrate this contrarian point—the regime's inability to implement full cultural hegemony—with just two instances of public reaction to cultural planning.

In 1994 the Department of Information withdrew the publishing licenses of several periodicals, including *Tempo,* the leading newsweekly at the time. Based in Jakarta, *Tempo*'s editors had been warned that they were overstepping official bounds. The crackdown when it came triggered widespread anger, especially among Indonesian intellectuals, journalists, and writers. A particularly direct response came from Emha Ainon Nadjib. Muslim-educated, a poet, essayist, and founder of a drama group, Emha countered New Order rhetoric by noting the "self-serving nature" of the power to determine what was "subversive," however much that power might wish to control what words meant and try to disguise its control in "a jargon of common good." Nor were Emha's critical views expressed privately. They were printed in a publicly available journal that was circulated among the members of Indonesia's rapidly growing urban middle class.[5]

Such opinions were not new. Back in the 1970s another well-known and widely published poet-cum-dramatist, W.S. Rendra, had written in a similar vein. The very title of Rendra's poem, "I Write This Pamphlet," had challenged the idea of an official monopoly on expression. "I write this pamphlet," he had written, "because institutions of public opinion / are covered in cobwebs / people speak in whispers / and self-expression is suppressed / into a 'Yes' ... "For Rendra, "when criticism comes only through official channels / life is like vegetables without salt. . . . [But] I see no reason / to stay suppressed and dumb / I want us to . . . sit in debate agreeing and disagreeing."[6]

Just as one should not in retrospect exaggerate the cultural power of the New

4. *Buku Repelita,* p. 150.
5. "Kafir Politis" ["Political Infidel"], *Tiras* [Jakarta], 9 February 1995, p. 30.
6. *Potret Pembangunan dalam Puisi* [*Development as Portrayed in Poetry*] (Jakarta: Lembaga Studi Pembangunan, 1980), pp. 27–28.

Order state, neither should one underestimate the risks undertaken by Emha and Rendra, among many others, in challenging it. Virtually all of the writers, dramatists, and artists who tested the limits on expression learned how hazardous the effort could be. *Tempo* in print was, after all, shut down and not allowed to reappear, although an electronic edition would later be disseminated over the Internet. Also, it was illegal to circulate the novels of Indonesia's most widely known author, Pramoedya Ananta Toer.

Pramoedya's work will be cited later in this chapter. But now, having illustrated both sides of the opposition between control and autonomy in the struggle over expression, I want to return to the state and its methods. The next sections will review how New Order authorities tried to limit and harness the representation of culture—by depicting a united nation, requiring a single national creed, and privileging certain more or less hierarchical conceptions of Indonesian society and history.

Depicting the Nation

In November 1971 the president's wife, Siti Hartinah ("Tien") Suharto, announced plans to build a theme park on the outskirts of Jakarta, where Indonesia's regional cultures would be on permanent display. To be called Beautiful Indonesia in Miniature (Taman Mini Indonesia Indah, or TMII, also Taman Mini), the park would enable Indonesians and foreigners lacking time or money to travel around the archipelago to experience the country's diversity and unity without leaving the capital. The exhibition, in Mrs. Suharto's words, would be "a concrete way" for Indonesians "to come to know and love" their own cultures. By knowing themselves better, she argued, Indonesians could develop their love of their nation, state, and national culture, and thus "greatly strengthen the union and unity of Indonesia, which belongs to us all, and which we defend and develop for the happiness of us all."[7]

Designed to encourage unity, the project quickly triggered discord. To avoid burdening the public budget, the park was supposed to be privately funded and was to become self-supporting. But financial projections were vague. Land for the project had been acquired by compulsion at low rates of compensation. Mounting criticism by students and intellectuals led the president himself to intervene. These critics' real target, he said, was not TMII but the armed forces, the government, and himself. If there were people acting in defiance of the constitution, he would "smash them, whoever they are."[8] The park was duly built. In 1975 it was officially opened by Mrs. Suharto, who managed it on the government's behalf with the aid of a foundation until her death in 1996.

---

7. Quoted in Greg Acciaioli, "A Tale of Two *Taman* (-*Mini*): National and Local Representations of Regional Identity in Contemporary Indonesia," unpublished paper, 1994.

8. As quoted by Hamish McDonald, *Suharto's Indonesia* (Blackburn, Victoria, Australia: Fontana, 1980), p. 127.

Beautiful Indonesia in Miniature was a quick success. Some 2 million people visited the park in its first year of operation. By 1994 annual attendance had tripled to more than 6.5 million. Among these were schoolchildren being taught about their country, adult Indonesians seeking recreation, and overseas tourists whose entrance fees brought needed foreign currency.

A huge billboard at the approach to Taman Mini announced in the Indonesian language that the park was "a vehicle. for conserving, developing and serving culture."[9] In the middle of the front entrance, sculptures portraying the struggle of the Indonesian people flanked an imposing monument to national ideology, the "Flame of Pancasila." The contents of the park included full-scale traditional houses from the country's twenty-seven provinces (including East Timor); a theater showing three-dimensional films depicting "Beautiful Indonesia"; and an extensive artificial lake dotted with islands representing the Indonesian archipelago. An imposing mosque, less imposing Catholic and Protestant churches, a Hindu temple, and a Buddhist stupa epitomized the country's religions.

Life-sized male and female mannequins dressed in traditional costumes from the relevant province occupied each of the houses, which were furnished with artifacts illustrating local traditions. At least weekly in every house a cultural performance was staged, typically a traditional dance. Reportedly, in order to keep the province's cultural heritage alive, the performance had to take place even if no visitors happened to be present to witness it.[10]

A ring of museums encircled the traditional houses. The museums celebrated Indonesian progress in fields such as national defense, oil and gas, telecommunications, and science. The arrangement of the two sets of buildings was said by one observer to portray development and modernity as an encompassing shelter that protected regional cultures and allowed them to thrive.[11] By bounding the provincial houses, the modern perimeter also helped to aggregate them and their contents into a single national whole, presented to visitors who would, in the words of a park brochure, leave "Beautiful Indonesia" feeling as though they had actually traveled around the real thing.[12]

It has been said that "One Country, One People, One Language"—a nationalist slogan dating from anti-Dutch days—"is a hope not a description" of Indonesia.[13] Taman Mini made national unity visible and tangible—as islands surrounded

---

9. The quote and the description that follows are based mainly on a visit I made to the park in February 1995.

10. "Untuk Menjaga Warisan Budaya" ["To Safeguard the Cultural Heritage"], *Gatra* [Jakarta], 29 April 1995, p. 110.

11. Acciaioli, "Tale," p. 8.

12. *Buku Acara Pekan HUT 15 dan Pekan Lebaran Taman Mini Indonesia Indah* [*Booklet of Events Commemorating Beautiful Indonesia in Miniature's 15th Anniversary and Muslim Fast-Breaking Week*] (Jakarta: [TMII], 1990), p. 36.

13. Clifford Geertz, "Afterword: The Politics of Meaning," in Claire Holt, ed., *Culture and Politics in Indonesia* (Ithaca, NY: Cornell University Press, 1972), p. 323.

by a lake, or as houses surrounded by progress. The park made the archipelago subject to easy mastery—on foot, in a minibus, or by overhead cable-car. But the exhibition suggested, too, that all this had been made possible through the accumulation and exercise of a higher mastery: the power of President Suharto to rule and therefore to represent the country. Shrinking the nation's 6,000 inhabited islands down to a theme park had made them "manageable" in this double sense of being easy to take and subject to higher control.

For all its emphasis on regional cultures, Taman Mini embodied what Michael Malley in this book describes as the dominance of the center over the regions. There were twenty-seven traditional houses, not because Indonesia had that many cultures—it had and continues to have many more—but because the central government had divided the country into that many provinces for purposes of uniform administration. In compartmentalizing cultures for the convenience of Jakarta, the pavilions overlooked the fact that ethnic identities diversified provinces and straddled provincial boundaries. What Greg Acciaioli called the "homogenizing hand" of the modern Indonesian state was especially evident in the representation of the cultures farthest from Jakarta. Compared with their counterparts from Java, Sumatra, and Bali, the traditional costumes and dances of Irian Jaya, for example, were less authentically reproduced.[14]

Shot on location, although produced in California, the three-dimensional films of "Beautiful Indonesia" screened in the park's theater reinforced the idea of Indonesia as a manageable and managed entity. Images filmed from the air and interpreted in voice-overs whisked audiences above dazzling scenery and, on the ground, through selected impressions of everyday life. The traditional and the contemporary were artfully juxtaposed: the uproar and color of a Balinese cremation on the one hand, Jakarta's nighttime traffic gliding down ribbons of freeways on the other. Past was linked to future: Scenes of children learning traditional dances or training for sports were said by the narrator to show the next generation striving for excellence by acquiring skills from its elders. Diversity was linked in unity: Remote hilltops on far-flung islands sprouted satellite dishes. One film ended with a large group of children, apparently representing the country's many provinces, posed on the grounds of the presidential palace in Bogor, West Java, singing a song whose lyrics urged all Indonesians to work together, serving their country and God through "Unity in Diversity"—the omnipresent national motto.

Finally, worth noting among Taman Mini's exhibits was a large mural inside the Museum of Indonesia. In this painting the national archipelago was depicted and framed by images of mythical animals drawn from Indic tradition: a white *garuda* (a bird) and a red *naga* (a serpent). An accompanying text explained to visitors that the *garuda* stood for the mother country (*tanahair,* or

---

14. Acciaioli, "Tale," p. 9.

"homelandwater"), while the *naga* represented the underworld (on which the mother country rested). Located at opposite ends of the mural, the two beasts were nevertheless connected: The *naga*'s long tail extended under the mural so that the *garuda* could rest on it. According to the text, the animals' relationship symbolized the movement of nature toward harmony between opposing, yet indivisible, elements.

The lesson of the mural was the message of the park: Among Indonesians, differences existed, but they were and always would be contained within the unbreakable entity that was the Indonesian nation. In contrast to the complex, dynamic, and sometimes conflicted realities of the archipelago explored in previous chapters in this book, this "Beautiful Indonesia" was simplified, fixed, and forever harmonious. In the mural's uniting of air, land, and water, the integralist ideology of the New Order had become a law of nature.

Requiring a Creed

Indonesian visitors to the Museum of Indonesia had no trouble recognizing the *garuda*. It is featured on the official seal of the Republic, where the bird's claws grasp the ends of a banner proclaiming in Sanskrit the national catchphrase, Unity in Diversity. At the center of the seal, on a shield drawn on the *garuda*'s chest, five objects symbolize the five principles of Pancasila: Belief in God; Nationalism; Humanitarianism; Democracy; and Social Justice.

Beginning in the late 1970s, and with increasing efficiency, Pancasila was taught in special "upgrading" courses. These were aimed at all citizens, but especially schoolchildren, students, and civil servants. From the mid-1980s onward, all political parties and sociopolitical organizations were required to subscribe to Pancasila as their sole ideology. The goals of this indoctrination deepened in the 1980s from understanding and observing Pancasila to making its principles integral to personal belief and behavior.

In classrooms, for example, Pancasila's values were incorporated into the teaching of subjects such as history, Indonesian language and literature, and religious education. Students mentioned the five principles in answers to standard questions such as "What does it mean to be an Indonesian?" and "What are the purposes of Indonesian education?" References to Pancasila were ubiquitous in official speeches and ceremonies. Even inside mosques sponsored by the regime, Muslims who looked up to the apex of the roof saw, hanging there, the five-sided Pancasila emblem framing the word "Allah" in Arabic script.

New Order authorities also used Pancasila to shape and contain the range of acceptable expression in the arts. In Bali, for example, the official mission of the government-sponsored College of Indonesian Arts was to educate its students, "in accordance with the Principles of Pancasila and the Constitution," to work "in a pluralistic society" with "love for and a desire to" further their culture in the context of service to social development and "dedication to God"—the latter an echo of the first of the five principles.[15]

As a hallmark of national unity, religious tolerance, and social order, Pancasila was used to warrant artistic expressions that did not endanger these values. As a badge of national identity, Pancasila was deployed against the perceived risk to morality and culture posed by Indonesia's openness to the modern world. Anti-Pancasila outlooks that Indonesians needed protection from, according to the 1994–99 development plan, included "individualism," for example, alongside more home-grown prejudices such as "narrow regionalism" and "exclusive" or "feudal" attitudes.[16]

For all its emphasis on harmony, the New Order was itself substantially responsible for the tensions that made harmony seem necessary. It was precisely the regime's success in opening and developing Indonesia's economy that expanded the country's middle class and linked its members to the wider world, including democratic-capitalist societies valuing individual freedoms. When the authorities used Pancasila to inoculate society against alienation, they were to an extent treating a consequence of their own policies.

Most of the artists whose works criticized the regime aimed less at the content of New Order ideology than its use by the authorities to constrain the range of tolerated expression. What Emha, in the article cited at the outset of this chapter, called "the jargon of the common good," was so tightly linked to Indonesian unity and progress as to be virtually unassailable on its own terms. Rather, the issue was the monopolization of meaning by the state and the lack of a freely bestowed mandate that would have legitimated the state's claim to speak for the Indonesian people. For Emha, Rendra, and others like them, open debate was needed to revitalize, humanize, and democratize Indonesian society and politics. For New Order ideologues, on the contrary, free expression would merely reopen the Pandora's box of instability and conflict that had bedeviled the country in the 1950s and 1960s.

Democracy and Hierarchy

Alongside "Beautiful Indonesia" and Pancasila, another tool used by the New Order to shape and limit expression was Javanism. This further illustration of culture as an official project will show how traditional sources of metaphors were put to political use.

The term *wayang,* broadly understood, encompasses rituals and entertainment

---

15. As quoted by Brett Hough, "*Sekolah Tinggi Seni Indonesia Denpasar and the Tri Dharma Perguruan Tinggi,*" ["The College of Indonesian Arts in Denpasar and the Three Duties of Higher Education"], conference paper, Third International Bali Studies Workshop, University of Sydney, Sydney, Australia, 3–7 July 1995.

16. *Buku Repelita,* p. 157.

in various forms—flat leather puppets lit to cast shadows on a screen, three-dimensional wooden puppets, dance dramas, even comic books—that share a repertoire dating from the Indianization of the islands in the premodern era. Central to that repertoire are the Indic epics, the *Mahabharata* and the *Ramayana,* as these have been reworked in local contexts, most notably the culture of the Javanese ethnic group to which perhaps half of all Indonesians belong, including Suharto and many of the fellow generals and ministers who accompanied him in his regime.

A character called Semar illustrates the indigenization of Indic mythology within Javanese *wayang.* A uniquely local figure, Semar is simultaneously a servant and a god. In the first role, Semar follows the hero Arjuna. In the second role, Semar outranks even the great god Bhatara Guru (Shiva in India). Semar has been associated with Suharto ever since 11 March 1966, when Sukarno, under duress, authorized Suharto to exercise emergency powers— de facto transfer, in effect, of the power of the presidency itself. This authorization, the New Order's virtual birth certificate, became known as "Supersemar"—an acronym for the "Letter of Instruction of 11 March" ("Surat Perintah Sebelas Maret").

Periodically thereafter, Suharto used *wayang* to legitimate the New Order and popularize its objectives. In April 1969, for instance, inaugurating the first in what would become a sequence of five-year development plans, the president brought shadow-play puppeteers from around the archipelago to the presidential palace in Jakarta. There he encouraged them to assist in the process of national development by disseminating its goals and priorities.

Early in 1995 Suharto met with another group of puppeteers. This time he called for the creation of a new *wayang* story or episode (*lakon*) that would revolve around the identity and significance of Semar. Accordingly, the Jakarta office of the Javanology Institute—itself a reflection of the New Order's interest in cultural research and development—organized a day-long seminar to discuss the many dimensions of Semar. The *wayang* puppeteers' association then formed a team to draft the new *lakon.*

The president hoped that in this new tale, Semar would be portrayed as someone without a formal leadership role who nevertheless speaks out. Suharto was not disappointed. Ruler-subject relations in old Javanese kingdoms were hardly democratic in a modern sense. But the puppeteers who created the new *lakon* presented Semar in a way that suggested that Javanese culture did have democratic aspects. To do this, the puppeteers emphasized Semar's interest in, and identification with, ordinary people and their welfare—Semar not only as the servant of a prince but as "the lowliest of the low" (*batur kedibal songolikur* in Javanese).[17]

But Semar was chosen to stand for much more than a kind of democracy. As an

---

17. Dwitri Waluyu, "Belajar Demokrasi ala Semar" ["Learning Semar-Style Democracy"], *Gatra,* 25 March 1995, p. 36.

all-powerful god and guardian spirit of Java, who does not appear in the versions of the *Mahabharata* known in India, Semar is a respected and autochthonous figure. The political use of Semar in 1995, while it appeared to favor a populist sort of democracy familiar to Westerners—*vox populi, vox Dei*—could also be taken as recommending limits on the right of ordinary people to express grievances. For beneath the lowliness of Semar lies a godliness to which ordinary mortals cannot aspire. And the Javaneseness of Semar could be read as lending indigenous authenticity to this erasure of the political importance of social class differences. Viewed in this context, democracy Semar-style appears fundamentally antithetical to Western political liberalism, at least to the extent that the latter calls for structural solutions to problems of inequality frankly acknowledged.

Semar illustrates the ambiguity that typifies high Javanese culture. The president seems to have wanted this archetypically Javanese figure to embody a democracy in which speaking out can and should occur inside the polity, but without transforming it. The enemies of the prince whom Semar-the-servant follows are always defeated, but the world in which servants accompany princes goes on. *Wayang* in this ritual sense reenacts "the triumph of good over evil so that order and stability are maintained."[18]

Yet just as Pancasila's principles could be held up critically as goals the New Order had not attained, and might even have violated, so could Indonesians differently understand Semar. One may wonder to what extent Suharto would have agreed, for example, with the way *Gatra,* the weekly newsmagazine that replaced *Tempo* after the latter was banned in 1994, welcomed the new *wayang* story's equation of Semar with the people. *Gatra* called it an invitation to ordinary Indonesians to have their own political aspirations.[19] One may also wonder whether any Indonesians saw irony in the new *lakon*'s performance inside TMII. For that resolutely pan-archipelagic setting could have been seen as underscoring by contrast the president's choice of a thoroughly Javanese character to represent all Indonesians in a performance conducted in Javanese—a complex language fully understood by less than half of the country's population.

Javanism and Familism

The diversity of expression in Indonesia necessarily involves the languages through which expression occurs. Hundreds of local and regional, not to mention foreign, languages are spoken in Indonesia. But there is only one national lingua franca, and that language, Indonesian, is a crucial part of what being an Indonesian means. Instruction takes place in Indonesian in all subjects at all levels. It is the language of virtually all media—newspapers and magazines, radio and televi-

---

18. "The Media," in Anthony Milner and Mary Quilty, eds., *Australia in Asia: Comparing Cultures* (Melbourne, Australia: Oxford University Press, 1996), p. 210.

19. "Belajar Demokrasi," p. 36.

sion. Corporations conduct business, make contracts, and advertise in Indonesian, which is also the language of government and public affairs—administration and justice, propaganda and memoranda. It is the language of modern culture and the arts—novels and poetry, films and plays. Small wonder that during the New Order, billboards in the larger cities proclaimed, "The Indonesian Language Is the Identity of the Nation."

It is nevertheless understood and accepted that an individual citizen should also have his or her own regional, ethnic, and religious identity, including a language other than Indonesian. Roughly speaking, if the national language is considered appropriate for discourse in public, ensuring comprehension in trans-ethnic settings, regional languages are preferred in private contexts. It is inside the household, for example, that a Javanese would communicate with other Javanese—parents, siblings, a spouse—using the Javanese language.

The association of regional languages with one's childhood and family lends them an intimacy that Indonesia typically lacks. And because it tends powerfully to evoke one's personal identity-from-childhood, a regional language or "mother tongue" is an attractive tool for glossing abstract political subjects such as democracy and hierarchy. Suharto's use of Semar shows that at the higher reaches of the regime, Javanese language and ritual performance could surface in the public realm as sources of support for a particular interpretation of what being Indonesian ought to mean.

Many public symbols of Indonesianness themselves have Javanese origins. The red and white colors of the national flag, the national formula—Unity in Diversity—and the *garuda* on the national emblem can all be traced to the fourteenth-century central-Javanese kingdom of Majapahit, whose territory the modern Republic claims roughly to inherit. Just as Suharto tried to use *wayang* and Semar to nest democracy within hierarchy in the ideology of a regime, so do these connections to myth and history illustrate how "High Javanism"—Javanese elite culture idealized and reified into something noble and profound—has been a source of symbols of national identity.

And if during the New Order Javanese was not entirely limited to the private or family realm, neither was the concept of the family itself. If President Suharto was portrayed as a Semar-like servant of the people, he was also given the title, "Father of Development." And along with other older male Indonesians, he merited being called simply "Father" (*Bapak*). An Indonesian lawyer active in defense of human rights once lamented that Indonesians could not criticize the president as a figurative father because it was unseemly for children to disagree with their biological father. The application of the family analogy to public life, in this lawyer's view, had made chiding the president a crime interpretable as subversion.[20]

---

20. Yap Thiam Hien, "Preface: Law, State and Civil Society," in Arief Budiman, ed., *State and Civil Society in Indonesia* (Clayton, Victoria, Australia: Monash University Centre of Southeast Asian Studies, 1990), pp. vii–viii.

The family in this context was made to stand for the common good. A good father made his children understand what was good for them as members of the family. When individuals failed to do what the government wanted them to, they were said not to understand that the government was furthering the common good. To cite but one example: Once a taxi driver told me that the people who were reluctant to turn over their land to the government to build "Beautiful Indonesia" simply did not understand what the government was planning for their own good.

The family metaphor has a long and broad history. Words for family roles such as "father" and "child" have been applied to relationships of social or political status, including the one between the ruler and the ruled, throughout the Malayo-Indonesian world. When they ruled the Indies, the Dutch also made use of such terms to elicit compliance and manipulate consensus. Familist rhetoric was employed then, as it would be later, to legitimate one sort of inequality, the hierarchy of parents over children, while masking others—notably differences of race, class, and gender. Implications for gender are discussed by Kathryn Robinson in this book.

A danger in reviewing these ways in which Suharto's regime tried to limit and shape discourse is that a reader will conclude that they must all have been effective. That would be a mistake. Perversely for New Order ideologists, their very emphasis on unity and compliance stimulated a desire to maintain and express difference and originality. Similarly, official support for deference to a *bapak,* or for taming democracy with hierarchy à la Semar, triggered counterhegemonic notions of creative autonomy—if not in politics, given the risks, then at least in matters of artistic expression to which this chapter now turns.

Region and Status

During the New Order, in the name of preserving regional cultures, the center tried to classify and standardize them. But it would be wrong to conclude that in matters of expression the regions passively accepted whatever Jakarta imposed. Outright rejection of central guidance was rare, but the reinterpretation of central ideas to suit local priorities was not. In this sense, the spectrum of permissible expression in Indonesia included room for the regions to tell their own stories and draw their own pictures in their own ways, as long as these ways did not contest the national frame or its symbols.

Two cases in point involved regional uses of the center's construction of Beautiful Indonesia in Miniature—the taming of the archipelago's diversity inside the physical unity of a theme park inside the national center that was, and is, Jakarta. Following the capital's lead, a Mini Park (Taman Mini) was erected in South Sulawesi. But this regional echo of a central project differed from its Jakarta-based inspiration in significant respects. It was established not on historically neutral ground but inside an old fort linked to the history of the local Gowa kingdom. At its zenith early in the seventeenth century, before the establishment of Dutch colonial rule, Gowa had been a renowned and powerful center. The siting of South Sulawesi's Mini Park thus emphasized the power and achievements of a once famous non-Javanese culture.

In Jakarta's version of "Beautiful Indonesia," cultures were made provincial—classified and confined in twenty-seven pavilions. Taman Mini, in effect, reduced the republic to a New Order organizational chart. In contrast, exhibits in South Sulawesi's Mini Park acknowledged local identities that ran along ethnic and spatial lines, lines that transgressed the neat borders between administrative divisions. Finally, the Mini Park's local organizers did not bow to pressure by the governor and the provincial branch of the Jakarta-based national office of tourism to standardize the traditional houses to be displayed by using prefabricated models. Instead, in Sulawesi, actual structures were copied. The result, in Acciaioli's opinion, was a living sign of resistance to Jakarta's modular view of local cultures as generically Indonesian.[21]

A second illustration of local creativity within a national frame occurred in Bali. As noted when discussing the official promotion of Pancasila, the national government established a College of Indonesian Arts in the capital of Bali, Denpasar. The institution's explicitly national name omitted any reference to Bali or to Balinese arts. Jakarta expected the College to ensure that the arts of Bali met quality standards, and to present Balinese culture to the rest of Indonesia and the world beyond. On important national occasions, for example, the College might be called upon by central authorities to stage performances drawn from one or another Balinese genre. Such evidence seemed to support the idea that the College was an "upstream" industry for Jakarta's national culture project: processing Balinese culture to make it fit the provincial showcase reserved for it in the national culture displayed on state occasions in the national capital.

Yet it was precisely the legitimacy of the college in Jakarta's eyes, seen as a national institution, that enabled it to express Balinese identity creatively in various forms. Thus did a major production by the college, tellingly entitled "Beautiful Indonesia," become a national vehicle for the assertion of a uniquely Balinese identity. The genre used on this occasion was "dance drama" (sendratari)—a modern form created in Bali in the mid-1960s.[22]

It may be argued that the central organization of museums enabled Jakarta to impose national classifications on local cultures. Yet during the New Order, inside some regional museums, offerings were regularly made to the sacred royal regalia of long-defunct kingdoms—behavior hardly in line with the monotheistic first principle of Pancasila. One might also think that reproducing culture for

---

21. Acciaioli, "Tale," p. 28.

22. Brett Hough, *Contemporary Balinese Dance Spectacles as National Ritual* (Clayton, Victoria, Australia: Monash University Centre of Southeast Asian Studies, 1992), p. 19; see also pp. 15, 20 (n. 4).

mass audiences in formats such as audiocassettes would have reduced its diversity by enabling the exact same performance to be replayed again and again. Reportedly in parts of eastern Indonesia, when a visiting ethnomusicologist asked to record a performance of some local genre, performers preferred to save themselves the trouble by presenting their own cassette recording of the event. But while such behavior may have limited the variety of recorded performances available, one can empathize with the desire of local producers of art to influence the "downstream" reproduction and processing of what they do. And while the large-scale circulation of traditional Javanese music in recorded form may temporarily have favored an especially popular rendition, too many other versions were available, or recordable, for uniformity to endure.

Finally, although controversially, one may ask at what point cynicism about central power becomes unrealistic. How, for example, should the following use of Taman Mini in Jakarta be interpreted? In 1995, on the officially designated occasion of Children's Day—23 July—the park hosted a live broadcast by the state television network. From all over the archipelago, children were linked visually by satellite to President Suharto in Jakarta, ostensibly to enable them to speak "directly" to him. Another four hundred or so children from all provinces had been brought to Jakarta to visit the park and "meet with" the president.

It would be easy to see in this event, as in the commissioned story of Semar, an authoritarian regime self-servingly locating democracy within a context of palatable inequality: technology replacing Semar as the locus of a politically convenient fusion of polar opposites—omnipotence and impotence, god and commoner, mature wisdom and immature youth. The children were hardly free to criticize the president or give him advice. Only propagandistically could their encounter with him be called a "dialogue."

And yet these youngsters will long outlive the president, and in the course of their lives, they may well come to believe things he did not believe, and do things he would not have done. And who is to say that the national experience of gathering with peers from all over Indonesia in the national capital may not have left a more lasting impression on Suharto's young audience in "Beautiful Indonesia" than the president's presence among them? If this use of the park was meant to propagandize the next generation into revering Suharto as the embodiment of Indonesian nationhood, one can doubt both the ability of the president to accomplish this trick and the inability of the children to distinguish their country from their head of state. Suharto's young listeners in 1995 already represented the potential of "Indonesia beyond Suharto" to alter or replace his legacy while retaining a diversity that lies beyond the capacity of any authoritarian leader of so vast and multiform a country to contain.

If Indonesians varied by region and generation, they were differentiated as well by relative wealth and status—made visible in towns and cities by differences between neighborhoods. In Jakarta on a Friday afternoon, for example, a visitor to TMII could easily be swept up in a river of worshippers leaving the large Diponegoro mosque. And as the crowd thinned, she or he would notice the change in surroundings: from the didactic orderliness of the park to an urban village (*kampung*) of small, dilapidated houses and narrow muddy roads replete with the bustle of specific lives being lived. The visitor had been swept out of the sanitized realm of Taman Mini into a genuine world of ordinary people whose *kampung* happened to share a boundary wall with Beautiful Indonesia in Miniature. The *kampung* dwellers slipped easily between these worlds. Some used the Taman Mini mosque for their Friday worship; some worked in the park. Unlike those who had been obliged to make way for the exhibition when it was built, these people appeared to have retained their land and remained in the shadow of Beautiful Indonesia.

Such people found entertainment in, for example, Indonesian popular music and songs, street theater performances, and cheap movies screened in rundown (or outdoor) cinemas. Something of the contrast between this vibrant culture and that of well-to-do Indonesians was captured by Indonesians themselves in the contrast between *kampungan* and *gedungan*—adjectives roughly translatable as "unsophisticated" or "retaining village ways" on the one hand, and "well-to-do" or "living in a house made of concrete [*gedung*]" on the other.

In Suharto's Indonesia, inside the social world of Jakarta, what separated these categories was wealth. *Gedungan* had it, *kampungan* did not. Seen from the *kampung* abutting Taman Mini, middle-class people were *gedungan*—better educated, earning higher incomes, living in buildings. A Jakarta newspaper once listed the forms of expression the *gedungan* favor—poetry recited by Rendra, drama and comedy performed by Teater Koma and Sri Mulat, jazz by Sergio Mendez—and noted their taste for Western and Japanese restaurants.[23]

The gap between *kampungan* and *gedungan* tastes can be bridged. The theatrical performances put on by Rendra in Yogyakarta early in his career, for instance, were *kampungan* in their origin and venues. But with growing popularity came opportunities to appear in established locales before higher-class audiences able to afford higher ticket prices.[24] The poems he read in these settings, however, continued to invoke the suffering and oppression of "the people" (*rakyat*) and to decry the corruption and avarice of those in power, whom Rendra openly portrayed as responsible for injustice.

Well over four-fifths of Indonesian adults can read and write, but the habit of reading is not widespread; in the early 1990s the circulation of newspapers per

---

23. "Young Professionals of Jakarta: Millions in Salary, Lack of Hard Work," *Kompas* [Jakarta], 11 May 1986, trans. Daniel S. Lev, in Richard Tanter and Kenneth Young, eds., *The Politics of Middle Class Indonesia* (Clayton, Victoria, Australia: Monash University Centre for Southeast Asian Studies, 1990), p. 167; see also pp. 44–48 (Lev's "Notes on the Middle Class and Change in Indonesia").

24. Alison Murray, "Kampung Culture and Radical Chic in Jakarta," *RIMA* [*Review of Indonesian and Malaysian Affairs*] [Sydney], 25:1 (1991), p. 3.

capita was the lowest of any ASEAN country. Hence the impact of Rendra's poems was greater in performance than in print. Theatrically declaimed by their author, projected on the strength of his personality and reputation, Rendra's poems of social criticism typically moved his mainly *gedungan* audiences to wild applause. Thus did Rendra and other poets "represent" the *rakyat*—from the poor farmers who lost their land to Beautiful Indonesia, to the factory workers who suffered unhealthy conditions for substandard wages.

Rendra expressed himself in national terms. By writing and performing in Indonesian rather than his native Javanese, he could sustain a broader, ethnically more diverse following. At the same time, however, his choice of the national language reinforced the *gedungan* character of his audiences, who typically used Indonesian more, and local languages or dialects less, than their *kampungan* counterparts did.

Expression and Repression

Creative expression under the New Order, it has been said, began with a burst of originality in the regime's early years. This florescence followed the end of a bitter debate between socially committed and "universal humanist" writers and artists. Seeing the first group as treacherously leftist, the new regime imprisoned its members, including Pramoedya Ananta Toer, and proscribed their works. The second group, including the poet and journalist Goenawan Mohamad, were thought safely apolitical if not anticommunist, and were encouraged to work. Then, in the mid-1970s, widespread student protests broke out against repressive government policies. The authorities responded by jailing "liberal" student leaders and banning several newspapers.

The crackdown reinvigorated the earlier tradition of social and political commitment and criticism, albeit in noncommunist form. In the art academies, for example, some students criticized the pedagogy of art education for slavishly following Western models. In 1975 these critics formed a New Art Movement (Gerakan Seni Rupa Baru) to ground artistic expression in social conditions. In cinema there were also calls for social realism and engagement: films that would go beyond describing personal and moral conflicts to protesting unjust social conditions. Poets and playwrights also took up the summons to social relevance and political critique.

In his own work, Rendra frequently derided the state, until in 1978 he was forbidden to perform onstage. The ban lasted seven years. This and other warnings led a number of writers and artists to retreat from social criticism toward less pointedly political topics in fantasy and history. But contemporary comments could be read into fantasies. Caustic portrayals of Dutch colonial rule could be taken as satires on post-colonial Indonesian elites. Official intimidation and repression were never wholly effective.

Thus in the mid-1980s, a decade after the turn toward social criticism in the visual arts, a similar movement arose among some Indonesian authors, who called for a return to a "contextual literature" that would spotlight the country's real social and political ills.[25] The new movement soon triggered disapproval from writers who rejected social realism as just another straitjacket. Although the New Order had been able to terminate by fiat the polemics between contextualists and universalists toward the end of Sukarno's rule, the questions of diversity and commitment in artistic expression that had animated that earlier debate had not gone away.

In 1981, for example, Rendra publicly criticized what he considered the timidity and conformity of Indonesian writers. "The function of the artist, the poet and the intellectual," he argued, was "to guide or lead social change."[26] For Pramoedya, who had been arrested for leftism and kept in prison or internal exile by the New Order for fourteen years (1965–79)—his internationally acclaimed novels were still banned in Indonesia in 1997—"the greatness of a literary creation" depended on whether it could foster awareness of and responsibility toward "the infinite variety of life."[27] Writing in 1993, a year before the banning of his news weekly, *Tempo,* Goenawan Mohamad pictured cultural expression as an open-ended process of challenging preconceptions and stimulating "dialogue, exploration, liberation."[28]

These rationales omitted self-expression as a justification for artistic endeavor. Thematic instead in New Order Indonesia was the artist's moral responsibility to engage with an "other." Widespread among Indonesian writers and artists was this recognition of an "other," meaning something or someone that lay beyond the self, such as the life force, God, one's fellow human beings, and especially the exploited or oppressed. Still rare in modern Indonesian literature, even late in the Suharto period, were extended portrayals of the interior world of a striving or doubting self disconnected from social context. Ironically, as Indonesian writers struggled to resist the regime's exhortation to conform, their emphasis on responsibility to others might be said to have implemented, however variously, the New Order's own repeated themes of family obligation and social service.

The next sections will review three thematic areas in contemporary Indonesian writing, painting, and film: social critiques; uses of history, *wayang,* spirituality and religion; and depictions of women. While necessarily subjective and incomplete—strictly traditional arts, for example, will not be covered—this se-

---

25. The ensuing controversy was reviewed in Ariel Heryanto, ed., *Perdebatan Sastra Kontekstual* [*The Contextual Literature Debate*] (Jakarta: CV Rajawali, 1985).

26. *Kompas,* 30 June 1981, as quoted in Sutan Takdir Alisyahbana, "Literature's Role in the Emergence of a New Culture," *Prisma* [Jakarta, English edition], 29 (September 1983), p. 11.

27. As cited by Astri Wright, *Soul, Spirit, and Mountain: Preoccupations of Contemporary Indonesian Painters* (Kuala Lumpur: Oxford University Press, 1994), p. 155.

28. *Horison* [Jakarta], 27:7 (July 1993), p. 8.

lection should convey something of the vitality and variety of contemporary Indonesian expression.

Bearing Witness

"A poet is someone who gives witness."[29] Rendra, who wrote this definition, exemplified it not only in his poetry but in political dramas such as *Mastodon dan Kondor* (*The Mastodon and the Condors*), *Perjuangan Suku Naga* (*The Struggle of the Naga Tribe*), and *Sekda* (*The Provincial Secretary*). Staged before large and appreciative audiences in the 1970s prior to his banning, these plays openly censured oppressive and exploitative regimes and leaders—by implication, the New Order—and defended the *rakyat*—the Indonesian masses. "Because we have only sandals / and you are free to use rifles . . . ," Rendra raged in an especially popular poem, "Because we must be polite / and you have jails . . . / So [we say] NO and NO to you." And time was on the people's side: "Because we are the current of the river / and you are the stones without heart . . . / So the water will erode away the stones."[30]

Rendra's themes were visible in the stark paintings and drawings of Semsar Siahaan and Dede Eri Supria. A recurring image on Semsar's canvasses was a skeletal maternal figure with hungry children: mother Indonesia unable to provide for her people. In the late 1980s, Semsar called on his fellow artists to stop romanticizing poverty. He defined his own work as "liberation art—individual freedom for the liberation of the majority of humanity."[31] Note again the emphasis on family obligation and social service.

Dede Eri Supria preferred the ultra realism of photographic images: unrelieved cityscapes against whose cold, uncompromising lines were set the figures of the *rakyat*. There was no vegetation and rarely even a glimpse of sky or any other natural feature to relieve the complex geometry of buildings—mazes without exits—as in his aptly named painting, *Labyrinth* (1987). Compared with Rendra, Semsar and Dede appeared more pessimistic about overcoming the oppression and alienation they depicted. Several of Semsar's exhibitions were closed by the regime, or not allowed to open.

Compared with the scathing imagery of Rendra, Semsar, and Dede, socially critical films were less pointed. Film censorship was more thoroughgoing, and the financial stakes were higher than for poetry or art. Typically in the 1970s, for

---

29. W.S. Rendra, "Gita Durma" ["A Psalm"], trans. Max Lane, *Inside Indonesia* [Northcote, Victoria, Australia], 2 (May 1984), p. 30.

30. "Sajak Orang Kepanasan" ["Poem of an Angry Person"], trans. Max Lane, *Inside Indonesia,* 2 (May 1984), p. 25.

31. Quoted in Brita L. Miklouho-Maklai, *Exposing Society's Wounds: Some Aspects of Contemporary Indonesian Art since 1966* (Adelaide: Flinders University of South Australia Discipline of Asian Studies, 1991), p. 97.

example, filmmakers who pictured poverty and injustice treated them as personal misfortunes to be transcended through hard work and moral behavior.

Exceptional in this context were *Si Mamad* (*Mamad* [1974]) and *Perawan Desa* (*Village Virgin* [1978]). In these films individuals fell victim to the social system through no fault of their own. Mamad was a good man whose obsessive honesty proved to be, literally, the death of him. *Village Virgin* was bolder still. Its plot was drawn from the actual gang rape of a 17-year-old schoolgirl by the sons of senior Indonesian officials. Because of police corruption, the perpetrators were not brought to trial. The filmmakers chose instead to picture a trial, and to end it with a dramatic court scene: The victim, having been intimidated by the police, is unable to give full evidence, and the case is dismissed. But the censors refused to allow the film to be shown with this conclusion. A new ending was shot, and the revised product released. The approved version ended with the rapists being "punished" by "natural justice"—in a car crash.[32]

In Indonesia under the New Order there were no approved versions of the writings of Pramoedya Ananta Toer, and the originals were banned. Nevertheless, the most widely—globally—read portrayal of the past in modern Indonesian literature was an epic four-volume novel by Pramoedya. It became known as "The Buru Quartet" because Pramoedya composed it while in internal exile on the penal island of Buru.[33] The novel brilliantly recreates the transitional years of the late nineteenth and early twentieth centuries by integrating history with fiction. The hero, Minke, a young, Dutch-educated Javanese aristocrat inspired by the real-life nationalist Tirto Adisuryo, emerges in the course of the narrative as a prototype of the Indonesian intellectual seeking to blend modernity with his own culture. Readers were quick to notice parallels between Pramoedya's portrait of the colonial Indies and the authoritarianism of the New Order. But the novel is genuinely historical—not mere political allegory. The Quartet stands out among fiction written during the New Order because it explores the interior thoughts and feelings of Minke as he struggles to find his own way in the world.

Hendra Gunawan (1918–83) also depicted colonial exploitation in ways that allowed those who viewed his paintings to think of post-colonial injustices, and he, too, suffered for his politics. He and Pramoedya both had been active in the Institute of People's Culture (Lembaga Kebudayaan Rakyat, or LEKRA), which flourished under Sukarno, claiming 100,000 members by 1963. LEKRA championed socialist realism and sharply criticized the work of artists and writers deemed

---

32. Full details are given in Krishna Sen, *Indonesian Cinema: Framing the New Order* (London: Zed Books, 1994), pp. 114–120.

33. Pramoedya Ananta Toer, *This Earth of Mankind* [*Bumi Manusia* (1980)], *Child of All Nations* [*Anak Semua Bangsa* (1980)], *Footsteps* [*Jejak Langkah* (1985)], and *House of Glass* [*Rumah Kaca* (1988)], trans. Max Lane (reprint, New York: Penguin Books, 1996 [*Earth, Child, Footsteps*], 1997 [*House*]). The Indonesian originals were published by Hasta Mitra in Jakarta.

unprogressive. Arrested in 1965, Hendra spent the next thirteen years in prison. After his release, he returned to painting historical scenes. In one of these, a Javanese prince meets with the nineteenth century Dutch Governor General H.W. Daendels against a background showing the maltreatment of native laborers mobilized to build coach roads on Java.

Released in 1978, Teguh Karya's well-received film *Nopember 1828* (*November 1828*) focused on a Javanese village occupied by Dutch troops in response to an uprising by another Javanese prince, Diponegoro. But within this political context, known as the Java War (1825–30), the film told the story of a family facing disaster and the sacrifices it has to make. The inclination of audiences to read back into the drama of Diponegoro's local revolt—the much later national struggle for Indonesian independence—may help to explain the success of *Nopember 1828*. Also contributing to its popularity may have been the director's use of the family as a metaphor for unity. On the screen it is the village elders' authority that binds the villagers together in a time of crisis.[34]

The past also could be put to nonpolitical use, as in *Ancient Time,* a 1987 oil and mixed media canvas by Nyoman Erawan. In this painting, a traditional Balinese calendar, which is also a grid of miniature scenes of daily life, foregrounds a thrusting triangular shape composed of smaller triangles. The whole is rent by curling cracks, evoking transience and decay. Apparently Nyoman drew on his native Balinese tradition—the calendar and the related ritual of cremation—to picture the interlocking of life and death.

Myth and Faith

Suharto's use of Semar has been described earlier. A more blatant case of a regional tradition's manipulation to embellish the New Order was the award-winning pseudohistorical propaganda film, *Serangan Fajar* (*Attack at Dawn*). Directed by Arifin C. Noer, the film presented Suharto as a major figure in the war of independence against the Dutch, and used *wayang* symbols and themes to enhance the heroism of the revolution and the president's role in it.

But *wayang* could be made to serve counterhegemonic ends as well. In 1995, for instance, Goenawan Mohamad chose the *wayang* medium to comment on the closure of his news weekly, *Tempo,* one year before. He worked with a puppeteer to present a new *lakon* spotlighting Arjuna's son Wisanggeni, who is banned from heaven for inappropriate behavior, but then proceeds, down on earth, to lead the peasantry in revolt against injustice. This is not to suggest that Goenawan seriously identified himself with Wisanggeni, any more than Suharto imagined himself to be Semar. It is rather to note that, in the New Order, mining *wayang* for allusions was a game not only the regime could play. *Wayang* could also inspire creative expression along more personal or spiritual lines, as in Danarto's

---

34. Sen, *Indonesian Cinema,* pp. 85–86, makes these points.

1974 short story "Nostalgia" ("Longing") and Y.B. Mangunwijaya's 1981 novel *Burung-Burung Manyar* (*The Weaver Birds*).

In the visual arts, Heri Dono painted figures inspired by *wayang* puppets. He also was a puppeteer who performed *lakon* that could be given contemporary relevance. He believed that *wayang* should represent all Indonesians—not just the Javanese—and hoped that regional folk tales would inspire the crafting of new *lakon* and thus help to nationalize the form. In 1995 controversy greeted an effort to do this in an animated *wayang* film for children centered on the role of Burisrawa. The film's characters spoke in regional languages and dialects; Burisrawa himself used a Sumatran language, Batak. But this attempt to nationalize *wayang* attracted criticism from some Javanese. In their view, Javanese-language shadow puppetry could be neither translated nor filmed.

A more successful effort to fashion a national genre from regional components was undertaken by the design group DECENTA at the Institute of Technology in Bandung beginning in the 1970s. The group collected indigenous motifs from around the archipelago and used them to express a national identity in architecture and interior decoration. The group's work could be seen in a number of buildings, particularly in Jakarta.

As with *wayang* in Javanese culture, the presence of Islam in Indonesia made it an obvious subject for writers and artists throughout the New Order. But putting Islam to creative use was far more sensitive than doing so with *wayang*. It was easier to criticize the ruling regime than even to seem to criticize a divinely revealed religion. Indonesians were enjoined by Pancasila to be, and they mostly were, tolerant of one another's faiths. But even appearing to insult Islam, and therefore God and the Prophet, risked the wrath of Muslim activists. In Jakarta in 1990, furious Muslim youths stormed the office of a tabloid weekly, *Monitor,* for having conducted and printed a popularity poll that ranked the Prophet Muhammad behind Suharto, Sukarno, and Iraqi President Saddam Hussein. The authorities shut down the paper, found its editor guilty of blasphemy, and sentenced him to five years in prison. Earlier, in 1987, the national parliament had debated allegations by some of its Muslim members that the proposed filming of a long prose poem by Linus Suryadi—*Pengakuan Pariyem* (*Confessions of Pariyem*)—should be outlawed because it questioned the existence of God.

Nevertheless, Islam did kindle creativity. Ahmad Sadali (1924–87), who pioneered abstract art in Indonesia, worked with Islamic themes. References to Qur'anic calligraphy in the paintings of A.D. Pirous were inspired by the Arabic writing he had seen in mosques and on gravestones as a child growing up in the devoutly Islamic province of Aceh. Younger artists, too, drew on Islamic backgrounds and identifications, notably in their use of Arabic script. Muslim themes resonated as well in the verses of contemporary poet Emha Ainon Nadjib.

In principle—literally, in Pancasila's first principle—monotheism was mandatory in New Order Indonesia. In practice, however, as long as believers were not offended, tolerance was widespread. And this enabled Javanism and mysticism to survive, even flourish, in their own right and as material for artistic use. Javanese mysticism, for example, empowered the hero in *Rembulan dan Matahari* (*The Sun and the Moon*), a 1979 film by Slamet Raharjo. On this subject too, however, elites were known to express concern. Thus in 1980 the jury of the Indonesian Film Festival warned directors not to make movies that could encourage people to believe that mystical beliefs and practices could overcome real problems.

Such advice did not inhibit creative Indonesians from wondering and challenging what reality might "really" be, and crafting "disordered" images that invited comparison with the "ordering" of reality by the New Order regime. In Danarto's "Rintrik," for instance, an old, blind, and black woman with a white piano buries babies abandoned by their mothers. One reviewer found in her a "mystic unity of opposites" and "the fluidity" of "mystic truth." Also known for experimenting with reality was Putu Wijaya, a prolific creator of fiction and drama. The same reviewer said of Putu's fiction that it invited "awareness of the arbitrariness of all codes, all structures of meaning, all forms of truth."[35] Two Javanese painters, Ivan Sagito and Lucia Hartini, both influenced by Salvador Dali, also stretched the bounds of the real. In 1984 Sagito depicted a skeletal man half-transformed into a fluid-looking cow and titled the disturbing result *I Want to Become a Sapi* [Cow]. Other works by Sagito defamiliarized everyday items in a manner reminiscent of Danarto's fiction.

Images of Women

Danarto's story "Rintrik" was but one of many representations of the woman in art and literature in Indonesia during the New Order. The messages connoted by these images of women might be subtly or boldly conveyed. At first glance, for example, Tatang Ganar's oil painting *Three Classical Dancers* (1989) seems unexceptionally classical: a representation of three goddesses in the Hindu-Javanese style of the well-known Prambanan temple complex in Central Java. Closer inspection, however, reveals the trio to be strongly built and holding slightly martial poses, with challenging gazes, as if to project their solidarity and power as a female group. Gender-linked issues of control and autonomy are more explicit in Mangunwijaya's three-volume historical novel *Roro Mendut* (1983). Indeed they appear to have been too explicit for Ami Priyono, who made the film version of the novel less "feminist" by rewriting the ending to reduce the heroine's role. The stereotyping of women was especially common in New Order cinema.[36]

---

35. Keith Foulcher, "Post-Modernism or the Question of History: Some Trends in Indonesian Fiction since 1965," in Virginia Matheson Hooker, ed., *Culture and Society in New Order Indonesia* (Kuala Lumpur: Oxford University Press, 1993), pp. 31 [on Danarto], 37 [on Putu].

36. This point has been made by Krishna Sen, "Repression and Resistance: Interpretations of the Feminine in New Order Cinema," in Hooker, ed., *Culture and Society*, pp. 126–127.

Part of this stereotyping involved contextualizing women in society and linking their motivations not to their thoughts and goals as individuals but to their social roles in meeting the needs and demands of others, notably children and husbands. Based on a real event, the 1988 television movie *Sayekti dan Hanafi* (*Sayekti and Hanafi*) told the story of a woman, Sayekti, who because of an emergency gives birth in an expensive hospital. She cannot pay the medical fees, so is not allowed to take her baby home with her.

Sayekti's courage and determination eventually result in her baby being restored to her. But if the text of this message is that women can overcome adversity to achieve their goals, the subtext is that such goals must fill a social role—for Sayekti, motherhood. Suci, the heroine of Arifin C. Noer's 1977 film *Sang Primadona* (*The Prima Donna*), displays similarly impressive resolve in following her aims. But her individuality is also circumscribed by her roles as a singer and prostitute and her ability to manipulate others—in this instance, men. A third illustration is Linus Suryadi's prose poem *Confessions of Pariyem,* which celebrates a Javanese girl's acceptance of her own social position—as a household servant.

Strong and striving women are present in the literature written during the New Order. Nyai Ontosoroh and her daughter Annelies in Pramoedya's *Child of all Nations* from the Buru Quartet come to mind, as do Bawuk and Sri Sumarah from the 1975 novellas of the same names by Umar Kayam. Harder to find in Indonesian fiction of the period, however, are the thoughts and feelings—the internal struggles—of women considered as distinctive persons apart from their external roles.

When personal disclosures do occur, they can be shocking, as in two self-portraits by the painter Kartika Affandi-Koberl: *Rebirth* and *The Moment of Beginning* (both 1981). In *Rebirth* Kartika's own head emerges from a naked female torso. The head is old, wears an expression of great anguish, and is surrounded by an angry aura of red. In *The Moment of Beginning* the naked and distorted breasts and genitals of another female body flow over the canvas. Streaming from the empty skull are a face and a mask, both distended in pain. To Indonesian viewers, the tortured woman's self-disclosure may be at least as disturbing as her nudity. Noteworthy in this context, among writings by younger writers, are the private worlds of the self explored in the short stories of Leila Chudori.

Mainly written and read by women in New Order Indonesia were "pop novels" (*novel pop*), a genre dating at least to the appearance, in the 1970s, of women's magazines—*Femina* and *Gadis* (the latter meaning "young woman"), *Kartini* and *Sarinah* (two famous women's names)—where a number of such works were serialized before republication in book form. These works were much more lucrative than "serious" literature. Marga T.'s best-selling pop novel *Karmila,* for instance, ran through more than a dozen printings, averaging 70,000 copies per print run. Inside the country, no "serious" Indonesian novel approached such success.

Pop novels were preoccupied with love. But they did not confine it within the family frame, or presume that a male-female relationship had to be sexual. They tended to present such situations plainly, without lecturing the reader. The authors' own professional backgrounds influenced their work: Hospitals and patients figure in the novels of Marga T. and Mira W., who were themselves doctors, while the plots of V. Lestari and S. Mara G.D., both psychologists, tend to involve families and problems of personal adjustment. La Rose, on the other hand, wrote about sexual problems, including, in her pop novels, *Si Bunga Mawar* *(Rose)*, the rarely covered topic of so-called sexual deviance.

In the New Order period, compared with works such as *Confessions of Pariyem,* which searched the past for values usable by women now, pop novels tended to address the present more realistically, and as their circulation shows, they did so in ways that spoke to the contemporary condition of many Indonesian women, especially in cities. Typically these novels did not, however, challenge the regime's exhortations to women to fulfill their *kodrat*—their God-given nature—to strive to be good wives and mothers.

Commerce and Youth

Women's pop novels imply pop culture, which implies capitalism, which transformed Suharto-era Indonesia while opening it wide to the world economy. Rising affluence buoyed spending on housing, clothing, travel, education, and entertainment in "mass cultural" forms such as television. Purchasing power, together with satellite technology, dramatically expanded the proportion of Indonesians with access to television programming. Beginning in 1988, several privately owned networks were established alongside the state-run Televisi Republik Indonesia. An estimated two-thirds of all Indonesians were viewers by 1991.

As entertainment and the media grew into big business, big businesses used mass culture to enlarge their markets. Cigarette firms sponsored rock concerts to promote their products. Audiocassette companies competed for air time to promote their latest releases. While established publishing companies expanded, wealthy Indonesians funded new media ventures and events.

Measured by the numbers of people they reached, these mass forms of culture were far more influential than the genres of literature, painting, and even film that have been reviewed here. And although the latter endeavors yielded a remarkable variety of artistic creations, one may ask whether Indonesia's new mass culture was homogenized by commercialization, reducing diversity of expression after all. The rest of this chapter will consider diversity and conformity in two relevant settings: youth culture and the press.

For the moral guardians of the New Order, Indonesian pop culture was a problem, for its inspiration came not from Pancasila but from international pop culture. And the global phenomenon, although it prompted apolitical local imitations, acknowledged individualism, spontaneity, and the spirit of rebellion—

all problematic from the standpoint of those inside and outside the regime wishing to defend supposedly Indonesian values from the onslaught of American youth culture.

In Indonesia the number of young people with higher education and the number of unemployed young people had never been higher. Small wonder that themes of frustration and anger in global youth culture, over issues such as conformism, hypocrisy, and pollution, found local appeal. The lyrics of Western rock music were easily adapted to criticize the New Order policies. The result was a kind of stalemate: In Jakarta, for example, the authorities allowed the subculture of rock to flourish, but kept it under surveillance.

My emphasis on writers and artists in this essay should not be misunderstood. Then as now, most young Indonesians were cultural consumers not producers. Nor, in focusing on protest, do I mean to exaggerate the expression of discontent. The range of expression associated with younger-generation Indonesians amounted to a microcosm of the country itself, and was similarly diversified—by location, class, income, education, and exposure to the larger world. And even when the t-shirt slogans and the rock music favored by urban Indonesian teenagers indicated dissatisfaction, or even alienation, such badges did not necessarily imply political action.

The work of the popular rock performer Iwan Fals illustrates this point. In the song "Aku Bosan" ("I'm Bored"), a child complains of being left alone at home by materialistic parents and older siblings. But boredom is a passive emotion—no action is called for—and the child's access to a maid and a television set described in the lyrics limits one's sympathy. While "Hura-Hura Huru Hara" ("Fake Riot") denounces loan sharks as blood-sucking Draculas, it offers no solutions. As its title suggests, the song is skeptical about social change. Addressed to members of parliament, the words of "Surat buat Wakil Rakyat" ("A Letter to the People's Representative") do plead for action: "Please hear [our voices] / and convey what they say / Don't be hesitant / Don't be scared ... / Speak up clearly ... / Don't go to sleep ... " More typical, however, were audiocassettes such as *Hijau* (*Green*), whose songs bemoan pollution but offer no way out of the bleak conditions they portray.[37]

Two other genres were genuinely gloomy: sentimental songs (*lagu cengeng*) about unrequited love, which the authorities criticized for undermining the optimistic spirit needed for national development; and the sometimes censored work of more or less nihilistic rock groups such as Thrash Metal and Grindcore, whose evocations of death and destruction appealed to yet another subculture of young Indonesian consumers of rock and pop.

---

37. The three songs cited by title in this paragraph are from audiocassette albums by Iwan Fals: the first two from *Dalbo*, the third from *Wakil Rakyat* (*The People's Representative*). The album *Hijau* is also by Fals.

Contradicting such despondence, still other groups and albums affirmed and celebrated life and faith. The title song from the rock spectacular *Kantata Takwa* (*Devotional Cantata*), for example, begins by reavowing the Muslim confession of faith: "There is no god but God." The idiom is rock, but the lyrics are Islamic and sung to an Arabic style of music. Such popularizations of Islamic piety further diversified the repertoires of Iwan Fals, Rendra, and Emha among other performers. And here, too, one may see the expanding role of business. In 1990–91, for instance, an oil-tanker magnate, Setiawan Djody, underwrote an extravagant premiere of *Kantata Takwa*. And in this case the involvement was more than financial: While Fals and others had composed the music, Djody himself had written the lyrics.

If the great majority of those who consumed youth culture in New Order Indonesia were not moved by the experience actually to engage in certain behaviors—to oppose repression, say, or to improve conditions—it does not follow that the producers of this culture partitioned expression from action. For all the multiformity of youth culture, many of its protagonists did articulate a need for social responsibility.

On 16 August 1990 around a thousand young people gathered at the Jakarta Arts Center to commemorate the forty-fifth anniversary of their country's independence with a program of music, drama, and poetry. But rather than laud their nation's achievements and progress, the young artists used their work and the occasion to dramatize a long agenda of social and political ills. Alongside unemployment and overpopulation, corruption and pollution, prejudice and injustice, they targeted the lack of democracy in Indonesia, including what they decried as the lack of opportunity for them to participate effectively in solving the country's many problems. Political criticisms of this kind amounted to a justification, as if the critics were saying: We are willing to better the country, but how can we do so under these conditions?

All over Indonesia, in study circles and poetry readings, rock bands and theater groups, producers of youth culture were expressing impatience for social change. Much of this activity was intended to make their own youth cohort less apolitical and more willing to act to improve the country. "This is not a tale about the idealism of young Indonesians," a student in Yogyakarta acknowledged. "Young people should want to ask [where] our civilization [is] going ... We have to try and make our future better."[38]

Other young artists directed their energies toward even younger Indonesians, as in these illustrations from Central Java: Wiji Thukul Wijaya organized theater workshops and a painting group for the children in his *kampung* in Solo. The

---

38. Quoted in Rosslyn von der Borch, *Art and Activism: Some Examples from Contemporary Central Java* (Adelaide: Flinders University of South Australia Discipline of Asian Studies, 1988), p. 71; my retranslation.

Anak-Anak Merdeka (Free Children) movement helped young *kampung* dwellers there and in Yogyakarta to express themselves in art. On 17 August 1988, Indonesian independence day, a group of students and recent graduates of one high school presented a play in a village near Magelang. They improvised dialogue from their own experiences and stopped the performance at intervals to ask the audience to respond. A witness later praised the experiment for its potential to resist the social order by "emboldening its subjects to seek ways to change it."[39] Expression, in short, could raise awareness, which could encourage action.

Censorship and Subtlety

The diversity of expression in Indonesia during the New Order was great. But, as has been shown, it was not unlimited. Consider the press in relation to the state. Most of the country's newspapers and periodicals were not affiliated with the government. And just as there was a youth culture, so did journalists work in a distinctive milieu with its own characteristic discourse. That discourse put a premium on indirect expression: subtlety, allusion, parody, and the dressing of objections in cultural terms less likely to offend the regime.

Enhancing these self-applied rules of style was the censors' practice of evaluating publications after they appeared, not before. Post facto censorship ensured that officials were not responsible for what got into print, and invited writers and cartoonists incrementally to test and stretch the limits of what was allowed. At the same time, however, it encouraged self-censorship and discouraged directly negative reporting or commentary on specific public personalities, most notably Suharto and his family. For their part, readers became adept at reading between the lines.

The sheer volume of information that the media conveyed, directly and indirectly, led one social critic to observe that the power of the Indonesian press, while less visible than that of the military, was not less significant.[40] Daily newspapers ran editorials on national and international events, next to columns of socioeconomic, political, and religious commentary by scholars, legislators, and retired public figures, among other authors. Before *Tempo* was banned, it carried an especially popular column by its editor, Goenawan Mohamad, entitled "Catatan Pinggir" ("Sidelines").

In one of these essays, Goenawan wrote that the business community had never supported artistic expression as lavishly as they had the Indonesian national soccer team. Yet he did not go on to ask for subsidies. Instead, he noted wryly that for all its commercial backing, the soccer team "loses anyway." The requisite to

---

39. Barbara Hatley, "Theatre as Cultural Resistance in Contemporary Indonesia," in Budiman, ed., *State and Civil Society,* p. 344.

40. Ariel Heryanto, "Introduction," in Budiman, ed., *State and Civil Society,* p. 297.

having a national theater and poetry that could win international respect and
acclaim was not money. It was "liberty," and that was something whose supply
he personally could not "guarantee."[41] Goenawan's humor and his mock humil-
ity—as if guaranteeing liberty were up to him rather than the regime—illustrates
political journalism New Order–style.

In a second piece, Goenawan commented on Indonesian perceptions of individualism:

> Individuals are still seen as trouble makers. When in 1945 Bung Karno [Sukarno]
> rejected the proposal to include human rights in the constitution, this was be-
> cause he regarded the *individu,* the *aku* [the "I"], as the basis of social unrest
> and disharmony. And even now, when we frequently see individuals being bashed
> up by the masses, tortured by the rulers and slandered by the public, we are still
> afraid of *aku*. We feel safer using the [first]-person-plural inclusive pronoun
> *kita,* meaning all of us, to refer to "I". We do not yet regard the individual as
> someone who dares, needs and has the right to stand out, and [who] is solitary
> and threatened always.[42]

Compared with the first essay, the language here is harsher, but the subtlety
remains. Political criticism is softened with historico-cultural allusions. The strong
phrase "tortured by the rulers" is moderated by association with Indonesians at
large: "the masses" who bash, "the public" that slanders, and the all-inclusive
"we" who are still afraid. Goenawan implies that the communal nature of Indonesian society is not yet able to accept the notion of individuality. By using "we"
he includes himself as a member of that communal group. Yet his writings provide evidence that it is also he, himself, who is expressing the individualism that
"dares" to speak out, but which results in vulnerability and social alienation.

Political journalists in Suharto's Indonesia may be likened to acrobats balancing between regime and conscience. That image at any rate is in keeping with
another of Goenawan's ostensibly softening remarks: "Every time in history, it
seems, has a moment when it is not easy to speak, but when also it is not easy to
remain silent."[43] Under the New Order, reinforcing their conscience was the tendency of many creative Indonesians to feel a social obligation to speak out.

Thirty-eight Indonesian writers, artists, and intellectuals did speak out on 8
May 1995. They signed a statement initiated by Arief Budiman, Emha, Goenawan,
and Rendra. Because its sponsors were leading national figures, the declaration

---

41. Goenawan Mohamad, *Sidelines: Selected Writings from Tempo,* trans. Jennifer
Lindsay (South Melbourne, Victoria, Australia: Hyland House and Monash Asia Institute, 1994), p. 94. The original appeared in *Tempo* for the week of 16 November 1985.

42. Goenawan, *Sidelines,* p. 13; originally in *Tempo* for 19 September 1992; my
brackets.

43. Goenawan, *Sidelines,* p. 101; originally in *Tempo* for 28 January 1978.

received wide publicity. In it they called for less control by the authorities, and for more freedom and justice. What is powerful, they argued, should not determine what is right. Otherwise, "those without power, whose expression is liberal and proper, will be pushed aside. The nation will bear the loss of their creative energies and abilities, while freedom and justice [are] choked" to death or near-death.[44] The terms of this "May Statement" were not revolutionary, nor did they threaten anyone. They noted the 1945 constitution's own approval of the creative energy of artists as a legitimate aspect of national culture.

It was this energy that the signatories believed to be at risk. But in the discussion that accompanied the statement's launching, the idea of creativity—and the related concept of expression—was not confined to the arts, but was extended to include all areas of human activity, including politics, economics, religion, and technology. Emha made the point later with reference to entrepreneurship: "Your creativity as the manager of a business is restricted if the mechanism for the distribution of capital is not 'democratic.'"[45] And his discourse also displayed the familiar preference for suasion over confrontation. For Emha knew that, in the eyes of the regime, entrepreneurship enjoyed a legitimacy that theater and poetry lacked, not to mention creativity in politics.

Conclusion

In the New Order years, how diverse was expression? How did it fare against homogenization and repression? As was shown, even in this incomplete survey, Indonesian expression abounded in creativity and talent applied to diverse topics in diverse forms and styles. Expression occurred in venues from Jakarta to the regions, from elaborate official occasions to spontaneous events in small towns with amateur performers, from mass-circulation magazines to poems recited in small gatherings. Commercialization and censorship made a difference, but they did not quell the wellsprings of variety and creativity in contemporary Indonesian culture.

That culture extends far beyond the bounds prescribed in five-year plans. It cannot be contained in artificial sites such as Beautiful Indonesia in Miniature. Contrary to the park's message, the nation's culture cannot be reduced to objects on controlled display, nor to the mere sum of the selected "best" in regional cultures. Commercialism and propaganda aside, culture is being produced by Indonesians who care passionately about their country and its people, and who want to contribute in their own way to its future.

Finally, in treating first the authorities' cultural guidelines and then the criti-

---

44. "Pernyataan Mei" ["The May Statement"], *Panji Masyarakat* [Jakarta], 1–10 June 1995, pp. 10–12.

45. Emha Ainon Nadjib, "Pernyataan Mei, Juni, Juli . . ." ["The May, June, July Declaration"], *Tiras,* 1 June 1995, p. 28.

cal responses to such constraints by writers, artists, and performers, the gap between the two may have been overdrawn. Between leaders and creators there was some common ground. Their constitution abjured Indonesians not to reject material from foreign cultures that could enrich national culture or facilitate participation in world civilization. Nor did the regime oppose individualism across the board. Certainly the censors were not idle—*Tempo* was closed—but they failed to keep expression within narrow bounds.

In 1997 the New Order still could not accept Emha's case for the indivisibility, universality, and democracy of creative expression, not least because Suharto was still in charge. The next and final chapter in this book considers the 1997–98 transition beyond Suharto. Suffice it to conclude here that the record of expression during his rule, the pattern of creativity and constraint, in no way precludes a future evolution toward greater official tolerance of the remarkable dynamism and diversity of modern Indonesian culture.

PART FOUR: TRANSITION

Chapter 10

Exit and Aftermath: The Crisis of 1997–98

Donald K. Emmerson

When the words finally came, they were not a simple "I resign." They conveyed an act of deliberate will by a speaker whose language bore instant consequences: "I have decided to announce my resignation from my office as president of the Republic of Indonesia, effective from my reading of this statement."[1] The utterance was self-executing in a way reminiscent of the power ascribed to the god-kings of ancient Java—that merely by saying something, they could make it happen. But the efficacy of these words mixed paradox with caricature, as if somehow the power of this king had been reduced to his ability to cease being one.

From Suharto to Habibie

In Jakarta, standing in a dark safari suit before the television cameras, President Suharto betrayed no emotion as he read the words that made him a former president. It was nine o'clock on a Thursday morning, 21 May 1998. Thirty-two years, seven months, three weeks, and a few hours earlier, on 1 October 1965, a leftist conspiracy had assassinated six of Suharto's fellow generals in the army. He had taken advantage of the occasion to destroy the left, acquire power, and launch his authoritarian New Order. Now, at last, his long rule was coming to an end.

Right after the president's resignation, the Supreme Court administered the

---

1. "Pak Harto: Saya Menyatakan Berhenti" ("Suharto: I Announce My Resignation"), *Kedaulatan Rakyat* [Yogyakarta], 22 May 1998.

oath of presidential office to Bacharuddin Jusuf Habibie. Habibie had been Suharto's own chosen vice president since March, and a minister in New Order cabinets continuously for two decades prior to that. The transfer implemented Article 8 of the Indonesian constitution, which reads, "Should the president die, resign, cease to perform, or be unable to perform his or her duties during his or her term of office, he or she shall be replaced by the vice president until the end of its duration."[2]

Five days later, coming into Jakarta from the airport, I looked out the windows of my taxi for signs of political change. There were none. A billboard on the right still touted Suharto's youngest son Tommy's Timor sedan as "The Pioneer of Cars for Indonesia's Future." Suharto's eldest daughter, Siti Hardiyanti ("Tutut") Rukmana, and his youngest daughter, Siti Hutami ("Mamiek") Endang Adiningsih, co-owners of the company that ran the toll highway I was on, were still entitled to some portion of the Rp 7,000 I was paying to use it. A roadside billboard still announced the opening of a new eighteen-hole golf course, as if Indonesia's property bubble had not burst, but had room to grow.

Eventually we did pass a building with broken windows, and soon after, Trisakti University, where four students had been shot dead by security forces during an anti-Suharto demonstration on 12 May 1998, just two weeks before. A white banner, hung from the university's main building, identified Trisakti as a "CAMPUS FOR REFORM" ("KAMPUS REFORMASI").

Later I took another cab through the city's Chinese-commercial quarter, Glodok, past the blackened and gutted hulks of buildings. Beginning on 13 May, spurred in part by the deaths at Trisakti the previous day, mobs had rampaged in Glodok and elsewhere in the capital. The looting and burning had left some 1,200 dead and thousands more wounded, and gutted hundreds of buildings and vehicles. Later, evidence would surface that in the course of the violence—by far the worst rioting seen in Jakarta during the New Order—dozens or more Indonesian women of Chinese ancestry had been raped. As I viewed the damage the chaos had done, I thought of another Indonesian-language sign I had seen on the airport road: "Make a Success of the Movement for National Discipline."

From the protests at Trisakti to the arson in Glodok, anti-Suharto anger had swept from the top of the social pyramid to the bottom. Trisakti, a highly regarded private university, recruited the sons and daughters of well-to-do Indonesians who could afford its costs. Its students had demonstrated peacefully against Suharto and his regime. But repeated protests by these and other students from around the city had contributed to an atmosphere of uncertainty and disorder that others had quickly turned to their own, less principled advantage—ambitious officers in the army, perhaps, as discussed below, but certainly the mobs of un-

---

2. The translation is from my essay, "Indonesia's Coming Succession: Constitutional Text, Historical Context, and Recommendations for U.S. Policy in a Time of Crisis," *NBR Analysis* [Seattle], 9:3 (May 1998), p. 59.

employed young men menacing terrified ethnic-Chinese Indonesians, or smashing their show windows for the goods inside.

A week after the May 1998 riots, Suharto resigned. The students who believed they had brought him down were jubilant. But they were not satisfied. Sporadically, they continued to demonstrate against Habibie, whom they did not trust, and for "total reform," which they wanted now.

Six months after the succession, protesting students again filled the streets of the capital. President Habibie had called the People's Consultative Assembly (MPR) into special session on 10–13 November to prepare the way for political liberalization, including plans for a democratic election to be held in 1999. But his long association with Suharto had compromised Habibie. Some of the students wanted him to step down and hand power to opposition leaders. Popular, too, were demands that Suharto be arrested, put on trial, and deprived of his presumablly ill-gotten wealth. Students also urged that the military's "dual function," which had entitled it to political influence, be cancelled outright, once and for all.

"We have proved to the people that we are not just ignorant boys and girls," said a 23-year-old philosophy student, as confrontations between students and police again spread through the city. "I have an obsession that this week will be as great an event as May, only without the riots."[3] Nevertheless, on 13 November the looting and arson began again. Again ethnic-Chinese Indonesians were victimized. And again, there were shootings and casualties. On this occasion, according to preliminary reports, sixteen people died, including eight students at Atma Jaya Catholic University gunned down in a particularly brutal attack by security forces. Suharto's half-brother, Probosutedjo, portrayed—had the gall to portray?—the ex-president as sympathetic to the students by quoting him as saying, "I resigned from my position to avoid bloodshed. Why does the government now cause bloodshed?"[4]

Why had Suharto resigned? Had the New Order merely been decapitated—its head replaced, but its body left intact? Or had the new head, Habibie, inaugurated a "Reform Order" that would live up to its name? To the complex—impossible?—task of trying to answer these questions soon after the crisis they recall, and without knowledge of the future they implicate, the rest of this chapter is devoted.[5] Primary attention is paid to the first query because, though controversial, it is the most historical of the three; because addressing it allows me

---

3. Seth Mydans, "Indonesia's Students: An Unrelenting Force for Change," *New York Times,* 13 November 1998, p. A3.

4. Seth Mydans, "Indonesian Chief Takes Tough Line on Protests," *New York Times,* 15 November 1998, p. 6.

5. In preparing this account I have drawn on diverse sources, including reporting, commentary, documentation, and notes of interviews I was able to conduct in Indonesia during stays there in January, May, and again in June 1998. For lack of space and because the unfolding drama in Jakarta tended to influence the country's political direction more than what happened in the regions, the chapter focuses mainly on events in the capital.

to update the account of the New Order begun by my coauthors in this book; and because informed speculation about the future requires an understanding of the crisis of 1997–98. For it was in the decisive context of the crisis that Indonesia moved beyond Suharto—or that Suharto, one might also say, failed to keep up with Indonesia.

Why did Suharto fall? In 1998 there were many different answers to this question. For clarity in analyzing them, it will be helpful to distinguish these answers by the extent to which the causal arrows they drew pointed in one of four directions: (1) inside-out; (2) bottom-up; (3) top-down; and (4) outside-in.

These pathways imply, respectively, four different but complementary explanations: (1) Suharto's resignation was the outward implementation of a decision reached inside his own mind. (2) Broad and intensifying opposition from below—from society—obliged him to quit. (3) He was felled from the top of the regime by his own collaborators' defections and urgings to resign. (4) Inescapable lateral pressures, from outside Indonesia, brought him down. In an already overlong volume, I cannot thoroughly explore and compare these understandings. But I will try to weave them into an account of Suharto's exit and the many-faceted crisis that, in some overall sense, caused it.

The resulting interpretation must be provisional and incomplete. But it will encompass most of the diverse actors and conditions that shaped the drama: from generals and Muslims in Jakarta, through fire and smoke in Kalimantan, to Michel Camdessus and the International Monetary Fund (IMF) in Washington, DC; and from the streets where students chanted and mobs looted, to the rooms where Suharto maneuvered in vain to remain in power. Since it was the president around whom the events of May 1998 revolved, it is with him that I begin.

Leaving the Kingship

"I have decided to announce [my] resignation . . ." The obvious sense in which these words mattered—they withdrew from the country's highest office the man who had held it for more than three decades—concealed something less evident, yet not trivial. That something was the assertion of choice: "I have decided . . ."

Since 1968 Suharto had succeeded himself six times, and outlasted as many vice-presidents.[6] Imagine that all the heads of governments in the world's independent countries had been racing each other to see who could stay continually in office the longest. By 1998, when finally he dropped out, Suharto had passed everyone in the pack but Cuba's Fidel Castro. Long before, most observers had concluded that the Indonesian president would hang on to his office for as long as he could. And he did.

---

6. Hamengku Buwono IX (1968–78), Adam Malik (1978–83), Umar Wirahadikusumah (1983–88), Sudharmono (1988–93), Try Sutrisno (1993–98), and B.J. Habibie (1998).

Or did he? One may speculate that by 21 May 1998 Suharto's appetite for power had been eroded by personal events. His wife, to whom he was quite close, had died in 1996. Signs of his own mortality had surfaced the following year. In December 1997, apparently for health reasons, he cancelled a trip to a meeting of the Association of Southeast Asian Nations in nearby Malaysia. Rumors circulated that he might have had a stroke. But if that is what happened, it did not prevent him from having his presidency renewed by the MPR in March 1998 for a seventh five-year term, which he appeared fully to intend to serve, or from flying to Cairo to attend a summit of developing countries in mid-May.

Such personal (inside-out) concerns, if they facilitated Suharto's decision to resign, could only do so in the context of larger circumstances, including substantial and intensifying (bottom-up) pressures on him to quit the presidency. Major and multiple upheavals were underway. Indonesia's economic engine had been thrown into reverse. Unrest was spreading. On campuses around the country, calls were mounting for an end to his rule and his regime. On 13–14 May, while he was still in Egypt, rioting engulfed Jakarta. Speaking informally to an audience of Indonesians in Cairo, the president said that if he no longer had the confidence of the people, he would resign. Reverting to the language of Javanese *wayang,* he said he was prepared to "leave the kingship and assume the position of a sage" (*lengser keprabon, madeg pandhita*).[7]

Was he using the metaphor of kingship to distance himself from his own presidency—aware that he might lose it and that he was not, in reality, a monarch at all? Or did he, at some deeper level, actually consider himself a kind of king, or at any rate identify with kingship? Whatever he intended by the phrase, or whatever else it revealed about him,[8] it showed just how alien to his world democracy was. Building on, but going well beyond, the argument made by Robert Cribb in this book—that twentieth-century Indonesian history can be understood as a nation's search for modernity—one might say that Suharto's insistence on modernizing his country economically but not politically is what, in the end, brought him down.

In the second half of 1998 this explanation for what had happened to Suharto was ubiquitous among observers in the United States and other places where faith in the necessity of democracy was especially strong. But if democracy's absence had ended Suharto's rule, why had he been able to stay in power so long? Merely through force and fear? While acknowledging the importance of repression, my coauthors in this book suggest the possibility of other answers as well.

One of these answers highlights the legitimating effect of rapid economic

---

7. English-language coverage of his remarks may be found in "If I'm No Longer Trusted, No Problem," *Jakarta Post,* 14 May 1998.

8. Compare, for example, Ben Abel's interview with Ben Anderson about Suharto, "A Javanese King Talks of His End," *Inside Indonesia,* 54 (April–June 1998), pp. 16–17; and Onghokham, "Soeharto Embodied Javanese Ruler," *Jakarta Post,* 25 May 1998.

growth. From that standpoint, what toppled Suharto was less democracy's absence than the economy's collapse. In reply, however, a democratist could describe the New Order in 1997–98 as an incompetent autocracy, in contrast to the relative economic resilience and political pluralism of the Philippines, South Korea, Taiwan, and Thailand at the time—and conclude that a more accountable regime than Suharto's would have been able to limit the vulnerability, stop the hemorrhaging, and speed the recovery of the Indonesian economy as well.

Whatever the role of autocracy in the undoing of his rule, we should not think that Suharto consciously chose not to democratize Indonesia, as if a lower ratio of benefits to costs might have led him to select a different strategy. The manner in which he rationalized his "abdication" suggests instead that he did what came naturally, in the context of his personality, upbringing, and career, embedded as these respectively were in familial, social, and military hierarchies. And there were other aspects of his life that had limited his exposure to ideas that might possibly have tempered his position, as president, to rule with an iron hand: his lack of an education beyond junior high school, for example, and his lack of experience traveling, let alone living, abroad.

As for the argument that the turbulence of 1997–98 made Suharto actually want to quit—as opposed to obliging him to do so—it is more likely to have strengthened his resolve to retain power, especially earlier in the crisis when his and the country's problems appeared less insoluble than they would turn out, by mid-May, to be. By threatening to derail economic growth and destroy political stability, the crisis endangered the two most important justifications for his regime. In a televised appearance on 19 May 1998, two days before he finally resigned, Suharto explained why in March he had not refused a seventh presidential term. Had he withdrawn his name then, he said, people would have criticized him for "sneaking off the battlefield"—fleeing his responsibility to the country in the middle of a crisis.[9]

It does not follow from this self-justification, however, that if the turmoil of 1997–98 had not occurred, Suharto would have willingly given up his presidency on schedule in March of the latter year. As president he was sensitive to criticism, a sensitivity that may be traceable in part to insecurities he experienced as a child. But among those who worked for him, the president had a reputation for being aloof, taciturn, and stubborn—not the sort to follow the winds of public opinion. And this almost regal quality of self-regard had grown more pronounced over the course of his decades in office. Interviewed early in 1998, one of his ministers remarked that far from taking the views of others into account, the 76-year-old general-turned-president had grown so accustomed to power, and so

---

9. "Pak Harto: Saya Ini Kapok Jadi Presiden" ["Suharto: Me, I've Had It with Being President"], *Kompas* [Jakarta], 20 May 1998.

insulated from bad news, that he could not imagine himself having become an obstacle to resolving his country's problems.[10]

Again, as with *lengser keprabon,* it was another improvised and oddly self-distancing reference in Javanese that may have given unintended voice to Suharto's true feelings: "There are those who say," he told the press on 19 May, "speaking frankly in Javanese: Not being president would be no skin off one's back [*patheken*]."[11] He seemed merely to be observing, in a detached way, the views of others. But the subtext could be understood differently: that it was he who was speaking "frankly," that the skinned back (literally, skin disease) would be his own, and that being president mattered to him very much.

On the same occasion he virtually confirmed this interpretation by asking Indonesians not to think of him as an obstacle. He was still in office, he said, "only because of" his "responsibility" to the nation. What he did not say was that this responsibility inhered in the office of president, which he still held. For that would have meant acknowledging the infinite circularity of his rationale: that as long as he was president, he would have to remain president. That he could speak "frankly" in this manner merely two days before ending his presidency shows not that he was ready to quit, but how long he could cling to the hope of avoiding that result.

And when, on the same occasion, Suharto promised personally, as president, "to execute and lead national reform as rapidly as possible"—as if he could coopt the movement for change by outrunning it into the future—he further confirmed his actual unreadiness to risk his neck by stepping down. And by November, six months after his resignation, "Hang Suharto!" had indeed become a chant of choice among student demonstrators in Jakarta.

Leaving the King

By the nineteenth of May, when he tried to turn the tide, it had reached sweeping proportions. Thousands of anti-Suharto students had taken over the parliament building. Televised images of their rallies and banners were flashing by satellite around the world. High-status women in business and higher education were helping to sustain the occupiers by keeping them supplied with snacks and bottled water. From the unemployed to the elite, it seemed, attitudes toward Suharto had shrunk to a short gamut from outright hostility to cynical indifference.

Animosity toward the president was severe in the capital. But students and others were voicing comparable enmity in cities around the country. Indeed, the sympathy for such criticism being shown by Sultan Hamengku Buwono X in

---

10. Adam Schwarz, *A Nation in Waiting: Indonesia in the 1990s* (Boulder, CO: Westview, 1994), p. 44 [aloofness]; interview, Jakarta, 16 January 1998.

11. "Pak Harto."

302 • INDONESIA BEYOND SUHARTO

Yogyakarta, the site of massive student demonstrations, was making him popular enough to become a player in post-Suharto opposition politics.[12]

High up in his regime, the president's own collaborators began to defect, adding (top-down) force to the momentum against him. On Monday afternoon, 18 May, inside the parliament building, surrounded by its student occupiers, MPR head Harmoko (who also chaired the legislature, or DPR) told them what they wanted to hear: Suharto should resign. Flanking him, and thus reinforcing his appeal, were all four of the vice presidents of the DPR, representing the government's pseudoparty, Golkar; the armed forces (Angkatan Bersenjata Republik Indonesia, or ABRI); and the two officially authorized and subsidized "opposition" groupings—of self-identifying Muslims in the Development Unity Party (PPP), and of nominally Muslim, non-Muslim, and secular Indonesians in the Indonesian Democracy Party (PDI). The implied message to Suharto was: Resign, or be impeached.

Harmoko was an unlikely rebel. Aptly described by William Liddle in this book as a "long-loyal associate" of Suharto, Harmoko had during his years as minister of information obligingly censored the media, including banning *Tempo* in 1994. On 29 May 1997, election day, as head of Golkar, Harmoko had mobilized a record 75 percent share of the vote for that political buttress of the regime. (In the resulting 500-member DPR, alongside the 75 appointive seats reserved for the military, Golkar claimed an overwhelming 325 seats, compared with 89 for PPP and a mere 11 for PDI.)

On 10 March 1998, Harmoko had proved his loyalty to Suharto one more time. On that day, as head of the MPR, in the same building where barely more than two months later he would call for Suharto's resignation, Harmoko had succeeded in getting the assembly to renew Suharto's presidency for another five years. Two months later, in mid-May, in the context of escalating antiregime violence, rioters burned down Harmoko's family home in Solo. That loss appears to have shaken whatever confidence he still had in the regime and its founder.

At the parliament complex in Jakarta on 18 May, hearing Harmoko defect, the students cheered. If such a lapdog could turn against his master, some of them thought, Suharto's rule must be over. Instead, Harmoko's record of obeisance may have stiffened Suharto's resolve not to be toppled by such a man. Harmoko had spoken out against the president in mid-afternoon. Early that same evening, in Suharto's residence on Cendana Street, ABRI Commander-in-Chief General Wiranto met with the president to discuss the situation. We do not know what was said, but we can surmise that Suharto refused to budge.

Later that night Suharto's top ministers also gathered at his home. Reportedly, they urged him to dissolve the cabinet. Reportedly, he refused. Later still, at 11

---

12. Useful on the sultan and his support is Dwi Marianto, "Orphans No More," *Inside Indonesia,* 56 (October–December 1998), pp. 21–22.

P.M., Wiranto released a statement. In it, he characterized Harmoko's public advice to Suharto to resign as nothing more than the MPR head's personal opinion, lacking legal force, and thus null and void. Having so recently soared, the students' hopes plunged.

On the nineteenth, Suharto consulted with a variety of figures from within and outside his regime. They alluded to the mounting disorder: the deaths of the students on the twelfth, the city-wide anarchy on the thirteenth and fourteenth, the reeling economy, the ongoing calls for his resignation, and plans to mobilize a million people to march against him on the following day, the twentieth. His visitors were respectful. But merely by underscoring the gravity of the situation they were, in effect, reminding the president of the possible costs to him and the country if he refused to quit.

On that same day, 19 May, the now beleaguered president made a final effort to coopt his opponents. He promised reforms, including a new, or at least reshuffled, cabinet. But later in the day his leading economic official, Coordinating Minister for the Economy, Finance, and Industry Ginandjar Kartasasmita, politely informed Suharto that his senior economic advisers, men who had played central roles in the New Order's development strategy, opposed the president's proposals. Suharto's last-ditch promises were, in these advisers' eyes, futile efforts to delay what had become necessary and inevitable—the president's resignation.

The next afternoon Ginandjar and Minister for Public Housing and Resettlement Akbar Tanjung led a dozen other incumbent ministers responsible for the economy to write Suharto a letter declining, in advance, to serve in a reshuffled cabinet. Suharto told his vice president, Habibie, to reverse the ministers' decision. Instead, Habibie used the assignment to ask the economic ministers to support him were he to replace Suharto in the event the president did resign. Ginandjar and Akbar were rewarded by Habibie two days later when, as president, he appointed them both to his first cabinet—Ginandjar in the same position he had held before, Akbar as head of the state secretariat. A few months thereafter, at the first congress of Golkar under Habibie's regime, Minister Akbar led pro-Habibie forces to a victory that gave him (Akbar) the chairmanship of that organization as well.

The ministers' defection on the twentieth was the final nudge, or rather the closing of the last alternative path of escape. Late that night Suharto decided to resign. The next morning he did.

These top-down betrayals at the eleventh hour appear to have surprised Suharto. The fact that they came from his economic ministers may have been, for the president, an especially bitter pill to swallow. Indonesia's material success had been the pride and preoccupation of this "Father of Development." Disloyalty on the part of one or two peripheral ministers might not have been fatal. But his longstanding zeal for growth—statistical indicators of its achievement filled his speeches—probably rendered all the more devastating to Suharto, first, the collapse of the economy on whose expansion he had focused so heavily, and second, the apostasy of those to whom he had entrusted its recovery.

Muslims of Last Resort

On the morning of 19 May, while he still harbored hopes of somehow surviving the onslaught against his presidency, Suharto met with nine leading Muslim figures from a variety of organizations and professions. The president cared enough about their views to hear what they had to say, and they in turn wanted a peaceful transition badly enough to have accepted the invitation to meet with him while other Indonesians were denouncing him. But Suharto also hoped to coopt these prominent Muslims into supporting an agenda for reforms that he himself would promise to carry out—reforms bold enough to outflank his critics, yet modest enough not to scuttle his presidency.

Among these Muslim visitors was the well-known intellectual Nurcholish Madjid. He had been involved in discussions with other influential Indonesians, including ABRI leaders, as to how the president might bow out, and what reforms should ensue. Many other influential Muslims, however, were not among the group that saw Suharto on the nineteenth. Absent, for example, was Amien Rais, the general chairman of Muhammadiyah, who had been particularly outspoken in opposition to Suharto's rule.

Nevertheless, the Muslim notables who did visit the president that morning were numerous and diverse enough to be of use to him. They had a moral status that Harmoko, in Suharto's eyes and the eyes of the public, lacked. If Suharto could generate the impression that these Muslim notables supported his plan for political survival through limited reform—better yet, that they had proposed it—he might be able to rescue his chance of staying on.

The visitors did not take the bait. Afterward, Nurcholish made it clear that Suharto's ideas of reform, including a cabinet reshuffle, were Suharto's alone. But by agreeing to meet with the president precisely when he was being vilified in the streets and on campuses around the country, his Muslim visitors did foster an impression: that the leaders of Indonesia's Islamic community greatly preferred peaceful change from inside the New Order to its violent overthrow from without. Such a judgment will not surprise readers of Robert Hefner's chapter in this book. Notwithstanding Western temptations to link Islam with violence, he argues, historically in Indonesia the Muslim community has not blocked but facilitated "the civility needed to achieve and sustain democratic politics and social peace in radically multicultural conditions."

Indonesian Muslims know that they constitute, at least statistically, the great majority of their country's population. That majority is diverse. Yet its existence heightens, in principle, the willingness of Muslims to entertain a peaceful evolution toward an electoral democracy that would empower the majority—"their" majority—to rule. Suharto's Muslim guests on 19 May 1998 differed in many respects. But they all understood that, compared with the violent destruction of Suharto's presidency, its peaceful transfer to Habibie was far more likely to favor the political fortunes of Indonesian Muslims as Muslims. Proliferating acts of mass violence against the New Order could provoke martial law and rule by an army historically suspicious of political Islam. Alternatively, such acts could lead to uncontrollable disorder—and who knew what that might breed?

Compared with such outcomes, a Habibie presidency did not look so bad in the eyes of Muslim leaders. Thanks to Suharto's decision at the turn of the decade to narrow the perceived distance between his regime and Islam, Habibie had become the patron of the Muslim thinkers and doers in the Indonesian Muslim Intellectuals' Association (ICMI). Beyond wishing to preserve civility by avoiding violence, some Muslims hoped that a Habibie presidency would serve their political interest, enabling Islamic parties and groups to usher in a democracy that would, at long last, enable the Muslim majority to acquire influence commensurate with its size.

Not every Muslim figure who spoke with Suharto that morning was inclined to think along such lines. Nahdlatul Ulama (NU) General Chairman Abdurrahman Wahid, for example, had little regard for Habibie or ICMI. Wahid was, in outlook, a "red and white" Muslim. He wanted to reach out, beyond the "green" agendas of those eager to defend and advance Islam in public arenas, to encompass and entertain the views of nominal or private Muslims and non-Muslims as well—men and women whose understandings of the nation-state were less explicitly religious, or more explicitly trans-religious, than those of assertively Muslim Indonesians. But others who were present that morning saw themselves, and their country, in noticeably "greener" terms.[13]

The next day brought further evidence that Suharto's self-consciously Muslim opponents were unwilling to press their opposition to the point of risking violence on a scale so large as to endanger democratization and, with it, their own political future. Muhammadiyah's Amien Rais had planned to lead a huge demonstration against the president on Wednesday, 20 May. Suharto's stubborn refusal to give up power had motivated more and more Indonesians to take part. The event was being described as the "march of one million" that would settle the president's fate once and for all.

At the very last minute, it was called off. Many marchers were unwilling to

---

13. The Indonesian flag is red and white, while green symbolizes Islam. Indonesians use these colors variously to distinguish individuals and groups. In this essay, the colors are meant to convey information about a person's outlook, not about his or her religion or religiosity. A pious Muslim can be a "red and white" nationalist, as long as that piety is accompanied by tolerance of non-Muslims and does not imply a desire to Islamize the state. A nominal Muslim or even a non-Muslim can believe in a "green" agenda to improve the economic or political position of the Muslim community, in hopes of thereby reducing Muslim resentment of nominally Muslim and non-Muslim Indonesians. Unfortunately, in polarizing times, these possible combinations of background and belief may be criticized as betrayals because they happen to cross a line drawn between "us" and "them"—as these identities might be defined, and the "us" defended, by anti-Christian Islamists, for example, or Christians hostile to Islam.

risk what could have turned into a bloody confrontation with security forces. But these moderates were opposed by radicals who insisted that the time had come to deliver the final blow to the regime. Tilting the balance decisively against the radicals was the last-minute decision by Amien Rais not to take part and to discourage his substantial following from doing so. He, too, was loathe to risk a major loss of life. But he also feared provoking an army crackdown that could have postponed or canceled the democracy that he needed to transmute popular support into national office. Nor was it coincidental that, in the months after Suharto's resignation, Amien and other Muslim leaders hoping for democracy were more disposed to give President Habibie the benefit of the doubt than many of their counterparts in nominally or non-Muslim opposition groups.

Soon after the presidency changed hands, a curious incident occurred. Commander-in-Chief General Wiranto of ABRI appointed Major General Johny Lumintang, a Christian, to replace Lieutenant General Prabowo Subianto, a Muslim, as head of the Army Strategic Reserve Command (Komando Strategis Angkatan Darat, or Kostrad). Eighteen hours later, Wiranto removed Lumintang from Kostrad and replaced him with a Muslim general. Religion definitely figured in Wiranto's reversal. Wiranto was told that appointing a Christian, however competent, to such an important position—as if there were no Muslim qualified to hold it—would offend Muslim sensitivities. Immediately the appointment was withdrawn on those grounds, although of course they were too discriminatory to be publicly acknowledged.[14]

In promoting Lumintang, Wiranto was thought to have taken a "red and white" line, basing his choice on merit not religion. Coordinating Minister for Defense and Security General Feisal Tanjung was a Muslim, too, but his attitudes and those of his closer associates were considered "greener" than Wiranto's. It is highly probable that Feisal influenced the ABRI commander to reverse the appointment; Habibie, newly inaugurated as president, may also have been involved. And both men reportedly were close, as noted by Liddle in his chapter.

However it occurred, the countermanding of Lumintang's promotion started off Habibie's rule on a controversial note among politically aware Christians, for whom Habibie's ties to ICMI were already a worrisome sign of bias. By the same token, Lumintang's fate encouraged assertive Muslims to believe that under Habibie their time might finally have come. These Muslims still resented Suharto's having named a Catholic general, Benny Murdani, to head ABRI and the ministry of defense consecutively in 1983–93.

Wiranto and Prabowo

In 1998, during the critical ten days from 12 May, when the Trisakti students were shot, to 22 May, Habibie's first full day as president, Indonesia's armed

---

14. Sources for this interpretation include an interview with a particularly knowledgeable source, Jakarta, 2 June 1998.

forces were implicated behind the scenes in two murky, overlapping, and potentially explosive fields of maneuver. The first of these involved questions about the loyalty and patience of Suharto's generals. Would they back him to the bitter end, regardless of how massive popular opposition to him and his regime became, ignoring the army's own origins as a popular force in the struggle against the Dutch? Or would they more or less quietly disassociate ABRI from its supreme commander, perhaps even to the point of moving to remove him, hoping to be judged as having saved, not subverted, the country?

The second field involved Prabowo—the head of Kostrad and, not coincidentally, Suharto's son-in-law—in conspiracies reportedly instigated to advance his chances of replacing General Wiranto as ABRI commander-in-chief. His critics later wondered whether Prabowo's ambitions might even have encompassed the presidency itself.

There were ample reasons to connect these areas of tension, the one between ABRI and the presidential palace, the other internal to the army within ABRI. Prabowo's ambition gave him a motive to want his father-in-law to fire Wiranto, and a reason to hope that the president would then either promote Prabowo, whom Suharto had previously fast-tracked up through army ranks, or give Prabowo emergency authority to reestablish order, or perhaps even do both of these things.

But how to persuade Suharto to embark on such a course? A number of possibilities might have occurred to Prabowo. Among these, several entailed violence, to which this reputedly brutal and quick-tempered former commander of the army's special forces (Komando Pasukan Khusus, or Kopassus) might not have been averse: to stoke public disturbances massive enough to discredit Wiranto for being unable to put them down; to earn favor with Suharto by excelling at the repression of the New Order's enemies; or even to start violence precisely in order to reap credit by ending it.

In late 1997 and early 1998, a series of allegedly radical opponents of the regime were abducted by unknown persons and held incommunicado while being interrogated about possibly subversive activity. Some of these detainees, we know from their own accounts, were tortured. More than a year later, perhaps a dozen were still missing and, in all likelihood, dead. At the time these kidnappings occurred, Prabowo still headed Kopassus. A subsequent investigation convincingly assigned responsibility for the round-up to Kopassus and, through it, to Prabowo. By this evidence, Prabowo did try to excel at destroying the perceived enemies of the regime. And if his ensuing promotion by Suharto to Kostrad chief was an indication, doing so paid off.

Prabowo was also implicated, after the fact, in the fatal shootings at Trisakti University on 12 May 1998, and in the anarchy that swept Jakarta on 13–14 May. But rather than getting Suharto to fire Wiranto, if that is what Prabowo wanted, Prabowo was himself fired by Wiranto in the wake of Suharto's resignation. Initially demoted from commanding Kostrad troops in Jakarta to heading a military academy in Bandung, Prabowo was later removed from the armed forces altogether, while Wiranto continued to lead ABRI.

Compelling with regard to the kidnappings and shootings, the evidence that Prabowo had instigated the city-wide violence of mid-May was less substantial. With Prabowo sacked, disgraced, and circumspect, and his allies already purged from key military positions, observers were left to depend, more or less, on Wiranto's rendition of events. And although Prabowo's version of what had happened on 13–14 May might be disingenuously self-serving, Wiranto, too, had a stake in how recent events would be read. Intriguing in this context was Wiranto's decision not to initiate court-martial proceedings against Prabowo.

Wiranto had good institutional reasons to want to render Prabowo harmless with minimum fuss. A prolonged or public investigation could have prompted disagreements within the army, injured further its already damaged reputation, and thus distracted Wiranto's attention from other issues, including ongoing political unrest and the consolidation of Habibie's nascent Reform Order. Less innocuously, however, investigating and punishing Prabowo too thoroughly or openly might also have uncovered evidence and induced accusations damaging to others, conceivably not excluding Wiranto himself.

Accounts of the mid-May rioting agree that security forces were very slow to respond. Below Wiranto, responsibility for the security of the capital lay with Prabowo and his allies, including the head of Jakarta's Regional Military Command, Major General Sjafrie Syamsuddin. If members of this group did not actually help to spark or fuel the violence, at least they allowed it to blaze away. Why? Arguably because they hoped that Suharto, in Cairo, would blame Wiranto for not extinguishing it.

Less conspiratorial explanations are possible, however: Security forces were overwhelmed by events. Officers calculated that it was safer to let the riots unfold than to risk the fatalities it would have taken to stop them. Perhaps Wiranto himself ordered restraint to avoid repeating on a larger scale the shootings at Trisakti the day before. Conspiracy and restraint could even be combined: Wiranto insisting on passivity to avoid provoking a clash that he knew Prabowo would have exploited.

It would be helpful to know what communications may have passed between Suharto's commanders, including Wiranto, in Jakarta, and the president himself in Cairo, or in the air en route home during the night of 14–15 May. Perhaps Suharto withheld permission to Wiranto or Prabowo to crack down in such unclear circumstances, preferring to return at once to Jakarta and decide for himself what to do. As for bestowing emergency authority on Prabowo, the president would have been leery of allowing history to be repeated. For in 1965–66 it was Suharto himself, holding and using the same Kostrad commandership that Prabowo now held, who had gained control of the armed forces, obtained a presidential grant of emergency powers (Supersemar), and wielded it to sideline and replace

President Sukarno. This time around, Suharto did not let himself fall into a comparable trap—if indeed Prabowo had meant to set one.

We do know that immediately following Suharto's return to Jakarta, the armed forces sent tanks into the streets in a major display of military force. The display ensured an eerily quiet weekend on 16–17 May, and figured in Amien Rais' ultimate decison, in effect, to cancel the massive demonstration planned for the twentieth. We know as well that when the chips were down and he could have backed Prabowo, Suharto did not. The president chose instead to let Wiranto remain in charge of ABRI. And that prepared the way for a mutually beneficial understanding between Wiranto and Habibie that had appeared unlikely almost up to the time it was reached: Wiranto would support Habibie as president, if Habibie would support Wiranto—not Prabowo—as head of the armed forces.

Why did Suharto abandon Prabowo? Prabowo was known for impulsive behavior. Although the president had authorized the younger man's rapid climb through army echelons, Suharto may have been wary of Prabowo to begin with. Although Prabowo was married to Suharto's middle daughter, Siti Hediati ("Titiek") Harijadi, reportedly she and her husband were estranged. And promoting Prabowo may have reflected not only Suharto's approval, but also his habit of balancing potential rivals—here Wiranto and Prabowo—against each other to strengthen his own grip on power.

If Prabowo did in fact secretly spur or worsen the mass violence of mid-May in order to further his own position against Wiranto's, Suharto in the end may have fallen victim to his own longstanding inclination to keep his lieutenants divided, up to a point, the better to rule them. Sukarno's position in 1965 and Suharto's in 1998 were hardly the same. Nevertheless, on the eve of the New Order and again in its final days, a president of Indonesia had overestimated his indispensability within a field of forces grown fatally unstable.

On 21 May, shortly after Suharto's resignation, Prabowo was relieved of his post as Kostrad commander. Prabowo was furious. He appealed to Suharto to overturn the decision. But by then Suharto was no longer president. Nor was he sympathetic. Reportedly, Prabowo's father-in-law and other Suharto family members criticized the general for making trouble. Prabowo did not stop there. He went to the presidential palace in full battle gear, and demanded to see Habibie. He was eventually persuaded to leave. But he frightened Habibie enough for the new president to spend the night in the guest house adjoining the palace, in case the angry general returned.

Absent at the Transition?

The story of how Prabowo gambled for power and lost was dramatic. But it was less important than what did not happen during that pivotal week: The army did not split apart, despite being divided at the top between Wiranto and Prabowo.

Wiranto was linked to officers and civilians with "red and white" views. Prabowo had cultivated supporters on the extreme "green" end of the political spectrum. And the mid-May riots had made less unthinkable the nightmare scenario: that vicious Sinophobia might spread quickly and widely enough to drown the New Order in carnage. If massive violence had carried Suharto to power thirty years before, perhaps nothing short of mass violence would bring him down.

But that did not happen, notwithstanding the estimated 1,200 Indonesians—many of them *pribumi* victims trapped in buildings torched by fellow rioters—who died on 13–14 May. The Wiranto-Prabowo rivalry and the anti-Chinese rioting did not sunder the military; did not ignite civil war; and did not precipitate racial slaughter on a national scale. Nor did the incentives for intervention offered by the disastrous economy, widespread unrest, and proliferating clashes, among groups and between them and security forces, produce a military coup—or even a declaration of martial law that the army might have used to take control. Compared with the devastating assault on civilian actors and institutions that might have been launched, but was not, Prabowo's blustering outside the palace, while it rattled those inside, never rose above farce.

For longtime Indonesia-watchers, these nonevents were puzzling. The origin of the New Order in a military appropriation of civilian authority and institutions, the insertion of active or retired officers into government positions at all levels, the justification of military intervention under the "dual function" doctrine, the latter's codification as national law, and Suharto's own army career were all reasons to deem the New Order a military regime. But if that were so, why were the armed forces, in effect, absent at the transition? Why had they not played a more decisive role?

Perhaps the explanation lay not in any characteristic of the military itself, but in the suddenness and velocity with which events had spun out of its control. By this logic, collapsing currency and equity markets in 1997 and spiraling unrest had caught the armed forces unawares, paralyzing them the way an onrushing truck's beams at night might cause a staring animal to freeze in place.

But this reasoning does not go far. The military had ample time to intervene. Like everyone else, the generals knew all along that eventually, Suharto would leave, or have to leave, the palace. Over the course of the 1990s, especially in the cities, politically aware Indonesians had grown almost endemically cynical toward the president's never-ending hold on power, his refusal to countenance political reform, and the ever fatter and more ubiquitous rents accruing to his kin and friends. And nearly eleven months elapsed between the fall of the Thai baht on 2 July 1997, which prompted downward pressure on the rupiah, and Suharto's resignation on 21 May 1998. (The economic crisis is taken up below.)

If surprise and speed fail to explain why ABRI as an institution did not seize the initiative in the transition of 1997–98, perhaps it was preoccupation. Military leaders may have been too busy putting out fires to plan or manage a change of regime. The fires were literal on drought-ravaged Kalimantan. And the armed forces, including the police, were absorbed on other fronts, too: political clashes related to the 1997 national election; flare-ups of ethnoreligious violence sparked or fanned by the election campaign; major bloodshed involving Dayak and immigrant Madurese communities in Kalimantan; rising unrest in Irian Jaya connected to Freeport's huge mining operation there; intensifying guerrilla activity in East Timor; and proliferating student and labor unrest and related urban disturbances—not to mention the distraction represented by the existence, within the army, of pro- and anti-Prabowo camps. On the other hand, the sheer multiplicity of the country's crises, if it could be construed as having diverted the military's attention away from system-changing intervention, could also be taken in the opposite sense: as an emergency that could have been used to justify a coup to "rescue" the country from such manifold travail.

The trouble with these answers is their failure to consider how the character of ABRI itself had changed. Suharto had subordinated the military to his own presidency so thoroughly and for so long that when the opportunity came when they might have acted as one body, they lacked the ability to do so.

To recapitulate history: In the 1960s, Suharto used the armed forces to help him acquire the presidency. He proceeded to make sure that they would not, in return, use him—to make policy, select personnel, or decide anything of importance to their position. The docility of officers was not complete or constant. But loyalty to the president was prized, and the feisty were shunted aside, along with their friends. When Benny Murdani lost presidential favor for speaking his mind, his associates inside the army lost their chance for advancement. Nor did grumbling in the ranks against Sudharmono prevent Suharto from making him vice president in 1988.

The choice of Try Sutrisno for that job in 1993 was different. Army leaders appeared to be using Golkar to promote Try's vice-presidential chances independently of the president's wishes. But Try was not anti-Suharto. He had served as Suharto's adjutant. Confident that a Try vice-presidency would not threaten his position, Suharto could allow it to develop.

Habibie was different still. He was a civilian. For the fifteen years from 1983 to 1998, vice presidents had been generals. As research and technology minister, he had antagonized more than a few officers for treating the armed forces as a captive market for the equipment that he insisted on ordering from abroad or instructing his strategic industries to manufacture. Compared with all of Suharto's previous vice presidents, the one to be named in March 1998 would have a greater chance of replacing him—given Suharto's age, the uncertainty surrounding his health, and the severity of the economic and political crises then underway. Army leaders knew all this. Yet they did not act, as a group, to thwart Habibie's ascent. Why?

The answer may lie in Suharto's policy of keeping a balance between generals. Even the subtle signs of autonomy evinced by ABRI during its "Murdani era" (to use Liddle's phrase) had caused Suharto to tilt the institution against

Murdani's more or less "red and white" associates by sidelining them in favor of "greener" officers. Suharto was careful, however, not to allow such a "green"-ward tilt to become steep enough to reduce his own centrality to the balance. Early in 1998, for example, he promoted the ostensibly "red and white" Wiranto to replace the "green" Feisal Tanjung as head of ABRI. Some thought at the time that this might foretell the further advancement of Prabowo, who cultivated "green" connections. And far from being put out to pasture, Feisal was made coordinating minister for political and security affairs in the cabinet announced by Suharto in March.

Thus, even if he had wished to, Wiranto could not have moved against Habibie without risking a potentially dangerous split with Feisal. And why should Wiranto have wanted to act so disloyally toward the protégé of the president whom Wiranto himself had faithfully served as an adjutant in 1988–93—the president more responsible than anyone for his own rapid ascent? As for blatantly launching a coup, and thus violating the constitution, that would have subjected Wiranto to fierce opposition from outside and inside ABRI's ranks.

These converging logics illustrate the mutually reinforcing character of the two main elements in Suharto's strategy for keeping ABRI in line: to counterbalance its leaders as individuals, while at the same time ensuring their collective loyalty and subordination to him. The success of these gambits reflected as well what was, from Suharto's standpoint, the optimal nature of the gap between the "red and white" and the "green"—deep enough to curb the pretensions of prospective rivals to the president, yet shallow enough not to open an intramilitary rift that could swallow him up.

In a sense, Suharto's tethering of the military to himself outlasted even his presidency. On 21 May 1998, immediately following the president's resignation, Wiranto announced that ABRI would remain responsible for his safety. Without such a guarantee, Suharto might not have quit. But with it, Wiranto was placed in a position that would become increasingly difficult over the ensuing months, as students massed in the streets and marched on Suharto's house, pressing their demands that he be arrested and tried—even hanged—for crimes against the people.

Wiranto retained conmmand of ABRI and kept his promise to protect the physical safety of his former superior. But the pressure was mounting against Wiranto, the army, and the police as repressive protectors of a status quo that appeared merely to have changed hands. Meanwhile the army's reputation had deteriorated badly, dragged down by revelations and reports of past and present abuses in Aceh, East Timor, Jakarta, Java, and Irian Jaya, among other places. Probably at no time since independence had the military been more manifestly unpopular than it became in 1998. Such was the legacy of the decades-long subordination of the armed forces to one man—a man for whom repression had been a method of rule.

Prolonging the Kingdom?

The more factors one finds that explain a momentous event, such as the exit of Suharto, the easier it becomes to think that it had to happen. But even as late as 19 May, in his remarks on that day, the president did not evince a clear willingness to resign. He promised not to run for president again, but that still left him up to five more years to rule.

He also promised to set up a committee to draft reforms, including new laws on elections, parties, and representative bodies, and against monopolies and corruption. He pledged a new election to be held on the basis of these new laws. The MPR formed by the election would then meet to choose a president (other than himself) and a vice president. Meanwhile, the existing "Development Cabinet" would be replaced with a new, "Reform Cabinet." But although Suharto may have wanted Indonesians to consider these proposals democratizing, nowhere in his statement, as it was reported,[15] did he make that clear. His remarks were about rescuing the nation, not about democracy at all.

The Indonesian economy was reeling. The smoke from the mid-May riots had barely cleared. From the campuses and the streets, bottom-up opposition to his presidency had spread to the heights of his regime. Eventually, had Suharto continued to refuse to cede power, it would have been taken from him. In "choosing" to resign at the eleventh hour, the president did not snatch victory from the jaws of defeat. By resigning, he accepted defeat. The inside-out hypothesis cannot explain why he left office, only how.

Nevertheless, in the nature of this "how"—the pseudovoluntary and minimally face-saving manner of his departure—Suharto did preserve the potential, however slim, for another kind of exit: out from the likelihood of being forever judged as a man whose addiction to power had destroyed his country, and into the chance of assuming, someday, a less odious role in Indonesian history.

We know that one of Suharto's favorite sayings in Javanese was *menang tanpa ngasorake*—to be victorious without causing a feeling of defeat. We may at least speculate that by resigning he hoped to reverse this sequence: *asor tanpa ngunggulake*—to be defeated in a way that denied his enemies a feeling of victory. The notion may sound fanciful. Later, however, one anti-Suharto activist, looking back on the president's announcement, commented wryly, "The end of the New Order was like sex without orgasm." The activist recalled watching Suharto resign on television, remembering how long the New Order had lasted, and thinking to himself, "That's it?"[16]

---

15. See "Pak Harto."

16. The Javanese phrase may be found in *Soeharto: My Thoughts, Words and Deeds—An Autobiography,* as told to G. Dwipayana and Ramadhan K.H. (English ed., Jakarta: PT Citra Lamtoro Gung Persada, 1991), p. 495. The quotes are from a conversation I had in Jakarta on 3 June 1998.

Some dubbed what had happened "the May revolution."[17] But it was not that. The New Order had not been overthrown. In some respects, it had been extended. On 19 May the president had promised reforms at the eleventh hour. Doing so had not salvaged his presidency. But his plans had not disappeared with him. Upon replacing Suharto, Habibie had taken them over and made them his own agenda. Nor was it surprising that Habibie should try, in effect, to keep his patron's commitments. Habibie had long resided inside the political house of Suharto, and it was Suharto who had placed him in the vice-presidency—a heartbeat away from the top job. This is not to belittle Habibie's plans for reform, but to note how their origin implied continuity: Suharto's regime would be improved, not replaced, at least not right away.

Habibie had what analysts of American politics would call "high negatives." I have noted his unpopularity with the military. His lavishing of public money on high-tech industry did not endear him to the technocrats, who found him economically illiterate. (A particularly risible example of "Habibie-nomics" was his notion that inflation could be reduced by progressively lowering interest rates.)[18] Secular, non-Muslim, and nonpracticing Muslim Indonesians worried about his connections through ICMI to political Islam. For these reasons he lacked the confidence of most Western governments and multilateral agencies as well. Coincidentally or not, in February 1998, when rumors surfaced that Habibie would be named vice president, the rupiah plummeted from some 8,000 to about 17,000 to the dollar—the first of two nadirs reached by Indonesia's currency during the crisis—before recovering temporarily.[19]

Why, then, did Suharto choose Habibie, of all people, to become his vice president in March 1998? It almost seemed as though Suharto had embarked on a strategy of self-defense by the logic of lesser evil: selecting to succeed him a person so obviously unfit to rule as to cause second thoughts among those wanting the incumbent to resign. In his comments on 19 May, Suharto asked rhetorically whether by quitting he might make matters worse: The vice president (Habibie) would take over, "but soon he too would have to withdraw," potentially leading to further chaos, as if the country had no basis for safeguarding public life.[20]

---

17. For example, "Indonesia's May Revolution," *Far Eastern Economic Review* [*FEER*], 28 May 1998, cover; Aboeprijadi Santoso, "Jakarta's May Revolution," *Inside Indonesia* [Northcote, Australia], 56 (October–December 1998), pp. 15–16. See also "Scenes from the Indonesian Revolution," *Institutional Investor,* 32 (June 1998), pp. 14–16; Clare Fermont, "Indonesia: The Inferno of Revolution," *International Socialism,* 80 (Autumn 1998), pp. 3–33.

18. Ross H. McLeod, "Habibie's New Inflation Theory," *Bulletin of Indonesian Studies,* 33 (April 1997), pp. 8–9.

19. The spread of violence in May accompanied the second such downward spike—again, roughly from 8,000 to 17,000 to the dollar. The rate had been about 2,400 prior to the baht's fall in July 1997.

20. "Pak Harto."

And yet, when Suharto chose Habibie, the older man knew that some sort of succession had become more imminent than ever before. Suharto was 76. He had lost his wife. He had been ill. To complete his 1998–2003 term, he would need to remain healthy into his eighties. In this context, his apparent lack of confidence in Habibie on 19 May looks more like a last-ditch excuse for not ceding power than evidence of a "lesser evil" ploy two months before. In March, unsure where the worsening crisis might lead, Suharto would have wanted above all to name as his potential successor someone of long association with, and proven fealty to, himself—qualities that Habibie supplied.

Suharto may have intended to groom his eldest daughter, Tutut, to replace him in the long run. Of his six children, she was the most prominent politically, within Golkar. Perhaps he had that eventual assignment in mind when he named her to his new cabinet in March. In the meantime, however, he needed an admiring pupil who could be relied on to obey his mentor absolutely, as long as the latter remained in office, and to defend him faithfully thereafter, whatever misfortunes an increasingly uncertain future might bring. He needed Habibie.

Patron and Protégé

The two men had met nearly half a century before, in Habibie's home town of Ujungpandang, South Sulawesi. It was 1950, the year Suharto turned 29 and Habibie 14. A young army officer, Suharto had been sent there to help put down a local rebellion against Jakarta—one of the uprisings discussed by Cribb in his chapter. They met again much later in Germany, where Habibie, by then an engineer, was on a fast track up the ranks at the aircraft firm Messerschmitt-Boelkow-Blohm, where eventually he would become a vice president. Suharto asked Habibie to return to Indonesia and join the New Order. In 1974, Habibie did.

During his long tenure as research and technology minister, Habibie would lavishly praise the president, calling him "SGS"—"Super Genius Suharto." Suharto, in return, was impressed that Habibie would give up his high salary in Germany to return to Indonesia. And if Habibie looked up to his patron, the patron looked down on Habibie. "He always seeks my advice on the principles of life," recalled Suharto in his "as told to" autobiography. "He thinks of me as his own parent. . . . He always asks for my advice. He takes notes on the philosophy that I impart to him"—a philosophy, Suharto added, that would serve the younger man well in his future work.[21]

One can make too much of this. Habibie's sycophancy toward Suharto-in-power did not guarantee that, upon gaining power in his own right, the ex-protégé

---

21. *Soeharto*, p. 392. I have slightly reworded the quote in English in light of the original, *Soeharto: Pikiran, Ucapan, dan Tindakan Saya* (same authorship and publisher, 1989), p. 457.

would implement the ex-president's authoritarian philosophy of governance. In fact, as noted later in these pages, President Habibie quickly reversed much of his predecessor's legacy. Nevertheless, from the New to the Reform Order, the continuity of leadership was unmistakable. Of the ministers named to the "Development Reform Cabinet" announced by Habibie on 22 May, the day after his inauguration, more than half (twenty of thirty-six) were holdovers from the Development Cabinet that Suharto had formed—his last—in mid-March. And among the four top-ranked (coordinating) ministerships, the holdover rate was 100 percent.

Habibie did separate from the cabinet two positions that Suharto had kept within it: the attorney generalship and the governorship of the central bank. The new president's intent was to depoliticize these positions, encouraging in the first instance a more impartial application of the law, and in the second, a more independent monetary policy. But anti-Suharto students, who wanted the former president investigated and punished for corruption, were soon calling for the attorney general's resignation on the grounds that he was protecting not prosecuting Suharto.

In the quick shift from one head of government to another, the New Order's institutions had not changed. After Suharto's resignation, the one thousand members of the assembly (MPR), who had unanimously reacclaimed Suharto president in March, still held their seats. So did the five hundred MPR members who doubled as legislators in the tame house of representatives (DPR). The "dual function" justifying military intervention in politics was intact. So were the positions held by active and retired officers throughout government, including the DPR, where military personnel still filled 15 percent of the seats, alongside Golkar's 65 percent. Indonesian troops still occupied East Timor. And all of the New Order's laws, including those that had reflected and bolstered its authoritarian character, remained on the books. In effect, the body of the regime had remained, while the head had been replaced—and the "new" head was extremely familiar. The old one, Suharto, was not dead, not in jail, not even in exile.

One morning in May 1998, a few days after Suharto's fall, I happened to be in the Jakarta office of *Ummat,* a Muslim biweekly. On one wall a staffer had posted a mocking retranslation of the famous New Order acronym "Supersemar." The original, laudatory formula—discussed by Virginia Hooker in her chapter—had been invented to commemorate the 1966 transfer of authority from Sukarno to Suharto, and to aggrandize the New Order's founder by association with the *wayang* character Semar. The poster on *Ummat*'s wall redefined "Supersemar" to mean "Suharto Is Exactly like Marcos" ("Suharto Persis Seperti Marcos"). But was he? In 1986 public anger against Philippine President Ferdinand Marcos had obliged him to flee Manila for Honolulu. Yet as of November 1998, Suharto was still in Jakarta, living as he had throughout his regime in a modest residence on Cendana Street in the heart of the city.

Following his exit, sightings of Suharto around the capital became a journalistic equivalent of ornithology. More often than not he would be glimpsed entering or exiting this or that mosque to pray. The first of these sightings occurred at the mosque in "Beautiful Indonesia in Miniature"—the national exhibition-and-recreation-area discussed by Hooker. For Suharto personally, major change had occurred. His empire had shrunk to a park. But he remained free to visit this microcosm of what he had once ruled. .

From May to November 1998, frustration grew among anti-Suharto students that not enough had changed. In the latter month, interspersed between chants for reform, there were new slogans calling for what May's segue from Suharto to Habibie had denied the protesters: Revolution. Suharto had not been able to retain power. But he had been able to relinquish it in a manner that infuriated his most vocal critics. Significant changes, reviewed toward the end of this chapter, were underway or planned in Habibie's Reform Order. But if one focused instead on the new president's own background and appointments, it was hard not to share the judgment of his critics that the New Order had been more renamed than repudiated.

Fires and Haze

My argument so far has attributed responsibility for Suharto's exit to Indonesians: Suharto himself, at the last minute, deciding to resign; his collaborators, not much earlier, disassociating themselves from his presidency; and his opponents, in preceding weeks and months, generating wider and louder protests against him in the streets, where looting mobs in their own way also defied his regime. These actions illustrate, respectively, explanations from the inside out (Suharto deciding), the top down (Harmoko defecting), and the bottom up (students demonstrating).

The explanations are not mutually exclusive. And they interact: Bottom-up pressure, including the torching of his family home, heavily influenced Harmoko's decision, as head of the MPR and DPR, to break regime ranks and, in effect, threaten Suharto with impeachment from the top down. And if Suharto's resignation was partly a response to bottom-up protests and riots, so were the latter open to top-down manipulation by the likes of Prabowo. But this account of exit remains incomplete without the addition of a fourth and last set of causal conditions and events that arose outside of Indonesia, yet were far-reaching enough to deliver inward pressure on Suharto to resign.

American political nudging was a part of this outside-in story. In Washington, hours before Suharto resigned, the State Department issued a vaguely worded statement that, in effect, advised him to. But no convincing evidence has come to light that this last-minute prompting made much of a difference. Indeed, the statement probably stemmed from a desire to appease Congressional liberals demanding that the United States push Suharto out, rather than from any eagerness in the executive branch actually to do so, given the considerable risks that a concerted American effort to remove Suharto would have posed. These risks included triggering a nationalist backlash against interference; giving Suharto a self-defense based on sovereignty; and splitting his opponents between those welcoming and those opposing American "help."

These objections might be countered by arguing that a major American campaign against him could have ended Suharto's rule sooner, and thus averted the horrors of the rioting in Jakarta in May. But the premise is unrealistic: The United States had been too close to the New Order and had too great a stake in Indonesian stability to foment a coup. And the inference is unwarranted: Anti-Americanism could have lifted the death toll even higher. Finally, if such a major American push had succeeded, the credit for ousting Suharto would have gone abroad, to the United States, draining moral authority from the local reform movement and implicating Washington deeply and controversially in the incoming, Habibie regime.

In any case, given what actually happened, an observer would have to conclude that the forces endangering the New Order from outside of Indonesia were much less political in origin than environmental and economic. Indeed, future historians may recall what happened to Indonesia in 1997–98 as the most severe combination of environmental disaster with economic inversion—boom to bust—experienced by any country in the second half of the twentieth century.

The phenomenon known as El Niño, a periodic warming of Pacific waters east of Indonesia that reverses weather patterns, had afflicted the archipelago before, most notably in the drought and fires of 1982–83. But the severity and timing of El Niño's visit in 1997–98 could hardly have been worse, arriving as it did on the eve of, and in time to speed, the crash of the rupiah and the Jakarta Stock Exchange (JSX).

The new round of drought, apart from its impact on growing seasons and food supplies, delayed the onset of wet weather enough to make the "rain forest" a misnomer. And the dryness made clearing by fire—for settlement, subsistence, and agribusiness—too easy to resist. A total area in excess of 20,000 square kilometers, larger than the American state of New Jersey, burned in Indonesia during the prolonged dry season of 1997 alone, according to estimates reached provisionally in 1998 and likely to be enlarged in future with better data.[22]

For varying periods of time, the resulting pall of smoke hung over all or parts of eight countries. An estimated 75 million people were directly affected. Worst hit, aside from Indonesia, were Singapore and Malaysia, given their proximity to Sumatra and especially to Kalimantan, where the most out-of-control fires were. "The haze," as it was called, soon damaged the health of 20–50 million Indonesians.[23] The losses of life and life expectancy may never be known. Eventually

---

22. Lew Simons and Michael Yamashita, "Indonesia's Plague of Fire," *National Geographic,* August 1998, p. 104.

23. Simons and Yamashita, "Indonesia's Plague," pp. 104 [20 million], 105 [75 million], 109 [50 million].

the rains arrived, but by February 1998 new fires were being sighted, and old ones had flared again. El Niño finally subsided in 1998. But the damage to Indonesia's economy had been done—in ruined or unplanted crops, closed schools and businesses, cancelled flights, lost tourism, and medical expense.

The biospheric origin of the disaster suggests that it could not have been avoided by Indonesians, and therefore did not implicate them. But dry wood was only a necessary, not a sufficient, cause of the fires on Kalimantan. Some were set, often on land previously cleared by timber firms, by indigenous people practic- ing slash-and-burn agriculture: burning the cover to enrich the soil with ash, dropping seeds for a crop, harvesting it, and moving on to repeat the cycle. Other fires were lit to clear land for habitation and farming by transmigrants brought to the island from more crowded parts of the archipelago. But the biggest fires were set by companies to convert overgrown areas into plantations, notably to produce palm oil that could be sold abroad for use in soaps, salad dressings, and cookies, among other products. And many of these companies were linked to people around President Suharto, including his golfing partner Bob Hasan—an ethnic-Chinese Indonesian and the country's leading timber tycoon at the time.[24]

Suharto was lucky that most of the fires were located off Java, and that prevailing winds blew most of the smoke north and west, not south. From 1 August to 31 October 1997, the maximum extent of the haze encompassed the air over parts of the South China Sea and the Indian Ocean, and blanketed the Java Sea as well. But all of Java, including Jakarta, was spared.[25] Had the skies over the Indonesian capital been as lethally polluted as they became over Singapore and Kuala Lumpur, the embarrassment to Suharto and his regime would have been greater.

As it was, the fires and haze did lead the minister for the environment at the time, Sarwono Kusumaatmadja, to drop the pretense that slash-and-burn farmers were mainly responsible and, instead, blame the close-to-Suharto companies involved. In retrospect, Sarwono's message was top-down evidence that the president could not assume that his ministers would remain loyal forever. But Suharto ignored it, preferring to replace the messenger with a new environmental minister in March 1998.

Also named to Suharto's new cabinet in March, as minister of industry and trade, was the man who had profited more than anyone from the destruction of the country's forests, Bob Hasan. Hasan was the first—as it turned out, the only— ethnic-Chinese Indonesian to be named a minister in the history of the New Order. It may have helped that he was Muslim. But his having broken the taboo against cabinet members of Chinese heritage was less a breakthrough into equal

---

24. See Christopher M. Barr, "Bob Hasan, the Rise of Apkindo, and the Shifting Dynamics of Control in Indonesia's Timber Sector," *Indonesia,* 65 (April 1998), pp. 1–36.

25. As shown by the map in Simons and Yamashita, "Indonesia's Plague," p. 105.

political opportunity for all Indonesians than a sign of how close to the president Hasan had become.

Who Pushed the Rupiah?

The economic crisis that ravaged Indonesia in 1997–98 resembled the environmental one in appearing to have assaulted the New Order laterally, from the outside in. As an external catalyst of disaster, the falling baht in Thailand to the northwest was an economic "El Niño"—just as rising water temperatures east of the archipelago could be taken for an environmental "devaluation" that, by drying Kalimantan's forest cover, made it cheaper to burn. The economic and the environmental crises were also alike in that, however external their origins may have been, both calamities deeply implicated Indonesian actors.

In the economy's case, one may ask: How deeply? To what extent was the New Order victimized by—or, conversely, responsible for—the devastation of Indonesian markets, firms, jobs, and incomes in 1997–98? In 1998, unable to agree on an answer, analysts explained the crisis variously along a spectrum of judgments—from those that made external factors most accountable for what had happened to the economy, to those that assigned such power most wholly to domestic phenomena.

The sequence of events is not in dispute. On 2 July 1997 the Bank of Thailand succumbed to mounting pressure against the baht by abandoning the peg that had linked the Thai currency to the U.S. dollar. The baht quickly fell by nearly a fifth in dollar value. Nine days later, having failed to repulse a comparable selling wave against its own currency, the Philippine central bank temporarily stopped buying the peso, which promptly depreciated by more than a tenth in dollar terms. Three days later, the central bank of Malaysia suspended its unsuccessful defense of the ringgit, which dropped to a thirty-three-month low.

Indonesia was next. Its central bank, the Bank of Indonesia, had been implementing a "downward-crawling peg." This policy allowed for a slow depreciation of the value of Indonesia's currency, measured by the number of rupiah needed to purchase one dollar, between the ceiling and floor of a moving band whose width had been set at roughly 8 percent of that gradually weakening number. Within this downward-slanting corridor, the actual number was permitted to fluctuate, as long as it did not strengthen in value through the ceiling or—the actual risk—weaken to the point of falling through the floor. Only to deter the latter breach would the Bank of Indonesia take steps to defend the value of the rupiah, by spending foreign exchange to buy it and make it more scarce, for example, or by raising interest rates to make it more attractive to save and lend.

In July 1997, Indonesia tried to cope with a swelling rush to sell its currency by lifting the ceiling and—more to the point—lowering the floor between which the exchange rate could vary. The height of this taller corridor equaled 12.5 percent of the rupiah's value against the dollar. But to no avail. On 14 August, the

Bank of Indonesia felt obliged to abandon these limits. The rupiah quickly fell by 6 percent against the dollar. Nor did it stop there. Within a matter of weeks Indonesia's currency had given up roughly half of its earlier value—from 2,449 to the dollar on 30 June to between 3,600 and 3,800 by the latter part of October.

It is hard not to infer from this chronology the inexorable force of conditions and actors beyond Indonesian control. The chain of events seems to favor an economic version of the "domino theory" popularized during the Vietnam War, with the Thai baht replacing the South Vietnamese government as the first domino, which fell against the peso, which downed the ringgit, which in turn toppled the rupiah.

But this apparent chain reaction cannot be traced to a conspiracy by foreign speculators who had "attacked" the baht merely because it was there. The extreme venality of the government of Prime Minister Banharn Silpa-archa, and a series of financial scandals, including the collapse of the country's ninth-largest bank, had preceded a September 1996 decision by the international credit rating agency, Moody's, to downgrade Thailand's short-term debt. And it was not foreign but Thai interests, responding to a local real estate firm's default on a foreign loan and rumors of trouble at the kingdom's largest finance company, who mounted the first concerted pressure on the baht at the end of January 1997.[26]

Similarly, it was Indonesian actors who initiated what would later turn into a stampede away from the rupiah. It was the increasing incidence of dollar buying by Indonesian companies, beginning in July 1997, that attracted the attention of foreign money traders.[27] These domestic firms, notably the *konglomerat* discussed by Ahmad Habir in his chapter, had contracted huge debts in dollars on the expectation that the loans could be converted to rupiah and invested in booming local markets, and that a portion of the profits could be converted back into dollars to service and retire the debt. The second conversion would likely be less favorable than the first, but not onerously so, due to the gradual pace of the downward-crawling peg. As soon as these debtors sensed the likelihood of a more steeply weakening rupiah, however, they began selling Indonesian currency for dollars in order to hedge against that possibility.

Foreign money managers, already alerted by Thailand's crisis to the riskiness of other "emerging markets," quickly joined the rush. They borrowed rupiah to buy dollars in the increasingly realistic expectation that the American currency would strengthen. For they knew that if it did, they could use their newly bought dollars to buy more than enough rupiah to pay off the original debt. The remaining rupiah could then be converted into dollars for a profit. Meanwhile, fearing

26. Callum Henderson, *Asia Falling: Making Sense of the Asian Crisis and Its Aftermath* (New York: McGraw-Hill, 1998), pp. 88–90 [Banharn, scandals, Moody's], 99 [concerted pressure].

27. Richard Mann, *Economic Crisis in Indonesia: The Full Story* ([no place]: Gateway Books, 1998), p. 26.

devaluation, foreign and domestic investors in the JSX sold securities and used the rupiah proceeds to buy dollars. Thus did a rising number of individually rational Indonesian debtors collectively contribute to precisely the outcome they feared—a smashed peg and their country's currency in free fall—with the "help" of speculators who, depending on the direction and timing of their own positions, gained or lost from that result.

Among the economic conditions that led to the currency's deterioration and prolonged weakness, two were vital, and both were local. The first comprised the already mentioned debts—large, private, short-term, and owed by Indonesians in foreign currencies—that pressured the rupiah to fall; became unrepayable when it did; and motivated enough selling pressure against occasional recoveries to make them unsustainable. The second was an opaque panoply of grossly overextended private banks whose high debt-equity ratios and noneconomic loans exacerbated the collapse, ruining the banking system and, with it, whatever role it might have played in restoring to the economy a semblance of financial health.

In June 1997, among countries that would be affected by the repercussions of the imminent decline of the baht, two indicators of financial vulnerability were positively correlated, and they were both particularly high in four countries. The two indicators were the ratios of short-term indebtedness and of domestic money to foreign exchange reserves. The four countries where both ratios were highest were Indonesia, Russia, South Korea, and Thailand[28]—precisely the economies that would fall the farthest, although at different speeds and to varying depths, in the course of the crisis. Without doubt, imprudent investing and lending by foreigners contributed to this vulnerability in Indonesia, just as their aversion to the rupiah helped send it lower. But the origins and unraveling of these conditions were rooted in the political economy of the New Order—as described by my coauthors in this book.

Repealing Sadli's Law

"In Indonesia, bad times foster good policies." By the 1990s, this rule had become reliable enough, and the role of Suharto's economists in its execution sufficiently crucial, for admiring foreign observers to have given it a name, "Sadli's Law," after the longtime technocrat and former economic minister Mohammad Sadli.

Sadli's Law had proved its worth at three key moments of economic crisis in the history of the New Order: In the 1960s, empowered by Suharto, the technocrats had repaired an economy ruined by Sukarno's neglect and intervention. In the 1970s, still licensed by Suharto, they had fixed the fiscal mess left by the profligacy and near-collapse of the state oil company, Pertamina. In the 1980s, with Suharto's authorization as always, they had used the shock of falling world prices for Indonesia's

---

28. *East Asia: The Road to Recovery* (Washington, DC: World Bank, 1998), p. 8. "Domestic money" (M2) includes rupiah in circulation and in checking and savings accounts.

main export, oil, to justify reforms that had helped to reorient the economy toward manufactured exports, returning it one more time to the path of growth.

This is an oversimplified account. It omits the influential roles of foreign donors, lenders, and investors. Domestic investors mattered too, especially in the 1980s. But, as recounted by Anne Booth and Richard Borsuk in their chapters, the technocrats thrived on adversity. Bad times favored their sober agenda of deregulatory reform based on respect for the power of the market—a respect acquired by the technocrats during their training as economists and reinforced by their experience as advisers.

Boom times had the opposite effect. They lifted public revenues and popularized optimism, buoying the policy leverage of those, many of them trained as "can do" engineers, who wanted the New Order to rely less on the market and more on the state as the engine of growth. As described by Borsuk and Habir in their essays, many of these supposed "nationalists" also wanted to use state resources to help less well-off "indigenous" (*pribumi*) firms and households compete for wealth with the economically ubiquitous ethnic-Chinese (*nonpribumi*) minority.

A boom-fed overexpansion leads to a bust conducive to reforms whose success permits an ensuing boom, which encourages overexpansion . . . By 1997 the rhythm of this cycle had become blindlingly familiar. "Blindingly" because it led observers of the onset of the New Order economy's fourth major emergency to believe that Suharto would remain true to form, again letting the technocrats rise to the occasion and implement Sadli's Law.

But Suharto was not his old self. Or, rather, at the age of 76, he had become his all-too-older self. I have noted the loss of his wife in 1996, and his illness in late 1997. We cannot know how he might have handled the crisis had he been younger. But this fourth time around, in 1997–98, he was less decisive than he had been during the three earlier crises. A grave case in point was his vacillation in January and February between the guidance given to him by IMF chief Michel Camdessus (backed up by the U.S. Treasury) on the one hand, and the contrary advice of an American economist, Steve Hanke, on the other.

On 8 October 1997 the IMF and the Indonesian government had announced an agreement that traded the Fund's promise of eventual access to a total of $43 billion worth of support funds (from three multilateral agencies and five countries)[29] in return for Indonesia's commitment to implement specified reforms.

---

29. Participants (and amounts pledged, in billions) were the IMF ($10), Singapore ($10), the World Bank ($4.5), the Asian Development Bank ($3.5), Japan ($5), the United States ($3), Brunei ($1.2), and Malaysia ($1), with the remaining $5 billion to come from "'Indonesia's own foreign assets.'" Mann, *Economic Crisis,* p. 50. The resulting $43.2 billion was from the beginning conjectural, because it might not all be needed, for lack of exact specification of contingent terms and purposes, and because the generosity of some pledging countries would soon be constrained by their own experience of the spreading regional crisis.

IMF (and American) dissatisfaction with Indonesian compliance led to a second agreement on 15 January 1998. This letter of Indonesian intent listed fifty specific reform measures that Suharto's government would have to undertake in order to qualify for continuing access to the original $43 billion package. Perceived Indonesian foot-dragging led to a longer and stricter third agreement, announced in full on 10 April, listing 117 actions that the government would have to complete by specific times to avoid losing further access to the package. Of the $43 billion agreed to more than five months earlier, merely $3 billion—7 percent—had been disbursed.

Steve Hanke, an economist from Johns Hopkins University, did not advise Suharto to break with the IMF. But he did urge the establishment of a currency board that would automatically exchange dollars for rupiah, or vice versa, at a fixed rate within a radically closed and homeostatic system. The board would begin with exactly enough dollars on reserve to match, at the set rate, the value of rupiah in circulation. And if enough Indonesians rushed to convert enough rupiah into dollars to dollarize the economy, so be it. The board would, in effect, replace the central bank and be entirely autonomous from the government, which would permanently cede the right to influence interest rates to the interplay of supply and demand.

The IMF and the U.S. government strongly opposed Hanke's idea as unrealistic. And it was. A successful board—avoiding dollarization—presupposed a government with sterling credibility, whose promise never to intervene would be forever kept. Yet credibility was just what the New Order lacked. If a $43 billion provisional carrot held by the IMF could not prevent Suharto from reneging on his promises to the IMF—reviving cancelled megaprojects, opening loopholes in reforms, resisting fiscal restraint—how could he be expected to live up to the permanent self-discipline required by a currency board, especially as the days of his rule became more and more clearly numbered? Camdessus (and the U.S. Treasury) also feared that Suharto might view the board as a surgical strike that would rescue the rupiah and somehow save Indonesia from having to engage in reform at all, that is, from following IMF (and American) advice. Suharto called the currency board idea "IMF-Plus" to allay such fears, but to little effect.

Eventually the dwindling of Indonesia's foreign reserves made Hanke's proposal moot. But not before it had taken up precious time and attention at the top of the regime. The one positive effect that might be attributed to Hanke's idea was that it helped make the IMF, the Bank, and the U.S. Treasury realize just how desperately Indonesians wanted to restore lost value to the rupiah. A stronger rupiah was needed to enable the repayment, or at least the renegotiation, of private foreign debts, and thus to save the real economy from shutting down for lack of credit—indeed, as the crisis worsened, for a lack of foreign banks even willing to accept Indonesian letters of credit to finance trade.

Alongside Suharto's indecision as an aging leader under conflicting pressures to make risky choices for rising stakes, other conditions distinguished the economic crisis of 1997–98 from its predecessors: Suharto's success in maintaining growth had opened up many more opportunities for his relatives and friends to enrich themselves. By 1997 the dealings and holdings of Suharto's children and cronies were everywhere. Necessarily, therefore, the IMF's reforms affected these rent-seekers and their appendages far more than if the crisis had occurred a few decades before. And the Fund went further, as we shall see, earmarking for destruction precisely these redoubts of "crony capitalism." But the president was loathe to undercut his kin and friends. And from this it followed that he would not comply—or would only half-comply, or feign compliance—with the IMF's lengthening lists of things for him to do.

Another key difference was the mixing of economics and politics. Not since the New Order's founding trauma in the mid-1960s had an economic crisis and a political crisis been so closely intertwined. In the first catastrophe, Suharto had been able to blame and oust Sukarno. Now Suharto was being blamed, if not for causing the crisis then for failing to resolve it while postponing an already overdue succession.

In the first emergency, the IMF, the World Bank, and American officials had sided with Suharto. Now they were pressing him to abandon the gambits that he had grown accustomed to using to help make the New Order work—inducing loyalty through patronage, trading access for rent, avoiding transparency to ensure control. In the 1960s, the Cold War and, within it, the Vietnam War had been in full swing. Then, his anticommunism had been sufficient to gain Western support. Now, to earn Western economic relief, he would have to risk reform.

Generations mattered too. The students demanding his resignation had not been born in 1965–66. They had grown up assuming economic growth. That growth had exposed them to notions of democracy and individuality in, for example, the robust counterculture reviewed by Hooker in her chapter. Suddenly, growth was gone, leaving the students to face rising prices and disappearing jobs in an economy expected to shrink in 1998 by 10 percent, a figure later revised downward to -15 percent.[30] Suharto and his relatives and associates had become part of the problem, if not the problem itself. And the students knew the solution: Show him the door.

Scale also mattered. The economic damage done by this crisis greatly exceeded that of the near-bankrupting of a single state corporation, Pertamina, in the 1970s, or the decline of oil prices in the 1980s. And unlike all three previous emergencies, this one was rooted in the private sector: the many businesses and banks that had borrowed so heavily abroad and spent so recklessly at home. Suharto was accustomed to revising the government's economic policies. So were

---

30. "Economic Indicators," *FEER,* 4 June and 26 November 1998, pp. 76 [10] and 104 [15], respectively. Even more pessimistically, using estimates from Goldman Sachs (Asia), "Economic Indicators," *FEER,* 17 December 1998, p. 58, put growth at -18.4 percent in 1998, rising to a still subzero -1.4 percent for 1999.

the technocrats. It was another matter to bring hundreds of disparate and suddenly insolvent debtor firms in Indonesia into fruitful negotiations with private creditor banks in multiple countries.

Indonesian officials were not even sure how much debt was involved. A "Frankfurt agreement" was finally drawn up to work out these debts, but it took months of meetings to negotiate. And because its repayment provisions, for a borrower entering the compact, depended in part on the exchange rate then in effect, Indonesian firms hung back from doing so in the hope that the rupiah would strengthen.

Reform or Replenish?

The role of the IMF bears further discussion. In the past, the technocrats had used the Fund and the World Bank to convey and bolster their own recommendations. Doing so helped these advisers compensate for their lack of a political base independent of the president. Suharto could easily reject the recommendations of people whom he had appointed and could dismiss, but the advice of the IMF and the Bank was harder to discard. From its inception the New Order had relied on their funds and approval. And in 1997, as in previous shocks and contractions, the value of IMF and Bank endorsement rose as the rupiah fell. By August the technocrats were in frequent and intensifying touch with both institutions.

As more than a few after-dinner speakers on East Asia's downturn pointed out at the time, the Chinese word for "crisis" combines "danger" with "opportunity." But not every crisis mixes these ingredients in the same proportions; and over time within the same crisis, the proportions change. In Indonesia, for example, from July until mid-December 1997, when Suharto's illness sent the rupiah down its first steep slope, the crisis plausibly could be seen as more of an opportunity to press for reform, including political reform, than a danger necessitating rescue. And that is more or less how it was understood, at that time, by many of the technocrats in Jakarta and their counterparts in Washington at the Fund and the Bank.

Already by mid-1997 both institutions were stressing the need for policy changes in developing countries, including measures against corruption. The World Bank's annual report on Indonesia, issued on 30 May 1997, for example, included language that by euphemistic Bank standards amounted to a bluntly political critique. Under "governance issues," the report pointed to conditions that "favor the well-connected over the efficient . . . inflate costs . . . engender cynicism and perceptions of unfairness . . . [and] make it difficult to do legitimate business." The implication was unmistakable that Indonesia lacked and needed

> an independent judiciary; . . . credible penalties for malfeasance; policy reforms to reduce the discretionary authority of government officials; and greater ac-

countability for poor performance or abuse of power. . . . [T]ime-tested policies (such as deregulation) are losing their edge, while the quality of growth—including fairness—remains a concern for the great majority of the nation.[31]

The IMF shared and advanced similar views of the New Order. Fund personnel were especially eager to attack three monopolies: two exclusive arrangements, one in cars, one in cloves, benefiting Suharto's youngest son, Tommy; and a third enabling the Food Supply Agency (Bulog) to assure stable prices for basic necessities. In its early months, the crisis had not worsened sufficiently to give the IMF or the technocrats enough leverage to take on the first children. But on 20 August 1997 the top-ranking technocrat, Saleh Afiff, as coordinating minister for the economy, was able to announce that Bulog's monopoly would be ended.

In 1998, by deregulating the importation of sugar, soybeans, wheat flour, cooking oil, and other necessities, the government did, for a time, reduce Bulog's purview to a single commodity: rice. But the delay illustrated a point made by Borsuk in his chapter: that market openings were easier to announce than accomplish. And in this case there were serious arguments to be made against deregulation: that Bulog had not been responsible for the crisis; that it had a reasonably good record of keeping prices within the reach of less affluent Indonesians; and that if the crisis spread to the real economy and lowered the buying power of millions of ordinary citizens—exactly what happened—the agency's services would be needed all the more, to keep the newly impoverished fed and prevent unrest.

Borsuk's essay describes the cozy set-up in soybeans enjoyed by their sole legal importer, Bulog, and their sole authorized crusher (for soymeal), Sarpindo, whose monopoly-rent-taking owners included, along with two of Suharto's children, two of his closest associates, the *nonpribumi* tycoons Liem Sioe Liong and Bob Hasan (see Table 6.1). If Indonesia's sudden travail was an opportunity to liberate markets from the distortions forced on them by the nepotistic and crony-rewarding hand of the state, then Bulog was fair game.

But the damage being done to currency and crops (from the drought) was bound to show up in higher domestic prices, especially for food—not to mention

---

31. *Indonesia: Sustaining High Growth with Equity* (Washington, DC: World Bank, 1997), pp. xxxi–1. The Bank was also prescient. It found the macroeconomy "currently performing very well," but went on to note that more

careful scrutiny of the data gives reason for pause. . . . [P]rivate external debt is increasing rapidly; . . . the growth of non-oil exports has declined markedly; . . . adverse developments in neighbouring countries could spillover into Indonesia; there is increasing dependence upon volatile capital flows; common local practices are coming under increasing international scrutiny; and financial markets continue to assign high risk to rupiah-denominated assets.

the downward pressure on the jobs and incomes that consumers would need in order to buy food, or the food-price volatility built into the approaching Muslim holiday cycle, from fast to celebration, in January 1998. In November 1997, food prices confirmed such fears by gaining 17.3 percent, while the year-on-year percentage increase in the overall index of consumer prices (CPI) that month was the highest Indonesians had seen since February 1996. And, as feared, the year-on-year average increase in the CPI during the first quarter of 1998 did rise ominously high, to 29.7 percent, compared with an average annual growth in the CPI of merely 8.8 percent in 1990–96.[32]

In the first months of 1998, price riots exploded in cities and towns throughout the archipelago. Ethnic-Chinese shopkeepers suspected of hoarding were subjected to looting. The first fatalities occurred. In Jakarta, panic buying and stockpiling emptied supermarket shelves. And students in different parts of the country began demonstrations that would continue off and on through, and beyond, Suharto's resignation in May. If the crisis had become a danger to the livelihoods of millions of Indonesians, if the most urgent priority therefore was on making necessities widely available and affordable to reduce mass suffering, and if Bulog's track record in this regard was at least adequate, one could ask: Why revamp the agency precisely when its services were most badly required?

Reformers could reply that it was precisely by deregulating Bulog and opening its markets to competition that prices of basic necessities could be lowered, insofar as the agency's monopoly had kept them artificially high. But "replenishers"—those wanting above all to make necessities again widely available and affordable—could answer this argument by noting the lack of alternatives to Bulog. The country's cooperatives were weak, corrupt, and no less subject to manipulation by the state. As for profit-seeking private firms, with credit already drying up, where would they find the capital to enter mass markets in basic commodities in the middle of a runaway crisis, especially knowing that the state expected them to sell at the lowest possible price?

Nor was the record of reform in less frenzied times encouraging. As Borsuk recalls, when monopoly licenses to import key materials had been cancelled in the past, dislodging the president's relatives or friends from upstream control, the same rent-seekers had tended to reappear downstream with fresh privileges. In the midst of an ordeal demanding simultaneous attention to many fronts, could the Fund stop that from happening again?

The debate over Bulog among New Order advisers, and between them and the IMF, paralleled disagreement about how to resolve the larger crisis. Especially early on, when the rupiah's troubles could still be depicted as a monetary fiasco that might largely spare the real economy, most of the technocrats and, above all,

---

32. Henderson, *Asia Falling,* p. 204 [November 1997]; "Economic Indicators," *FEER,* 4 June 1998, p. 76 [early 1998]; *World Development Indicators 1998* (Washington, DC: World Bank, 1998), p. 231 [1990–96].

the IMF saw the crisis as an opportunity to unshackle Indonesian markets from collusion, corruption, and nepotism (KKN). These reformers looked to the curative power of austerity. In contrast, just as they would later emphasize restocking food supplies, replenishers wanted above all to restore the supply of affordable foreign exchange. They believed in the curative power of liquidity.

The scarcer dollars became in rupiah terms, the more the ranks of the replenishers grew. Mounting danger and damage to the real economy reinforced the opinion of this group—some technocrats, many "nationalists," most credit-starved entrepreneurs, the first children, and above all Suharto himself—that the highest priority should be given not to reforming markets but to rescuing the rupiah. Its shrinkage against the dollar somehow had to be slowed, stopped, and reversed, in order to replenish the dried-up supply of capital and credit. (Early in the crisis the government had raised interest rates, which remained in late November 1998 among the highest in the world.)[33] Among the replenishers were economic "nationalists," credit-hungry businesspeople, some of the younger and more politically minded technocrats, and increasingly vocal critics of the IMF outside Indonesia such as Steve Hanke and Jeffrey Sachs, the latter a policy economist at Harvard University.

Shutting the Banks

Each of the two camps had a powerful argument on its side. The replenishers could point to the destructive consequences of the IMF's early insistence on reform by austerity. In Jakarta in October and November 1997 the Fund had pressed the government to keep interest rates high and cut public spending enough to achieve a budget surplus equal to one percent of GDP. Critics later claimed that such advice tipped what could have been a temporary—because unjustified—loss of confidence in the rupiah into a full-scale recession. The Fund had also wanted to shut down a fifth of the country's banks.[34] How and to what effect the Fund's desire was carried out bear more than cursory attention.

On the heels of its agreement of 31 October 1997 with the IMF, the government issued a surprise announcement that sixteen small, private banks would be closed, including several with links to the president's family and friends. To prevent a panic, the public was told that depositors with accounts of less than Rp 20 million (roughly $6,500 at the exchange rate then in effect) would be able to recover their money from one of three state banks beginning on 13 November. Ninety-four percent of all deposits in the closed facilities were of this size—and

---

33. Over a six-month period from late May 1998, interest rates declined only slightly, from 60 to 50 percent. "Economic Indicators," *FEER,* 4 June 1998, p. 76; "Emerging-Market Indicators," *The Economist,* 5 December 1998, p. 122.

34. Reportedly the Fund urged the closing of 42 of the least viable of the 222 banks in Indonesia at the time. Mann, *Economic Crisis,* p. 52.

therefore, guaranteed.[35] To depositors with larger accounts, the government held out the hope that their money too could be recovered, wholly or partly, from the eventual sale of the shuttered banks' assets.

Far from reassuring depositors and winning back investors, however, the closures bred alarm. The shutdowns' suddenness implied that the central bank had known, but had refused to admit, just how bad things were. And if that were so, how much more bad news about other banks was the government keeping to itself? Because the sixteen targeted entities were small, the IMF and the government may have doubted that closing them would trigger a rush of withdrawals from larger, healthier banks. But the bigger banks suddenly became reluctant to lend to any of the smaller ones for fear that among the latter, many more than sixteen might be too ill to save. And depositors went further, rushing to pull their savings from all private banks, large or small.

To retain depositors, the private banks raised already high interest rates higher, which further choked off credit. To stop the frenzy, the government promised that no more banks would be closed. But that assurance directly contradicted the reformist intentions of the IMF. To put it mildly, the Fund's effort to "help" Indonesia had not begun well. It might even have turned a problem into an emergency. The Fund itself later admitted that the early November closures had been maladroit. And in the course of its many consecutive agreements with Indonesian authorities—three prior to Suharto's exit, more thereafter—the Fund did shift its priorities away from austerity and toward liquidity, as if having mended its earlier ways.[36]

But reformers had replies: Strong medicine had been needed. It had taken time to work, but it had worked, and more rapidly than many expected. By November 1998, apparently satisfied with the pace of reform, the Fund had settled down to drip-feeding the economy—nearly a billion dollars every month. Inflation had been at least temporarily slashed, and the rupiah seemed to have stabilized, albeit at a value—7,500 to the dollar—roughly three times weaker than in July 1997. Among East Asian countries with convertible currencies, Indonesia still had the worst-performing bourse, but by a less embarrassing margin. Perhaps the economy had turned the corner.

But had it? Pessimists thought not. They pointed to continuing economic uncertainty and political unrest. And even if things were improving, it was not clear

---

35. Mann, *Economic Crisis,* p. 53.
36. These documents were of various kinds, including memoranda and letters of intent. In addition to those on 31 October 1997 and 15 January and 10 April 1998, discussed above, a memorandum on 24 June took into account the transfer of power and the economic costs of the May riots. A supplementary memorandum on 29 July revised macroeconomic targets and timing and addressed the need for a social safety net. Letters of intent on 11 September, 19 October, and 13 November, respectively, focused mainly on rice, dealt with banking and corporate debt, and expressed optimism that the economy might finally have begun to recover.

how much of that trend reflected IMF medicine rather than other factors, including the competitiveness of Indonesian exports, boosted by devaluation, and the strength of overseas markets, including the still expanding American economy.

There was another, more machiavellian argument available to the reformers for use in defending what they had done. They could accept the replenishers' critique as an economic proposition, that more liquidity and less austerity would have allowed the economy to land more softly and take off again sooner, while rejecting liquidity as a strategy on moral and political grounds. For decades Suharto had delivered economic growth. He had used that success to justify his corrupt, rapacious, and authoritarian rule. Why stop a recession if it could bring him down? Why restart growth just in time for him to bask in it? He would have used it to rewarrant and reextend his rule, including its venality and repression. Recovery was fine—but whose?

The IMF is not in the habit of claiming to have overthrown those who ask it for help. Nor do I believe that it intended to, or did, overturn Suharto. In a widely circulated photograph taken on 15 January, Michel Camdessus could be seen standing with his arms crossed, looking down at Suharto while the Indonesian president bent over to sign the second of his government's agreements with the Fund. But Indonesians with whom I spoke in Jakarta at the time did not draw from this image the lesson that Suharto would have to go. They saw the picture in broader terms: By appearing to lord it over Suharto, the IMF chief was lording it over Indonesia—the way a Dutch governor-general might have earlier in the century. The photograph did not strengthen Suharto's position. On the contrary, it made him look craven. But the nationalist tone of the reaction to it signaled the risk of carrying such an outside-in explanation of Suharto's exit too far.

On 4 May another event occurred that could be cited, in retrospect, as linking austerity-promoting IMF reform to Suharto's political demise. On that day the government announced cuts in fuel and electricity subsidies. Price hikes ensued for gasoline and kerosene, suddenly making public transport and heating for cooking costlier. Protests by students and workers quickly followed, notably in Medan, North Sumatra, where demonstrations led to violent anti-Chinese riots.

Antigovernment and anti-Chinese disturbances already having raised political temperatures around the country, the timing of the cuts could not have been worse from Suharto's standpoint. Apparently, however, the Fund did not decide their timing. Suharto did. Indeed, he felt confident enough of his position to fly to Cairo five days later. But the cuts had infuriated not only students, but also the poor and the unemployed, including the mobs whose depradations in Jakarta on 13–14 May brought the president back to Jakarta to face the consequences of his policy.

The IMF had inclined Suharto to cut the energy subsidies. But he had taken the step himself. On 15 May, his first day back in the capital, he cancelled the cuts. But that did not stop the momentum against him.

Accounting for Exit

The best way to understand the diverse sources of Suharto's resignation is not to choose between them, but to distinguish their interactions and effects. Sometime toward midnight on 20 May, the president decided to resign. We cannot dismiss his own agency in the matter, as if by then circumstances had made quitting inevitable, and therefore trivial. He could have attempted to crush his enemies. He could have tried, for example, to trade Prabowo's promotion for the use of the latter's troops against the students, replaying in Jakarta the Tiananmen Square massacre in Beijing in 1989. And the actual manner of Suharto's exit, which he chose, was not trivial at all. By maximizing continuity within change, the transfer on 21 May left the country squarely within the ambit of his legacy, ruled not by one of his enemies, but by Habibie, a former acolyte.

Sitting in his Jakarta home at year's end, Suharto had reason to worry that an investigation of his wealth and behavior in office might still deprive him of the safe retirement he sought. He may have been disquieted to learn of the detention, in London, of another ex-president, Augusto Pinochet Ugarte, accused of responsibility in the deaths of more than three thousand Chileans. At the time of Suharto's ascent in the 1960s, many more had died. Nevertheless, he had not been arrested, or been driven into a risky exile. Wiranto, true to his promise, had kept student demonstrators a safe distance from his house. And at least, by resigning, Suharto had avoided the humiliation of being outmaneuvered and sidelined by his successor—the fate that he himself had inflicted on Sukarno thirty years before.

Bottom-up pressures were critical, especially those generated by the students. The students could claim to be the conscience of the nation. And while they disagreed about a lot, they could and did agree that Suharto had to go. "REFORMASI," the word stamped on their headbands, was an abstraction. It implied a potentially endless process as much as it did a finite goal. By centering their protests on Suharto, the students kept their diverse ranks united, their movement focused, and their goal feasible. Whatever else the president could or could not do, he could always quit.

Simply asking Suharto to leave may seem a curiously modest demand for the students to have made, compared with the revolutionary campaign for structural transformation that they might have launched. It should be remembered, however, that censorship during the New Order was geared to preventing and punishing criticism of the president above all. Abstractions, Marxist ones aside, were considered much less harmful. In this context, denouncing the president was brave.

Violence, unfortunately, mattered a lot. If the economic crisis demolished the New Order's promise of development, urban rioters sent its other hallmark, order, up in flames. And in doing so, both students and mobs weakened support for the president high up in his own regime, shaking the confidence of his collaborators enough to prepare and unleash disavowals from the top down. The clearest illustration of this effect was Harmoko, his house in Solo destroyed, turning against the president at last, and, at the very end, the ministers responsible for the economy, who refused further service after watching it collapse. Apart from students and the underclass, of course, bottom-up pressures also came from other quarters, including workers, Muslims, journalists, NGOs, and members of the culture of creative expression charted by Hooker in this book.

As for the factors that worked from the outside in, they affected the economic crisis in differing ways and to varying degrees without ever becoming its primary cause. That cause was excessive domestic private-sector debt, coupled with panic by domestic actors: debtors buying dollars; savers withdrawing deposits; buyers emptying shelves; and wealthy ethnic-Chinese moving their capital offshore, if not themselves as well—all of them acting fast, while they thought they still could. In this busy context, foreign arbitragers mattered somewhat, but not much.

The IMF mattered more. Replenishers were right to fault its initially relentless attention to reform as overdone. At first, the Fund behaved as if it did not understand that this was mainly a crisis of the private sector, not a case of official profligacy along the lines of earlier emergencies, driven by public debt, in Latin America. An organization of and for governments, the Fund was not mandated to deal with private firms. And yet it could recommend that the Indonesian government close down dozens of ailing private banks, notwithstanding the panic this might produce—and which the closing of sixteen such facilities did produce, in November, on a major scale. Had Fund personnel focused more on resuscitating the rupiah, they might have been led to consider ways of working out the private debts that were keeping it down. Had they been more sensitive to the potential for panic, they might have considered first putting in place mechanisms for restructuring and resolution, before trying to board up banks.

But what if successful economic reform had wound up prolonging in power a man renowned for standing in the way of meaningful political reform? This question makes no sense if Suharto's mid-May exit and what led up to it were inevitable—foreordained to happen when and how they did. But among the many roads not taken, surely there were some that could have been.

What if Sadli's Law had worked again? What if the IMF had not been called in? What if the sixteen banks had not been so precipitously closed? What if the Fund had given the highest priority to stabilizing the rupiah, performing triage on the banks, and working out foreign private debt? What if a currency board had been tried? What if the fuel-price subsidies had been left in place? What if Suharto had not flown to Cairo? What if the Trisakti students had not been shot? What effect would that have had on the student protests? Might the violence of mid-May then not have occurred? And what combination of these and other alternative events would it have taken to leave Suharto in power?

Three arguments from the premise of inevitability might be made in reply:

First and most narrowly, by his own behavior, Suharto already had doomed his presidency. After decades of repression, his comeuppance had to come. But this claim rests less on evidence than on a need to believe in justice. Not all dictatorships are programmed to self-destruct. In Havana in 1999 Fidel Castro was still fending off the future. Despite Tiananmen, Deng Xiaoping died in bed. If Suharto's hold on power was doomed, why did it last so long?

The answer cannot be sought merely in the iron quality of the president's fist. Much of the credit must go to what amounted to "Suharto's Law": If you open and grow the economy, people will not mind a closed and stunted polity. This was never fully true. Some people did mind, from the beginning, and their numbers grew. But it took them three decades to gather enough momentum to end his rule, not only because of repression but also because the growing economy made political opposition less attractive, and easier for the regime to coopt. Indeed, when the president's tenure finally did end, there was a sense in which Suharto's Law, or at any rate its necessary corollary, had been vindicated after all: If you shrink the economy, people will mind an also stunted polity.

A characteristically American argument from inevitability might be called "Clinton's Law": Closed polities cannot survive open markets. But although Indonesia opened its capital account in 1970, much earlier than its neighbors, democracy did not follow. Perhaps one can rescue Clinton's Law by claiming that markets under Suharto were freed only enough to coopt his opposition, and not enough to give it the resources and motivation to bring him down. But then proponents of Clinton's Law must acknowledge its contingent character: that by manipulating markets, while still providing growth, an authoritarian leader can postpone his rendezvous with democracy. And if there are circumstances under which Suharto's Law can trump Clinton's, and Clinton's override Suharto's, neither is truly a law at all. Perhaps we should resolve the conflict by crediting Suharto's proposition as plausible in the short run, with Clinton's holding up in the long. But the New Order lasted more than three decades—not exactly a short run.

A third and final inevitability imbues the laws of the economists who argue that you cannot keep an open capital account, manage the exchange rate, and set interest rates all at the same time. But in relation to Indonesia this law does not even deserve a name, since Suharto violated it so successfully for so long. Perhaps he did so in ways that make the New Order an unfair test of its validity. But to acknowledge that would again mean rescuing an abstraction at the expense of its power to explain specifics.

Many things together brought Suharto down, his own actions not least among them. But as a matter of preconditioning or context, the most important of these was the economic crisis in all its severity and implications. Had it not occurred, Suharto might have survived, at least for a time. And that brings me back one last time to the role of the IMF. If, in years to come, Indonesians can say to themselves with confidence that they are better off without Suharto than they ever were beneath him, some of them may in retrospect appreciate the insensitivity of the Fund's insistence on reform, while continuing to regret the human costs of the crisis to which that insistence contributed.

It is hard to imagine that austerity-seeking international bankers, resignation-demanding Indonesian students, the mobs who charred parts of Jakarta, and the collaborators who jumped ship to avoid going down, could have had anything in common. They did. All of them treated the crisis as an opportunity, and thereby helped to change it into a danger that Suharto came to believe he could not escape without leaving his presidency behind.

Habibie Schedules Reform

Over more than thirty years, the sheer strength of Suharto's position had turned into its weakness: The president's unaccountability had hardened into isolation. In contrast, in the first six months of his own presidency, B.J. Habibie defied his critics' predictions and advice—that he would fail, that he should quit—by turning his weakness into a kind of strength. Being seen as a merely transitional figure allowed him to claim the transition as his specialty, and make it more than mere. For he knew that just as the unraveling of the economy in 1997–98 had proven fatal to one long-lasting regime, so would the nature and longevity of the next one be determined by his success in reforming the polity in 1998–99.

But what, in the months following Suharto's resignation, did *reformasi* mean? Its prescriptions may be clustered and listed very roughly in order from the most to the least popular: (a) institute the rule of law; end collusion, corruption, and nepotism (KKN); hold free and fair elections; and limit presidents to serving no more than two five-year terms; (b) make Suharto legally accountable for the corruption and repression associated with his rule; terminate the political role of the armed forces; and assure the full autonomy of all the regions; (c) make Habibie resign and cede power to an independent presidium or committee that would accomplish clusters (a) and (b); (d) rewrite the constitution to make Indonesia a federal state; and (e) free East Timor. Again roughly speaking, from May to November, Habibie's answers to these clusters of demands were, respectively, (a) yes; (b) maybe; and (c) through (e) no.

I am not suggesting that Habibie did only what was popular, and did it simply to increase his own popularity. But it suited him and his weakness—his "high negatives" from long association with Suharto—to seek legitimacy wherever he could find it. He found it in promising, scheduling, and designing the accountability that Indonesians had been denied for so long. True, in a way, to his original vocation, Habibie became a political engineer.

Particularly valuable to him, if not also to Indonesia, was his early initiative in scheduling political reforms. A timetable suited his vulnerable position well: It was useful without being presumptuous—stating when decisions would occur, not what they would be. By placing procedure first, before content, it encouraged all those who wished to influence reform and run for office, including Habibie's many opponents, to believe that they could do so. By negotiating the schedule with the leaders of the DPR and the MPR, including Harmoko (still chair of both bodies), and by going to the parliament building to do so, Habibie signaled his deference to representative institutions. Never mind that Harmoko had obligingly renewed Suharto's presidency just two months before; that, thanks to Suharto, the DPR and the MPR were not really representative; and that Habibie probably could not have acted unilaterally in the matter anyway.

The upshot was a timetable calling for a special session of the existing assembly (Sidang Istimewa Majelis Permusyawaratan Rakyat, or MPR-SI) to be convened in December 1998 to mandate a fresh election to be held in May 1999 under new laws, which the existing DPR would adopt, making the balloting truly free and fair. The MPR thus constituted would meet in December 1999 to elect the next Indonesian president and vice president, whose inauguration would coincide with the dawn of a new millennium.

Habibie's critics found the last touch too creative. On 19 May 1998, Suharto had said he would not seek the presidency again. Habibie had made no such promise. As of November, he still had not. His critics feared that, at best, the new president wanted to prolong his term to the end of the century. At worst, they suspected him of trying to obtain six months (June–December 1999) in which to use his position as president to manipulate the MPR into enabling him to succeed himself.

Nevertheless, with minor changes, President Habibie's timetable took hold. The MPR-SI met as planned in mid-November 1998. A few weeks later, following another consultation with the president inside the parliament building, Harmoko announced an only slightly revised schedule: a national election on 7 June 1999, and a meeting of the resulting MPR in October and November to choose a president and vice president, who would be inaugurated on 10 November 1999, less than two months earlier than previously scheduled. Whether even this revised schedule would be kept or not, of course, remained to be seen.

From the onset of his administration, responding to the demand for reform, Habibie moved rapidly on other fronts as well. He relaxed restrictions on expression, more than doubling the number of publishing permits and allowing media criticism to flourish. He released a number of high-profile political prisoners, although the East Timorese resistance leader Xanana Gusmao was not among them. Several of these ex-detainees soon began organizing against the president. Indeed, they were encouraged to do so by his announcement that henceforth anyone could organize a (noncommunist) political party—a decision that scrapped the New Order's ban on political organizing outside Golkar and the recognized "opposition" parties, PPP and PDI.

Around the country, new parties quickly formed, at least on paper. In November 1998 the DPR had not yet decided what criteria they would have to meet in order to compete in the 1999 election, yet by the end of that month the Department of Home Affairs had taken note of more than a hundred such organizations. There were parties for all kinds of groups: religious, ethnic, regional, occupational. Parties with more or less feminist agendas took up the issues raised in this book by Kathryn Robinson in her chapter. Parties concerned with ethnicity in business debated the issues discussed by Habir in his. There was even a party for older people, and a more or less tongue-in-cheek party for artists and comics.

On 13 November, the MPRI-SI authorized holding a national legislative election in May or June 1999, to be organized by an independent committee including representatives from political parties and nongovernmental organizations in addition to the government. The MPR-SI also limited presidents and vice presidents to two five-year terms; reduced presidential access to emergency powers; made it easier to amend the constitution; halted compulsory indoctrination into Pancasila; and promised that Indonesia would ratify and enforce all UN human rights conventions.

Meeting separately, the DPR took up draft legislation on election procedures, political parties, and the composition of representative institutions. The drafts raised many controversial issues.

One such issue concerned the nature of the electoral system to be put in place. Voters in New Order elections had been asked to choose between Golkar, PPP, and PDI, not between individual candidates, in a system of proportional representation in multiple-member districts corresponding to existing administrative units. Some reformers wanted to set aside some legislative seats in single-member districts. The electorate would fill such seats by voting not just for a party symbol but for the party's candidate, by name. This reform, it was said, would decrease the distance between parties and constituencies, give voters more control over their representation, and thus ensure a more accountable democracy. Some national-level politicians at party headquarters in Jakarta, on the other hand, preferred the old system for this same reason, reluctant as they were to relinquish power to their counterparts in the regions. Still others argued from convenience, that redrawing constituency boundaries would be too difficult in the limited time remaining before election day on 7 June.

Reformists lost this battle to the politicians. Single-member districts were not instituted after all, reducing the potential for an electoral decentralization of power. This outcome was consonant with the cautiously skeptical view of decentralization expressed by Malley in his chapter.

Parties and Mobs

As to who would win the election in June 1999, if Habibie's schedule could be followed, that was not clear at all. What did seem clear was that, with so many prospective contenders to split the vote, no single party was likely to win, in its own right, an absolute majority of seats in the DPR, let alone in the larger MPR.

And that implied a possibly unstable politics of making and breaking coalitions in the MPR, where the new president and vice president would be elected.

Already in November there were several political parties worth watching. One of these was led by Sukarno's daughter, Megawati Sukarnoputri. The regime had engineered her removal from the chairmanship of PDI in 1996. Her breakaway party, the Struggle PDI (Partai Demokrasi Indonesia Perjuangan, or PDI-P), had gone beyond opposing PDI and contesting her ouster to become a nationally organized "red and white" contender with a good chance of doing well. But few observers expected Megawati's movement to gain a majority of seats in the DPR, let alone in the larger MPR. And some criticized her for what they saw, fairly or not, as her passivity in the face of rapidly changing events.

In his earlier criticisms of President Suharto, Amien Rais had shown that he was anything but passive. He left his post as chair of Muhammadiyah to lead a new National Mandate Party (Partai Amanat Nasional, or PAN), and spent much of the rest of 1998 traveling the country to rally support. His background in Muhammadiyah drew him to rely on his popularity among modernist urban Muslims, and to mobilize them for PAN as much as he could. But he also knew that to gain the presidency he would have to resist being pigeonholed as sectarian, a danger heightened by some of his own past statements and associations.

Amien knew what Hefner tells us in this book: that to be an Islamist in culturally pluralist Indonesia is to risk being marginalized by the more open-minded Muslim mainstream, not to mention the fears of religious minorities. So instead of organizing just another party for Muslims, Amien tried to make PAN a "rainbow" grouping that would appeal to nationalist and populist Indonesians of differing faiths and backgrounds. This same logic of inclusion, however, made it harder for him to ally PAN with other groups, lest his proto- "rainbow" be identified within such a larger and even more diverse coalition as mainly "green"— assertively Muslim—after all.

A third serious contender was the Nation's Revival Party (Partai Kebangkitan Bangsa, or PKB), inspired by NU's Abdurrahman Wahid and led by Matori Abdul Djalil. Its problem was the opposite of PAN's. Its identification with Wahid, and his identification with secular-liberal democracy and with Megawati and her transreligious outlook, potentially limited PKB's ability to mobilize NU's large base of more traditional and rural followers of Islam—many of them "lighter green" in outlook than the modernists, but Muslims all the same.

Effectively blind and in a wheelchair from the effects of a stroke, Wahid was an unlikely candidate to run the country. Hence a coalition between his PKB and Megawati's PDI-P was more likely to serve her presidential chances than his. Wahid welcomed such an outcome—he distrusted Amien Rais—but some members of NU did not want the organization used in this way. By November, various factions within NU had launched their own political parties.

One NU figure, Hamzah Haz, even wound up leading the holdover "opposition" PPP. Hoping to refashion itself from a fixture of the New Order into something more independent, PPP planned to redeploy as its campaign symbol a picture of the *ka'bah,* the stone structure in Mecca that Muslim pilgrims circumambulate. (Suharto had banned the PPP's use of the *ka'bah* on the grounds that the political use of religious symbols could provoke disorder.)

Many other groupings of Muslims sprang up in the period of decompression that followed Suharto's resignation. They included, for example, a somewhat "deep green"—Islamist—Moon and Star Party (Partai Bulan Bintang) of modernist Muslims; a Justice Party (Partai Keadilan) of Muslim student activists; a modernist Islamic Community Party (Partai Ummat Islam) based in Sumatra; and a New Masyumi (Masyumi Baru) claiming to continue the interrupted history of the original Masyumi, banned since 1960 as an ostensible threat to Sukarno's and then Suharto's regime.

But if the politicking was novel, the violence was not. As noted at the outset of this essay, on 13 November, while the MPR delegates made decisions that appeared to democratize the country, in the streets outside, student protests against Habibie and the MPR led, once again, to shootings and riots. Student fatalities at Atma Jaya Catholic University exceeded the death toll at Trisakti University six months before. Yet Habibie, unlike Suharto, did not fall.

That antigovernment students could not repeat in November what they had achieved in May reflected how much things had changed. Habibie's timetable had gained general support. The students' action in seeking to disrupt the MPR could be portrayed as an effort not to speed but to derail the process of democratization. This view appealed, of course, to pro-Habibie elements, including "green" Muslims who hoped that elections would enable them to build a political majority. But it also resonated with those members of the middle class who felt frightened and exhausted at the prospect of endless violence and unrest.

Habibie himself tried to take advantage of the situation by calling in several of his more vocal opponents, including retired military officers who had called for his replacement by a presidium. They and their group, the National Front (Barisan Nasional), wanted him and Suharto tried for stealing public funds and abusing human rights. The accusations had been issued on 12 November, the day before the protests and deaths at Atma Jaya. Yet it was improbable that these retired officers, who sympathized with the students, would have had a hand in shooting them. Nor were the accusations uniquely provocative; among the students, lambasting Suharto and Habibie already had become routine. One could even wonder whether Habibie might be reverting to his old mentor's tactics—resorting to intimidation, Suharto-style.

The Atma Jaya shootings further stigmatized and demoralized the armed forces. Wiranto took out newspaper ads offering condolences and promised investigations to assign responsibility. But the students who had hoped to use the MPR's convening to topple Habibie failed to do so. Indeed, the students' own ranks were divided between radical and moderate groups.

There was more violence to come. On 22 November, a Sunday, in northern

Jakarta, reacting to reports that Christians had broken windows in a local mosque, Muslim youths attacked churches and slaughtered thirteen Christians. Some of the victims belonged to ethnic groups on the outer islands. On 30 November in Kupang on the west coast of Timor, in the Christian-majority province of East Nusatenggara, Muslim-Christian tensions flared into riots that led to the burning of local mosques. Soon after, in retaliation, Muslim mobs torched churches in Sulawesi.

Muslim and Christian leaders deplored the violence and urged calm. But they could not dispel the specter of further bloodshed along religious, ethnic, and economic lines. And one could picture Suharto in his living room on Cendana Street thinking, "I told you so." Had he been more tolerant of democracy, such cleavages might have grown less deadly as people gained experience in handling them more responsibly. But that argument offered small comfort to Indonesians appalled by what their country seemed to be disintegrating into. "The government is losing control," Wahid despaired. "We may not make it to the election."[37]

Democracy?

Among the many Indonesians who badly wanted their country to become at long last a successfully functioning democracy, some worried that this goal, finally within reach, could fall victim to the rush to achieve it. These Indonesians feared that differences of religion, ethnicity, region, and class were being turned into battlefronts of political identity and competition.

This fear harked back to the experiment with parliamentary democracy in the 1950s discussed by Cribb, Liddle, and Malley in this book. Many factors had combined to ruin that experiment. But more than a few Indonesians, including senior military officers, still associated that failure with excessive freedom— freedom as license to engage in conflicts and rebellions—rather than with, for example, the unwillingness of Sukarno and the military itself to give democracy a chance.

Nevertheless, spiraling violence did not breed sentiment for armed intervention to curtail Indonesia's second experiment with democracy. There were several reasons for this. Having itself been implicated in causing violence, the army's posture was defensive, not offensive. Its officers were preoccupied with introspection, not expansion. Democracy was being planned, but had not yet begun, making it easier to blame the outrages in the streets on Suharto's New Order— the violence equivalent to steam exploding from a pressure cooker whose lid had only just been lifted—or on the continuing economic crisis. And notwithstanding the conspiracy theories clogging rumor circuits in Jakarta, the consensus for

---

37. As quoted by José Manuel Tesoro, "Ceaseless Maneuvering," *Asiaweek* [Hong Kong] via <SEASIA-L@LIST.MSU.EDU>, 13 December 1998.

reformasi was real, deep, and widespread enough to cause any officer to think more than twice before acting in a way that could be seen as trying to block the process.

Then again, given Habibie's timetable and whatever lay beyond, it was still early days. In the run-up to the election, new rivalries would be opened and old ones intensified, inviting further violence. And the more shredded by such violence the social fabric became, the larger the constituency of Indonesians wanting order would grow, and the higher the likelihood that civilian or military authorities, or both, would take steps to stop the juggernaut—however much such measures might be denounced by radical students as a restoration of repression.

Would such a sequence of events—disintegration spawning reaction—wind up reviving ABRI's "dual function" just as that license to intervene was about to be phased out? Conceivably. But momentum was still running in the other direction. At its special session in November 1998 the MPR did agree to continue the practice of appointing ABRI members to the DPR and the DPRDs. But the assembly also ruled that the number of such appointees would be incrementally reduced. The ABRI leaders accepted this directive on the understanding that the process of drawing down such representation would be stretched out over six years. On the other hand, as with Habibie's electoral timetable, this one, too, was subject to change.

The November MPR also specified that "efforts to combat corruption, collusion, and nepotism must be undertaken resolutely with regard to anyone—officials, former officials, the families and cronies, as well as private firms/ conglomerates, *including former President Soeharto*."[38] In Jakarta coffee shops, this prospect inspired many scenarios. According to one of the more inventive: Unable to prevent legal proceedings against his former boss, Habibie would go to Suharto to ask the ex-president to let himself be tried and sentenced, on the secret understanding that Habibie, in his capacity as president, would immediately pardon him.

Indonesians also worried that Suharto might be able to protect himself from prosecution, at least to any vigorous degree, by discreetly channeling portions of his family's still considerable wealth to preferred candidates in the coming competition for political power, possibly in return for assurances of future immunity. Were that to happen, it would be ironic: "crony capitalism" under noisy attack, "crony democracy" quietly underway.

One could also wonder whether efforts to end "crony capitalism" itself might turn out merely to reduce the cronies' average size. The MPR in mid-November required the government to discourage the concentration of assets in the hands of conglomerates, and to encourage economic democracy by giving opportunities

---

38. "Ketetapan Majelis Permusyawaratan Rakyat Republik Indonesia Nomor XI/MPR/ 1998" ["Republic of Indonesia People's Consultative Assembly Decision No. XI/MPR/ 1998"], Jakarta, 13 November 1998; italics mine. The delegates added an acknowledgment of the principle of presumed innocence and basic human rights.

and incentives, including top priority in the extension of credit, to cooperatives and small-and-medium-sized enterprises (SMEs). This directive did not mention rent-seeking, race, or politics, but potentially it implicated all three.

In November, a qualified cooperative could borrow money at a special government-subsidized rate of interest roughly three times lower than the commercial rate available to depositors in cash-hungry private banks. Money borrowed on such advantageous terms and then placed in such a bank yielded handsome rents. In theory these rents could finance income-producing activities by the co-operatives. Or they could line the pockets of cooperative leaders and their patrons higher up, especially since co-ops were not expected to turn a profit the way a private firm would be.

The rhetoric of helping cooperatives and SMEs had a racial dimension as well. Helping them was taken to mean helping to boost *pribumi* participation in the economy, in the hope of lessening the hegemony of ethnic-Chinese conglomerates. But to generate self-sustaining productive activity, such assistance would have to be transparently allocated to avoid suspicion of favoritism, and used to prepare its beneficiaries for success in market competition rather than for extended dependence on the state. Would these and other necessary conditions be met? Too often in the past they had not been, as Habir shows in his discussion of the failed policy of building *pribumi* "fortresses" in the 1950s.

Finally, one could wonder how much of the money—Rp 10 trillion or $1.3 billion at November's rate—being funneled into cooperatives by the minister in charge of helping them, Adi Sasono, was being used, and how much more would be used, for political ends. In a still badly damaged economy, with resources scarce and a key national poll in prospect, there was more than a minor chance that the MPR's mandate to give economic "incentives" to cooperatives and smaller-scale enterprises might be taken to mean also giving them incentives to return the favor by voting for a particular party. Suharto had used the civil service, in cities, towns, and villages throughout the islands, to deliver the votes that he wanted. Would Sasono enlist the nationwide network of thousands of cooperatives to the same end?

I asked at the start of this chapter: Was Suharto's New Order really finished? Would Habibie's Reform Order achieve reform? The New Order was over in the sense that a return to power by its founder seemed inconceivable. But if that regime had amounted to more than just one man, if it had been a set of institutions, a cohort of officials, and a way of doing business, these were still in place. Democratizing Indonesia meant trying to dismantle a system of fear and favor, deference and influence, talent and venality, by turning its own elements against it—elements that for three decades had been used to entrench it.

Repressive though it was, the New Order had delivered, with qualifications and exceptions, on its two main promises, development and stability. The costs had been high in lives lost and rights abridged. And the future was, as always, obscure. But under Habibie, the country was neither developing nor stable, and people were being hurt, even killed, in strife that an election seemed destined to make more common, not less.

In November of 1997, the opportunity to reform had bred the danger of chaos. Closing banks to stop "crony capitalism" had triggered panic. In November 1998, the danger of chaos threatened to foil the opportunity for reform. If democratization meant dispersing power, disintegration was an excuse to concentrate it.

One could hardly blame idealistic students for creating this dilemma. At Trisakti and Atma Jaya, they were not the ones with guns. And yet it was possible to imagine future analysts looking back on the crisis of 1997–98, and the vortex of opportunity and danger that it was, and asking whether somehow the perfect— *reformasi total*—had become the enemy of the good. Or would the blame for failure be pinned on Habibie's ambition, or on the brutality of the army and the police, or on some other factor as yet uncovered in November 1998?

Or was the premise of failure too pessimistic? Perhaps the economy would recover and the violence recede in time for this and future elections to be held successfully, free and fair, permitting the Reform Order to implement both parts of its name.

As the next and last chapter will briefly relate, reasonably democratic and remarkably peaceful elections were in fact held in June 1999. The pessimism of many observers was proven wrong. But additional challenges awaited the polity and the economy alike. These included the selection of a new president, the formation of a stable government, the maintenance of social order, and the implementation of political and economic reforms. Uncertainties also swirled around the referendum scheduled to take place in East Timor at the end of August. Would the territory's long-suffering people be able to choose freely between "autonomy" inside or "separation" from Indonesia—and would the losing side accept the outcome?

I first visited Indonesia in 1967. Grass grew in the cracks in the city's main thoroughfare, Thamrin Street, so few were the vehicles on it. The New Order proceeded to transform Indonesia's economy. But it took decades. It will take years if not decades for democracy to take hold, if it ever does. One may hope that it will, without believing that it must.

Chapter 11

Voting and Violence: Indonesia and East Timor in 1999

Donald K. Emmerson

Minutes after landing in Jakarta on the morning of 3 June 1999, four days before Indonesians would hold their freest elections in forty-four years, I joined what I had come to observe.

The Struggle [for] Indonesian Democracy Party (PDI-P), led by Sukarno's daughter Megawati ("Mega") Sukarnoputri, had turned the center of the capital into a field of red. Crimson headbands, shirts, and banners sported pictures of Mega, her late father, and the party symbol, a fierce black bull. Their faces painted red and black, teenagers laughed and shouted from cars, on motorbikes, and in the backs of trucks. The PDI-P handsign was everywhere: index finger to thumb in a circle symbolizing unanimous support.

These red legions slowed to a crawl the bus that was carrying me and other foreign election monitors into Jakarta from the airport. Our driver quickly obtained and displayed through his windshield a large PDI-P poster with Mega's picture on it. That laissez-passer helped get us through her festive gridlock, which continued to rev and roar outside our hotel for the rest of the day.

Four mornings later—7 June, election day—I found myself outside a polling station next to a church in a village an hour by jeep from Ambon city in Maluku province, some 2,500 kilometers northeast of Jakarta. While waiting for the voting to begin, I spoke with a PDI-P representative from the village. He too had come to monitor the balloting. Unlike the PDI-P crowds in Jakarta a few days before, however, he was in no mood to celebrate. He likened himself and his fellow villagers to an unmoving crocodile—apparently asleep but in fact alert and ready to attack if provoked.

Such a provocation had occurred weeks earlier when, as another Christian resident told the story, the village had been assaulted by machete-wielding men from two nearby Muslim communities. Caught by surprise, several villagers had died. Others had been wounded. But the village would not, I was assured, be taken unawares again. It would be awake and waiting.

On a zig-zag course between euphoria and dread, the world's fourth most populous country was lurching toward reform. Would it arrive? After three years of sporadic violence, worsened by the economic crisis of 1997–98, was the archipelago finally stabilizing? After three decades of authoritarian rule by Suharto, was the country at last democratizing? Or, despite half a century of independence, was the very existence of Indonesia at risk in the post-Suharto transition?

Clashes and fatalities had mounted in the closing years of Suharto's presidency. To recapitulate briefly: In July 1996, apparently instigated from within his regime, thugs had ousted Megawati's supporters from her party's headquarters in Jakarta, triggering deadly riots. In 1997–98 a string of lethal clashes—ethnoreligious, economic, political—had exploded around the archipelago. One of these had flared in May 1997 in Banjarmasin, South Kalimantan, in the heat of the campaign for what would be the last of Suharto's quinquennial elections, engineered as usual to assure a victory by Golkar. On that occasion, tensions between Golkar and the Development Unity Party (PPP) had been implicated in ethnoeconomic rioting that had taken more than a hundred lives. A year later, having already "disappeared" a series of dissidents, security forces had shot and killed four protesting students, setting the stage for the looting, burning, and raping that had swept Jakarta on 13–15 May 1998, precipitating Suharto's resignation and replacement by his hand-picked vice president, Habibie.

The violence spiraled into 1999, including isolated but horrific instances of Muslims killing Christians and vice versa. A few of these incidents ricocheted from place to place, as news or rumors of Muslims or Christians being murdered in one city or village triggered vengeance by coreligionists in another. Some of the parties scheduled to compete in the June elections identified themselves, wholly or partly, with Islam or Christianity.[1] Small wonder that most observers expected the balloting to be bloody.

It was not. Neither the campaign prior to the 7 June elections nor the voting itself incited violence on a significant scale. Conceivably, "morning after" emotions—embarrassment, remorse—had a quieting effect. Certainly, by mid-1999, economic conditions had grown less dire. Anger-triggering inflation, in particular, had begun to abate.

It mattered too that the novel prospect of competing on a level field had encouraged the contending parties to rate their electoral chances highly, and hence to want to cooperate in keeping order. Parties focused on winning votes and seats

---

1. *Almanak Parpol Indonesia* ([Jakarta]: [API, 1999]), pp. vi-viii, 589, 592.

had a stake in preventing the cancellation of a contest through which they hoped to gain power and influence in post-Suharto Indonesia.

Heartening though it was, the relative absence of violence on election day did not mean that underlying tensions had been resolved. At the end of that peaceful day on the island of Ambon, my Christian informants still feared attack. Fortunately, their fears were not fulfilled. But weeks later in another part of Maluku province, violence linked to religion did recur.

Islam in Moderation

In 1999 Indonesia's estimated 216 million people included roughly 190 million Muslims. No country had more. As related earlier in this book, in the 1940s and 1950s some Muslim leaders had wanted to use the state to enforce Islamic laws. To accommodate religious diversity while deflecting Islamist demands, Sukarno had proclaimed the doctrine of Pancasila, including tolerance of all monotheistic faiths. His successor, Suharto, claimed to have rescued Indonesia from matching calamities—communism on the extreme left, Islamism on the extreme right. The New Order occupied what its critics derided as the "extreme center."

Suharto destroyed and banned the Indonesian Communist Party (PKI), and required adherence to Pancasila, including religious tolerance. Under Habibie, the left did not come back. Marxism remained illegal. But religion in politics was reallowed. Although Pancasila remained the national ideology, organizations were no longer required to swear allegiance to it. The four dozen parties that contested the 1999 elections were free to base themselves on Pancasila, but they could also choose some other (non-Marxist) credo, including Islam.

In his engineered elections, Suharto tolerated but three contenders: Golkar, PPP, and the Indonesian Democracy Party (PDI). In the 1999 electoral campaign, Golkar, PDI, and Megawati's breakaway PDI-P preferred to base themselves on Pancasila. But PPP, self-identified as Muslim, chose Islam. PPP leaders took satisfaction in selecting as their party's logo the stone structure in Mecca at the hub of Muslim pilgrimage-a powerfully Islamic symbol whose partisan display Suharto had expressly forbidden.

Since the 1980s Islam had enjoyed a rising profile in Indonesia—ethically and culturally, if not politically as well. In the 1990s, with Suharto's blessing, Habibie had become an official patron of sorts for modernist Muslims who resented what they saw as the disproportionate access of Christians to positions of influence in the New Order. Conversely, some non-Muslim and nominally Muslim Indonesians worried about the possibly toxic effect of reinjecting religion into politics. Muslim-Christian clashes prior to the campaign for the 1999 elections only deepened such apprehension.

Nine of every ten Indonesians, on average, are Muslims, and democracy entails majority rule. The June poll, though far from perfect, was democratic enough to reflect the will of this majority. Yet there was no landslide for Islam. Only a fourth of the 48 parties competing on 7 June identified themselves wholly or

partly with Islam, and most of these emphasized its moral values not its obliga-
tory laws. In the national legislative election, merely 15 percent of all voters
chose any one of these twelve relatively Muslim contenders. And of this dozen,
the two most militant were among the least successful, receiving together less
than half of 1 percent of all ballots cast.

In contrast, four-fifths of all the competitors in the June poll (including all of
several small Christian parties) identified either wholly or in part with Pancasila—
and reaped, in the national parliamentary poll, the vast majority of the votes.
Provincial and district legislative results showed a comparably widespread aversion to intransigence in religion.

Certification of the results of the elections was inordinately delayed. Poll
watchers noticed many irregularities, but these were on the whole minor, and
appeared to reflect not massive skullduggery but logistical obstacles, poll worker
inexperience, and the difficulty of applying new and complex rules simultaneously
across so many islands, including the need to wait until all votes were counted at
one level before reporting the results to the next higher level. Each voter had to
pierce, and poll workers later publicly had to count, three separate ballots—for
national, provincial, and district legislatures. With 48 parties per ballot, the voter
faced, in theory, 144 choices.

Presented with such an array of alternatives, it was feared, the electorate might
spread its votes too evenly to permit a majority coalition to form. Voters instead
drastically winnowed the pack. Of the 48 contending parties, only 19 parties won
at least a single seat in the national legislature, and of these only 5 did well
enough to become major players.

Megawati's PDI-P came in first. Of the 105.8 million votes cast in the national
legislative election, her party received 33.74 percent. Golkar's 22.44 percent gave
it second place. In third place, with 12.61 percent, was the Nation's Revival
Party (PKB), associated with Abdurrahman Wahid and his tolerant understanding of Islam. The somewhat "greener" PPP came in fourth at 10.71 percent. That
left Amien Rais' National Mandate Party (PAN) in fifth place with 7.12 percent.
The 43 other parties split the remaining 9 percent of the votes.[2]

To be listed on the ballot, a party had to have established a presence in at least
half the districts in each of at least nine provinces. This requirement kept regionalist parties out of the contest. Departing from the pro-Golkar role it had tended
to play under Suharto, the military did not interfere. Nor did the electoral competition unsettle the economy. Interest rates kept trending downward. The rupiah,
its fall already broken, continued to firm. Foreign reserves rose. The Jakarta
Stock Exchange soared. Such news bolstered hope that the 1999 poll would bring
an end to violence and the start of a stable democracy.

---

2. These data were taken from *The Jakarta Post's* website on 16 August 1999; <http:/
/www.thejakartapost.com:8890/elec99.htm>.

More Trouble Ahead?

Elections are like weddings. They promise, but they do not guarantee. The June marriage of accountability and diversity in Indonesia may well prove sustainable. But many things could still could go wrong.

Nationally, turnout at the more than 300,000 polling stations around the country exceeded 90 percent—an encouraging sign. Facilitating this high level of participation was the generally peaceful atmosphere on polling day. Nevertheless, across all provinces, turnout was not uniformly high. In Aceh, one of the most troubled parts of the country, only 69 percent of registered voters exercised their choice—the lowest rate of any province.[3] Acehnese alienation from Jakarta had been stoked by revelations of atrocities committed by national troops against a long-smouldering local rebellion. Acehnese also resented the siphoning of revenue from local resources, notably natural gas, to distant Java. In certain districts where poll workers were too afraid of reprisals to administer the voting, the effort to hold the elections had to be abandoned.

Nor did higher turnouts in other restive parts of the archipelago signal a relinquishing of grievances. Papuans in Irian Jaya still resented Jakarta's capture of returns from local resources, including copper and gold. Voting day in Maluku was not a resolution but merely a suspension of the intermittent Christian-Muslim strife that had caused mounting fatalities and damage in parts of that province since January 1999. Deadly intercommunal strife flared again in that province within a matter of weeks following poll day.

In East Timor the elections amounted to a chance to answer the wrong question. Voters were not asked whether they wished to remain inside Indonesia. There were no expressly East Timorese parties among the four dozen whose logos crowded the ballot. Choosing between Jakarta-based parties within an Indonesian frame presupposed a negative answer to the key question—independence. In this sense, however free the vote in East Timor might have been, it could not have been fair. As if to make this point, proportionally more ballots were defaced by those who did go to the polls in East Timor than in any other province.

The success of elections as means of legitimation depends not only on how many people come out to vote, and how free and fair the voting is, but on what happens afterward. Counting the votes should not take too long, and not long after the results are in, the party or person with the most votes should form or lead a government.

By these measures, in 1999, Indonesia's electoral process was multiply flawed: First, it took more than a month for a final result to be officially announced. Second, the People's Consultative Assembly (MPR), the body with constitutional authority to elect a president and vice president, was not scheduled to do so for several months.

---

3. International Election Observation Mission, *Post-Election Statement No. 3* (Washington, DC: National Democratic Institute for International Affairs, 1999), Appendix I.

Third, the June balloting for the national legislature (DPR) determined the composition of only two-thirds of the 700-seat Assembly, or 462 seats. DPR members automatically hold Assembly seats as well. But the remaining 238 Assembly members were to be decided later: 135 to be chosen by provincial legislatures; 65 to be proposed by social organizations for approval by the General Election Commission; and, most controversially of all, 38 to be appointed by the armed forces from within their own ranks.

Fourth, the ratio of votes to seats favored the sparsely settled outer islands against densely populated Java. Fifth and finally, the prospect of quickly forming a new government with a decisive mandate faded as it grew clear that no party would end up occupying an absolute majority of the 462 Assembly seats that had been at stake at the polls in June. Despite winning a third of the vote, for example, Megawati's PDI-P could expect to fill, with its own representatives, only about a fifth of the Assembly seats.

As noted above, the slowness of the count was evidence less of any concerted effort to manipulate it than of the inexperience of election personnel and their priority on accuracy over speed. Nor was delay necessarily dysfunctional. The parties that did best on 7 June needed time to negotiate a stable majority in the Assembly that could elect the next president and vice president. Yet the longer these negotiations went on, at least partly out of the public eye, the more the authority of the June mandate risked being undercut, and with it the credibility of the post-Suharto transition. Observers speculated whether kingmakers striking secret deals and buying Assembly votes in July and August might manage to supersede the verdict of the voters in June.

According to the rules in effect, a party could have won in June enough votes to occupy a majority of the 462 directly elected seats in the 700-seat Assembly, and yet still lose the presidency. For this to have happened, the opponents of such a party would only have had to coax—bribe?—enough of the 238 nondirectly elected Assembly members to form a majority of all 700. In actuality, on 7 June, none of the competing parties came close to winning an absolute majority of the directly elected seats. But the resulting fluidity enlarged the chance that a minority of Assembly members, who had not been directly elected, could in the presidential race wind up tipping the balance against a plurality who had—in effect, circumventing the electorate's will.

Perfidious Golkar?

At election central in Jakarta, the earliest returns to arrive and be announced came in from the core islands of Java and Bali, where PDI-P had its strongest support. Proximity to the capital and superior telecommunications favored prompt reporting from these core islands. Later, however, results began trickling in from the less accessible and infrastructurally less equipped periphery of Indonesia, and it was there that Golkar had long been strongest.

The addition of these later-arriving votes eroded the early national lead that Megawati's party had seized, while Golkar's showing steadily improved. In early July, PDI-P's total was still running well ahead of Golkar's. But the electoral law's bias toward the late-reporting outer islands favored Golkar. Java locates three-fifths of all Indonesians but only half of the 462 directly elected Assembly seats.

Most reform-minded Indonesians did not trust Golkar. They remembered how, and for how long, its politicians had decorated Suharto's corrupt autocracy. In the eyes of more radical student leaders and activists, Golkar and Habibie were the enemy: holdovers from a heinous past who would do almost anything to bring it back. The longer the tabulation of votes dragged on, and the larger Golkar's share grew, the more suspicious such critics became that Habibie and his minions were stealing the election.

By July, it almost seemed as though, in Jakarta, the traffic in rumors outnumbered its counterpart in cars. Some said that Suharto had decided to commit all of his and his children's reportedly vast wealth to bribing the Assembly into protecting them from prosecution for corruption. According to another rumor, Golkar had already won the June poll and election officials were delaying the public count on purpose, lest news of a Golkar plurality trigger chaos. By the beginning of July, anti-Golkar radicals in Jakarta were sufficiently convinced of a Golkar conspiracy-in-progress to demand that the party be disqualified and its ballots disallowed. For these critics of the ruling party, disenfranchising the millions of voters who might have sincerely chosen it was a minor price to pay for blocking its attempt to stay in power.

Was Golkar stealing the election? Irregularities did mar the voting and the counting. On 7 June, for example, after casting (actually, piercing) his or her ballot, but before leaving the polling station, each voter was supposed to dip a finger into indelible ink to help prevent readmission. In Maluku, at the eleven mostly rural polling stations that I visited, mainly at random, on election day, poorly trained poll workers did not always confirm that the fingers of those who were about to vote were, in fact, ink-free. And some monitors worried that the ink was too easily rubbed off—though when I stained my own finger, the mark remained, despite washings, for more than a week.

But the devil was not, at least on any major scale, in these details. Nor did major problems arise in the very first counting of the ballots, scrutinized as that procedure typically was by monitors, including party representatives, and a crowd of onlookers awaiting the outcome. Golkar's effective monopoly in some of the most remote islands did create occasions for manipulation. In a few places, the party did well enough to cause its rivals to demand a recount—or even (in North Sulawesi) a revote. But it was also plausible that at some of the archipelago's more remote polling stations, villagers chose Golkar from habit or for some other innocuous reason.

Suharto's patronage had linked Golkar to his inability to prevent or mitigate the economic shocks of 1997–98, not to mention the extent to which they implicated the "crony capitalism" in which he and his family and friends had been engaged. Such guilt by association hurt the party, especially in Jakarta and other urban constituencies on Java where the economic jolts had hit people hard. But it was not a liability in those more rural or semi-urban places, including some on the outer islands, where producers of food and makers of labor-intensive products for export had benefited from the higher local prices, cheaper labor, and greatly cheapened rupiahs that the crisis had entrained.

The electoral process was more vulnerable to malfeasance at later stages, higher up the reporting chain, as allocations by party and place were totaled and forwarded to the next level. There were checks at these stages too. But they were insufficient to guarantee the exactitude of the slowly growing final count. Nevertheless, the likely deviation of announced from actual results was not great enough to invalidate the ordinal ranking of the five main parties: (1) PDI-P, (2) Golkar, (3) PKB, (4) PPP, and (5) PAN.

Making a Rainbow

Of greater concern was the anomaly that could result from the maneuvering of politicians trying to form a majority-for-president in the Assembly. Megawati and Wahid, respective leaders of the first-place secular-nationalist PDI-P and the third-place liberal-Muslim PKB, had informally agreed to cooperate. But Mega's advisers worried that her presidential hopes could be dashed by a counteralliance of Habibie's second-place Golkar with the avowedly Muslim fourth-place PPP, several other assertively Muslim parties, and recruits from the military, regional, and social blocs of seats that had not been filled by direct election at all.

Some Indonesians worried that such a two-bloc pattern, should it materialize, could reverse the moderating effects of Muslim tolerance and Islamist weakness at the polls in June. But a polarizing face-off between Megawati and Habibie was not inevitable. The fluidity of the political scene made other scenarios possible. If in trying to counterbalance Mega, for instance, Golkar tilted too far toward political Islam, secularists within the party might leave it to support her and her explicitly nonconfessional coalition. Nor could Habibie rest assured that Golkar's bloc in the Assembly would remain loyal to him, especially if, after repeated divisions of the house, his presidential candidacy still could not achieve majority support.

Like the Indonesian flag, Megawati and her PDI-P are "red and white": nationalistic; pro-Pancasila; tolerant of religious diversity and secularism; and suspicious of political Islam, especially its "darker green"—more militant—varieties. PDI-P's most influential partner, PKB, could be termed "light green": tolerantly Muslim; pro-Pancasila; and committed to democratic pluralism, including personal freedoms and amity between faiths. Following the elections, PDI-P strategists hoped to make its alliance with PKB the core of a broad majority coalition—a "rainbow"—that could elect Megawati president and stably rule the country.

But it was not clear that such a project could succeed. Efforts to slow Mega's momentum could already be discerned. In "greener" circles, doubts circulated as to how good a Muslim she was and whether Islam countenanced rule by a woman. The relative weakness of PDI-P and PKB on the outer islands, compared with Golkar and PPP, further complicated her ability to project an image as the nation's choice. So did signs of second thoughts inside PKB, whose willingness to support Megawati for president depended on Wahid's ability to deliver his party's conservative rural Muslim base, and on his own willingness to cede the presidential post to her. In August, PAN's Amien played on the latter uncertainty by trying to coax Wahid into a potentially anti-Mega coalition.

Alongside her gender, Megawati's qualifications and abilities also attracted controversy. Some analysts dismissed her as a housewife out of her depth. They pointed to her lack of political or professional experience, apart from persecution by Suharto. They regretted her silence at times of crisis when she could have bolstered her popularity by speaking out. They contrasted her limitations as an orator with her father's golden tongue, and chafed at her preference for vague rhetoric over concrete proposals. Also subject to gossip were her failure to complete higher education, and the business dealings of her third and current husband. Sometimes her critics were not even consistent, as when they faulted her for poor attendance as a member of the national legislature under Suharto, but then derided that same body as a rubber stamp.

Mega's reticence distinguished her from her rivals. Wahid gave frequent media interviews. In them he vacillated between supporting her for president and suggesting his own readiness to run. Habibie was never at a loss for words, and they could be surprising. Indonesia-watchers were amazed in January 1999 when he said that he would offer the people of East Timor full autonomy inside Indonesia, and (in effect) push them out if they turned it down. Amien, campaigning at full speed, also took specific stands on policy issues. He was willing to let East Timor go, he said, and went on to suggest that it was time to consider scrapping Indonesia's unitary republic for a federal system.

But these ideas were controversial in Indonesia. They generated buzz at the cost of backlash. For middle-class urbanites weary of ongoing conflict and displays of ambition, Megawati's vague populism, artless politics, and personal reserve may actually have seemed refreshing. And in this sense her strategy was not amateurish at all: Better to bask in the myth of her father as the great unifier of Indonesia than to risk getting into potentially divisive details about what she, as president, would or would not do.

Particularly problematic in this context was the future of East Timor. Army leaders had agreed, in principle, to a gradual disengagement of the military from politics. But they were not happy with the idea of East Timor's independence. Since invading the territory in 1975, Indonesian units had fought and taken casualties trying to keep it inside the republic. Some Indonesian officers had acquired East Timorese wives and property. Local militias had been trained and armed to resist separation—and had done so with a vengeance, terrorizing pro-independence Timorese. Because of the resulting insecurity, the United Nations Assistance Mission in East Timor (UNAMET) twice postponed implementing Habibie's offer to let the territory's people choose between autonomy within Indonesia or separation from it.

The military establishment appeared unwilling, perhaps even unable, to halt the process of national political reform. But the views of one general I interviewed, who supported reform but drew the line at East Timor's independence, reflected the integrationist sentiment of other officers as well. Habibie's sudden offer of take-it-or-leave-us autonomy had unsettled these men. They worried that the territory's loss could precipitate the unraveling of Indonesia. And they disliked Amien, in part, for his willingness to unhook the province from the republic and replace the latter with a federation.

Compared with Amien, Mega was less amenable to letting East Timor go, and that made her presidential candidacy more attractive to retired officers who favored integration. One could even see why her front-running status in the presidential race might motivate some of these men to want to keep East Timor insecure. Its insecurity could become an excuse to keep postponing the territory's self-determination until a newly inaugurated and popularly empowered Indonesian government, led by Megawati, might just decide not to allow it. On the other hand, such an outcome was bound to trigger an outcry from Western governments, which favored self-determination and on whose willingness to help rescue the economy Jakarta had come to depend.

The population of East Timor was scheduled to choose on 30 August to accept "special autonomy" (integration) within unitary Indonesia, or to reject and set in motion the territory's "separation" from Indonesia. Earlier that month Megawati traveled to East Timor to express her hope that this "popular consultation"—Jakarta did not want to call it a referendum—would result in a vote for autonomy within. She also said that as president she would honor the choice of the East Timorese. But if that choice favored separation, as many expected it to, would she go along? And even if she did, would the Assembly?

Catastrophe in Timor

The East Timorese voted on their homeland's future on 30 August 1999. I spent the previous night trying to sleep in a tent pitched on a high bluff in Tutuala at the easternmost tip of the island. I was there for the Carter Center, which had sent a team of monitors to observe the popular consultation.

The view from the bluff was spectacular, but not convincing. The climate onshore was too marked by signs of fear and violence for the scenery to seem real. I had felt the danger since arriving on the island five days before. The Carter Center had warned me and my fellow monitors not to travel after dark, lest we encounter one of the roadblocks thrown up nightly by militias bent on intimidating pro-independence Timorese. On my first afternoon in East Timor's capital, Dili, two pro-integration relatives of a driver of one of the Carter Center vehicles were slashed to death in Becora, a neighborhood whose inhabitants strongly favored separation from Indonesia. A thirteen-year-old survivor of the killings blamed them on pro-independence Timorese.

My Carter Center colleague Annette Clear of Columbia University and I were camping at Tutuala on the eve of the vote because the man in whose house we had planned to stay in Los Palos had been murdered, also by machete. He was a local notable known for his pro-independence views. The killers had splashed gasoline on his house and burned it out.

Witnesses described an apparently methodical raid by men of military build. A knowledgeable source blamed the killing on pro-integration elements, including the district chief.[1] At the funeral of our would-be host, his distraught younger sister, dressed in black, vented her misery in one continuous stream of Portuguese that no one dared interrupt. At one point, perhaps thinking that I worked for the United Nations Mission in East Timor (UNAMET), she threw herself at my feet while continuing to keen, as if I could relieve her grief. I don't recall ever feeling more powerless than I did then.

Early on the morning of polling day, on the road to Mehara where we planned to begin monitoring the vote, Clear and I passed hundreds of people walking to the polls. At the seven voting centers we visited that day, from Mehara westward to Baucau, we found thousands of Timorese patiently waiting to mark a ballot for or against autonomy (integration) inside Indonesia. UNAMET ran the balloting professionally, without obvious bias toward either side, and guaranteed the secrecy of each individual act of choice.

Of the more than 400,000 Timorese who had registered to vote—perhaps half of the territory's total population—a stunning 98.6 percent went to the often considerable trouble to cast a ballot. And of these ballots, an unmistakably large majority—78.5 percent, or almost four-fifths—rejected integration with Indonesia. Also firmly rejected, in effect, was the pro-Indonesian militias' campaign of intimidation prior to the vote.

The relative calm that had marked Indonesia's national elections on 7 June was repeated, with some exceptions, in East Timor on 30 August. On 31 August Clear and I traveled to Quelicai on the flank of Mount Malobu only to find it eerily vacant save for Indonesian security forces and militias. The people had fled for fear of reprisals. Ominous too were the five militia roadblocks that we had to negotiate that same afternoon east of Dili.

The reprisals soon came. Within twenty-four hours the militias were fully engaged in what might be termed "political cleansing": killing independence supporters, injuring them, or hounding them out of the territory. In this vicious

---

1. Interview, Los Palos, East Timor, 29 August 199.

process the militias torched or otherwise damaged a significant portion of East Timor's already scant urban infrastructure.

As the smoke plumes and the death toll rose, so did the outrage of people and governments around the world. The Indonesian authorities, who were supposed to assure the security of East Timor, were unwilling or unable to do so. Yet they refused to countenance an international force that would restore peace and order. The United States terminated all military-to-military relations with Indonesia, including aid and sales, and hinted strongly at economic sanctions if Jakarta did not stop the slaughter or allow others to do so.

On 12 September, President Habibie announced that his government would accept foreign intervention after all. By then, however, the Timorese had been subjected to nearly a week of killing, burning, and looting uncurbed and even abetted by Indonesian forces.

Indonesian complicity in this catastrophe cannot be denied. The Carter Center team saw incidents of intimidation or violence take place in full view of armed Indonesian soldiers and police, who stood by and did nothing or actually helped the perpetrators. But was this complicity limited to rogue elements within Indonesia's East Timor command? Or could responsibility be traced up through the ranks to Jakarta and, ultimately, to Armed Forces Commander Wiranto himself? (In mid-September, pending evidence to the contrary, it was less plausible that President Habibie would have masterminded the wrecking of his own proposed solution for East Timor, not to mention the ruining of Indonesian credibility abroad.)

In September, so soon after these events, it was not possible to explain them definitively. Yet I returned from East Timor skeptical of the "rogue elements" thesis that locally based Indonesian officers and units had acted without the knowledge, or with the knowledge but without the approval, of their superiors in Jakarta. Independence for the territory was anathema to the Indonesian army up and down its echelons, including high-ranking reformist officers who supported democratization and eventual civilianization for Indonesia. Letting East Timor go, they feared, could embolden other centrifugal provinces to secede as well. And that would destroy what these men were committed to defend: the territorial integrity of the nation. (Holders of this view were undeterred by the fact that East Timor had never been part of the homeland that Indonesian nationalists had claimed and wrested from the Dutch.)

The argument that rogue elements acted on their own is not without merit. Over the years of war and repression in East Timor, Jakarta's special forces and intelligence units had established a proprietary role for themselves in the territory. Indonesian battalions resident in East Timor had recruited thousands of Timorese into military and other roles. As already noted, some Indonesian officers had married Timorese and acquired property in the territory. Having fought a long and brutal campaign against independence, such people naturally feared for their own lives and livelihoods were it to come about after all. In these senses, Jakarta's forces were locally entrenched and not necessarily amenable to Wiranto's control.

Wiranto himself had reasons not to want to confront and discipline the East Timor command. In May 1998, as recounted in the previous chapter, he had fired Prabowo Subianto, a former chief of special forces (Kopassus) long active in East Timor. But instead of purging Prabowo's intra-army network of friends and allies, Wiranto chose reconciliation. The armed forces commander may also have been unwilling to discipline the Timor command for reasons of political ambition. By September he had become the most commonly mentioned candidate for the vice-presidency of Indonesia. But to be elected to that office by the MPR, he would need military support, including the votes of the thirty-eight Assembly members appointed from the armed forces. Knowing how much his fellow officers opposed Habibie's decision to hold a popular consultation, Wiranto would not readily have challenged that sentiment by overruling army hardliners bent on retaining the territory. Habibie himself had never been liked by the officer corps.

My account so far implicates Wiranto in the butchery and arson in East Timor through inaction, because of his failure to control his own men. Complementary evidence and logic, however, suggest that in addition to allowing the violence to happen, he was proactively complicit in making it happen.

The Indonesian military in September 1999 was not a warlords' affair. The army that Wiranto inherited had been streamlined and centralized by Suharto precisely to avoid intramilitary splits that might have endangered the New Order. And Wiranto had had time to establish his position. He had been in charge of the armed forces continuously since February 1998. He had served as minister of defense and security in Habibie's cabinet since May 1998, when he had turned back Prabowo's challenge to his authority. By September 1999 enough time had passed for Wiranto to have consolidated his control over the military and its policies.

The militias in East Timor had different names, and were active in different parts of the territory: Red Dragon (Naga Merah) and Thunderbolt (Halilintar) in Maliana, Red and White Iron (Besi Merah Putih) in Liquica, Thorn (Aitarak) in Dili, Legacy (Saka) in Baucau, Tim Alfa (Team Alpha) in Los Palos, and so on. Yet they all had in common the connivance of the Indonesian military, which had incubated, armed, and encouraged them to intimidate pro-independence Timorese. The militias were even represented aboveground in the United Front for Autonomy (UNIF), which campaigned, with Indonesian support, for integration in the run-up to the vote on 30 August. This intertwining of the military and the militias was not merely a local project. It reflected policies of Indonesia's high command dating back to the 1970s when Jakarta first began instigating irregular bands of young Timorese men to support its anti-independence war.

Wiranto and his advisers appear to have believed that pro-integration Timorese would either win the popular consultation by a small margin, or lose it narrowly enough to ensure that the outcome could be portrayed as indecisive—and therefore not binding on Indonesia. Such an expectation would explain why, despite mounting intimidation prior to the vote, the militias did not, by and large, disrupt the balloting itself. Possible restraint by the Indonesian army also helps to explain why none of the militias did what any of them could have: kill a few for-eigners working for UNAMET and thus stop the popular consultation from tak-ing place. As confirmed to me in conversation with a high-ranking UNAMET official, it would have taken no more than two such assassinations to cause the Mission to withdraw from the field, if not from East Timor altogether. That the militias did not take this step at least raises the possibility that they may have been under some discipline from above.

As for the violence that swept the territory following the vote, it seems to have been premeditated and coordinated. Pro-integration Timorese and their Indone-sian backers with whom I spoke on the night after the balloting vehemently ques-tioned the neutrality of UNAMET and warned that they would reject the result if it went against integration.[2] It was clear too from these conversations that my pro-Jakarta informants had been convinced by the overwhelming turnout at the polls that the balloting probably had gone strongly against them. Beyond trucu-lently rejecting independence, they did not say what they planned to do. But their intransigence was at least consonant with recourse to desperate measures. Al-ready that same day, UNIF had tried to cripple an official committee for recon-ciliation by boycotting its inaugural meeting.

Foreign intelligence reports, as these were summarized for me by reliable third parties, also contained evidence that the high army command was proactively implicated in the militias' backlash. Contingency planning among Indonesian officers may have yielded a fallback option to unleash the militias if the vote decisively favored independence. The aim of such violence may have been to render the result of the vote null and void by assuring that it could not be imple-mented—or, failing that, to cripple the newborn nation by killing its prospective leaders, or forcing them to flee, while torching and looting the physical assets such leaders would need to make independence work.

In sum: Ultimate responsibility for the catastrophe in East Timor must be assigned to the Indonesian military, not only local units but also their superiors in Jakarta, who by action or inaction inflicted, encouraged, or tolerated the vio-lence. Symbolic of the mockery of a security force that the Indonesian army in East Timor had become was the trashing and looting of the UNAMET compound in Dili by Indonesian soldiers shortly after its evacuation.

Recriminations and Backlash

The dimensions of this tragedy were massive. By mid-September, according to United Nations estimates, perhaps 7,000 Timorese had died and up to 300,000 had been displaced—out of a total population of perhaps 850,000. To the politi-cal and security crises, a humanitarian disaster had been added.

---

2. Interview with members of the East Timor People's Front (Barisan Rakyat Timor Timur), Dili, East Timor, 31 August 1999.

Recriminations were quick to come. In the agreements that governed the popular consultation, signed with Indonesia on 5 May 1999, how could the UN and Portugal have trusted Jakarta's promise to ensure the security of the process? How could the UN and Portugal have acquiesced in Jakarta's refusal to allow for the presence of an armed international force in case violence did break out? Had foreigners insisted on such a safeguard, Indonesia might not have allowed the popular consultation to take place. But thousands of lives would have been saved.

Without condoning the decision to go along with Jakarta and refrain from arming UNAMET, however, it is not hard to understand it. Habibie's January proposal to let the East Timorese express themselves on their future, and his willingness to allow the UN to administer the vote, had opened a unique window of opportunity to end the violent subjugation of the territory—a tragedy that Indonesian intransigence already had prolonged for twenty-four years.

Habibie was a weak leader whose presidency might not survive. From her initial statements on the subject, Megawati seemed less willing than he to permit East Timor's independence. The democratization of Indonesia might constrain its next government by enabling politicians to rally support for extreme nationalist gestures, including withdrawing Habibie's offer—refusing to entertain self-determination for East Timor lest other parts of the republic demanded the same right. For such reasons, diplomats in New York and Lisbon, and in Washington as well, were willing to relinquish responsibility for security in return for the chance, at last, to hold a plebiscite. It should be recalled as well that in Western capitals, in the wake of Kosovo, there was little appetite to insert troops in yet another hot spot barring a compelling imperative to do so.

Ever since the former Portuguese colony's invasion in 1975, the domestic politics of Indonesia and the struggle to end or defend Jakarta's subjugation of East Timor had run on separate tracks. East Timor was a burning issue for activist groups and political leaders around the world, but not for Indonesians. Suharto and the army kept their repression of East Timor, and its people's desire for independence, beyond the knowledge of most Indonesians.

These two tracks—politics in the republic and events in the territory—finally intersected in 1999, brought together by burgeoning press freedom in Indonesia, Suharto's replacement by Habibie, and the latter's decision, bypassing the army, to break with the status quo. East Timor became a topic on which candidates for office in Indonesia's newly democratizing polity could be expected to express opinions.

In September, after such a resounding mandate for separation from Indonesia, and with the formation of an international peace-keeping force under way to stop the killing and destruction, it seemed clear that East Timor's separation from Indonesia would become real. But how would the agony of Timorese self-determination affect the democratization of Indonesia?

Some Indonesians already had mounted a nationalist backlash against the West, replete with charges that Australians, Americans, and Portuguese were scheming to tear East Timor from the bosom of mother Indonesia. Hyperpatriots accused the West of wanting to destroy the republic. Habibie was pilloried, too, for allowing such an anti-Indonesian conspiracy to occur.

But there was also reason to believe that the hotheads would not prevail. Notwithstanding bank scandals that furthered weakened Habibie's position, the Indonesian economy was on the mend. Cooler heads knew that further recovery would require cooperation with the West and with Western-influenced institutions such as the International Monetary Fund and the World Bank. Plans for Asian participation in the peace force lessened the sting of having to relinquish East Timor to the West. And the vote for separation on 30 August was a massive reality check that only the most chauvinist and conspiratorially minded Indonesian could deny.

Democracy might well create incentives for nationalists to rail at the outside world. But it was hard to imagine the fourth most populous country democratically choosing to become an international pariah, merely for the sake of rejecting the clear desire of a small half-island to be free. The legacies of economic growth and social dynamism that my coauthors have explored in this book, and the stretching of public horizons beyond Suharto and his autocracy in 1997–98, had made Indonesians not less but more open to the world.

Indonesians by 1999 were not so malleable that they could be led to ignore that larger world, and their country's proper role within it, for the sake of a local delusion—least of all one involving a few people in a small place that the Indonesian revolution had ignored. Nor were Indonesians morally obtuse. Among the educated, who knew what was going on, many were sensitive to the plight of the Timorese, and ashamed at the evidence of atrocities committed and abetted by Indonesian hands.

The Indonesian military was another matter. Its culpability in the militias' rampage challenged the process of democratization. Political accountability could not be realized in circumstances that allowed the armed forces to operate beyond public control. Unless the commanders of the army and the police were willing and able to disarm and arrest the militias and bring them to justice, not to mention the need to bring the commanders themselves to account, Indonesia's democratization would remain subject to reversal by men with guns.

In 1999 thousands of Timorese died because the army exercised its "dual function." If that license to intervene somehow survives in Indonesia, not even an elected government will be able to claim to have instituted the rule of law. And without the rule of law, what will the country's next regime amount to but another self-serving obfuscation—from "Guided Democracy," to "Pancasila Democracy," to a third new name designed to hide the impunity of leaders and institutions?

Democratizing Indonesia

In Indonesia's complex political transition as it appeared in mid-September 1999, contingencies were plentiful and certainties scarce. One could, all the same, hazard these conclusions:

First, the growth of a kind of democracy was too far along to be entirely reversible. In 1999 Indonesians disagreed about how power should be allocated within newly accountable civilian institutions, but virtually no one wanted to bring them down. The 7 June elections were successful in that, by and large, votes did reflect actual preferences, not threats or bribes. Religious militants were few, and they received little support. As for the military, its leaders had no appetite to stop the process of reform even if they could.

Second, democratization had not led to a wholesale repudiation of the past. The constitution had not—yet?—been changed. A higher proportion of the seats in the People's Consultative Assembly had been filled by voter preference than before, but that body still was only partly elected. Pancasila had become less compulsory than it was, but Marxism remained illegal, and Suharto was neither in exile nor in jail. His health had begun seriously to fail, and if it worsened further, he might be expected to die before being held accountable for his deeds while in power.

Golkar, far from being banned or shunned for its role as a pillar of the New Order, had finished second nationally in the elections, while another fixture of New Order politics, PPP, had come in fourth. Such continuities were no reason to belittle the significance of real innovations—uncoerced elections, political pluralism, media freedom, and more downwardly responsive leaders and institutions. But they did suggest that if the reform process were not to stall, more attention would need to be paid to institutionalizing it.

Third, along with political accountability, Indonesia badly needed relief from social strife. Although it might frustrate observers eager for more rapid change, the conservative tenor of political reform could help to create and sustain an inclusive and thus prospectively stable ruling coalition. But there was no guarantee that such a government would be up to the task of curbing corruption and vested interests—a task central to restoring economic health and public credence in the fairness of development.

Fourth, it was clear in 1999 that in a more democratic Indonesia, the viability of national borders would depend, more than before, on whether the periphery had reasons to remain within them. Decentralizing laws had been passed, including provisions that would reallocate to places such as Aceh and Irian Jaya more of the national income earned from exploiting their rich resources. As always in Indonesia, however, the implementation of laws could not be assumed. In time, perhaps, following Amien Rais, federalism could be placed on the national agenda for dispassionate consideration.

Chances are that Indonesia will not break into multiple pieces, even if East Timor leaves. Violence is likely to recur from time to time, but not to the point of all-out civil war. It will not be easy for Indonesians to translate one calm day of voting in June into a stable and legitimate reformist government that can calm the country. But the elections did at least show that, for all their differences, Indonesians could campaign and vote for political office peacefully on a national scale.

Fifth and finally, the responsibility of the Indonesian military and its high command for decades of war and days of catastrophe in East Timor underscored the need to return that institution to the "sole function" of national defense. Without curbing the armed forces, so long and so broadly entrenched in public life under Suharto, Indonesians could not hope to shelter their democratic experiment under the rule of law.

To end on a note of concern is not, however, to lapse into pessimism about the future of Indonesia beyond Suharto. Whatever may await the people and leaders of this extraordinary nation, I doubt that one can have read this book without acquiring respect for their creativity and their resourcefulness in making, for better or worse, their own way in the world.

Sources: Readings, Websites, Videos

Information on Indonesia is available in many forms and places. Three criteria were used in selecting a source for inclusion below: that it augment in a particularly useful way the relevant chapter's coverage; that it be accessible to readers of English; and that it not already have been cited in a chapter or on the contributors' page. A fourth criterion, suitability for classroom use, guided the selection of videos. Space limitations further limited the list. The list can be used, however, to explore a rich array of additional sources on Indonesia, including many in the Indonesian language, through bibliographic notes in the readings and via electronic links in the websites to other databases.

Readings

Chapter 1: Nation: Making Indonesia

Bellwood, Peter. 1985. *Prehistory of the Indo-Malaysian Archipelago.* Sydney: Academic Press.

Dahm, Bernard. 1969. *Sukarno and the Struggle for Indonesian Independence.* Ithaca, NY: Cornell University Press.

Frederick, William H. 1989. *Visions and Heat: The Making of the Indonesian Revolution.* Athens: Ohio University Press.

Gardner, Paul F. 1997. *Shared Hopes, Separate Fears: Fifty Years of U.S.-Indonesian Relations.* Boulder, CO: Westview Press.

Leifer, Michael. 1983. *Indonesia's Foreign Policy.* London, UK: George Allen & Unwin.

Lev, Daniel S., and Ruth McVey, eds. 1996. *Making Indonesia: Essays on Modern Indonesia in Honor of George McT. Kahin.* Ithaca, NY: Cornell University Southeast Asia Program.

Ricklefs, M.C. 1993. *A History of Modern Indonesia since c. 1300.* 2nd ed. Basingstoke, UK: Macmillan.

Sato, Shigeru. 1994. *War, Nationalism and Peasants: Java under the Japanese Occupation 1942–1945.* Sydney: Allen & Unwin.

Singh, Bilveer. 1995. *Dwifungsi ABRI: The Dual Function of the Indonesian Armed Forces.* Singapore: Institute of International Affairs.

Sundhaussen, Ulf. 1982. *The Road to Power: Indonesian Military Politics 1945–1967.* Kuala Lumpur, Malaysia: Oxford University Press.
Taylor, Jean. 1983. *The Social World of Batavia: European and Eurasian in Dutch Asia.* Madison, WI: University of Wisconsin Press.

Chapter 2: Regime: The New Order

Anderson, Benedict. 1990. *Language and Power: Exploring Political Cultures in Indonesia.* Ithaca, NY: Cornell University Press.
Crouch, Harold. 1988. *The Army and Politics in Indonesia.* Rev. ed. Ithaca, NY: Cornell University Press.
Crouch, Harold. 1979. "Patrimonialism and Military Rule in Indonesia." *World Politics,* 31 (4), pp. 571–587.
Grant, Bruce. 1996. *Indonesia.* 3rd ed. Melbourne, Australia: Melbourne University Press.
Human Rights Watch/Asia. 1994. *The Limits of Openness: Human Rights in Indonesia and East Timor.* New York: Human Rights Watch.
Jackson, Karl, and Lucian Pye, eds. 1978. *Political Power and Communications in Indonesia.* Berkeley, CA: University of California Press.
McDonald, Hamish. 1980. *Suharto's Indonesia.* Blackburn, Victoria, Australia: Fontana Books.
Nasution, Adnan Buyung. 1992. *The Aspiration for Constitutional Government in Indonesia: A Socio-legal Study of the Indonesian Konstituante 1956–1959.* Jakarta: Pustaka Sinar Harapan.
Ramage, Douglas E. 1995. *Politics in Indonesia: Democracy, Islam and the Ideology of Tolerance.* London, UK: Routledge.
Said, Salim. 1998. "Suharto's Armed Forces: Building a Power Base in New Order Indonesia, 1966–1998." *Asian Survey,* 38:6 (June), pp. 535–552.
Vatikiotis, Michael. 1993. *Indonesian Politics under Suharto: Order, Development, and Pressure for Change.* London, UK: Routledge.

Chapter 3: Regions: Centralization and Resistance

Dick, Howard W., James J. Fox, and J.A.C. Mackie, eds. 1993. *Balanced Development: East Java in the New Order.* Singapore: Oxford University Press.
Drake, Christine. 1989. *National Integration in Indonesia: Patterns and Issues.* Honolulu, HI: University of Hawaii Press.
Dunn, James. 1983. *Timor, A People Betrayed.* Milton, Queensland, Australia: Jacaranda Press.
Hill, Hal, ed. 1989. *Unity and Diversity: Regional Economic Development in Indonesia since 1970.* Singapore: Oxford University Press.
Kahin, Audrey R., ed. 1985. *Regional Dynamics of the Indonesian Revolution.* Honolulu, HI: University of Hawaii Press.
Kim, T.J., G. Knaap, and I.J. Azis, eds. 1992. *Spatial Development in Indonesia: Review and Prospects.* Aldershot, UK: Avebury.
Krieger, Heike, ed. 1997. *East Timor and the International Community: Basic Documents.* Cambridge, UK: Cambridge University Press.
MacAndrews, Colin, ed. 1986. *Central Government and Local Development in Indonesia.* Singapore: Oxford University Press.
Osborne, Robin. 1985. *Indonesia's Secret War: The Guerilla Struggle in Irian Jaya.* Sydney: Allen & Unwin.

Reeve, David. 1985. *Golkar of Indonesia: An Alternative to the Party System.* Singapore: Oxford University Press.
Taylor, John G. 1991. *Indonesia's Forgotten War: The Hidden History of East Timor.* London, UK: Zed Books.

Chapter 4: Development: Achievement and Weakness

Arndt, Heinz W. 1984. *The Indonesian Economy: Collected Papers.* Singapore: Chopmen Publishers.
Booth, Anne, ed. 1992. *The Oil Boom and After: Indonesian Economic Performance in the Soeharto Era.* Singapore: Oxford University Press.
Booth, Anne, and Peter McCawley, eds. 1981. *The Indonesian Economy during the Soeharto Era.* Kuala Lumpur, Malaysia: Oxford University Press.
Cole, David, and Betty Slade. 1996. *Building a Modern Financial System: The Indonesian Experience.* Cambridge, UK: Cambridge University Press.
Dirkse, Jan-Paul, Frans Husken, and Mario Rutten, eds. 1993. *Development and Social Welfare: Indonesia's Experiences under the New Order.* Leiden, Netherlands: KITLV Press.
Glassburner, Bruce. 1971. *The Economy of Indonesia: Selected Readings.* Ithaca, NY: Cornell University Press.
Hardjono, Joan, ed. 1991. *Indonesia: Resources, Ecology, and Environment.* Singapore: Oxford University Press.
Hill, Hal. 1996. *The Indonesian Economy since 1966.* Cambridge, UK: Cambridge University Press.
Pangestu, Mari, and Yuri Sato, eds. 1997. *Waves of Change in Indonesia's Manufacturing Industry.* Tokyo: Institute of Developing Economies.
Prawiro, Radius. 1998. *Indonesia's Struggle for Economic Development: Pragmatism in Action.* Kuala Lumpur, Malaysia: Oxford University Press.
Woo, Wing-Thye, Bruce Glassburner, and Anwar Nasution. 1994. *Macroeconomic Policies, Crises, and Long-Term Growth in Indonesia, 1965–90.* Washington, DC: World Bank.

Chapter 5: Markets: The Limits of Reform

Aden, Jean. 1992. "Entrepreneurship and Protection in the Indonesian Oil Service Industry." In Ruth McVey, ed. *Southeast Asian Capitalists,* pp. 89–101. Ithaca, NY: Cornell University Southeast Asia Program.
Bresnan, John. 1993. *Managing Indonesia: The Modern Political Economy.* New York: Columbia University Press.
Chalmers, Ian, and Vedi Hadiz, eds. 1997. *The Politics of Economic Development in Indonesia: Contending Perspectives.* London, UK: Routledge.
Hadiz, Vedi. 1997. *Workers and the State in New Order Indonesia.* London, UK: Routledge.
Manning, Chris, and Joan Hardjono, eds. 1993. *Indonesia Assessment 1993—Labour: Sharing in the Benefits of Growth?* Canberra: Australian National University Research School of Pacific Studies.
Pangestu, Mari. 1996. *Economic Reform, Deregulation, and Privatization: The Indonesian Experience.* Jakarta: Centre for Strategic and International Studies.
Plunkett, H.J., W.E. Morgan, and J.L. Pomeroy. 1997. "Regulation of the Cement Industry." *Bulletin of Indonesian Economic Studies,* 33 (April), pp. 75–102.

Robison, Richard, ed. 1990. *Power and Economy in Suharto's Indonesia.* Manila: Journal of Contemporary Asia Publishers.

Robison, Richard, and Vedi Hadiz. 1993. "Economic Liberalisation or the Reorganisation of Dirigisme? Indonesian Economic Policy in the 1990s." *Canadian Journal of Development Studies,* December, pp. 13–32.

Schwarz, Adam. 1991. "Indonesia's Economic Boom: How Banks Paved the Way." In Richard O'Brien and Sarah Hewin, eds. *Finance and the International Economy (4): The AMEX Bank Review Prize Essays,* pp. 188–207. New York: Oxford University Press.

Winters, Jeffrey A. 1996. *Power in Motion: Capital Mobility and the Indonesian State.* Ithaca, NY: Cornell University Press.

Chapter 6: Conglomerates: All in the Family?

Anatomy of Indonesian Conglomerates. 1991. Jakarta: PT Data Consult.

Hill, Hal. 1988. *Foreign Investment and Industrialization in Indonesia.* Singapore: Oxford University Press.

Hill, Hal, and Terry Hull, eds. 1990. *Indonesia Assessment 1990.* Canberra: Australian National University Research School of Pacific Studies.

Kunio, Yoshihara. 1988. *The Rise of Ersatz Capitalism in Southeast Asia.* Singapore: Oxford University Press.

MacIntyre, Andrew. 1990. *Business and Politics in Indonesia.* North Sydney: Asian Studies Association of Australia with Allen & Unwin.

Mackie, J.A.C., ed. 1976. *The Chinese in Indonesia.* Melbourne, Australia: Thomas Nelson.

Mackie, J.A.C. 1992. Overseas Chinese Entrepreneurship. *Asian Pacific Economic Literature,* May, pp. 41–64.

Robison, Richard. 1996. "The Middle Class and the Bourgeoisie in Indonesia." In Robison and David S.G. Goodman, eds. *The New Rich in Asia,* pp. 79–101. London, UK: Routledge.

Robison, Richard. 1992. In Ruth McVey, ed. *Southeast Asian Capitalists,* pp. 65–88. Ithaca, NY: Cornell University Southeast Asia Program.

"The Role of the Indonesian Chinese in Shaping Modern Indonesian Life." 1991. Special issue of *Indonesia.* Ithaca, NY: Cornell University Southeast Asia Program.

Schwarz, Adam. 1992. "All Is Relative." *Far Eastern Economic Review,* 30 April, pp. 54–56.

Chapter 7: Religion: Evolving Pluralism

Frederick, William. 1982. "Rhoma Irama and the Dangdut Style." *Indonesia,* 34, pp. 103–132.

Geertz, Clifford. 1980. *Negara: The Theatre State in Nineteenth-Century Bali.* Princeton, NJ: Princeton University Press.

Geertz, Clifford. 1968. *Islam Observed: Religious Development in Morocco and Indonesia.* New Haven, CT: Yale University Press.

Geertz, Clifford. 1960. *The Religion of Java.* Glencoe, IL: Free Press.

Geertz, Hildred. 1963. "Indonesian Cultures and Communities." In Ruth T. McVey, ed. *Indonesia.* New Haven, CT: Yale Southeast Asian Studies with HRAF.

"Islam in Contemporary Indonesia: Proceedings of a Workshop." 1997. United States-Indonesia Society, 1625 Massachusetts Avenue, NW, Suite 550, Washington, DC 20036-2245; tel. 202-232-1400; fax 202 232 7300.

Johns, Anthony H. 1987. "Indonesia, Islam and Cultural Pluralism." In John L. Esposito, ed. *Islam in Asia: Religion, Politics and Society,* pp. 209–229.New York: Oxford University Press.

Madjid, Nurcholish. 1990. "Indonesia in the Future: Sophisticated and Devoutly Religious." *Prisma,* 35, pp. 11–26.

Mahasin, Aswab. 1990. "The Santri Middle Class: An Insider's View." In Richard Tanter and Kenneth Young, eds. *The Politics of Middle Class Indonesia,* pp. 138–144. Clayton, Victoria, Australia: Monash University Centre of Southeast Asian Studies.

Reid, Anthony. 1993. "A Religious Revolution." In Reid. *Southeast Asia in the Age of Commerce, 1450–1680.* Vol. 2: *Expansion and Crisis,* pp. 132–201. New Haven, CT: Yale University Press.

Warren, Carol. 1993. *Adat and Dinas: Balinese Communities in the Indonesian State.* Kuala Lumpur, Malaysia: Oxford University Press.

Chapter 8: Women: Difference Versus Diversity

Alexander, Jennifer. 1987. *Trade, Traders and Trading in Rural Java.* Singapore: Oxford University Press.

Brenner, Suzanne April. 1998. *The Domestication of Desire: Women, Wealth, and Modernity in Java.* Princeton, NJ: Princeton University Press.

Geertz, Hildred. 1961. *The Javanese Family.* New York: Humanities Press.

Kahn, Joel. 1980. *Minangkabau Social Formations.* Cambridge, UK: Cambridge University Press.

Locher-Scholten, Elspeth, and Anke Niehoff, eds. 1987. *Indonesian Women in Focus: Past and Present Notions.* Dodrecht, Netherlands: Foris.

Manning, Chris. 1998. *Indonesian Labour in Transition: An East Asian Success Story?* Cambridge, UK: Cambridge University Press.

Nadia, Ita F. 1996. The Political Role of Women's NGOs. In Rustam Ibrahim, ed. *The Indonesian NGO Agenda: Toward the Year 2000.* Jakarta: CESDA-LP3ES. Available from IAPC, P.O. Box 1160, Collingwood 3066, Australia; <ACFOAHR@PEG. APC.ORG>.

Oey-Gardiner, Mayling. 1991. "Gender Differences in Schooling." *Bulletin of Indonesian Economic Studies,* 27(1), pp. 57–79.

Sjahrir, Kartini, guest ed. 1985. *Prisma: The Indonesian Indicator: Special Issue: Women in Development: The Multiplier Effects,* 37 (September).

Suryakusuma, Julia. 1996. "Death of a Consort, End of a Dynasty?" *Inside Indonesia,* July–September, pp. 2–3.

van Esterik, Penny, ed. 1996. *Women of Southeast Asia.* 2nd ed. DeKalb: Northern Illinois University Center for Southeast Asian Studies.

Chapter 9: Expression: Creativity Despite Constraint

Anderson, Benedict R. O'G. 1966. "The Languages of Indonesian Politics." *Indonesia,* 1 (April), pp. 89–116.

Anderson, Benedict R. O'G. 1965. *Mythology and the Tolerance of the Javanese.* Ithaca, NY: Cornell University Modern Indonesia Project.

Aveling, Harry. 1975. *Contemporary Indonesian Poetry.* Brisbane, Australia: University of Queensland Press.

Guinness, Patrick. 1994. Local Society and Culture. In Hal Hill, ed. *Indonesia's New Order: The Dynamics of Socio-economic Transformation,* pp. 267–304. Honolulu: University of Hawaii Press.

Hatley, Barbara. 1994. Cultural Expression. In Hal Hill, ed. *Indonesia's New Order: The Dynamics of Socio-economic Transformation,* pp. 216–266. Honolulu: University of Hawaii Press.

Hill, David T., ed. 1998. *Beyond the Horizon: Stories from Contemporary Indonesia.* Clayton, Victoria, Australia: Monash Asia Institute.

Hill, David T. 1994. *The Press in New Order Indonesia.* Perth, Australia: Murdoch University Asia Research Centre.

Hill, David T. 1984. *Who's Left? Indonesian Literature in the Early 1980s.* Clayton, Victoria, Australia: Monash University Centre of Southeast Asian Studies.

Holt, Claire. 1967. *Art in Indonesia: Continuities and Change.* Ithaca, NY: Cornell University Press.

Schiller, Jim, and Barbara Marin-Schiller, eds. 1997. *Imagining Indonesia: Cultural Politics and Political Culture.* Athens: Ohio University Center for International Studies.

Sutton, R. Anderson. 1995. "Performing Arts and Cultural Politics in South Sulawesi." *Bijdragen tot de Taal-, Land- en Volkenkunde,* 151(4), pp. 672–699.

Chapter 10: Exit and Aftermath: The Crisis of 1997–98

Aspinall, Edward, Herb Feith, and Gerry van Klinken, eds. 1999. *The Last Days of President Suharto.* Melbourne, Australia: Monash Asia Insitute.

Baker, Richard W., M. Hadi Soesastro, J. Kristiadi, and Douglas E. Ramage, eds. 1999. *Indonesia: The Challenge of Change.* Singapore: Institute of Southeast Asian Studies.

Budiman, Arief, Barbara Hatley, and Damien Kingsbury, eds. 1999. *Reformasi: Crisis and Change in Indonesia.* Melbourne, Australia: Monash Asia Institute.

Eldridge, Philip J. 1996. *Non-Government Organizations and Political Participation in Indonesia.* Kuala Lumpur, Malaysia: Oxford University Press.

Gellert, Paul K. 1998. "A Brief History and Analysis of Indonesia's Forest Fire Crisis." *Indonesia,* April, pp. 63–85.

"Indonesia." 1998. *Granta,* 62 (Summer), pp. 59–143.

Indonesia in Crisis: A Macroeconomic Update. 1998. Washington, DC: World Bank.

Johnson, Colin. 1998. "Survey of Recent Developments." *Bulletin of Indonesian Economic Studies,* 34 (August), pp. 3–60.

Liddle, R. William. 1999. "Indonesia's Democratic Opening." *Government and Opposition,* 34 (Winter).

MacFarling, Ian. 1996. *The Dual Function of the Indonesian Armed Forces: Military Politics in Indonesia.* [No place given]: Australian Defence Studies Centre.

May, R.J., and G. Forrester, eds. 1998. *The Fall of Soeharto.* Crawford House Publishing, P. O. Box 1484, Bathurst, NSW 2795, Australia.

McBeth, John, et al. 1998. "Cover Story: Habibie in the Hot Seat." *Far Eastern Economic Review,* 3 December, pp. 10–16.

Schwarz, Adam, and Jonathan Paris, eds. 1999. *The Politics of Post-Soeharto Indonesia.* New York: Council on Foreign Relations.

Soesastro, Hadi, and M. Chatib Basri. 1998. "Survey of Recent Developments." *Bulletin of Indonesian Economic Studies,* 34 (April), pp. 3–54.

Websites

Note: Except for those using <GOPHER>, all of the following addresses begin <HTTP://>.

Governments:

Indonesian Embassy in the U.S.: <WWW.KBRI.ORG>
Indonesian Government: <WWW.INDONESIATODAY.COM>
U.S. Embassy in Indonesia: <WWW.USEMBASSYJAKARTA.ORG>
U.S. Department of State: <WWW.STATE.GOV>

Newspapers and Magazines:

Indonesian Observer:
<WWW.INDOEXCHANGE.COM/INDONESIAN-OBSERVER/>
Washington Post:
<WWW.WASHINGTONPOST.COM/WP-SRV/INATL/LONGTERM/INDONESIA/
ANALYSIS.HTM>

Other:

<WWW.IIT.EDU/~INDONESIA/JENDELA/>
<WWW.UNI-STUTTGART.DE/INDONESIA/NEWS>

Organizations:

East Timor Action Network:
<GOPHER://GOPHER.IGC.APC.ORG/11/PEACE/TIMOR.GOPHER>
Human Rights Watch: <WWW.HR.ORG>
International Monetary Fund: <WWW.IMF.ORG>
World Bank: <WWW.WORLDBANK.ORG/HTML/EXTDR/REGIONS.HTM>

Other:

Archive of news and commentary:
GOPHER://GOPHER.IGC.APC.ORG:2998/7REG-INDONESIA>
Business: <WWW.CASTLEASIA.COM>
East Asian economic crisis:
<WWW.STERN.NYU.EDU/~NROUBINI/ASIA/ASIAHOMEPAGE.HTML>Politics,
economics, culture, tourism: <INDONESIA.ELGA.NET.ID/>

Videos

Bitter Paradise: The Sell-out of East Timor. 1996. 56 min. Criticizes the New Order
and Western governments for depredations in East Timor. The Cinema Guild, 1697
Broadway, Suite 506, New York, NY 10019-5904, U.S.; tel. 212-246-5522; fax 212
246 5525; web <WWW.CINEMAGUILD.COM>.
From the Barrel of a Gun. 1992. 60 min. Compares nationalism in Indonesia (Sukarno)
and Vietnam (Ho Chi Minh). Part of a series: *The Pacific Century.* Annenberg CPB
Multimedia Collection, P.O. Box 2345, South Burlington, VT 05407-2345, U.S.; tel.
1-800-LEARNER; fax 802 864 9846; web <WWW.LEARNER.ORG>.
In the Shadow of Mount Ramelau. [Year not available.] 58 min. Defends New Order
policies toward East Timor. Information Section, Indonesian Embassy, 2020
Massachusetts Avenue, NW, Washington, DC 20036; tel. 202-775-5200; fax 202
775 5365.

Indonesia. 1993. 60 min. Focuses on economic inequality and tensions over the relative wealth of the ethnic-Chinese minority. Part of a series: *Mini Dragons II*. Ambrose Video Publishing, 28 West 44th St. (Suite 2100), New York, NY 10036, U.S; tel. 1-800-526-4663; fax 212 768 9282; web <WWW.AMBROSEVIDEO. COM>.

Indonesia: Islands on Fire. 1996. 25 min. Criticizes New Order repression and Western investors through footage of demonstrations and interviews with activists. Global Exchange, 2017 Mission Street (#303), San Francisco, CA 94110, U.S.; tel 1-800-497-1994; fax 415-255-7498; web <WWW.GLOBALEXCHANGE.ORG>.

Indonesia: Riding the Tiger. 1992. Three-part series: *Kings and Coolies*. 52 min. Covers Dutch rule, Indonesian nationalism, the Japanese occupation, and independence. *Freedom or Death*. 55 min. Reviews the nature and effects of Japanese rule during World War II. *The New Order*. 53 min. Portrays Suharto's regime, including its violent origin and emphasis on development. Films for the Humanities and Sciences, P.O. Box 2053, Princeton, NJ 08543-2053, U.S.; tel. 1-800-257-5126; fax 609 275 3767; web <HTTP://WWW.FILMS.COM>.

Indonesia: The Story of a Volcano. 1996. 20 min. Concerns Mount Merapi on Java, the eruption process, local residents, and government relocation. Films for the Humanities and Sciences, P.O. Box 2053, Princeton, NJ 08543-2053, U.S.; tel. 1-800-257-5126; fax 609 275 3767; web <HTTP://WWW.FILMS.COM>.

Indonesia: The Way of the Ancestors. 1978. 52 min. Portrays beliefs and practices related to animism—the imputation of special power to inanimate objects and natural phenomena. Part of a series: *The Long Search*. Ambrose Video Publishing, 28 West 44th St. (Suite 2100), New York, NY 10036, U.S; tel. 1-800-526-4663; fax 212 768 9282; web <WWW.AMBROSEVIDEO.COM>.

Indonesia: Urban Development in Jakarta. 1998. 20 min. Uses the daily life of a twelve-year-old boy to illustrate the capital's crowding and lack of services. Films for the Humanities and Sciences, P. O. Box 2053, Princeton, NJ 08543-2053, U.S.; tel. 1-800-257-5126; fax 609 275 3767; web <HTTP://WWW.FILMS.COM>.

Lords of the Garden. 1994. 55 min. Explores the meanings and methods of tree-house-building among the Korowai people of Irian Jaya. Asian Cultural History Program, Department of Anthropology, Smithsonian Institution, Washington, DC 20560-0112, U.S.; tel. 202-357-4135; fax 202 357 2208.

Portuguese Tears—Timorese Blood. 1995. 52 min. Interprets East Timor from the standpoint of the New Order. Information Section, Indonesian Embassy, 2020 Massachusetts Avenue, NW, Washington, DC 20036; tel 202-775-5200; fax 202 775 5365.

Ring of Fire. 1988. Four-part series: *Spice Island Saga*. 30 min. *Dance of the Warriors*. 30 min. *Dream Wanderers of Borneo*. 30 min. *East of Krakatoa*. 30 min. Records a journey through the archipelago. The Video Catalog, Audio Collection, P.O. Box 64454, St. Paul, MN 55164-0454, U.S.; tel. 1-800-733-2232.

Shadow over East Timor. 1991. 57 min. Addresses events in their homeland through the experiences of East Timorese in Australia. WUSF, 4202 East Fowler Avenue, SVC 0001, Tampa, FL 33620-6902; tel. 1-800-292-9873; fax 813 974 4806; web <WWW.WUSFTV.USF.EDU>.

Index

Italicized page numbers indicate pages which contain Tables or Figures; page numbers
followed by *n.* and number indicate pages on which a numbered footnote appears.